THE CRY OF TAMAR

"This is a major resource both for those teaching courses on violence to women and also for practitioners who support women in situations of violence. It is the only book I know that addresses a number of major issues of violence: sexual harassment, rape, battering, ritual abuse, child abuse, and others, as well as pornography as cultural violence. It has particular importance to religious people by bringing these issues into the context of biblical and theological reflection as well as psychological counseling."

> —Rosemary R. Ruether
> Georgia Harkness Professor of
> Applied Theology
> Garrett-Evangelical Theological
> Seminary

"I can't imagine a more authoritative accounting of the subject of violence against women than Pamela Cooper-White has accomplished here. She has given us a profound analysis of the cultural sources of violence and sexual boundary violations as well as practical remedies that can be applied by both individuals and congregations. Moreover, she does all this within a psychological and spiritual framework that does not blame, never loses hope, and maintains respect for both men and women. This is thoroughly researched, state-of-the-art scholarship. *The Cry of Tamar* has value beyond the church, in any setting where the restoration of the feminine voice to our culture is valued."

> —Peter Rutter, M.D.
> author of *Sex in the Forbidden Zone*

"If you don't have a vision of justice and a politics to implement it, you're just running a MASH unit in the war of the bodies of women and children. Pamela Cooper-White calls us to such a vision and such a politics—a superb effort!"

> —Susan B. Thistlethwaite
> Professor of Theology
> Chicago Theological Seminary

For my family,
all the victims and survivors,
and to the memory of Verneice Thompson

THE CRY OF TAMAR

VIOLENCE AGAINST WOMEN AND THE CHURCH'S RESPONSE

Pamela Cooper-White

FORTRESS PRESS

MINNEAPOLIS

THE CRY OF TAMAR
Violence against Women and the Church's Response

This publication is designed to provide accurate and authoritative information in regard to the subject matter covered. It is sold with the understanding that the publisher is not engaged in rendering legal or other professional services. If legal advice or other expert assistance is required, the services of a competent professional person should be sought. *From a Declaration of Principles jointly adopted by a committee of the American Bar Association and a committee of publishers.*

Scripture quotations are from the Revised Standard Version of the Bible copyright © 1946, 1952, 1971 by the Division of Christian Education of the National Council of Churches of Christ in the United States of America and are used by permission.

Scripture quotations are from the New Revised Standard Version Bible, copyright © 1989 by the Division of Christian Education of the National Council of the Churches of Christ in the United States.

Interior design: Northwestern Printcrafters
Cover design: Evans McCormick Creative

Library of Congress Cataloging-in-Publication Data
Cooper-White, Pamela, 1955–
    The cry of Tamar : violence against women and the Church's
response / by Pamela Cooper-White.
        p.   cm.
    Includes bibliographical references and index.
    ISBN 0-8006-2730-X (alk. paper)
    1. Women—Crimes against—Religious aspects—Christianity.
2. Violence—Religious aspects—Christianity.   3. Church work with
women.   4. Women—Pastoral counseling of.   I. Title.
BT704.C66   1995
261.8'32—dc20
                                                                94-23086
                                                                CIP

The paper used in this publication meets the minimum requirements of American National Standard for Information Sciences—Permanence of Paper for Printed Library Materials, ANSI Z329.48-1984.

Manufactured in U.S.A.   AF 1–2730
                            4   5   6   7   8   9   10

CONTENTS

FIGURES

TABLES

PREFACE

At the wedding of a friend last summer, the priest performing the ceremony addressed all the guests, exhorting us to take seriously our role as witnesses to the new marriage. It was hot. The glass-walled chapel at Pacific School of Religion was like a greenhouse. People smiled, fanned themselves with programs. Didn't the bride look lovely? Wasn't it an unusually summery day for the Bay Area? The priest's words rang out, suddenly calling us to attention, reminding us of our commitment—beyond the surface pleasantries and the etiquette of the wedding as a social occasion. He told us the biblical Greek word for witness is *martys*. He called us to pour out our lives, our selves, as witnesses, as *martyrs*, to this union now being created before God and before us.

I hope and believe that my friend's marriage, and her life, will be blessed with harmony and peace. But for so many women, that is far from the reality of their lives. All too often hope dies, crushed by the fist of a battering partner, overwhelmed by the violation of a rapist's attack, smothered even in earliest childhood by the devastation of sexual abuse.

This book—amazingly for the first time—gathers together by one author under a nontechnical framework the seemingly disparate strands of the violence-against-women movements. I say "amazingly" because with the research and advocacy advancing apace in the various strands, no introductory book from a unified perspective yet exists.[1] One reason for this lacuna, no doubt, is that each strand has often pressed ahead independently toward political initiatives for change, so vital for improving women's treatment within the North American context. A second reason is that many people have become engaged where they first encountered violence against women. A third is that the theoretical perspectives often shift as one moves from one area to another.

The envisioned readers of this book, then, are those who want to know more about the various forms of violence against women and some of what can be done to counter such violence. By the term *church's response* in the book's subtitle is meant the basic witness for what is healthy and against what is destructive. I am taking the hopeful stance that the church's response to violence against women can be increasingly helpful, even proactive. This book is an effort to support that response by suggesting starting points for advocacy (both pastoral and institutional) and by undergirding those suggestions with both theological and theoretical foundations.

I felt drawn, even compelled, to write this book for many reasons. In my first parish ministry setting in 1979, I opened a program for homeless people and had my eyes opened to the realities of battered women. The very first family to come to supper in our simple parish hall was a battered woman who had fled from her violent husband with her two children, preferring the streets to the terror of their apartment. Deeply convicted by that encounter, I went on to become involved in the battered women's movement, a commitment that I have carried throughout my ministry in secular agency, church, and seminary settings. More recently, while teaching at the American Baptist Seminary of the West, I discovered the lack of a book addressing the multiple forms of violence against women from one author's unifying perspective and analysis. I found myself assigning dozens of books and articles and wishing for one source that could serve as a primary text for the class.

As an Episcopal priest, I write with a Christian and, at times, distinctively Anglican voice. The book carries the assumption of a certain shared world with the reader, that of the Christian church in the U.S. I hope it may also be of some transferable value to readers of different religions, although I do not pretend to represent in a universal way all the complexities of their traditions.

Beyond these reasons for writing the book, there is another: I am a woman. As I have shared in various places throughout, I have personal experiences with some of the specific forms of violence I am describing. Additional stories in this book have been gathered from others. The stories of my friends and colleagues, if compiled, easily fill in any gaps in experience in my own life. The stories if laid end to end could be wrapped around my entire community, perhaps around the world. These stories are included in order to model an important aspect of our witness, namely, giving voice to the voiceless. The forms of violence against women are not limited to those detailed in this book. Medical violence, female infanticide, traffic in women, and economic violence against women are all areas for further exploration, but ones that go beyond the scope of this book. There are also controversial international and cross-cultural practices, such as female genital mutilation, which cannot be adequately dealt with here. These issues need to be incorporated someday in a comprehensive work on violence against women. What I have selected, however, is one central cluster of abuses out of which a community can build a stance against violence and model an important aspect of our witness, namely, giving voice to the voiceless.

In spite of our commitment as Christians to the good news of justice and peace, this breaking of silence seems an enormous and at times overwhelming task. Why should we be so often reluctant to hear and respond to the violence in our society and even in our own ranks?

Psychologist Judith Herman describes the tremendous pressures to minimize and deny violence, especially violence by human agency, because those who bear witness "are caught in the conflict between victim and perpetrator."[2] The witness is morally bound to take a side.

> It is very tempting to take the side of the perpetrator. All the perpetrator asks is that the bystander do nothing. He appeals to the universal desire to see, hear, and speak no evil. The victim, on the contrary, asks the bystander to share the burden of pain. The victim demands action, engagement, and remembering. . . .

Herman highlights the importance of a social context that values justice because this "affirms and protects the victim" by uniting the victim and witness. For individual victims this alliance is formed with friends; for groups, with political movements.

> In the absence of strong political movements for human rights, the active process of bearing witness inevitably gives way to the active process of forgetting. Repression, dissociation, and denial are phenomena of social as well as individual consciousness.

Moving from repression to awareness and expression is the goal of this book. All too often, with the best of intentions, those of us who collectively are the church, who call ourselves "the body of Christ," blind ourselves to Christ's wounds in our own communities, our contemporary world. We cannot bear the full brunt of the truth. Elie Wiesel wrote of the Holocaust survivors who tried to tell their stories, "To be believable, their tales had to tell less than the truth."[3] Yet we are called, again and again, to be witnesses, martyrs to the truth.

This book is an effort to support us all in that crucial work. The effort begins with Tamar, a woman whose voice calls from a distance through a biblical narrative (2 Sam. 13) from which her life is all too quickly dropped and forgotten. The invocation of Tamar's voice is the paradigm for this project. The work of restoring victims to voice is redemptive. Through it, we proclaim Tamar's vindication.

Many have sustained me in this work and contributed greatly to this project. First, I thank my editors at Fortress Press, Marshall D. Johnson, Timothy Staveteig, and Lois Torvik, whose enthusiasm for this project has meant so much. They have helped shape this book in many ways. I am also grateful to the many people who have read individual chapters and given feedback so generously from their respective areas of expertise: Marita Bausman, David Biale, Marsha Blackstock, Alan Creighton, Jim and Margaret Emerson, Margot Silk Forrest, Rich Garcia, Donna Garske, Charles Gibbs, Victor Gold, Barbara Green, Dale Griffis, Gina Hens-Piazza, Jaimee Karroll, Chilton Knudsen, Karen Lebacqz, Leslie Levy, Andrew Littman, David McCoy, Karlin Olson, David Owen-Ball, Kristin Rapsher, Melissa Reed, Carol Robb, Colin Ross,

Gary Schoener, Caryn Stardancer, Pat Stewart, Marti Stortz, Stephanie Townsend, Jim Ward, and Tamera White. Nancy Lemon also gave invaluable legal information.

I am grateful to the women faculty of the Graduate Theological Union, who collectively have been a great support. Especially I am grateful to Carol Robb, whose model for collaborative study groups for her book in progress on women and economic justice inspired the richly collaborative nature of this project. It was in those study groups that my idea for this book was first nurtured and encouraged. I am also grateful for the annual women faculty retreat, and especially Clare Fischer, Barbara Green, Gina Hens-Piazza, Randi Walker, and Anne Wire, who gave such helpful and clarifying feedback on chapter 1. Particular thanks go to Rosemary Chinnici, Liz Edwards, and Peter Rutter, who read the entire manuscript with great attention and care, and whose encouragement has meant so much.

This project has also been inspired by a number of groups and organizations. I am particularly grateful to the Center for Women and Religion (CWR) of the Graduate Theological Union, where I have had the great privilege of being employed as director to integrate my passion for the church with my passion for justice for women. I am also grateful to the Mid-Peninsula Support Network for Battered Women in Mountain View, California, where I worked as executive director; Sojourn Services for Battered Women in Santa Monica, California, where I was first trained in hotline and shelter work; Caroline Fairless, with whom I have co-led numerous workshops and trainings on domestic violence; and my many friends in the California Alliance Against Domestic Violence, for nurturing, challenging, and engaging me in our common work for battered women and their children. I especially remember my friend, the late Harrison Simms, founder of Oakland Men's Project, whose work with men and youth to unlearn racism and sexism taught me so much. I also thank my students at the American Baptist Seminary and throughout the Graduate Theological Union, as well as the CWR staff and board, who have given me so much of their wisdom and shared with me in stimulating, thought-provoking discussions. The Sexual Ethics Task Force of the Episcopal Diocese of California, of which I have been grateful to be a member, has also been an inspiration to me, as a model for the awareness, compassion, and dedication to making justice that is possible in our church.

I am grateful to all the women who have allowed their stories to be told in this book and the many women whose lives have touched mine through the various organizations in which I have been privileged to serve. They have graced me with their examples of courage and faith. I have in each case sought to protect their identities by conflating or otherwise altering identifying descriptions and circumstances.

Finally, there are a few people without whose support this project might not have been possible. Marie Fortune of the Center for the Prevention of Sexual and Domestic Violence in Seattle, whose pioneering efforts first promoted a widespread awareness of violence against women in the church, has been a boundless resource of information and helpful analysis over the years as well as of friendship and encouragement. My mentors in the therapeutic community, Steve Joseph, Peter Rutter, Marilyn Steele, and the late Verneice Thompson, have given richly of themselves and their wisdom—it is not too much to say that they have been influential in shaping the way I have come to see the world.

And last but not least, I thank my husband, Michael, who has lived with piles of books threatening to topple all over the house and articles on grim topics appearing at the breakfast table without warning, who has read and reread draft after draft, helped with technical matters ranging from Koine Greek to laser printing, and through it all has given me unflagging encouragement, support, and faith in the project. As a denominational leader, he has modeled unfailing commitment to justice for women—and others—in the church, and I am proud of our partnership.

"THE CRIME OF AMNON"

Now Absalom, David's son, had a beautiful sister, whose name was Tamar; and after a time Amnon, David's son, loved her. And Amnon was so tormented that he made himself ill because of his sister Tamar; for she was a virgin, and it seemed impossible to Amnon to do anything to her. But Amnon had a friend, whose name was Jonadab, the son of Shimeah, David's brother; and Jonadab was a very crafty man. And he said to him, "O son of the king, why are you so haggard morning after morning? Will you not tell me?" Amnon said to him, "I love Tamar, my brother Absalom's sister." Jonadab said to him, "Lie down on your bed, and pretend to be ill; and when your father comes to see you, say to him, 'Let my sister Tamar come and give me bread to eat, and prepare the food in my sight, that I may see it, and eat it from her hand.'" So Amnon lay down, and pretended to be ill; and when the king came to see him, Amnon said to the king, "Pray let my sister Tamar come and make a couple of cakes in my sight, that I may eat from her hand."

Then David sent home to Tamar, saying, "Go to your brother Amnon's house, and prepare food for him." So Tamar went to her brother Amnon's house, where he was lying down. And she took dough, and kneaded it, and made cakes in his sight, and baked cakes. And she took the pan and emptied it out before him, but he refused to eat. And Amnon said, "Send out every one from me." So every one went out from him. Then Amnon said to Tamar, "Bring the food into the chamber, that I may eat from your hand." And Tamar took the cakes she had made, and brought them into the chamber to Amnon her brother. But when she brought them near him to eat, he took hold of her, and said to her, "Come, lie with me, my sister." She answered him, "No, my brother, do not force me; for such a thing is not done in Israel; do not do this wanton folly. As for me, where could I carry my shame? And as for you, you would be as one of the wanton fools in Israel. Now therefore, I pray you, speak to the king; for he will not withhold me from you." But he would not listen to her; and being stronger than she, he forced her, and lay with her.

Then Amnon hated her with very great hatred; so that the hatred with which he hated her was greater than the love with which he had loved her. And Amnon said to her, "Arise, be gone." But she said to him, "No, my brother; for this wrong in sending me away is greater than the other which you did to me." But he would not listen to her. He called the young man who served him and said, "Put this woman out of my presence, and bolt the door after her." Now she was wearing a long robe with sleeves; for thus were the virgin daughters of the king clad of old. So his servant put her out, and bolted the door after her. And Tamar put ashes on her head, and rent the long robe which she wore; and she laid her hand on her head, and went away, crying aloud as she went.

And her brother Absalom said to her, "Has Amnon your brother been with you? Now hold your peace, my sister; he is your brother; do not take this to heart." So Tamar dwelt, a desolate woman, in her brother Absalom's house. When King David heard of all these things, he was very angry. But Absalom spoke to Amnon neither good nor bad; for Absalom hated Amnon, because he had forced his sister Tamar.

After two full years Absalom had sheepshearers at Baal-hazor, which is near Ephraim, and Absalom invited all the king's sons. And Absalom came to the king, and said, "Behold, your servant has sheepshearers; pray let the king and his servants go with your servant." But the king said to Absalom, "No, my son, let us not all go, lest we be burdensome to you." He pressed him, but he would not go but gave him his blessing. Then Absalom said, "If not, pray let my brother Amnon go with us." And the king said to him, "Why should he go with you?" But Absalom pressed him until he let Amnon and all the king's sons go with him. Then Absalom commanded his servants, "Mark when Amnon's heart is merry with wine, and when I say to you, 'Strike Amnon,' then kill him. Fear not; have I not commanded you? Be courageous and be valiant." So the servants of Absalom did to Amnon as Absalom had commanded. Then all the king's sons arose, and each mounted his mule and fled.

While they were on the way, tidings came to David, "Absalom has slain all the king's sons, and not one of them is left." Then the king arose, and rent his garments, and lay on the earth; and all his servants who were standing by rent their garments. But Jonadab the son of Shimeah, David's brother, said, "Let not my lord suppose that they have killed all the young men the king's sons, for Amnon alone is dead, for by the command of Absalom this has been determined from the day he forced his sister Tamar. Now therefore let not my lord the king so take it to heart as to suppose that all the king's sons are dead; for Amnon alone is dead."

But Absalom fled. And the young man who kept watch lifted up his eyes, and looked, and behold, many people were coming from the Horonaim road by the side of the mountain. And Jonadab said to the king, "Behold, the king's sons have come; as your servant said, so it has come about." And as soon as he had finished speaking, behold, the king's sons came, and lifted up their voice and wept; and the king also and all his servants wept very bitterly.

But Absalom fled, and went to Talmai the son of Ammihud, king of Geshur. And David mourned for his son day after day. So Absalom fled, and went to Geshur, and was there three years. And the spirit of the king longed to go forth to Absalom; for he was comforted about Amnon, seeing he was dead.

2 Samuel 13 (RSV)

Introduction:
The Rape of Tamar

The story of Tamar in 2 Samuel 13 is a touchstone for virtually all the themes of this book. There is a rape which combines elements of incest and domestic violence. There is a conspiracy of men aiding and abetting the perpetrator of the crime and a male conspiracy of silence after the fact. Finally, there is a raw form of retribution in the end, but this brutal act of revenge is done quite apart from the victim. Tamar is possibly the only rape victim in Scripture to have a voice, and yet all power to act or even to speak is taken away from her. It becomes men's business. In the end, the father to all three of the principal characters in this drama, as well as all the father's servants, are seen to mourn and weep bitterly day after day—not for the victim—but for the perpetrator and the victim's brother.

Tamar's voice may be imaginatively reclaimed through an act of subversive memory. *Subversive memory*, a term coined by Elisabeth Schüssler Fiorenza, describes a process of retrieving lost voices of biblical women through historical imagination and re-creation. She writes:

> *If the enslavement and colonialization of people becomes total when their history is destroyed because solidarity with the faith and suffering of the dead is made impossible, then a feminist biblical hermeneutic has the task of becoming a "dangerous memory" that reclaims the religious suffering and engagement of the dead.*[1]

What would the story sound like if told from the women's perspective? What different conclusions would that lead us to draw about the events themselves? Would we draw different morals from the story?

Retelling Tamar's Story

I am named for my aunt, who died a few years before I was born. I don't know too much about her, because my father and the other men have kept it hushed up. I'm not sure I have overheard all the details right from my mother's and the other women's whispering among themselves. They shake their heads and cluck their tongues, and sometimes still one of my aunts will get red in the face and cry, or another will make a fist and clench her teeth because it makes her so angry to think about. But they can do nothing, and so the few times they remember it, they whisper. And sometimes I hear it said, too, that Tamar, my aunt, should never have gone to my uncle's room. She should have known better. She should have hidden her beauty more carefully and been more humble. This is what they tell me, sometimes, because people say that I am very beautiful, too, and should carefully guard this treasure so that a good man will want me and bad things won't happen to me as they did to her. I am named after her in memory of her, but also as a warning to me, to avoid men's violent ways as best as I can. I'm the age now—fourteen—that she was when the terrible thing happened to her. It frightens me even to tell the story.

King David, my grandfather, had many sons and daughters from many different wives. One daughter in particular, Tamar, was noticed by one of her half-brothers, Amnon, early in her life while she was still a virgin and not yet betrothed to anyone. Amnon was terribly infatuated with her to the point of sickness. He thought constantly about her, even forgetting to eat. Because she was his sister he was hesitant to do anything about it, but he saw her as a prize that he wanted desperately to claim as his own.

His cousin Jonadab had more experience getting his own way at whatever cost to others. Everybody knew Jonadab was a sneaky conniver, but everybody, especially the men, just winked at his troublemaking and called him clever. I think they halfway admired him for getting away with things and being so crafty. I think they envied him. Jonadab planted an idea in Amnon's mind, a plan to make Tamar have sex with him. Amnon could pretend to be ill and get Tamar to tend him in his room. "Why not?" Jonadab said to Amnon in a confiding tone. "If she really wants you, too, as all women seem to, then she'll be only too happy that you arranged such a clever way to be alone together! And once it's done, then the king will have no choice but to give her to you. No one will even object, since you're a prince and she's a princess. It's quite natural that she should be in your room serving you, since that's her duty. And if she protests, well, what's to stop you anyway, then? What right does she have to refuse *you*, the heir to the throne of the whole kingdom? Wouldn't she want to be a queen? If she refuses, then teach her a lesson in obedience to her future king!"

Amnon liked the plan and added a trick of his own: the king *himself* would order Tamar to minister to him. This made Amnon feel even more powerful. So Amnon pretended to be sick, and everything went according to the plan that Tamar alone would cook in his presence and feed him . . . Tamar alone stood next to his bed.

He reached out and grabbed her hard, saying, "Come, lie with me, my sister." Tamar felt shocked and betrayed. She tried to pull away, but he would not let her go. Then she cried out, "No, my brother," reminding him of his relationship to her as kin. She cried, "Do not force me! Such a thing as this is not done in Israel! Don't do this reckless and crazy thing! Are you mad?" But still he kept pulling her closer. Then she began to cry, sensing her helplessness. She tried to appeal to his pity: "As for me, where could I carry my shame?" And to his pride: "And as for you, you would be considered a fool, a reckless fool!" Finally, trying desperately to stop him from hurting her, she tried to appeal to his reason, causing him to delay and giving her time, she prayed, to escape: "Listen, it doesn't have to be this way. Speak to the King—we could be married. I'm sure he would give his permission!" Everyone knew that King David had bent rules before, but all her appeals fell on deaf ears. "Enough!" he shouted, and although she fought back, he was too strong for her. Her refusal made him angrier, and now he didn't care how he hurt her. He called her names, threw her down on the floor, and raped her. The pain must have been terrible. She was terribly bruised and beaten; all she could think of for the whole time was that he was going to kill her. He kept her there as long as he wanted to, punishing her for her refusal, acting out every fantasy his mind had produced before when he had thought about her. Tamar didn't exist for him at all, except as an object for his possession and the release of his pent-up frustration.

Finally, he was exhausted and stopped. Tamar was crushed and could hardly move. She was terrified and just lay there waiting for his next move.

Then he looked at her with horror. She had become simply a reminder of all that had happened. She was no longer a beautiful, virginal woman, but a pathetic, bruised and bleeding, frightened girl, a reminder of his own brutality and his own weakness. She was no more his possession now than before. None of this had gone the way it was supposed to! He felt betrayed by Jonadab and enraged at Tamar. Why had she refused him? It was her fault! She was supposed to want him. It was her own fault that it had gone this way! "Get up! Get out!" he roared at her, filled with hatred.

Now Tamar was filled with a new horror. She knew that as a woman who had lost her virginity, she would be worthless in any marriage deal. What little rank she had as a princess was now far devalued. She might be completely shunned, left unprotected from any man's brutality, and left to a life of shame and poverty. "No, Amnon," she wept, "at least now give me the respect you owe me and honor me now, as your betrothed. I know that the law requires this, and if you refuse me your protection, I am lost! This is even worse than what you just did to me."

Amnon responded by shaming her further. Without another word to her, he coldly called his servant in, who saw her condition but said nothing. "Throw this woman out of here," Amnon said to the servant. "She's crazy, and she refuses to leave." The servant did as he was told, roughly pushing her out against her protests, as he had done with prostitutes before, as if Tamar had somehow offended Amnon. He quickly latched the door behind her, barring her return.

She went, weeping and distraught, barely able to walk. On her way she did not try to hide what had happened, but defiantly rent her robes and put ashes on her head so that others would see how she had been wronged. She arrived home and told my father, Absalom, the whole story. He did not say much, and did not join with her in expressing anger. Instead he tried to calm her down and reminded her not to betray the family's honor by speaking of this. "After all," he told her, "he *is* your brother, too." Yes, she thought, I called out to him as brother, but he did not honor me as his sister.

They tell me that after that Tamar went quietly around their house like a ghost, pale and ill and weeping. She was like an empty shell. Even her anger and outrage had been beaten out of her.

My father bided his time, and after two years, he plotted Amnon's death while they were traveling to work with the sheepshearers. Father came home to the family's tent full of the news, but then our family had to move quickly away that very night to Geshur, the land of his mother's father, for fear of my grandfather David's anger. My mother remembers from that time how my father's jubilation about finally having his revenge was cut short by fear of the king and also by anger that the king was so unwilling to see his side of the story. The whole family fled like criminals.

My aunt Tamar never really recovered from that move. My mother says that when Absalom came and told how he'd had Amnon killed, Tamar turned even paler and fell down screaming and crying. That night they all formed a caravan and fled. Tamar was so weak she couldn't ride and became so ill that when they arrived at Geshur, she no longer even knew who any of them were. She died a few days later.

Now my father is dead, too, killed by the king's general Joab, after my father's revolt against King David and many years of war. The king never really hated my father. He has forgiven him and mourns him still, so we are allowed to live in Jerusalem again. It's very confusing. I miss my father, and I know that all of this has to do with the control of the kingdom and how important that is for Israel. But I remember my aunt's story, too, even though no one speaks of her, at least not above a whisper. I remember this aunt for whom I was named, and I am afraid of what will become of me.

Tamar's Story in the Bible

Tamar's story, sadly, is still modern:

- Tamar was sexually assaulted, not by a stranger, but by someone she knew.
- The violation took place not in a dark alley or in a desolate park, but by a member of her own family in his home.
- Tamar was exploited through one of her most vulnerable traits—her kindness and her upbringing to take care of the other.
- Tamar said no; her no was not respected.

- When Tamar sought help, she was told to keep quiet.
- The process for achieving justice and restitution was taken out of her hands entirely and carried forward by her brother—it became men's business.
- In the end, it was her perpetrator for whom her father mourned, not for her.
- The end of Tamar's story happens without her.

Reading Tamar's Story

This Bible story is seldom heard in Christian churches. It is rarely read on a Sunday in lectionary-based traditions and not for any other saint day or other public occasion.[2] Yet this story needs to be heard,[3] and this hearing needs to be in a critical and questioning frame of mind or we will be misled, both by the ways we have traditionally been taught to hear a biblical text (that is, uncritically, as the word of God) and by the narrator's own viewpoint (that is, uncritically as the true and only telling).

This latter point needs expansion. Whenever a narrator of history (of any century) seems to present (whether intentionally or not) a neutral objectivity, hearers are lured into accepting this version of the story as the only version, that is, the truth. Readers, unless vigilant, fail to question the author's biases, adopting them without reflection.[4] In the telling of Tamar's story, whose viewpoints might we be led to? A note to biblical scholars: My method in approaching this text is purposely eclectic. I do not come to this exegesis with the methodological purity of a scholar using only a social-cultural, literary, rhetorical, or linguistic lens for analysis. Rather, I come as a hungry and passionate preacher and pastor, to glean whatever meanings I can about Tamar's shadowed history from whatever approaches seem to shed more light.

The narrator of 2 Samuel 13 at times portrays Tamar's situation poignantly, eliciting our sympathy for the female victim. But mostly, the narrator (I assume *he*) steers us in the direction of primary interest, even sympathy, for the men all around her. Even the poignancy of Tamar's humiliation is drawn out for the primary purpose of justifying Absalom's later murder of Amnon and not for its own sake.

The narrator aligns his perspective first with Tamar's brother Absalom: The statement "Now Absalom, David's son, had a beautiful sister, whose name was Tamar" (2 Sam. 13:1b) locates Tamar in reference to her brother, Absalom, and secondarily to David, but not first and foremost as a person in her own right. The sentence immediately goes on: "and after a time Amnon, David's son, loved her" (1c). Tamar is sandwiched between Absalom and David, Amnon and David. Because the first verb used to indicate any agency or intention is *loved*, the action of the story begins not with Tamar or Absalom or David, but with Amnon, aligning with his perspective.[5] Readers are drawn at the outset into *his* problem, that of a seemingly unrequited love, so overwhelming that it has made him (love)sick. What kind of love so quickly resorts to rape? Note that it did not seem possible to do anything "*to* her" or literally, to *do* her (*asah*). This is not love, but a lust to take ownership, a (temporarily) frustrated desire to dominate, control, and possess. The very use of the word *love* betrays a stunning lack of empathy for the victim and a complete absence of an understanding of the difference between relationship with a person versus ownership of property.[6]

The reader of 2 Samuel 13:3-5 may be drawn into further sympathy for the perpetrator because we are meant to see how he is being talked into a plot against his sister by their cousin, who is described as "a very crafty man," or as some commentators prefer, "wise."[7] A neutral term is used; Jonadab is not described as evil. He is "wise for doing evil," in the words of the rabbis.[8] He is also described as "a friend," using the same word that was used to mean "best man" in a wedding![9] Thus he becomes a perverted matchmaker of sorts, and readers are permitted to divert blame for the act of rape at least partially onto this Iago-like instigator. The perpetrator, Amnon, begins to look like the protagonist of a classical Greek tragedy, a basically good, even superior person like Othello, noble by birth, who by one tragic flaw—his "love" for his sister which blinds his reason and self-restraint? his gullibility and susceptibility to persuasion?—is brought to ruin. Perpetrator thus becomes victim, eliciting our sympathy.

In 2 Samuel 13:6-19, the rape incident is told with suspense. The father-king himself is apparently duped into being an accessory to the crime by ordering the victim to go to visit the perpetrator—ironically cast in a role like that of Uriah in the story of David and Bathsheba (2 Samuel 11-12).[10] Then we hear the victim's protests. Twice, we are tersely told, "But he would not listen to her," once before the act of sexual violence (14a) and again immediately following it (16b).

The actual act of sexual violence is also told tersely. "Being stronger than she, he forced her and lay with her" (14). The gentle English translations "he lay with her," or "had relations with her," are inaccurate according to the original Hebrew *shakhav*, after which the usual preposition for "with" is omitted (11), reading more accurately—and more brutally—as "he laid her."[11] *Shakhav* also has associations with death (for example, "to die" is "to *lie with* one's ancestors" in 1 Kings 1:21 and 2 Kings 14:22), and with defeat, linking sex and death[12]—the pornographer's own elision. The word translated as "force," *'innah*, can also be translated more forcefully as "humiliate" or "oppress."[13]

Here it can be argued that Amnon is no longer being portrayed in a sympathetic light. He has been led by Jonadab to the threshold of opportunity for this crime. His actions, however, are surely his own. Sympathy for Tamar is not the narrator's primary interest. The forcefulness of Tamar's oppression is drawn out, not to illuminate her pain, but to justify Absalom's anger at Amnon and subsequent murder of him.[14]

If his strength (*hazak*; 14b) was called into account, then she must have been physically resisting as well as verbally protesting—even fighting back as hard as she could. The story does not tell the whole truth here, which must have been at minimum that he forcefully restrained her, pushed her or threw her, and held her down and raped her. As shocking and even offensive as it is to see these words so starkly in writing—and all the more so considering our conditioning about the sacredness and the so-called beauty of the Bible as God's word—these are probably the minimal simple facts of the story.[15] To say less may be to belie both the terror and the excruciating pain of this young, virginal victim's experience. Is the brevity of this sentence dramatic, or is it minimizing, antiseptic, and even perfunctory?[16]

After the rape, the narrator goes on to report that Amnon "hated her with a very great hatred, so that the hatred with which he hated her was greater than the love with which he had loved her" (2 Sam. 13:15).[17] The story continues to report the perpetrator's viewpoint, the thoughts and feelings after the incident of violence; the victim's viewpoint is not presented. The rapist, having fulfilled his fantasy, perhaps now, for the first time, sees the real woman whom he victimized—bruised, bleeding, mortified. Rather than admit her anguish to himself, he fortifies his denial by hating her and ordering her out of his sight and, presumably, out of his consciousness. We are given no indication that he ever thought about her again—even in terms of fear of punishment or reprisal.

The victim again protests, this time at being thrown out of the house in disgrace, but again, "he would not listen to her" (2 Sam. 13:16). She is then further humiliated and degraded by the rapist's callously calling his servant to throw her out and bolt the door behind her. What are we to make of the victim's refusal to leave? Here we need to take care not to blame the victim with such formulas as she really wanted it, she really loved him all along, and this is proof. There is no question that she was suffering. But in the aftermath of the rape, she was expressing a legitimate cultural terror of being shamed and cast out of the community altogether as damaged goods.

Compare this to King David's own stealing of Bathsheba (2 Sam. 11:1-13). David's act is described not as a crime against the person of Bathsheba, but as a crime of property theft and murder against Uriah, her first owner-husband, by an unauthorized usurper—compared by David's prophet Nathan to the theft of a sheep from another man's fold (12:1-15).[18] At best, Tamar could expect a marriage to someone her father chose, who might also assault her in any way he liked as his property—but at least she would have what little honor was accorded to women in the community. This perspective is also expressed in her first words of protest before the rape, "Now speak to the king, for he will not keep me from you" (13:13c). Phyllis Trible writes, "Her words are honest and poignant; they acknowledge female servitude. Tamar knows Amnon can have her but pleads that he do it properly."[19]

Having sex with a woman—whether or not by force—was a time-honored means of declaring an engagement in Hebrew and other ancient cultures[20] and probably would have been accepted as a betrothal by the king if the perpetrator had properly assumed his ownership and responsibility over the victim.[21]

Even though her new situation in the aftermath of the rape was hardly comparable a marriage of mutual love, Tamar knew that the alternative to complete disgrace and desolation was to invoke ancient laws that gave her at least some rights.[22] A man who "seduced a virgin" was required to make her his wife by paying the bride-price (Exod. 22:16-17) and could not ever "put her away," or divorce her as in the case of a normally arranged marriage, "because he forced her" (Deut. 22:28).

Wherever and whenever women are generally regarded as property, their being raped and beaten remains a commonplace occurrence. In such a context, public honor may be the only thing left to a woman's basic sense of worth. Before the rape, Tamar was a princess whose virginity was a valuable commodity and could have ensured her a secure life with a wealthy and powerful protector against other male violators.[23] Now, if this perpetrator would not claim her after using her, no other man would want her. At best, she could obtain shelter from another brother, but no status, and also no children—the other main measure of a woman's worth besides the power of her husband. This wrong of sending her away was, then, greater in the long run than the wrong of the rape because it had devastating lifelong consequences. The physical and even psychological wounds of the rape trauma itself might eventually heal—or she might become numb after repeated marital rapes and battering, which she and the community around her might simply accept as part and parcel of a normal married life. But ostracism from the community could mean death—banishment as a pariah. Without the protection of a brother or other male family member, she would be exposed to further violence with no one to care and no honor left to avenge, consigned to a bitter life of poverty that would be brutal and short.[24]

After Tamar is put out, and the narrator briefly but poignantly reports her crying aloud (2 Sam. 13:19b), the perspective of the story shifts from the perpetrator to the victim's brother, and secondarily to the whole company of men at the king's court.

First, the victim's brother minimizes what happened. He asks not "Did Amnon rape you?" but "Has Amnon your brother been with you?" (20a).[25] The victim is told by her brother to keep the incident quiet.[26] She is even told to try to stifle her feelings: "He is your brother; do not take this to heart" (20b). She is not told even of his own anger, or apparently consoled in any way.

King David is reported to be "very angry" (13:21), but no communication is apparent between him and his victim daughter. His anger is no more likely to be out of sympathy with her than anger at the violation and devaluation of his property, which—until he chose to give it away, or more accurately, barter it away for a favorable political alliance—was his to dispose of. His son was a despoiler, not primarily of his daughter's personhood, but of his own property interests. One of his most valuable political pawns had been devalued. This was a triple abrogation of his rights, not only an act of property theft, but an act of familial disloyalty of a son against a father, and political treason of a subject and heir against his king.

Tamar ended up "a desolate woman in her brother Absalom's house" (13:20c). The word for desolate, *somema*, is poignant—it is used to refer to a land that is laid waste,[27] and contains not only social abandonment and psychological desolation, but also her fate of being childless—another blow to a woman's honor.[28]

Of Tamar we hear no more, even though the story goes on for nineteen more verses—roughly half the chapter. The rest of the story shows the machinations of the men, the revenge plot against the perpetrator, the confusion and scattering of all the king's sons, and the news to the king, and concludes with the general mourning not over Tamar, but over her rapist, and the flight of Tamar's brother, who—not incidentally—with Amnon out of the way was now first in succession to David's throne.

The narrator goes on at length in the next chapters to describe Absalom's return to court, his growth in popularity with the people, and finally the aborted coup against the king, resulting in Absalom's own death and one of the most well-known laments of the Bible, David's soulful cry, "O my son, Absalom, my son, my son Absalom! Would I had died instead of you, O Absalom, my son, my son!" (2 Sam. 19:1). So the whole story of Tamar, Amnon, and Absalom, ends with a truly heartrending outcry of grief for this second son. Tamar's voice is lost.

Tamar possibly died not too many years after the assault and never even lived to see this turn of events. Absalom named his only daughter after her (2 Sam. 14:27), and at least in some later Jewish traditions such naming is only done in memory of a deceased relation.[29]

Whatever Tamar's thoughts and feelings, whether her desire was for revenge or reconciliation or some kind of restitution, the power to act was taken out of her hands. Terrorized, betrayed, and, most likely, physically injured by the rape, then shamed and consigned to a life of desolation afterward, she was further disempowered by the brother who arrogated to himself the right to avenge her as he saw fit and the remote father-king who stayed out of the whole matter, only occasionally being duped—simply because he was inattentive—into complicity first with the rape and then with the revenge.

This telling of Tamar's story is men's history, told from a patriarchal viewpoint. In the words of one commentator, "Tamar is the tragic figure of the drama, but in the general context she is merely a subsidiary figure whose fate is only important for the light it sheds on the struggle between the two oldest princes and its further consequences for the history of the kingdom of David."[30]

Unpeeling Layers of Sexism

The authorship and political intentions of the narrator(s) of this story are not entirely resolved in contemporary biblical scholarship. The whole "succession history," recorded in 2 Samuel 9–20 and 1 Kings 1–2,[31] contains multiple *narrative* (original or close to original, whether written or oral sources) and subsequent editorial layers. Depending upon the scholar's viewpoint, either the narrative or the editorial layers are viewed as pro-Davidic/pro-Solomonic propaganda, whereas the other layers are viewed as quite the opposite.[32] Regardless of the theory, Tamar's own story is submerged under the male drama of political intrigue and destiny.

The story of Tamar likely belongs to one of the early narrative layers.[33] In many scholars' opinions, the narrator's bias was to show David as the rightful, foreordained, and even messianic king,[34] even though he exhibited particular weaknesses and failures that could not be ignored in the text since they were commonly known. The literary form is a court history, a "royal apology."[35] In alternative views, this narrative is intended to demonstrate King David's crimes and weaknesses.[36] In either case, the narrators are concerned with the succession of kings, the fulfillment of (patriarchal) prophecy concerning the establishment of an absolute monarchy, the politically unifying principle of monarchy in general, and the maneuvering of King David's sons to inherit or usurp the throne. They are concerned with theological questions of David's role in (male) salvation history.[37]

In a second layer (actually multiple layers) of the editors' voices found in 2 Samuel, patriarchal assumptions are carried forward by the Deuteronomic School (who crafted or compiled not only the Book of Deuteronomy but also a long Deuteronomistic history stretching from Joshua through 2 Kings).[38] Their agenda[39] was to restore centrality of religious and political power to Jerusalem with Josiah as king, the temple as a single consolidated place of primary worship, and the Law as a binding force of community behavior, a corrective reform following the fall of the Kingdom of Israel in 721 B.C.E. and centuries of political turmoil as described in 1 and 2 Kings.

For both earlier author(s) and later editors, the agenda was to bolster the principle of monarchy in general and David's lineage in particular. The rulership of men, or *patriarchy* (literally, rule of the fathers), is therefore not only the implicit cultural perspective of the book of 2 Samuel, but its explicit agenda. Suspense is generated in these stories around the central theme of David's power and authority and the political intrigues of those, including his sons, either to usurp his rule or to support it.

Commentators from our own century generally have passed on these biases unexamined and unchallenged to preachers and students of exegesis. As Elizabeth Schüssler Fiorenza states, "The historical marginality of women is therefore generated not only by the original biblical sources but also in and through the androcentric interpretations and patriarchal reconstructions of biblical scholarship."[40]

For example, the editor of the *New Oxford Annotated Bible* (Revised Standard Version),[41] writing in 1962, is laudatory indeed about the author of 2 Samuel (who, he believes, erroneously according to more recent scholarship, is "the Early Source, most of which was probably written by a single individual during the reign of Solomon"). He writes that this book

> is of such remarkable historical and literary quality that its author deserves the title "the father of history"—a title usually given to the Greek historian Herodotus, who lived 500 years later. . . . Thanks to the genius of the Early Source, 2 Samuel is one of the most clearly written, most homogeneous and most easily understood of all Biblical books; this is especially true of chapters 9–20, where the author seems to be writing from direct personal knowledge. Throughout the account of David's reign there shines the conviction that Israel is the people of the Lord and that his providence is at work in their history.[42]

The question might be raised: Providence for whom? Not for Tamar, whose voice vanishes from the narration long before the story is over.

In a more recent commentary, P. Kyle McCarter, Jr., frames the story of Tamar's rape as a matter of sacrilege:

> Most fundamentally, chap. 13 is a story of nebala, "sacrilege." . . . nebala is a violation of the sacred taboos that define and maintain the social structure and, as such, represents a serious threat to the society itself. The particular "sacrilege" committed here is incestuous rape. Although there is no certainty about the legal status of marriage between half-siblings in Davidic Israel . . . our narrator makes it unavoidably clear that incest is an issue by the extraordinary frequency of sibling terms he employs in vv. 1–14 ("brother" and "sister" six times each). Thus the particular incident that begins the story of Abishalom's revolt is an act of violence born of excessive love within the royal family, viz. Aminon's rape of Tamar. The immediate result is an act of violence born of excessive hate within the family, viz. Abishalom's murder of Aminon. There is, as Gunn aptly puts it, "excess of love at the beginning, excess of hate at the end."[43]

By framing the story as one of excessive love, McCarter, citing David Gunn,[44] bypasses the horror and violation of the rape altogether. He concludes the same paragraph with a focus on the "social fabric of all Israel":

> In the process of all this the son, Abishalom, is estranged from the father, David, and will eventually make war on him. The initial sacrilege, therefore, will precipitate the destruction of the entire social unit, the family. And because this particular family is the royal family, the social fabric of all Israel will finally be threatened.[45]

Does this view of the social fabric of all Israel encompass the women? Who is understood here as family—the women, the children, and the men? Or is family uncritically accepted as the patriarchal household, in which the harmonious relations among the men is what matters?

At least in two contemporary sources, Amnon's rape of Tamar is described simply as a "misdemeanor." Hertzberg, exegeting the word *nevelah* in 13:12, writes, "He does the 'wanton folly,' folly which is not simply 'stupidity' but a culpable misdemeanor."[46] In fact, *nevelah* is a strong word, far from "folly" or "misdemeanor," carrying the meaning of desecration, decay, and even corpse.[47] Here it is translators and commentators who dilute the strength of Tamar's voice, which is transmitted forcefully in the original narrative.

In a refreshing departure from scholarly collusion with the patriarchal bias of the sources, two women biblical scholars, Phyllis Trible and Judith Todd, have focused on Tamar's experience.[48] Trible, in a painstaking and pioneering exegesis of the text, highlighted Tamar as an exemplar of violence against women in the Bible and paved the way for more feminist readings of biblical texts about women.[49] Todd has further pointed to a justice theme directly relating to Tamar's own experience. Tamar pleads, "These things are not done in Israel." The question becomes: How *are* things done in Israel? Is the monarchy really any better than the justice system before it?[50] Todd writes:

> The literary connections of Tamar's rape with the rape of the Levite's concubine in Judges 19 point toward the question of justice in Israel. If . . . the implications of Judges 19ff are that the events there were the result of the fact that the monarchy, which ideally guaranteed justice, law, and order, had not yet been established,[51] then Tamar's counsel to Amnon and subsequent rape raise the issue of justice within the early monarchy itself.[52]

In this commentary, Todd not only raises the justice issue pertaining directly to Tamar—noting the parallel with the ghastly gang rape and murder of the Levite's concubine in Judges 19—but she also highlights Tamar's counsel, restoring to Tamar the status of a wise woman.[53] Tamar must not only have been well versed in the details of the law but also extremely astute politically and resourceful in the midst of crisis and trauma.

With few exceptions in the scholarly literature,[54] however, Tamar is disempowered not only by the many actors—her rapist-brother, his conspirator, her avenger-brother, and her father, and all the other brothers and other men of court who grieve her brothers' deaths but not her own—but also by the narrator who cannot see her viewpoint, and all the translators and commentators, ancient and modern, who extend the minimization and denial of the violent act of rape itself. Even our own inattention to the ways in which we are subtly led by the narrator to take not Tamar's point of view, but first her perpetrator's, then her brother's, and finally her father-king's hinders Tamar's voice.

Thus, we are dealing with layers of sexism around this story: First, we come as readers with our own very individual histories, wounds, assumptions, and blind spots. Our own reading of the text is both conscious and unconscious, and it can be argued that our engagement with any text is as complex and laden with projection as any other relationship.[55] Then come the prejudices of our own contexts and our larger cultural biases, all of which may obscure for us the fact that the narrator is biased. The sexism of these modern layers of interpretation that are our own, combined with the prevailing view of modern translators and commentators, leads us toward the (likely unconscious) assumption that the story is about sex, passion, or lust rather than power and property.

Questions of Canon and Redemption

The retelling of Tamar's story through historical and biblical imagination, this reclaiming of "subversive memory,"[56] is an act of resistance that raises the whole question of biblical authority. Often readers of the Bible are conditioned always to look for a moral to the story—and are then led to infer the moral intended by the particular narrator. If it is biblical, many assume that it establishes normative behavior. So, for example, if a crime is framed as a violation of property rather than of person, readers are likely to accept that framing as correct. Is everything that is in the Bible named *holy* to be accepted without reflection? Is the narrator's frame of reference, namely, that women are property rather than persons, above scrutiny? It is not enough to say that this was simply the cultural and historical reality of those times. It is not enough to recognize this cultural and historical bias while continuing to read the text from the perpetrator's point of view and, therefore, in tacit sympathy with him. As long as we ignore the victim's pain, or fail to ask about it, we have not located the text's truth—assuming that as "people of the Book," we have a stake in doing so.

Some readers may argue that the treatment of women as property was simply a cultural reality of biblical times, and that we cannot read back into the text a consciousness about women's equality and personhood that did not exist then. Of course there is truth in this argument, that we cannot imbue the biblical narrator with the perspective of a much later era. There are objections to this, however. First, the only recorded voice available to us is that of the men, who, to be sure, tacitly condoned and were embedded in the cultural view of women as property. However, did women of the time acquiesce to that view, or did they simply have no choice, no access to the power and privilege even to be accorded a voice? Does the value of women as property nullify women's experience of the physical and emotional pain of rape and the terror of being killed or cast out? Does the frequent silence of women in the Bible imply agreement, or simply exclusion? Even in the text we have, Tamar's voice is at least heard, and she is by no means acquiescent to Amnon's violence. Before she is silenced, she protests both in words and physical resistance, and after the rape, she protests in deed by publicly crying out her shame.

Second, to the extent that we simply accept the bias of the narrator as time- and culture-bound, rather than critically examining it and challenging it, we run the risk of becoming complicit with it. Especially where the cultural biases of the narrator may be consonant with our own, we may forget to question, and uncritically absorb his rendering of the story as the truth, rather than one of many possible truths.

If such stories in the Bible serve to subjugate women as property, then why should we read them? Why should they be accorded the honor of canon? I believe that such stories can be instructive, although never wholly redeemed in the sense that the narrator's own point of view can be somehow made a valid moral to the story. We must read the historical texts *as* history—with the full awareness that *all* historical narrative is biased. Our desire as Christians to read all historical narratives in the Bible as part of salvation history comes into conflict with the realization that many voices are excluded from that history—voices of women, children, and different ethnic groups—who were not recounted as victorious examples of God's vindication of the righteous. Tamar's troubles are lost, submerged in the great turmoil of male political strivings that swirl all around her.

Power and politics, however, are not all that the text relates. The Samuel stories taken all together blend political realism, a complex portrait of David himself as a central focus, and an account of divine providence in an artistic synthesis with God's providence as a central theme.[57] If God's hand was somehow providentially in the destruction of David's would-be usurper-son Absalom, and if the story of Amnon and Tamar was just a foil for Absalom's rise to power, and if this rise to power is then crushed as a demonstration of God's faithfulness to the preservation of the Davidic monarchy, then where was this same God of providence *for Tamar*? Where was God for Bathsheba? For the Levite's concubine?

To claim that the Bible "contains all things necessary for salvation"[58] is not to assert that each biblical story spells salvation for all people. Each story needs to be measured against the whole of Scripture. In particular, the biased perspectives of certain historical narratives and the morals to those stories implied by their narrators need to be measured against the larger theme (in both the Hebrew and Christian Bibles) of justice for the poor, the orphan, the widowed, and the vulnerable, against the ethic of care for the stranger and the sojourner, and against the overarching theme of love of neighbor as one's self.

Two elements are crucial in stopping violence and abuse of women and other oppressed groups. The first is to hear the stories from their own viewpoint insofar as this is possible. This is true whether the story is about the rape of a girl three thousand years ago in Jerusalem or of a next-door neighbor tomorrow.

The second crucial element in stopping abuse is questioning and opening for revision all forms of authority and power that are misused to perpetrate, incite, or collude with abuse—consciously and directly, as with Amnon and Jonadab, or unconsciously, as with King David. Such power and authority needs to be critiqued even when it appears in the Bible—or in the church.

PART
ONE

THE FRAMEWORK OF
VIOLENCE AGAINST WOMEN

Power and Violence against Women

Inscrutably involved, we live in the currents of universal reciprocity.
—Martin Buber, *I and Thou*[1]

My stepsons love to tell the story of how the younger boy, when he was three years old, ran pell-mell up to a giant saguaro cactus in the Arizona desert standing with its arms outstretched. He threw his arms around its middle in a bear hug. My husband and the older boy were horrified and rushed to him, expecting to be confronted by a frightened and crying human porcupine. But Adam was just little enough to have avoided the large stickers. He turned to them in amazement at their worry and with a broad smile on his face said, "The cactus likes me!"

What a wonderful world it must seem to three-year-olds who can still see and respond so spontaneously to the Thou in every living creature and feel themselves to be in real communication with plants, animals, waves, even rocks. This is akin to the seeing of native shamans all around the world, and is a respect, wonder, and expectancy that is born into everyone and that is only slowly eroded as we are civilized.

This capacity for deep seeing, this deep *faith* in the sacredness of all living beings, is not something we have to work to acquire. On the contrary, I believe it is something inherent in human consciousness. But we do lose it—or, rather, we lose access to it. It remains stored, but often buried under layers of conditioning that cause our conscious selves to forget. Remembering or "re-membering"[2] our sense of interconnectedness with all life is usually regarded as the eccentric activity of mystics—or lunatics.

This chapter begins with Martin Buber's well-known affirmation of the primary human longing for relation, for an unmediated encounter with a You.[3] All the abstractions and uses to which people put one another, and even subjective inner experiences of the other, constitute some manner of objectification, an I-It encounter.[4] He writes:

> *The basic word I-You can be spoken only with one's whole being. The concentration and fusion into a whole being can never be accomplished by me, can never be*

accomplished without me. I require a You to become; becoming I, I say You. All actual life is encounter.[5]

Buber did not actually address gross acts of violence or social oppression in *I and Thou*. Yet, the subtleties and complexities of interpersonal relationality that he explored lay a foundation for understanding human violence on a larger scheme. Heeding our own innate yearning for I-You relating, and resisting the many social and systemic forces that press us from all directions toward objectification, is at the heart of the Judeo-Christian commandment to love God and neighbor. We yearn for mutuality and unmediated connection. "In the beginning is the relation."[6] In these words of Buber, Christians may also be reminded of John 1:1 "In the beginning was the Word, and the Word was with God, and the Word was God." What is the *Logos*, the divine Word, if not a reaching out and toward, a primordial first spark of connectivity?

This chapter addresses two interlocking themes that help to define and analyze the nature of violence against women: relationality and power.

First, through the lens of Buber's *I and Thou*, we can understand violence against women—and violence more generally—as the annihilation of connectivity, the dulling and erasure of human relationality through objectification. Tamar's story is a poignant, even wrenching, example of a woman who yearned for I-You connection, who offered care, and who met unlove with reason and respect. And yet she was treated as property passed from hand to hand, cast out, and finally disregarded, *somema*, wasted.

Second, an exploration of I-It relating and its consequences leads to a discussion of power. Exploitative power and objectification go hand in hand. Tamar's story has taught us that violence against women is primarily a matter of power (especially political power and the power of property), not sex. The fact that her story is told in a biblical framework of salvation history also suggests that the saying coined in the rape crisis movement in the 1970s—"Rape is power, not sex"—is fundamentally a theological assertion.

Before the specific forms of violence against women and our pastoral response can be explored, it is essential that the question of power be addressed. Perhaps one of the reasons the church has been slow to take up the issue of violence against women as an issue of power is precisely because it has not yet come to terms with—even recognized—the extent and the limits of its own power, nor has it yet entered fully into the theological and ethical questions pertaining to a nonabusive understanding of power, both human and divine, in the world.

Power is an enormous and complex subject, and any brief discussion will necessarily be partial.[7] Nevertheless, some theological and ethical groundwork concerning the subject of power must be set down before an examination of the question of violence can be meaningfully undertaken. This will lead, in turn, to some suggestions for alternative understandings of power as nonabusive and for a basis for community that is built on accountability, relationality, and care.

I, Thou, and It

Sadly, the view of the world through the eyes of a three-year-old gets lost as we grow up and become used to a very different (often tacit) ethic. Our yearning for connection may be innate, but the *construction* of connection—how we go about achieving relations—is learned from our social context. Business as usual in our world encourages us to forget this sense of interconnectedness and to regard others as Its. Our entire social and economic structure depends upon the *use* of the It—regarding plants, animals, people, and the earth largely as consumable resources. This way of life, however, is now being caught up short by the dawning realization that none of these resources is in inexhaustible supply. Our abuse of them has not only resulted in extinction of species and pollution of the entire planet, but has also endangered our way of life and even our very survival.

Violence as Control and Loss of Connection

Our loss of connection with the world and with other human beings is also at the center of violence against women. In a battering relationship, just before the actual physical violence occurs, the batterer calls his partner a name.[8] There is a moment of decision, when the man consciously crosses the line and hits (or kicks or chokes): "You. . . ."

One common belief about domestic violence, rape, and other forms of assault on women is that somehow the man momentarily loses his head. As long as our Western civilization has existed, for example, there has been a lesser punishment for men who killed their wives in a so-called crime of passion, usually justified as being committed in a fit of sexual jealousy. In English and American jurisprudence, such crimes have been designated with the lesser charge of manslaughter, which is defined as killing someone, but without malice. Frequently this is determined by the presence of so-called mitigating circumstances—that is, those in which any "reasonable man" would also be likely to kill.

But the man does not really lose his head. (If this were true, then why does he manage to beat only his wife and not others who anger him at work or other settings? How is he capable, in the course of supposedly losing his head, of battering only in ways that do not leave marks, or targeting certain parts of her body only—her pregnant belly or her breasts?) Rather than losing his head, the abuser makes a critical shift in perspective, no longer seeing her as a human being, equally precious as himself, but only as an object to be manipulated—from a Thou to an It. The epithet he hurls at her becomes the key that opens a passage for him into a violence that in his mind at that moment seems justifiable.

The fact that wife-beating and the lesser charge of manslaughter for killing one's wife as opposed to one's neighbor were long accepted as a cultural norm, says more about the consensus of men over the decades regarding the possession of women as objects than about the ethical truth. Violence against women is connected to all other forms of violence, just as all living beings are, in reality and in spite of our forgetfulness or callous indifference, interconnected. We are confronted daily with the many forms of violence in our world. We often end up feeling that our powers are fragmented, as one worthy cause after another is lifted up for study, fundraising, or volunteering. We have a great agenda for social reform but are often overwhelmed by the myriad social problems confronting us. What is needed is a way for understanding how, from a personal and holistic perspective, all violence is one.

All violence begins with the personal, with the I, and with a point of decision, a crossing of a line, where each of us chooses momentarily to view another living being as an It rather than a Thou. The ultimate purpose of each act of violence, each reduction of another person from a Thou to an It, is to control the other. Our choices matter, even on what seems like a small scale. They have resonance in the universe. When we truly see another person or other living being as a Thou, we cannot dominate or control them. We then must enter into a different kind of covenant, where power is shared. This is the "universal reciprocity" that Buber recognized as mysterious, connected with the divine.

Impersonal Messages

Just as a critical moment of objectification occurs when a husband batters, a labeling or name-calling (spoken or unspoken) happens before every violent act in our world. Racist epithets usually emerge at the start of wars: Krauts, Japs, Gooks. Similar labels have been concocted in neighborhood turf wars when new ethnic groups would move into cities and towns during the natural unfolding and movement of generations: Micks, Dagos, Wops, Spics, Hymies, Niggers.

All are familiar with the terms children bring home from school, either as victims or as perpetrators of schoolyard bullying and violence, terms that usually echo multiple forms of racism, heterosexism, sexism, or able-bodyism: fag, queer, lezzie, geek. We learn to label in self-defense against those who would label us. Well trained from childhood experiences, name-calling is carried into adulthood—Communist, right-winger, hippie, liberal, feminist, fundamentalist.

The desensitization used, for example, by the military and media during wartime and practiced by all to decry or label others can lead to a lifelong desensitization to cultural and personal violence. According to one study, our youngest children watch an average of twenty-seven hours of television each week (with numbers as high as eleven hours each day in inner cities). Based on these figures, a study of the American Psychological Association concluded that children witness an estimated eight thousand murders and one hundred thousand acts of violence before finishing elementary school.[9] A *TV Guide* study conducted during eighteen hours (6 A.M. to midnight) on April 2, 1992, in Washington D.C., tabulated 1,846 individual acts of violence, 175 scenes in which violence resulted in one or more fatalities, 389 scenes involving "gun-play," 673 depictions of punching, pushing, slapping, dragging, and other physically hostile acts, and 226 scenes of menacing threats with a weapon.[10] In fictional programming, the study found more than 100 violent scenes per hour. Children's cartoons were the most violent program form, with 471 violent scenes per hour.[11] A number of nationally sponsored studies concur that violence on television does lead to more aggressive behavior by children and teenagers watching the programs.[12]

Children are not only passively exposed to violence on television. They are actively initiated into committing hundreds of symbolic acts of violence every hour "playing" video games. A new video game, "Mortal Kombat," released by Sega Genesis, includes a feature in which the action stops and the computer says to the player, "Finish him." By entering a code, the player then causes the character who is winning on the screen to rip off the head of the opponent, pull the spine off the body, and hold it up triumphantly, dripping blood.[13] In other so-called games already released or being developed by the same manufacturer, half-naked women are pursued by zombies and raped, and sexual acts are graphically depicted.[14] In "Night Trap," digitized video images of real teenage girls are stalked and killed by hooded assailants[15]—manipulated by children using joy sticks.

Drawing Connections

One of the great blessings of the church is that we insist on drawing the connections among persons and valuing each as precious as the next. For example, many of us have held the hands and gazed into the eyes of Salvadorans who were no more than targets for pilots of AC-37 fighter planes. Without the concern and involvement of North American churches, we might never have known the extent of the violence in El Salvador and other embattled countries.

The act of remembering (or re-membering) one's connectedness to all life has grave political consequences. Some time ago, I attended the first anniversary celebration for a village named Panchimilama. The village had been reclaimed one year before, with the help of the Lutheran church, by campesinos who had earlier been driven out by bombings in the region. That day, the chapel was dedicated and eight infants were baptized. How disturbing to learn that one year later, this village was surrounded by soldiers who pelted the inhabitants with grenades. The same week, the Lutheran Church of the Resurrection in San Salvador was bombed, and its offices were leveled to the ground. Bishop Medardo Gomez continued to receive death threats for carrying out the basic Christian mandate to minister to the poor. Like many other church leaders, he was called names, such as *subversivo* and *comunisto*, by the death squads. He has often had to live apart from his family and even, briefly, in exile out of the country altogether, but he insists on remaining in El Salvador, building the humanitarian mission of the church. He refuses to be bullied out of the country, but he knows that it may mean his death.

The I-Thou relationship is not simply an attitude of love toward others—although it is that—but also actions of making connections and actively working for justice. Had not hundreds of delegations of church people traveled to places like El Salvador and South Africa, meeting people and making friends with them, sharing their ministry, standing in small and large ways against oppression, a sense of I-Thou relationship would be no more than a vague commitment. It would be all too easy to say, "Well, that's just the way things are down there." The press reports very little of what happens there, and when they do, it seems distant and abstract, an It. But the gospel message which is the great ethic of our faith is that we do reach out across borders and across cultures, both within the United States and abroad, and we honor the millions of Thous of every race and creed whom we recognize as our brothers and sisters throughout our neighborhoods and throughout the world.

Examining Aggression

How easy it might be to romanticize the I-Thou moment of connection as something that good people simply choose before they attempt to stamp out I-It relations as hurtful. In 1922, the same year that Buber published *I and Thou*, Sigmund Freud was completing a different book, but with a similar title, *The I and the It* (*Das Ich und Das Es*, more commonly translated as *The Ego and the Id*).[16] Aggression, Freud maintains, is a core aspect of the structure of the human psyche from infanthood.[17] The most primal passion to survive within each of us, our internal It (or in Latin, our Id) begins with that primitive part of our psyches that demands to have its needs met heedless of others'. This internal It cannot respect the selfhood of another. Because it is pre-Ego, pre-I, it knows no I *or* Thou. It is incapable of sharing.

Far from ignoring or pretending that we have all risen above our inner It, our inner aggression or even violence, we need to acknowledge that it does, indeed, exist. Repressed into the unconscious, the internal It can wreak havoc unless it is brought into the light of conscious insight. We need to begin addressing violence, both in the microcosm of our households and the macrocosm of the whole human family, by courageously facing it within ourselves. We need to nurture our own ability to recognize another person as a Thou, and catch ourselves when we start to objectify that other into an It. In this way, we will all begin to be more comfortable with the complex challenges of sharing power, honoring differences, and entering into relationships with an open-mindedness toward being changed.

Freud's construct of the human personality was essentially pessimistic. He saw the normal narcissism of the newborn infant as a basic foundation of human nature. There is no question that this primary narcissism is a part of our personality structure, which we only partially successfully contain, for the most part at an unconscious level and very early, for the sake of interfacing with the world and surviving with other human beings. However, what Freud failed to see fully was the spark of universal connection, also present from birth, that spark which imbues early childhood innocence with a zest for relationship, a willing and eager trust, and an indomitable (at least for a while) sense of "yes!" to life.

One of C. G. Jung's significant contributions to the study of the psyche was precisely in his acknowledgment of this transpersonal dimension, which he thought moved through the larger Self (much larger than the conscious ego) via the "collective unconscious," the accumulated deposit of human species wisdom encoded deeply, and largely in symbolic form, in the human mind since the dawn of humanity itself.[18] He even considered the possibility that this transpersonal dimension, which when tapped gave one an oceanic sense of well-being and interconnectedness with all life, could be continuous with the divine.[19]

Seen in the perspective of honoring each person as both an I and a Thou, the Golden Rule of Jesus—"Do to others as you would have them do to you" (Luke 6:31; Matt. 7:12a)—is not simply a legislative quid-pro-quo ethic that maintains basic civilization, but it is deeply personal and relational. As other human beings are viewed as Thou, a sense of the deep interconnection is evoked. We begin to share the Native American wisdom which respects not only all other human beings, but also the animal world and our very environment, the earth, as Thou and not It. We are beginning to realize that by "having dominion" (Gen. 1:28) and holding power over other people, animals, and our environment, we have ended up exploiting them, destroying them, and using them up. As North Americans, every time we visit a so-called Third World[20] country we realize how rich in material things we are. Each of us can find new Thous in our midst to honor: Every time we let the water run or buy clothes made in a Two-thirds World factory, we participate in an "It" way of using the world. We are in desperate need of learning new, harmonious ways to live—ways that can only be learned by a conversion of perspective, a _soul conversion, from I-It to I-Thou_. Our very survival may depend on it. We are pushed by an I-Thou ethic beyond the simple notion of loving the neighbor as one's self, even beyond Jesus' sharpening of that commandment into loving one's enemy, the one who is different, challenging, even attacking us. We are pushed to view every creature in the whole creation—both animate and inanimate—as a Thou, and then to transform our relationships accordingly. This is not easy, heaven knows. We all struggle with this simplest yet most radical gospel imperative: to love God, neighbor, and even enemy unconditionally, as God loves.

Rereading Tamar's Story

Amnon from the beginning sees Tamar as an It: "It seemed impossible to Amnon to *do* anything *to* her" (2 Sam. 13:2). He plots to get her alone with him entirely for his own interests, and without regard to hers. Even after she reasons and pleads with him, he "would not listen to her; and being stronger than she, he forced her" (13:14). Absalom, too, it seems, thinks of Tamar more as an It than a Thou. When she returns to him weeping after the rape, he tells her to hold her peace. Nevertheless, in Absalom's case, there is some indication that he sees the humanity of his sister. She is referred to four times as his sister, even his "beautiful sister," emphasizing their relationship, and he himself addresses her as "my sister"—although negating her voice at the same time, by twisting Amnon's relationship as "your brother" into grounds for suppressing justice for the sister: "Now, hold your peace, my sister; he is your brother; do not take this to heart" (13:20).[21]

Amnon, too, calls her "my sister," but only *before* the rape. This form of address becomes a ruse in Amnon's mouth. He is interested not in relationship, but in use. Once the rape is over, he shows his true nature: "Put *this woman* out of my presence" (13:17).

David, too, apparently regards Tamar as an It, while he clearly loves and sees his sons as Thous. David goes to see Amnon when he hears that he is ill. He sends Tamar to minister to him—merely a tool in bringing about Amnon's recovery? Later he is "very angry" when he hears "of all these things," but there is no record of his calling Tamar to him for consolation or even a full report. In the whole story, it is only Absalom whom he addresses as "my son." We never hear him address Tamar as "my daughter." Finally, it is the deaths of his sons which make David weep. The rape and eventual death of his daughter is not worthy of any response, at least in the historical record.

It is Tamar who consistently regards both her brothers, as well as her father, as Thous. She trustingly follows her father's request to bake cakes for Amnon. She brings the cakes near to him without questioning. As soon as Amnon asks her to lie with him, her very first words are "No," and "*my brother*." She goes on, arguing her case like an equal, appealing to his reason. She concludes by reminding herself and Amnon of their larger context of relationship and acknowledges the authority of their father by naming him with his title: "speak to the king; for he will not withhold me from you" (13:13). Finally, after the rape, she continues to appeal to his relationship with her. Again, she says, "No, *my brother*; for this wrong in sending me away is greater than the other which you did to me" (13:16). But he would not listen to her and had her put out, using the words "*this woman*,"[22] denying their relationship and robbing her of the dignity that such relationship might have at least partially redeemed. The label *this woman* does not mean "this person," but rather "this property" (now used and to be discarded). Tamar goes into the unlit night of historical oblivion, without ever having lost sight of the Thous in relationship all around her—

her last days are spent in the house of her brother Absalom. Thereafter she is like so many women in history, a derivative being, with only her brother as a point of reference for her identity. She is reduced to a label, an It, a voiceless and desolate woman.

The Interconnectedness of Oppressions

The power shuffle is a dramatic exercise that is often used in workshops or classes on violence against women.[23] This exercise was developed by a small, visionary group of women and men as part of a larger program for unlearning racism, sexism, and homophobia; prevention education with young people of all races; and rehabilitative education for batterers and men working to stop their violence. The exercise begins by asking all the workshop participants to move silently to one side of the meeting room and to remain silent throughout. As various categories are called out, those people who identify themselves as belonging are asked to cross the room. They turn and face those remaining, and then after a moment are asked to walk back to rejoin the group.

One by one, the categories are called: "If you are a woman, please come to the other side of the room." "If you have ever been called fat." "If you or anyone in your family have ever had a mental illness." "If you are Latina or Latino." "If you grew up in a family where there was alcoholism." "If you are Black or African American." "If you are gay, lesbian, or bisexual." "If you grew up poor." And so forth.

The accumulated effects of these (and many other) separations and exposures, however voluntary, build in the silence. Participants are moved from initial unease and hesitancy, to fear, shame, anger, both personal and vicarious, and even despair at the gulfs between people. There are moments of guilt when people sometimes feel that they have had to stay too long on the seemingly safe side. There are also moments of liberation and defiance and pride as people claim their past, their identities, their uniqueness, their solidarity with others across the line. Few people are unmoved by the experience.

Afterward, a long period is spent, at first more quietly and privately in pairs of participants, and then as a whole group, reflecting on the feelings evoked by the experience. Then the theoretical basis of the exercise is shared. The categories that were called out in the exercise all have one thing in common: they represent groups that in our society are systematically targeted for oppression, or *target groups*. The participants then construct a chart of target groups and their counterparts, or *nontarget groups*, on the other. Privilege and power generally reside on the nontarget side of each category (see Table 1).

One of the most common objections to the experience is that it seems to create more divisions between people, and that they feel their separations from each other when, especially at such a workshop, their attention is especially tuned to moving toward unity and togetherness. The exercise evokes a

TABLE 1: OPPRESSION AND TARGET GROUPS

Nontarget/Power	Target
men	women
white	persons of color
adults	children and under-25
boss	worker
normal	developmentally disabled
Gentile	Jew
heterosexual	gay/lesbian/bisexual
rich/upper-middle class	working class/poor

powerful sense of frustration about the artificial separations that are imposed daily in our world and into which we are born—separations that serve no other purpose than keeping the various ranks on the power pyramid in their proper place.

A deeper basis for hope, however, emerges through an experience of a new form of connection, even though the initial feeling is that of separations. Nearly everyone finds himself or herself variously targeted, depending on the category that is called. Although the false unity by which we all sometimes try to remain optimistic, that "we're all in this world together, we're all the same," is disrupted, it is replaced by a fragile but deeper sense of real hope—a sense of empathy and compassion based on real common ground.

Even though the various forms of oppression have different, specific effects on the targeted groups and individuals, at a deeper level all oppressions are linked to maintain a pyramid or hierarchy of unequal privilege and access.[24] Most of us know personally what it is like to be on the targeted side. Thus, while we do not any longer assume we know the particulars of another person's experience, we do share the feelings of having been disempowered simply by virtue of who we were and are. On this shared experience, we can build a bridge.

The targeting system is maintained by violence. Children in the schoolyard learn either to beat up or be beaten. Deeper than physical bruises, however, is a psychological learning. The name-calling of the schoolyard—which is the same I-It objectification described earlier—is carried into adult life, only in more subtle ways. Stereotyping which insists on attributing certain traits, usually negative, to those on the target side, is not only learned at a young age by those on the nontarget side, but it is also internalized by those on the target side. So women as well as men come to believe that women are less logical, poor at math, poor at mechanics, and so forth. Blacks as well as whites come to believe that blacks are slow, lazy, violent, primitive, and more criminal. Gays and lesbians as well as straight people come to believe that they are sick for being attracted to the same sex. This internalized oppression—often born of the necessity for self-protection, even survival—is more insidious even than overt acts of oppression by those on the nontarget side, because it undermines the health, wholeness, and self-esteem of people on the target side from within. (It accounts for the subtlest and most difficult obstacles to overcoming oppression: the woman in the parish who "just can't see" a woman as her minister; the fearful and closeted gay man who writes an editorial on the sin of homosexuality.)

We all suffer from this social system. Nobody voluntarily chooses to be on one side of the chart or the other, at least not initially. We are born into most of the categories, or they happen to us because of aging, illness, or accidents. We suffer in several ways. We are set against each other, so that it is difficult to see any common ground. Our sense of horizons is limited, so that we accept that current injustices are natural or inevitable: (taking out of context) "the poor you will have with you always." We use reverse logic to justify oppression: "It's proof that blacks are inferior because there are so many more of them in prison," instead of asking what it is about our system that causes that inequality. This limits our relationships, because we tend to be segregated and stick with our own "kind." Ultimately we forget that we all need and are entitled to certain basic rights: good health care, stimulating education, and challenging work.

The workshop continues with addressing the question of bridging the many rifts between people. It is not a theory of quick fixes, like sharing ethnic foods or even making personal friends with people of another race or sexual preference—although spending more time together is certainly an invaluable prelude to understanding. It is a theory of *building alliances*, forging partnerships across lines of power and privilege for the sake of shared advocacy for social change. This goes deeper than a promise of support or politically correct rhetoric. (It requires a conversion of heart that recognizes solidarity in and across difference.[25]) It calls for deep self-reeducation and sacrificial listening when we find ourselves on the privileged side of the line, and self-empowerment and claiming of authority when we find ourselves on the side targeted for oppression.

Imagine a radiant, laughing, loving two-year-old, arms flung wide, saying "yes!" to life. We are born with natural curiosity, warmth, trust, and kindness. (Prejudice and oppression, both externalized and internalized, are *learned*. And they can be unlearned. Unlearning racism, sexism, heterosexism, classism, ageism, and all the other -isms, requires effort on the part of those on the nontarget side. It is not the responsibility of the targeted groups to teach their nontarget counterparts. It is not their job to take care of those on the target side in yet one more way.

The goal of those on the nontarget side is to become allies. An *ally* is a member of a nontarget group who educates himself or herself about the target group and is willing to help make changes in ways that he or she wants to have happen. An ally does not set the agenda for change or reform for the target group, but rather listens to what priorities and needs are expressed by those who know the experience of injustice from the inside out. To be an ally is challenging work: taking risks, making mistakes and admitting them, staying open to dialogue even though it sometimes hurts. There is no shame in having misinformation—the system has guaranteed that we all will be misinformed about one another. The responsibility an ally assumes is in being willing to give up those misconceptions.

Who participates in alliance building? Because everyone is now, has been, or will be at some time a target of some type of oppression, and because everyone is now or has been or will be at some time in a nontarget group and therefore in the position of power over others, alliance building is for everyone. The effect of alliance building is to interrupt oppression. Allies cease being Its and become Thous in each other's (and their own) eyes.

This training model is not without certain difficulties. It can tend to reinforce labels *oppressed* and *oppressor* even as it speaks about alliance building, mutual empathy, and the elimination of objectification across lines of privilege. Also, although the analysis in this model addresses cultural institutions and systems, the method still tends to be largely personal or interpersonal, and may inadvertently psychologize violence that is social and systemic and therefore beyond individuals' good intentions or even capacity for greater consciousness.[26]

The proposed solution, alliance building, is therefore a complicated matter. It is not accomplished by simply teaching individuals to listen better to one another, although that certainly is a prerequisite for any true mutuality. No one individual can represent the aims, experiences, and agendas for social change of an entire oppressed group. Anyone who has been engaged in social change work for very long knows of the changing and often competing agendas promoted by individuals claiming, often with very genuine concerns, to speak for an entire target group. Conversely, to pretend that, as a white woman, I have nothing to say to another who is, say, an African American woman, no challenge or disagreement because this other is African American, can incarnate another form of racism. Treating another with kid gloves is not mutuality. How can the basic premise of this antioppression training model, which is to mobilize empathy and relationality toward building alliances across lines of privilege and discrimination, actually be applied to creating larger, systemic change?

I-Thou-We: A Paradigm of Accountability

Wherever the sacredness of the I-Thou relationship is destroyed by exploitation, violence, or abuse, the power of relationship as peers is replaced by a dominating power. Tamar's story presents this picture of power—power that is equated with raw force, dominance, and violation. Dominating power presupposes and requires for its existence an I-It way of regarding other living beings. It feeds on objectification.

Even knowing about these outcomes and the costs and despite our best efforts and intentions we fail time and again to maintain an I-Thou relationship with others and with the world. We need a larger container to hold and reinforce our efforts and intentions to be in I-Thou relation. This container is *community,* creating a third dimension of "we-ness" to the sacred dyad of I and Thou.[27] Beyond the I-Thou pair there needs to be a "holding environment,"[28] which acknowledges all thoughts, feelings, and impulses, and at the same time reinforces I-Thou mutuality while containing or restraining I-It aggression. Accountability to community becomes the safeguard of mutual care and justice, in some sense providing a loving parental frame for both encouragement and healthy limits. This accountability to community itself, taking the role of parent, replaces the paternalistic and authoritarian parent-idol of unaccountable hierarchy that has dominated social structures for at least four thousand years.

holding environment

I-Thou-We also acknowledges that God is not only in the sacred interaction of the I-Thou pair but also surrounds the pair and transcends their particular binary unit. Although Buber primarily develops the twofold conception of relation, he hints at this mystery. True community must be built of subjects, not objects. Buber writes:

> Two basically different notions are confused when people use the concept of the social: the community built of relation and the amassing of human units that have no relation to one another—the palpable manifestation of modern man's lack of relation. The bright edifice of community, however, for which one can be liberated even from the dungeon of "sociability," is the work of the same force that is alive in the relation between man and God. But this is not one relation among others; it is the universal relation into which all rivers pour without drying up for that reason. Sea and rivers—who would make bold to separate here and define limits? There is only the one flood from I to You, ever more infinite, the one boundless flood of actual life.[29]

God is not only in the I and in the Thou but also in the We. God stirs us all to love and justice precisely in the matrix of the We—a loving web of connections that both includes us and reaches beyond us as far as the limits of the universe. The We is the *matrix,* literally, the *womb,* of all our being and all our relationships. Accepting the language of God as the "ground of our being,"[30] then the matrix of the We is God's womb, the warm and spongy place in which we are held and our creativity is fed. The capacity of each individual to have impact, grow, and create is both nurtured and also mediated within the larger context of all the other individual beings' unique impact, growth, and creativity.

What, then, brings about social change, especially if social change is understood to be more than a matter of purely personal, I-Thou commitment and empathy between individuals? How is I-Thou-We relationality nurtured and contained through community accountability? This brings us back to the question of power.

Power, Consciousness, and Mutuality

Power in the most fundamental sense is the power of the I to be able. The English word *power* derives from the Latin word *posse*, "to be able." This already implies the basic dilemma of community: How can we honor and satisfy the capacity of each I to do while at the same time honoring and mediating the complex striving of so many unique selves?

In psychologist Rollo May's terms, the *power to be*, basic to every infant's survival, is the knowledge that one can make an impact and feel one's own significance.[31] This is tied up with the power of self-affirmation and the power of self-assertion as well. May, in fact, draws the conclusion that what he terms the *power of aggression* and the *power of violence* emerge or erupt when the power of self-assertion is repeatedly blocked and denied expression.[32]

How do we exercise that power to be and to do in the context of an enormous society of others who also must have the freedom and the space to be and to do? What happens when these powers come into conflict? I believe the answer lies in our innate awareness of the interconnectedness of all life. The expression of our individual powers is tempered by our conscious and intentional awareness of our interconnectedness. In May's words, "the future lies with the man or woman who can live as an individual, conscious within the solidarity of the human race."[33] Neither the individual nor the solidarity is sacrificed in this picture. Our consciousness of the other, of the Thou, is as much a part of our own inner voice as our awareness of hunger, thirst, or sexual desire. Chronic hatred and fear are learned. Other beings become Its through our social conditioning, but we are born with the capacity to relate to all creation as a Thou.

Integration of our own personal power is essential to any real mutuality. Mutuality is not equality, not sameness.[34] Mutuality involves empowering each other to find and express what each can truly know and do, each one's unique contributions, not the dulling uniformity of the lowest common denominator. Differentiation of this sort threatens a falsely built unity that depends on merger and the suppression of disagreement. But by integrating disavowed anger, competition, envy, guilt, and fear, much greater power to do and to be is freed and released. Violence, ultimately, comes from not trusting and not believing in one's own power to do and be. It is only out of fear that one must control others, whether in overt or covert ways.

There is tremendous power in the integrity of one's own vision held in the awareness of solidarity with all life. This is the power of the cross. Being willing to surrender even life itself rather than surrendering the authentic power of self-in-compassion led Jesus to the cross, but also to resurrection.

Our language to describe power is impoverished by the narrowness of our culture's understanding of it.[35] We need new words, a new terminology to express the richness and complexity of this dimension of human relations. One response to this need has been a threefold typology of power that has been gaining consensus in feminist circles, articulated most succinctly by Starhawk:[36] *power-over* versus *power-within* and *power-with*.

Instrumental, utilitarian I-It ways of relating lead to only one kind of power, the currently predominant understanding of power as *power over others*. I-Thou ways of relating break down and melt this dominating view of power, replacing it with mutuality, justice, and care. This is a different kind of power, *power-with*, traded and shaped together through negotiation, struggle, and mutual concern and respect. Implicit in *power-with* is the power of the self, the authentic voice of the I, or true self.[37] This is *power within*, the charisma of the individual. Not until one's own self-authority is acknowledged and claimed can one enter into true mutuality. To expand Starhawk's paradigm, this might be called *power-owned*, to indicate a conscious claiming of one's power within.

An I-Thou-We framework extends this even further—power is not only owned and then shared, but also held within this matrix of community, a matrix of accountability, of containment and checks and balances. Here we need what I am calling *power-in-community*,[38] which recognizes the power that is *beyond* the individual and the relationship. This power enters the realm of the prophetic, which holds both individuality and relationality and transforms them into something much larger—something that finally approaches what Jesus referred to as the "Kingdom of God."

My own understanding of power-over, power-with, power-within, and power-owned—with power-in-community as an overarching category that embraces the other forms of power—both draws on, and also departs in some significant ways, from the threefold typology gaining consensus in feminist circles. In order to enter into dialogue with this view, it is first necessary to describe the logic and purpose behind it.

A Feminist World History of Power as Power-Over

The growing consensus in recent feminist scholarship regarding power begins with a view of world history. This issues in an indictment of the normative understanding of power in Judeo-Christian civilizations for approximately four thousand years—dating back to the earliest establishment of a culture that was both monotheistic and patriarchal—as the power to manage and control others.[39] Power in this normative sense means power-over, to "have dominion" or, literally, lordship (Gen. 1:28). The more people and creatures under one's care and authority, the more power one has. The worldview that accompanies this understanding of power is a Darwinian one of the world as an arena for struggle, striving, and competition. One is either over or under. One defends one's own self against rivals and defends those more vulnerable who belong, as it were, to him or her, while striving to stay on top. This understanding of power, however well disguised under a veneer of sophistication and social etiquette, is based on a harsh anthropology of eat or be eaten, an anthropology of fear. Power in this worldview is associated with virility, potency, masculinity, and even biological male sexuality, as revealed in our language: "the thrust of his argument," "a penetrating analysis."

This view is not confined to an analysis of ancient history, which can be studied at a distance by anthropologists and archaeologists. Even though many huge changes have occurred in terms of technology, culture, and specific forms of government over four thousand years, and although vast cultural variations exist between different countries and continents, many feminists point to a prevalence of modern patriarchal systems operating with an understanding of power as the power of dominion over others.

Caution needs to be taken regarding the universalizing inherent in some versions of this view. The temptation to homogenize different cultural systems of male-female relating and arrangements of power is considerable. This approach can function ideologically or reductionistically, and not reflect adequately the experiences of women and men, real subjects, even in different patriarchal cultures. This being said, patriarchy does prevail in a variety of ways in the modern world and appears deeply resistant to change.

The word *patriarchy* often causes alarm in church circles. We want to believe that women and men can and should be in relationship and partnership together and that men are simply human beings, some nice and some not so nice, but human beings nonetheless who as a group should not be blamed for the world's social and political distresses. It is helpful to make the distinction that to name patriarchy as the prevailing structure of power is not to blame individual men or to question most men's good intentions. More individual men than not do not find themselves in lofty positions on the power pyramid and, in fact, feel quite powerless.[40] To name patriarchy for what it is, however, is to point out that, even around the year 2000 C.E., after a century of reforms intending to grant more rights and more access to women and people of color, the vast majority of government officials, senior corporate executives, tenured university professors, high-ranking military officers, and senior church officials—the leaders of the main social institutions of government, business, education, the military, and religion—are men and, specifically, heterosexual Caucasian men. These facts are not in dispute. What becomes controversial is when this entrenched system is called to our attention and dredged up from the realm of unconscious acceptance, and the question is raised: Is this right? This question, after so long being ignored or suppressed, has deeply disturbed the world and, like a major earthquake, has caused deep fissures in the structure of the pyramid.

Power and authority, both for and over others, have been for four thousand years and still are seen, largely without question, as fitting hand in glove. In Judeo-Christian cultures, power is understood as distributed along a pyramid, upon which sits one God (whether Yahweh or the Christian triune God) at the pinnacle; below God come the ruling (male) government officials, (male) priests, and their (male) prophets (today, read advisors), all under "His" (read God's) direct orders; and then come the rest of the people generally distributed according to their social and economic status. Status has been defined differently in various centuries and locales, but the result has nearly always been that women, children, and serving-class people of whatever age and gender have been heaped near the bottom. Beneath them, scarcely noticed, are animals, plants, and the earth itself. The lower beings on the pyramid support the life of those higher up. Those lowest are cultivated, used, and exploited for their resources with little or no acknowledgment or compensation. Below a certain line (usually defined by gender, age, race, or serving-class status), beings always have been regarded as the property of those above the line. They are used, used up, and abused.

Power-Within and Power-With

From this analysis, feminist writers have sought to deconstruct and dismantle this notion of power as power-over. Power-over is recognized as death-dealing, both for individuals and for the planet. The alternative is simply to affirm power as power-within and power-with. Unlike power-over, both power-within and power-with are formulations of power intended to embody mutuality, justice, responsibility, and care.

Power-within is the power of one's own inner wisdom, intuition, self-esteem, even the spark of the divine. Theology that values power-within is joyfully incarnational, celebrating the inherent goodness or "original blessing" implanted in the human being,[41] not preoccupied with human sinfulness but rather with human goodness and inspiration. It is an *enthusiastic* theology, in the etymological sense of the word: *en-theos*, "God within."

Tamar demonstrated this clear, God-given power-within when she resisted Amnon's attack. In her valuing of her own powers of reason, in her learned argument, and in her attempts to salvage some dignity and respect even after the rape occurred, Tamar remained true to her own spiritual center and her own knowledge of her value as a human being. She managed this even while Amnon was relentlessly trying to reduce her to the status of an object. In her grief, Tamar respected herself with an act of resistance. She rent her robe and put ashes on her head. She went away, crying aloud, to let the world know of her innocence, her outrage, and her grief.

Power-with carries the dignity of power-within into relationship. Power-with is the power of an individual to reach out in a manner that negates neither self nor other. It prizes mutuality over control and operates by negotiation and consensus.[42]

It is Tamar's faithful and consistent relating to her father and her brothers as Thous, in spite of being endangered, objectified, unheard, and uncared for by them, that characterizes her relational stance as one of power-with. Although her options were limited by her time and culture, she approached them with dignity and dignified them in all her responses. The rupture of right relationship lay in the refusal of these men to meet her power-with stance in mutuality. Where she brought power-with, they met her with power-over. She was silenced by both the men in her family and by the historical record. But her commitment to a different kind of mutuality in relationship was never completely erased.

Limitations of the Threefold Typology

The understanding of power-with and power-within is a liberating and necessary alternative to power-over. The act of identifying these two forms of power, whether with this particular terminology or something similar, is a courageous act of reclaiming forms of power that have been largely unacknowledged or devalued by the dominant culture. Still, they do not go far enough, particularly in providing guidance for living. Power-over is undeniably a social construction that functions not only in the private, personal sphere of human relationships, but also at the level of society, politics, and institutions. Power-within and power-with often exist in the sphere of individuals and their relationships with other individuals and smaller groups. Yet they do not pose an adequate alternative to power-over because they do not operate primarily in the overarching sphere of community and society. I suspect this is likely because they have been formulated more in reaction against the predominant paradigm of power as power-over, and therefore primarily constitute efforts at deconstruction[43] rather than an effort at construction of a new social vision.

Much work has, of course, been needed in deconstructing the paradigm of power as power-over and beginning to recognize and defuse the destructive messages of oppression, both external toward other groups and internalized toward ourselves. While we are still immersed in patriarchal culture and structures, it is nearly impossible to envision anything beyond it. The work of deconstruction is demanding, even exhausting. It is the work of a lifetime, because the messages of oppression are so deeply ingrained. Is it too much to say that maybe we are all "racists, etc. in recovery"? Like the alcoholic who achieves sobriety, we can find ways to make our behavior healthier, but we can never eradicate all the messages of unhealth. It is frightening how early and how deep they are planted, and our awareness can sometimes lead us to despair. Deconstruction seems at times to be our only hope.

Perhaps for this reason, because so much energy is still needed in deconstructing the paradigm of power as power-over,[44] there has been very little successful work on constructing an actual workable alternative. More often than not, feminists have tended to shy away from the exercise of any explicit sort of authoritative power in women's organizations, experimenting instead with models that are largely collective and leaderless.[45] A few theoretical frameworks have been developed, including one by Starhawk based on her typology of power-within and power-with, as exercised in a collective with central coordinating function(s) but with no traditional leadership, and Riane

Eisler's social vision of a "partnership way."[46] The goal of such models has been to discover a way toward a more mutual exercise of authority.

It is complex and troubling to work on the constructive rather than the deconstructive side of the problem of power-over. It is easy to see the perils of a dominator understanding of power, because they are more blatant and because our world produces many examples, to our continual shame and horror. The damages of power-over range from the mildest forms of interpersonal harassment and petty exploitation to evils as global and incomprehensible as the massacres at Soweto and the Rio Lempo, and the extremes of genocide, as in the Holocaust. They include acts of war against entire nations motivated by the desire to maintain and protect a capitalist-consumer way of life, and the stockpiling of weapons of planetary catastrophe in the name of maintaining dominance as a so-called world power.

More subtle forms of abuse are also real, however, even in a collective social structure, yet harder to see. The constructive task of envisioning an authentic, just, and caring exercise of power is elusive, prone to both subjectivism and sentimental idealism.

Existing proposals often run the risk of falling into a largely untested utopianism, although they carry the seeds of a promising new paradise of mutuality and justice for all. There are aspects of both peril and promise with all three forms of power: power-within, power-with, and power-over.

The danger of overemphasis on power-within is solipsism: mistaking the voice of one's own neurosis or simply the more limited view of one's conscious self—in Jungian terms, the little ego—for the voice of the Self with its larger wisdom. Scars of old wounds can impede and block the free circulation of the human instinct for good, just as internalized messages of prejudice and self-hatred can also distort our perceptions. "The human being has an infinite capacity for self-deception." When this inner voice moves into the ethical arena as the governor of our choices and actions, can we really always access our inner wisdom to know what is healthy and right? Can we really tell the voice of our inner wisdom from the encoded voices of our parents, our peers, our society, and our own ego defenses? Or, in the more traditional terms of Christian faith, can the notion of sin, as defined as alienation from God and from each other, be quite so easily dismissed?

Also, when the power-within of one person seems to shine out and enthrall others, there are clear dangers if such charisma is neither healthy, caring, nor just. At the outer extremes, such power-within as charisma can lead to cult violence, and end in tragedy such as the Branch Davidian inferno or the mass suicide at Jonestown.[48]

On the other side of the power spectrum, *power-with* seems like a natural opposite to power-over and clearly has greater potential for mutuality and intimacy. In rejecting a dominator model, one sows seeds for nonviolence and revalues process as having as much value as tasks, goals, and outcomes. There are dangers here, too, however, dangers that have been felt by many in feminist and other collective organizations. There is a largely unacknowledged Shadow side to purely collective models for sharing leadership and authority, which is the banishment of open anger and an inability to tolerate direct disagreement. A longing for niceness, agreement, and mutual love can result in locking conflict in the closet. Affiliation and mutual care can lead to stifling merger. The disavowed parts of the collective then can become dangerous—anger and distrust are projected externally onto a shared enemy. The group psychological process becomes one of *splitting*—incapable of holding good and bad together in dialectical tension—so that the group tends to see people and things as either all good or all bad. Ideologies become rigid: "You're either a part of the solution or a part of the problem." Any member of the group who begins to challenge this is scapegoated. Disagreement is viewed as betrayal of trust. Terrible and vicious woundings take place with very little insight into the projections involved. This is a form of violence that is often cloaked in politically correct rhetoric and thus not named as violence at all. We talk about "calling each other" in a quest for greater and greater purity of thought and purpose. This drive toward unity and perfection is often understandable in groups whose ideals are so high, and whose mission is to confront an oppressive structure that is perceived as so overwhelming. It is easier to turn inward and focus on the internal conformity of the group than to face the hugeness of the task of outward-looking social reform.

This is likely to be compounded in women's groups, where the socialization of women to be polite and kind, to seek agreement and affiliation rather than to disagree and fight, causes conflict to go underground. Nurturing is the expected relational stance at all times, even when it is in conflict with competence.[49] Envy, competition, and anger are taboo, and so remain largely unacknowledged. (This in itself is a function of internalized sexism—unconsciously adopting stereotypes of femininity.) The feminist movement has been generally slow to examine this phenomenon, but the truth of it is perhaps confirmed by the charged quality of family secret which it carries for those who dare to discuss it.[50]

Another pitfall of power-with social organization is indecisiveness. So much attention can sometimes be devoted to process that tasks are not accomplished.[51] There is an inability to "bite the bullet" and make difficult decisions. This is especially true when the decision will cause pain even though necessary to set limits, maintain healthy boundaries, or be faithful to the overall mission of the organization over the long term.[52] This often arises in organizations particularly around the volatile issues of personnel and budget, and sometimes larger questions of structure, process, and communication are raised in crisis moments as an avoidance of making the painful decisions at hand.

Finally, collectives are susceptible to manipulation. Power-over cannot be banished simply by decree. Whether or not it is an innate part of the human psyche (and perhaps this involves a theological discussion of original sin), it is

nurturing

certainly ingrained in us from our absorption of patriarchal culture. Given this reality, power-over will always emerge. If authorized leadership is either weakened or disempowered by a distrust of power in whatever form, then power-over will erupt completely unauthorized. Collectives are thus susceptible to manipulation, covert exercises of power-over, and psychological bullying which the group is unable to acknowledge and address because power-over has supposedly been banished. Certain individuals, although not in any identified coordination or leadership function, can hold the entire group hostage to the extreme detriment of the group's original purposes or goals. Energy is diverted to placating or bargaining with the bully, and away from productive and healthy pursuits.

This is not to advocate for a return to a dominator model of power. At the same time, I would argue that domination does not need to be equated with leadership. Leadership can be valid and authorized. In this sense, power-over, or aspects of power-over, need to be reexamined in a positive light. Positive aspects may include legitimate authority, responsibility, nurture, and stewardship. Martha Ellen Stortz has helpfully described this aspect of power-over as "power-for," which is also similar to what Karen Lebacqz describes as "trusteeship," and to Rollo May's "nutrient power."[53] This is the power of the parent to protect and nurture the child[54] and the teacher to educate the student.[55] It is the legitimate charge of authorized police and fire corps "to serve and protect." It is the ancient power of wisdom of the elders.

Here, admittedly, we are on dangerous ground. Who is served and protected at the expense of whom? Do all really receive equal protection? Who assumes the responsibility to speak for whom? Are all voices equally heard? By what authority is this power being exercised? Who appointed those in power? To what ends? Problems inevitably arise when those vested with power-over, even in the form of power-for, do not have the wisdom, experience, accountability, and genuine care to exercise it for the good of others. And that good must be defined by those served, not by those serving. This leads to a pivotal criterion for the exercise of power-over, or power-for, which is that power must be proportionately linked with service, and the purposes of that service must be defined by those served.

One of the more subtle difficulties with even the most well-intentioned forms of power-for is that there is always a danger of the privileged presuming to speak for those without voice, rather than making room for them to enter the conversation and speak for themselves. Oppression was once aptly defined as "not needing to learn the other person's language."[56] This often hidden dynamic has rendered a great deal of the church's service and advocacy work, not to mention centuries of so-called charity, ineffective and ultimately revictimizing.

Nevertheless, there is a role for power-over in the form of power-for. Legitimate authority can cut through red tape and get things done. It can perform the necessary functions of setting limits, organizing, and coordinating. It is particularly needed in times of crisis when decisiveness is crucial. If the theater is on fire, there is not time for everyone to sit down and come to consensus about a plan of action.

Power-in-Community

The limitations with the current threefold typology of power-over, power-within, and power-with point to the need for another paradigm for power—one that embraces the power of the individual self and values relationality and mutuality, but also is large enough to meet the challenges of the larger sphere of social construction. While power-over has the most obvious potential for violence, violence can be a consequence of any of the three. To the extent that any of these forms of power are exercised within the larger social context of patriarchy, violence will fall disproportionately on those who reside lowest on the pyramid, including women, people of color, and the poor.

The term power-with comes closest to the idea but does not say enough, thus prompting my turn to the term power-in-community. In truth, every theory of power implies a corresponding theory of community.[57] Power-in-community can embrace all three forms of power—power-within, power-with, and power-over/power-for. It requires a differentiation of these forms of power, like St. Paul's frequent use of the imagery of the human body to describe the body of Christ. Power-in-community is organic. It needs a head (a leader or leadership group) to organize and direct the body.[58] But leadership in this model, unlike a patriarchal power-over model of hierarchy, is authorized by those who are served by that leadership and is accountable to them. Compassion[59] and justice are embraced as the goals of the community together with its leadership, rather than competition for dominance. Leadership also may be fluid and may rotate from one person or group to another as the task or mission may demand. Leadership in this model is based on a mutual I-Thou relationship. Seeing those served as Thous rather than Its does not mean abdicating responsibility, authority, or care for them. On the contrary, it means being careful, responsible, and authoritative (as in setting limits or confronting and stopping violence as it occurs) as the role of serving requires—rather than authoritarian. This leadership is consultative, consensus-oriented, and earned by the good faith it demonstrates.

One last caution must be raised here. As I reread my own writing, I can hear someone saying, "Aha! So it's right that men should have dominion in the home—just use it responsibly!" or substitute Caucasians, heterosexuals, or any other group of people who traditionally have held authority as power over other whole groups of people. A vindication of any concept of authority must be approached in our patriarchal culture with the utmost care, caution, and awareness of the horrors already perpetrated by those in power. I am not by any means proposing a new rationale for the status quo. I do not envision the same people holding all the power and privilege they do now, only doing it a little more nicely. This is not simply another version of paternalism, in which one holds power unto one's self for the good of the other.[60] Nor will it do simply to shuffle the cast of characters around, so that those who are currently oppressed can be on top.

I am, however, arguing that a leveling of authorized or overt power will not eliminate the emergence of violence through covert abuses of power. Power-over/power-for must be authorized by the community as a whole, not just by the privileged elite who already hold power-over. Power-over/power-for should never be conferred in society solely according to a given category (e.g., gender, age, religion, class, physical ability, skin color, sexual orientation).

Those who are authorized to serve in a power-over/power-for capacity do not *have* the power; it is on loan from the community. Power ultimately resides in the community itself, and every person is responsible for seeing that it is exercised well—or else to demand that it be reconferred or redistributed. Hannah Arendt located power ultimately in the power of the *polis*, the gathering of people:

> The only indispensable material factor in the generation of power is the living together of people. Only where men [sic] live so close together that the potentialities of action are always present can power remain with them, and the foundation of cities, which as city-states have remained paradigmatic for all Western political organization, is therefore indeed the most important material prerequisite for power. What keeps people together after the fleeting moment of action has passed (what we today call "organization") and what, at the same time, they keep alive through remaining together is power. And whoever, for whatever reasons, isolates himself and does not partake in such being together, forfeits power and becomes impotent, no matter how great his strength and how valid his reasons.[61]

Tyranny succeeds, according to Arendt, not primarily by force, but by isolating people from one another and from the leader.[62] Thus, power is reclaimed in community—where people talk to one another and name injustice, when mutual fear and suspicion are overcome and solidarity is achieved.

Because power resides in community, many more people may carry leadership and authority—carry it well—than is currently supposed. All our criteria for leadership need to be reexamined in the light of our prejudices and stereotypes. But authority, in and of itself, is not negative.[63]

Finally, privilege and power do not need to coincide. Powers to lead, care, govern, teach, and prophesy may be differentiated and distributed. Privilege, in contrast, can be shared. As privilege carries dignity and respect, then all should have equal access. As, in our society, privilege also means wealth and access to resources, then clearly our current system of privilege needs to be dramatically revised. As long as power-over is used to garner more and more resources for one's self, while others are freezing on the streets and starving, then clearly such power is not accountable regardless of its rhetoric.

The operative relationship within this power-in-community, then, actually goes beyond what can be described as I-Thou. Even in one-on-one relationships, if power is truly vested and held in the community, it is to that entire matrix that even the I and the Thou belong.[64] There is an expansion of relational consciousness that holds the preciousness of community together with the preciousness of the I and the Thou: I-Thou-We intertwine in a fluid, mutual dynamic.

Some Words about God

This brings us back to the assertion that the saying "Rape is power, not sex" is a theological statement. All the foregoing discussion, while grounded in theology, has been largely a discussion of ethics—that is, how human beings treat each other in the world. But Buber's *I and Thou* is theological, even if his intent was primarily to write an existential philosophy of human relations.[65] How we re-image our relations with one another and our planet has immediate and far-reaching consequences for how we come to re-image our God. Or, to turn that around, how we image our God has everything to do with how we image our relationships with each other.

Even as our society has rendered certain groups of people from Thous to Its, so we have rendered God into an It. Rather than seeking to know God as a Thou, and responding to the stirrings of the Holy Spirit in our midst prompting us to love and justice, we have created God in our own image—or, more accurately, the image of those at the top of the power pyramid. This idol appears to us as the old white man with the beard, above us rather than among us, more judge than advocate, and more ruler than friend.

To construct a new theology is the task for another book, and other authors have already made admirable beginnings toward deconstructing the authoritarian God-idol of old and reconstructing a God of love and justice. Feminist,[66] liberation,[67] process[68] theologians, and others[69] have begun to provide us with an array of new images for God, many of which have sound biblical sources, and, as well, have reclaimed ancient alternatives:[70] images of mother[71] (e.g., Num. 11:12-13; Deut. 32:18; Ps. 131:2; Isa. 42:14; 46:3-4; 49:15; 66:9; of midwife (Ps. 22:9-10; Jer. 49:15), of lover, friend, bakerwoman, (Matt. 13:33; Luke 13:20-21), mother bear (Hos. 13:8) one who enfolds humanity under a warm wing (Matt. 23:37; Luke 13:34-35; Ruth 2:12; Ps. 17:8-9; 36:7; 57:1; 61:4; 91:4; Luke 13:34).[72] The Hebrew word for God's compassion, *rahum*, and the word for mercies, *rahamin*, literally mean "womb love": "Can a woman forget her nursing child or show no compassion for the child of her womb? Even these may forget, yet I will not forget you" (Jer. 49:15). For some of these writers, the very task of theology is one of imagination, to re-image or even re-mythologize God.[73] Images are being reclaimed, as well, from ancient Hebrew, Native, and other non-Western-European cultures as well as from biblical sources—recognizing God in all beings rather than perpetuating a man-centered view of the world through a man-centered view of God: God as tree of life, as river, as fire (Deut. 4:24 and the Elijah story), as rock (Isa. 17:10). Sallie McFague also points out the strength of relational images for God in the Hebrew Bible.[74] Paul Tillich's phrase for God, "the ground of being," which is now being adopted in a number of liturgies, draws on Eastern understandings of God,[75] and recalls the God in whom we "live and move and have our being" (Acts 17:28).

Such images pose an alternative to the patriarchal God-father-judge. They are incarnational, immanent, working together with humanity on the side of justice and peace, and sorrowing with humanity when justice and peace are ruptured.

These images imply a different solution to the problem of how God can be both good and omnipotent, and yet allow evil to exist in the world. Rather than meting out catastrophe and pain as punishment for sin, God is seen as suffering with us when we suffer.[76] In such a view, God is *not* all-powerful to prevent human suffering, which would obviate humanity's free will, but, rather, stands in solidarity with a suffering humanity.[77] God's power lies not in the manipulation of the world like puppets, but in the constant and abiding energy for transformation of all things into good.[78]

The importance of a more inclusive language for referring in worship to both God and people is closely tied to these theological issues and to the issue of how oppressive stereotypes and paradigms are internalized early in life. If a God-idol is constructed in the image of those at the top of the power pyramid, then a vicious cycle is put into place in which subsequent generations of children are taught to believe that some people are more like God than others. Little girls grow up believing, usually at a deep, unconscious level, that they are created less in the image and likeness of God than their brothers. Black children, looking at Victorian paintings of a blond and blue-eyed Jesus, conclude that Jesus has less to do with them than with white people.

These considerations also extend to who functions as ordained clergy and religious leadership. To the extent that the most numinous or sacramental roles, whether designated as priest or some other term, are reserved for men alone, then only men will be seen as God's representatives. Children will infer that this is what God looks like as well, rather than being able to see God in the marvelous diversity and fullness of humanity and all creation.

Thus, considerations about how we image both God and humanity in our worship language have far-reaching consequences for the perpetuation of violence. Changes in language, finally, must be more than an exchange of masculine pronouns and images of masculinist values of domination for feminine pronouns and images of stereotypical feminine values of nurture. As soon as we think we have a fix on God, we have fallen into idolatry. Buber wrote, "God . . . the eternal presence, cannot be had. Woe unto the possessed who fancy that they possess God!"[79] Our attempts at naming God are little more than labels that objectify God and fail to embrace the vastness of divine being. A shift away from patriarchal consciousness in worship does not mean a

substitution of one set of formulas for another, but, rather, a shift from believing that we can name God to metaphorical thinking and imagining,[80]
which touch lightly on the impressions and experiences we have of God's relations with us—but never coming to rest as if we had found the truth about
the divine.

A shift, then, of relational consciousness is required in our theology as well
as our anthropology: Not only must we learn to challenge our I-It thinking in
relation to each other to become I-Thou and, as we invest power in the community, I-Thou-We; we also need to be open to the liberating breath of the
Holy Spirit, and to the movement of the Holy Spirit within the community
toward justice and peace, so that our relationship with God is fully I-Thou.
And as we more fully recognize God-in-the-matrix, as well—God's presence
and movement in the interstices of all our communal life—we can even relate
to God more mutually as "I-Thou-We."[81]

Tamar's Story

Where was God for Tamar? If we depend upon the biblical narrator's voice
to tell us, God was absent for Tamar. Tamar lived out her days, a desolate
woman, in her brother's house. God was somewhere else, pulling the strings
of the male power elite, maneuvering Israel's destiny through the men's
machinations for power and property.

But faith discerns a different end. How differently things might have gone
for Tamar had she had a community of faith to speak a liberating word of
hope to her! Our faith tells us that what happened to Tamar was a violation,
not of her father's property rights and political assets, but a violation of her
own personhood. Our faith tells us that Tamar did not deserve what happened
to her. It was wrong, and it should never have happened. And I believe that
our faith tells us that God did not cause Tamar's suffering. Rather, God stood
with Tamar, as silent in the narrative as the suffering woman herself. God suffered with Tamar, and although her story is lost to us down through the silence of the historical record, Tamar is not lost with God. With God, Tamar is
not alone, and she is vindicated for eternity.

Now it is up to us, as the church, to proclaim her vindication and make it
manifest in our truth-telling and vigilance to bring about empowerment, relationship, justice, and change. In speaking her truth, *our* truth, we reweave
the *concilium* and become the *re-concilers* that God has called us to be.

Images of Women: Pornography and the Connection to Violence

Now Absalom, David's son, had a beautiful sister, whose name was Tamar; and after a time Amnon, David's son, loved her. And Amnon was so tormented that he made himself ill because of his sister Tamar; for she was a virgin, and it seemed impossible to Amnon to do anything to her. . . . he would not listen to her; and being stronger than she, he forced her, and lay with her.

—2 Samuel 13:1-2, 14

And without more ado she stood up and shook the white wrappings from her, and came forth shining and splendid like some glittering snake when she has cast her slough; ay, and fixed her wonderful eyes upon me—more deadly than any Basilisk's—and pierced me through and through with their beauty. . . . Life— radiant, ecstatic, wonderful—seemed to flow from her and around her . . . and now stood out the incarnation of lovely tempting womanhood, made more perfect—and in a way more spiritual—than ever woman was before.

—H. Rider Haggard, *She* (1887)[1]

O was happy that Rene had whipped and had prostituted her, because her impassioned submission would furnish her lover with the proof that she belonged to him, but also because the pain and shame of the lash, and the outrage inflicted upon her by those who compelled her to pleasure when they took her, and at the same time delighted in their own without paying the slightest heed to hers, seemed to her the very redemption of her sins.

—Pauline Reage, *The Story of O* (1954)[2]

This chapter started out as the first in the series of chapters on different forms of violence against women—beginning at the seemingly milder end of a spectrum of violence against women, that of the portrayal of images of women in the media. Milder because no woman ever gets physically hurt by a billboard or a television ad, does she? But I discovered that I had fallen into a very deep swamp. A swamp of hatred, fear, and the most brutally murderous regions of violence against women. By stepping into the territory of society's portrayals of women, I had stepped into the whole territory of misogyny, hatred, and fear of women.

I found myself easily misled into thinking this would be a milder chapter, a way of easing into the relentless parade of horrors in the chapters to come. It is tempting to use an image of a *spectrum* of violence against women, and, indeed, the original conception of this book was as a string of chapters moving from one end of the spectrum to the other. The spectrum would range from the "mildest" forms of media exploitation and "playful" sexual harassment to more serious forms of sexual harassment, to economic and medical violence, then, perhaps, to pornography, then stalking and threats and phone harassment, then battering, then sexual assault and abuse (including incest), with ritualistic abuse and murder at the outer, most extreme end. Viewing all these forms of violence against women as a continuum is valuable because it demonstrates their connectedness and the cumulative effect on women's lives of so many different but related threats to their daily well-being. The cumulative effect is nothing less than terrorism.

Even so, this notion of a spectrum is misleading, because it seems to support the argument that certain forms of violence are less dangerous than others—and therefore not to be taken overly seriously. From the point of view of many perpetrators, almost nothing short of murder warrants much of a fuss—the victim exaggerates, she couldn't take a joke, she misinterpreted, she's crying wolf. But even the seemingly milder forms of violence against women are dangerous. The entire spectrum supports the entire spectrum. It might be tempting to put objectification of women through media images on the opposite, mildest end from the most blatant and sadistic forms of physical violence. And in one sense, that is felt to be true. On one level, no woman is as damaged by seeing a billboard of a woman in a stereotypically sexy pose as she would be by being gang-raped or murdered. But when we consider the deepest root causes of violence against women, it becomes clear that every specific form of violence supports and maintains the systemic perpetuation of them all.

This also raises more questions out of the previous chapter. The entire foregoing analysis describes *what is*, in terms of power relations and abuses, and how the objectification of people is maintained and justified. It also offers a vision of what *might be* if these abuses were eradicated, a vision no smaller than the Realm of God. Still, as I step into the morass of how women are portrayed, I see not only a method of propaganda for the woman-subordinating status quo—although it surely is that. I see glimpses of deeper meanings, meanings that frighten me terribly. I see glimpses of fear and loathing and hatred. In pornography I see mirrors held up to my own female body, shattered mirrors of shattered bodies, things somebody in his imagination wants to do to my body, to all women's bodies. And when I make the return voyage from stuff that is labeled "pornography" to stuff that is labeled "advertising" and even "art," I see some of the same gestures, the same arrangements of people, the same poses, the same messages. And I begin to shift my understanding of unaccountable power-over as not the *cause* of violence against women but the mediating *structure* through which individual acts of violence are meted out. It is a description of the status quo. I am left asking the question "Why?" and I am driven deeper for an understanding of the cause.

In pornography and in media images of women, I begin to understand that the social structure of patriarchy is merely the exteriorization of a deep psychological landscape—a major component in the "collective unconscious," to use Jung's terminology—containing a great deal of fear. Structure, whether in the individual personality or in the culture, represents a need for containment of forces that are feared. Against what deep forces is patriarchy erected?

Rather than looking to the more extreme, overtly violent end of the spectrum of actual, physical violence against women, the answer to this question is better understood by beginning at the apparently more mild end—in the images of women in the mainstream media, and in pornography. We can begin, in fact, with the supposedly mildest forms of all—socially accepted, public media images of women. Because herein lies the *mythos* of misogyny. Public imagery of women is the text for all the other forms of violence.

Images of women saturate the culture, as emblems or as mascots for products ranging from cars to mechanics' tools to boats to designer jeans. These images become icons for sale, valued as objects for their own sake—Barbie dolls, centerfolds, the silvery nude women on the mudflaps of trucks. These images instruct both men and women on what a "real" woman should be like: an "It-woman" with vacant eyes, large breasts that never sag, a frail and even anorectic waistline, a body that complies uncomplainingly no matter what you do to it. Dress It, undress It, throw It, leave It lying around; fold It and carry It in your pocket or briefcase, masturbate on It; display It and let It catch all the mud thrown up by your fast-moving wheels. It never cries.

Misogyny is hatred of women fused with fear, fear of woman's power (and here I mean authentic power from within), the numinous power of woman's energy to bear and sustain life, the mystery of woman's bodily cycles. Woman's monthly bleeding is said to have awed and terrified ancient man. She could bleed and not die. Her blood had magical power.[3] And she could sustain life in her body and through the magic of her breasts. Her power was inextricably joined to the earth and to the enigmas of life and death. The most ancient religious artifacts venerated her power and saw it as one with the life-giving and life-taking power of the goddess, the earth mother.[4] Regardless of whether there ever was, in fact, a utopian matriarchal era of the goddess, there is wisdom to be gained from whatever strands of goddess culture we can uncover, particularly in the redemption of the body and the earth as sacred and worthy of reverence. An entire, important line of feminist spirituality now focuses on reclaiming that power, submerged and subverted by patriarchal culture, and also bringing its wisdom to bear in the healing of the wounded and plundered earth.[5]

Myths are constructed to explain the world and, more to the point, to try to control forces that are perceived as mysterious and threatening. For patriarchy, Woman is such a force. Patriarchal myths attempting to control women's power serve to lock unique individual persons—both women and men—into stereotypes that are constricting, damaging, and ultimately death-dealing. Myths about woman, like all myths, are often founded in some biological reality. However, biology is not destiny. Individual women, as persons, are much more than the biological realities of their lives. Women menstruate, make love, miscarry, give birth, nurse babies, have hot flashes, and feel the ebb and flow of hormones like the lunar tide in cycles, not only monthly, but in great cycles over the lifespan. Women also read and write books, drive buses and tractors, perform surgery, conduct orchestras, and manage businesses and governments. Images that focus only on women's biological realities confine women's lives to the level of myth, just as a stereotype (in the literal sense of the word) can only produce a single picture.[6]

Six Myths

Stereotype-bearing myths about women abound in our culture. I will point to six as having both theological significance and particular relevance to the issue of violence against women: woman as fused with nature, woman as sub-species, woman as mother (whether all-nurturing or devouring), woman as bearer of sin to humanity, and woman as gateway to death. These myths are, of course, intertwined. I separate them out for the sake of closer examination, but they flow easily together and are often seen merged in public images.

Woman as Nature

A young Nastassia Kinski reclines, naked, draped only with a six-foot boa constrictor. A billboard advertisement for beer shows a woman in a tiger suit. Even in serious films, women are portrayed as part of the earth itself, for example, *Woman of the Dunes*. Such images go deep in the mythological imagination. Venus is not born from the body of a woman, but emerges from the sea naked, dripping, with long hair like seaweed, on a giant shell—an image immortalized by the Renaissance painter Raphael.

Modern commercial imagery contains faint echoes of such ancient mythological representations. But whereas the ancient symbols retained some sense of the numinous power of woman in a positive light, modern imagery trivializes and reduces them to "visual property,"[7] objects either overtly or subliminally aimed at men's power fantasies. And again, while the stimulation of sexual fantasies is the more obvious intent of such image-making, these are actually a mediating structure for the more basic power fantasies that are based on fear and the need to be in control.

Why should man fear the natural? Why this need to subdue it? Man's linking of woman with animals and with nature, "the natural," is related to his denial of the body, the desire to transcend physical limitations, which is seen most fully developed philosophically in classical Greek "mind-body dualism" (not incidentally, the cultural backdrop of the New Testament, especially as seen in the writings of St. Paul). Ultimately, the denial of the body becomes an obsessive denial of death.[8] The struggle to deny mortality involves hiding from one's own natural bodily functions. Sex becomes a momentary losing of one's self rather than a deeper finding. Illness, weakness, disability, even defecation, are reminders of an inescapable mortality that must be denied and hidden at all costs.

Thus, childbirth is contained in a sanitary, surgical environment by white-coated physicians, the mother (and emerging baby) drugged with anesthesia, so that the blood, the screaming, the sweat—and also much of the joy—are kept under control. Death most often occurs in our culture in a sterile white-and-steel environment, surrounded by tubes and electronic devices, rather than at home surrounded by family. American funeral practices shield mourners as much as possible from the reality of death, behind a screen of bad organ music, heavy make-up, satin padding, and rolls of fake grass. Etiquette takes the place of true ritual.

Women, animals, and nature become linked in masculinist culture because they all irrepressibly carry reminders of the bloody reality of life, and therefore must be corralled and tamed.[9] Although they provide things necessary to survival, they must be carefully controlled. They are plowed, planted, bred, harvested, and eaten. The art of *husbandry* is the marshalling of these frightening forces into manageable, consumable resources. Thus, Woman becomes the icon for all that Man needs in order to survive, and at the same time fears and wishes to control. Children, because of their impetuosity and innocence, are similarly objectified and domesticated as early in their lives as possible as part of the same mentality. Both the romantic (pseudo-idealizing) and monstrous (i.e., "savage") stereotypes of people of color (especially Native Americans and blacks) also link them with nature and the body. Wild and free, or wild and dangerous, they are seen by "white" people as forces to be subdued. Darkness of skin is tied in a fearing and hateful way with the so-called "dark" forces of the unconscious where irrationality, primal physical impulses, darkness, and evil are all lumped together under a thick wall of denial. The jungle itself becomes a metaphor for the deepest regions of the unconscious, where things grow wild and uncultivated, pushed back beyond the light of ego consciousness.

Man's fear of Woman as nature, then, is bound up in the fear that nature itself will overwhelm or devour him. As bodily realities are more and more pushed underground and left to grow to nightmarish proportions in the shadows of the collective unconscious, woman and nature both become monstrous Its. Hence, we have images of snakes and basilisks, as in one of the epigraphs to this chapter,[10] the old tradition of naming hurricanes only with women's names, and the numerous portrayals of Mother Nature: "You can't fool Mother Nature." Implacable woman and implacable nature bring their terrifying and impersonal forces to bear against Man. He believes he must tame and subdue this Woman/Nature in order to maintain his denial of death. To survive, Man must control those forces that would challenge his fantasy that he will never die.

It is no surprise, then, that, as Woman is identified with nature, Man identifies himself with culture (and hence with technology).[11] And so the mind-body split of centuries of male rationalism constructs a dualism in which woman and man represent opposing forces of instinct or irrationality vs. reason, darkness vs. light/enlightenment, matter vs. idea, wildness vs. cultivation, and procreation vs. creation. Woman is the raw material to be cultivated and brought to heel by Man. In reality, the so-called "cultivation" of both women and the natural world have been rape, plunder, and devastation. Tamar was left a desolate woman in her brother's house, *somema*, a land laid to waste.

Woman as Eternal Mother

Mother Nature brings us to the second misogynist myth: the myth of woman as Eternal Mother. While the Father archetype dominates in our religious depictions of God, and Mother is either devalued or left out of religious iconography, to the detriment of both women's and men's spirituality, the devalued and suppressed Mother archetype is projected onto real women as an expectation of being perfect suppliers of every need, both physical and emotional. When women fail to live up to this impossible standard and assert their own individuality, limits and needs, those who believe they should be recipients of their care fly into infantile rage. The stereotype of the all-bountiful mother invades nearly every relationship men and women have with women, from the subtle expectation that all women will bear children and automatically be capable and loving mothers, to the expectation that women will treat them only out of a desire to nurture and never out of any other motive, however justified. The inevitable frustration of such expectations has given rise to frightening and negative stereotypes on the flip side of the Eternal Mother: the sterile and withholding mother, or the devouring mother. In the one, the need originating in infancy for affection, care, and touch is frustrated; in the other, the primal need for autonomy and space is invaded and overwhelmed. While real infants and real mothers need, and do find, the delicate balance between abandonment and enmeshment, real women are continually enslaved by the myth that they should innately know how to achieve this balance perfectly from the moment of their child's first cry, and that women should reenact this perfect mothering in every other relationship as well. Women are reduced to their function as mother. Their failure to live up to myths of maternal perfection become pseudo-grounds for rage and violence against them: women must be kept under control so that their primary function will be maintained. Nothing less than survival is (unconsciously) believed to be at stake.

Strong psychoanalytically-based arguments have been made that as long as women are the primary caretakers of small children, Woman will be identified with providing—or, as is inevitable, not providing—our most basic survival needs. In a poignant and profound theory too complex to describe in detail, psychoanalytic thinkers including Melanie Klein, Nancy Chodorow, and Dorothy Dinnerstein have showed the link between mother, breast, and nature; or, in another version, woman, body, and death. At a preverbal and primal stage, we are programmed to meet Mother as It, whereas we meet Father somewhat later in the process as a subject, an I. At the most primitive level of our socially constructed, but perhaps biologically influenced, psyche, power is therefore invoked to keep Woman, nature, and ultimately mortality, contained and under control. These authors advocate a major overhauling of our social and sexual arrangements and, in particular, a sharing of early parenting.[12]

Again, the link is made between maternity and mortality. In order to keep the tremendous power of the life force, that is, the *erotic*, in its literal sense, under control, childbirth is carefully contained within social and medical constraints. In spite of its miraculous and deeply numinous power, "procreation" is devalued far beneath the more masculine "creation," as these two words imply (the prefix "pro-" meaning "proto-" or somehow not yet complete or at its highest form). "Creation" is reserved for acts of the creative mind: art, literature, technological innovation. One is considered "creative," not for giving birth, which is regarded by our culture as *mundane* (which in the literal sense it is) and, hence, relegated with all things earthy to a place of little value, but for transcending the *mundane* by making something *artificial* (also in the literal sense) that did not exist before—a book, a building, a painting, a machine.[13] Thus the fearsome and numinous force of Eternal Mother as it is projected onto individual women is corralled, tamed, and controlled in the service of biological survival, while the creative Father is exalted through individual men's thought and achievement.

Woman as Crazy

One of the most effective means of silencing women and invalidating women's experience—and protest—has been the pervasive myth of women's inherent emotional instability and faulty perception of reality.[14] The figure of the Madwoman is familiar throughout patriarchal history, from ancient mythology to the modern cinema, assuming the proportions of an archetype.[15] In the most benign sense, "women's intuition" is sometimes held up as a positive trait. However, this is dangerously close to an essentialist portrayal of women as emotional to the exclusion of rational competence.

The root of the word *hysteria* is the Greek word for womb, *hysteron* (hence, the word *hysterectomy*).[16] The term was coined because, as Plato wrote in the *Timaeus*, hysteria was assumed to be a women's disease, in which a wayward uterus somehow became detached and floated around the body, wreaking havoc. "Don't get hysterical" entered the popular vernacular as a caution—almost always directed at women—against expressing too much feeling. Descriptions of hysteria read as an exaggeration or caricature of stereotypical feminine behaviors: overly emotive, wanting too much sex or none at all ("frigid"), having irrational fears, and fainting.

Historically the "cure" could be as extreme as mutilation of women's bodies. Women's reproductive organs were often surgically removed in the nineteenth century as a supposed cure for psychological disorders. This practice continued to be documented as late as 1946.[17] Female sexuality and female madness were viewed as inextricably linked. Not only were ovaries and uteruses removed routinely, but female circumcision and clitoridectomy were practice in the United States into the twentieth century as a "cure" for masturbation.[18]

The myth of women's madness has proved to be self-fulfilling prophecy in some instances. In fact, a number of mental disorders disproportionately affect women in our culture,[19] including agoraphobia (fear of leaving the house), dysthymic disorder (a chronic low-level depression, once called "depressive neurosis"), anorexia nervosa (self-starvation prompted by a misperception of being fat), bulimia (compulsive binge eating followed by self-induced vomiting), somaticization disorder (recurrent, multiple physical complaints that cannot be traced to any evidence of physical illness), dissociative identity disorder, and others. Many of these can easily be considered to relate to stereotypical definitions of femininity—for example, "a woman's place is in the house" can be translated into agoraphobia,[20] and anorexia and bulimia can be understood as an exaggerated attempt to meet society's standards of thinness.[21]

The prevalence of these disorders in women is often used to support the myth of women as crazy. It is more accurate, however, to assign the disproportionate nature of these disorders as *legitimate psychic reactions to patriarchal conditions*, and not as inherent weaknesses or instability in women. Thus, the etiology of a variety of hysterical neuroses and characterological problems is most often linked to childhood sexual abuse, a position which Freud himself initially espoused, but from which he later retreated. (This will be elaborated further in chapter 8.) To the extent that women *act* crazy, it may well be a normal response to abuse and repression. It is easier for both men and women to label a woman as crazy than it is to face the truth of the violence and hatred directed against women in our culture.

Woman as Subhuman

In the year 584, forty-three Catholic bishops and twenty men representing bishops voted, after lengthy debate at the Council of Macon, whether women were human. Women were declared human by one vote in a count of 32 to 31.[22]

The question of women's inferiority ranges from trivializing her worth to even disregarding her life. A sampler from centuries of Christian writing reveals a consistently callous and inhumane regard for the value of women.

St. Augustine, whose own struggles with sexuality and with women are well known, considered that woman is only formed in the image of God when she is married to a man, because it is their union that constitutes the image of God.[23] He also wrote, "Any woman who acts in such a way that she cannot give birth to as many children as she is capable of, makes herself guilty of the many murders."[24]

The widely revered scholastic theologian Thomas Aquinas wrote in his *Summa Theologica* in 1266:

Father and mother are loved as principles of our natural origin. Now the father is principle in a more excellent way than the mother, because he is the active principle, while mother is a passive and material principle. Consequently, strictly speaking, the father is to be loved more.[25]

And in another passage:

. . . in a secondary sense the image of God is found in man, and not in woman: for man is the beginning and end of woman; as God is the beginning and end of every creature.[26]

Such attitudes were not confined to the Middle Ages. Martin Luther wrote in the sixteenth century:

Women should remain at home, sit still, keep house and bear and bring up children. . . . If a woman grows weary and, at last, dies from childbearing, it matters not. Let her die from bearing—she is there to do it.[27]

Luther also wrote of his wife Katherine von Bora:

The inferior ought not to glory over the superior. Katie can rule the servants but not me. David gloried in his own righteousness before men, not before God. When Katie gets saucy she gets nothing but a box on the ear.[28]

John Calvin and John Knox also insisted on women's submission. Knox wrote, "Woman in her greatest perfection was made to serve and obey man."[29] Calvin even took up the question of wife abuse, but on scriptural grounds exhorted battered women to "bear with patience the cross which God has seen fit to place upon her; and meanwhile not to deviate from the duty which she has before God to please her husband, but to be faithful whatever happens."[30]

Such thoughts about women's inferior humanity have not been banished from the writings of modern divines. Episcopal Bishop James Pike wrote in 1968:

Women are simple souls who like simple things. Our family Airedale will come clear across the yard for one pat on the head. The average wife is like that.[31]

And the greatly esteemed theologian of the twentieth century, Karl Barth, wrote—in spite of an assertion that women and men are equal in dignity, access to God, peril, and promise—that men are above and women are below, in accordance with the created order in the Book of Genesis: "A precedes B, and B follows A. Order means succession. It means preceding and following. It means super- and subordination."[32] He speaks against the exploitation of women by men as an offense against divine order, but holds the man responsible because of his prior status in creation. The man must understand "the order and sequence and therefore the obligation in which he is the first."[33]

Woman as Bearer of Sin

The church's legacy of woman-blaming dates at least as far back as Tertullian in the second century C.E.:

Do you know that each of your women is an Eve? The sentence of God on this sex of yours lives in this age; the guilt must necessarily live, too. You are the gate of hell; you are the temptation of the forbidden tree. You are the first deserter of the divine law . . . you are the one who persuaded him whom the Devil was not strong enough to attack. All too easily you destroyed the image of God, man. Because of your desert, that is, death, even the Son of God had to die.[34]

John Chrysostom wrote in the late fourth century, "Among all savage beasts, none is found so harmful as women."[35]

This theme was echoed by the greatly admired seventeenth-century poet John Donne, writing about Eve's temptation of Adam:

> For that marriage was our funerall
> one woman at one blow, then kill'd us all.[36]

Eve-blaming became the rationale for keeping women subordinate.[37] If left to her own wicked devices, who knew what harm might result? Nor was this a matter simply of inferior discernment or intelligence on the part of women. Women were not viewed as merely ignorant or stupid. They were viewed as intrinsically evil. This view was of long standing in the church. It is perhaps most dramatically represented in the work of the eminent theologians who compiled the best of fifteenth-century authorities (Scripture, the church fathers, and classical sources) and marshalled them with Aristotelian logic against the crime of witchcraft in their enormously influential treatise *Malleus Maleficarum* (The Hammer of Witches) in 1486:

> *Now the wickedness of women is spoken of in Ecclesiasticus xxv: There is no head above the head of a serpent: and there is no wrath above the wrath of a woman. I had rather dwell with a lion and a dragon than to keep house with a wicked woman. And among much which in that place precedes and follows about a wicked woman, he concludes: All wickedness is but little to the wickedness of a woman. Wherefore S. John Chrysostom says on the text. It is not good to marry (S. Matthew xix): What else is woman but a foe to friendship, an unescapable punishment, a necessary evil, a natural temptation, a desirable calamity, a domestic danger, a delectable detriment, an evil nature painted with fair colours! . . . Cicero in his second book of The Rhetorics says: The many lusts of men lead them into one sin, but the one lust of women leads them into all sins; for the root of all woman's vices is avarice. . . . When a woman thinks alone, she thinks evil.*[38]

The fact that the entire edifice built around the blaming of Eve was a misreading of the story made no difference. Phyllis Trible has convincingly argued that the man Adam was with Eve throughout the dialogue with the serpent:

> *Taking, eating, giving: these actions by the woman do not tell the whole tale of disobedience. The story is careful to specify that the man is with her ('immah), just as it earlier included him by the use of the plural verb forms in the dialogue. Yet throughout this scene the man has remained silent; he does not speak for obedience. His presence is passive and bland. The contrast that he offers to the woman is not*

strength or resolve but weakness. No patriarchal figure making decisions for his family, he follows his woman without question or comment. She gives fruit to him "and he ate." The story does not say that she tempted him; nor does its silence allow for this inference, even though many interpreters have made it. It does not present him as reluctant or hesitating. . . . Simply put, the serpent has tempted both the woman and the man. Instead of consulting the God who gave them life, one flesh disobeys.[39]

Women were equated with evil. "The word 'woman' means 'the lust of the flesh.' And it is said: I have found a woman more bitter than death, and a good woman subject to carnal lust."[40] And because of this essential defect, women were naturally susceptible to becoming instruments of Satan:

> *But the natural reason is that she is more carnal than a man, as is clear from her many carnal abominations. And it should be noted that there was a defect in the formation of the first woman, since she was formed from a bent rib, that is, rib of the breast, which is bent as it were in a contrary direction to a man. And since through this defect she is an imperfect animal, she always deceives. . . . And all this is indicated by the etymology of the word; for* Femina *comes from* Fe *and* Minus, *since she is ever weaker to hold and preserve the Faith. And this as regards faith is of her very nature. . . . This is so even among holy women, so what must it be among others?*[41]

In the same treatise, it was also proposed that the theory of the atonement, in which Christ died as the second Adam to redeem men (literally) from Adam's fall, applied to men only and protected them from becoming witches: "[Christ died] to preserve the male sex from so great a crime: since He was willing to be born and to die for us, therefore He has granted to men this privilege."[42] The vast proportion of people killed in the witch trials were women. Witchcraft was a woman's crime, and believed to be wholly consistent with her supposed innately evil nature.[43]

Woman as Gateway to Death

Misogynist reasoning takes Eve's scapegoating as the bearer of sin to its logical conclusion: ultimately, Woman, as Bearer of Sin, brought death into the world. As such, her just deserts are death. This doctrine was not an abstract theoretical assertion. The *Malleus Maleficarum* was far from an academic exercise. It became the theological basis for the torture and murder of as many as nine million women during the "witch-craze"[44] of the sixteenth and seventeenth centuries in Europe, the British Isles, and colonial America. Inspired initially by a Papal Bull by Pope Innocent VIII in 1484, in which he overturned the church's long-standing rejection of belief in witchcraft as a heathen belief punishable by death,[45] the *Malleus Maleficarum* became law. In an era when few people could read, it was printed and distributed widely, and was a required text for every judge.[46]

The result, as with any genocidal movement, was to destroy the culture, heritage, and wisdom of an enormous segment of society, including much valuable knowledge of healing, midwifery, agriculture, and spirituality, which was lumped together with other supposed indicators of witchcraft and punished by death. For the women who survived, there were profound consequences as well, for the fear of being accused of witchcraft made women conform to rigid standards of behavior. Any apparent deviation from the norm—even doing more good deeds than the average person—exposed one to accusations. Imprisoning, torturing, and murdering women for witchcraft became a pervasive means of social control of women.[47]

We consider ourselves more civilized than the people of those supposed "Dark Ages," and like to dismiss the "witch-craze" as a bizarre aberration, a phenomenon of mob psychology that could never be repeated. But the witness of the mass rapes of women in Bosnia contradicts this. Women continue to be specifically targeted for violence, as a means not only of conquest, but of social control.

The mass murder of women in an engineering department at the University of Montreal in 1989 by a twenty-five-year-old man who shouted "You're all f--ing feminists" further shatters our complacency. The specter of intentional woman-killing comes even closer to home. We comfort ourselves falsely with the idea that he was deranged, aberrant. But male identification with Marc Lepine's violence quickly spread to other campuses.[48] Graffiti "Kill Feminist Bitches" appeared at the University of Ontario shortly after Marc Lepine's rampage in Montreal. At the University of Alberta, a female engineering student who had complained about sexism in the engineering faculty was subjected to chants of "Shoot the Bitch!" from hundreds of her "fellow" students at a skit-night shortly after the Lepine shootings.

We still want to deny and distance ourselves from such atrocities, especially in our own country. But a huge industry—estimated at $4 billion[49]—legally exists in the United States that publishes and promotes images of the torture and mutilation of women that exceeds even the lurid punishments for witches prescribed in the *Malleus Maleficarum*.

The link between pornography and actual violence is well established.[50] Jane Caputi, an expert on sex crimes against women, in summarizing numerous studies, describes this connection:

> *1. In many cases, pornography actually is sexual violence, a document of actual degradation, rape, torture, and even murder (as in the snuff film).*
> *2. Pornography is used manipulatively to undermine women and children's capacity to avoid or resist abuse.*
> *3. Pornography causes sexual violence through its capacities to normalize that violence, give ideas to receptive male viewers, and break down some men's personal and social inhibitions against behaving in a violent manner.*[51]

In an FBI study of thirty-six serial killers, pornography was determined to be the primary "sexual interest" of 81 percent of them, and Ted Bundy, in a highly publicized statement, confessed that pornography was linked with his becoming a serial killer.[52] Serial killings, or "recreational murder," has dramatically increased since the 1950s, and the vast majority of serial killers are white men targeting women as their victims.[53] Serial killings are not only the stuff of pornography—they are mainstream entertainment. Much hoopla was made of the hundredth anniversary of Jack the Ripper a few years ago in a spirit of fun and tourism.[54] The blending of murder and mutilation with sexuality is not confined to pornographic or even low-budget "slasher" films, but is found in highly regarded mainstream and art films as well. The shower scene in *Psycho*, with its symbolically sexual knife-murder of a naked woman, opened the door to much more explicit eroticized violence against women— now a commonplace in movie "entertainment."[55] Popular "splatterpunk" horror novels aimed at teenage boys, dimestore "romance" novels aimed at women themselves, superhero comic books, and slasher videos all depict rapes and other forms of violence against women which the victims supposedly enjoy and crave, are all readily available and constitute a multimillion-dollar industry.

Nowhere is the link between woman and death made more explicit, perhaps, than in the horror of "snuff films," an extreme type of underground pornographic film in which a woman who thought she was hired to act a part is actually raped, tortured, and murdered as the camera rolls. Both the filmmaker and the viewer achieve, through participating in this atrocity either directly or vicariously, a false and temporary sense of ultimate control over both woman and death. Woman and death are merged in a sadistic fantasy of ultimate mastery through abuse and total annihilation.

While actual snuff films are an underground phenomenon, much material that Jane Caputi describes as "snufflike" abounds in films and even in mainstream advertising. The most fashionable magazines in the late 1980s showed models in poses of bondage, torture, and death, with men's hands or feet violently posed on their bodies, and even "shown suffocated under plastic bags, run over by cars, or buried under the sand in order to sell such products as boots, perfume, stockings, and shoes."[56] Up to the present moment, images of violence against women are used to sell blue jeans and other fashion items. The recent movie *Boxing Helena*, in which a man cuts off the arms and legs of a woman, was advertised with soft-focus artistic photography and the text: "His obsession tore her apart! . . . controversial, erotic . . . a visual feast, as titillating as it is haunting." The effect of such material is to make victimization chic and to normalize and desensitize an entire culture to misogynistic violence.

Within this larger context, explicitly violent magazines and movies do, sometimes, desensitize, disinhibit, and at least help to shape the fantasies of boys and men who rape and murder women.[57] In 1988, an eighteen-year-old murderer in Greenfield, Massachusetts, was undergoing psychological evaluation at the time of his crime for his obsession with slasher films and his identification with "Jason," the murderer in the *Friday the 13th* series. In Japan in 1989, a group of men and teenaged boys who serially murdered and dismembered young girls were found to have thousands of pornographic videos and comic books, known as *manga*—especially of the "Lolita" type.[58]

One of the most dangerous aspects of pornography that blends sex and violence is the depiction of the woman as experiencing arousal, orgasm, or other enjoyment, as a result of sexual assault. This is a common theme, and this kind of material has increased in the last decade.[59] Researchers have identified that the likelihood of sexual violence stemming from exposure to such materials does not vary with the extent of sexual explicitness so long as the violence is presented in an undeniably sexual context. The U.S. Attorney General's Commission on Pornography concluded: "Once a threshold is passed at which sex and violence are plainly linked, increasing the sexual explicitness of the material, or the bizarreness of the sexual activity, seems to bear little relationship to the extent of consequences. . . . "[60]

Pornography is often misunderstood by those who have never seen it and who equate it with a vague idea of pictures of nude people engaged in sexual activity. This innocence may then be exploited by arguments in favor of pornography as free speech.

For this reason, it is important to view pornography. Adult women's first exposure to pornography is often a shocking, destabilizing experience. Not only underground publications, but also such mainstream and supposedly soft-core publications as *Playboy* and *Penthouse* sold next to bubble gum and comics at the convenience store feature cartoons and photographic images of women that explicitly link sexuality and violence. In a *Penthouse* cartoon, a rapist is shown leaving the scene of a rape, and a bruised, naked woman, presumably his victim, cries after him, "Encore!"[61] A *Hustler* photograph of a man driving a jackhammer into a woman's vagina is captioned "at last a simple cure for frigidity."[62] Two themes of cartoons and photographs appear again and again; that women deserve sexual assault and abuse, and that women want and enjoy rape. A photograph titled "Battered Wives" in *Hustler*[63] shows a naked woman covered with batter, her neck being grabbed by a man with tongs. The caption reads "Battered wives: this photo shows why it's no wonder that wife beating has become one of society's stickiest problems! But today's liberated women should have expected this kind of response when they decided that men should do more of the domestic chores like cooking. Still, there's absolutely no excuse for doing something this bad. Now he's going to have to beat her just to smooth out all those lumps." Violent contempt for women and messages of backlash against women's efforts to achieve social equality are clear in this single example.

Racist indoctrination also frequently goes hand in hand with misogyny in pornography. Black women are shown as animals, as enjoying sex with animals, and in scenes depicting sexual slavery and battering. Asian women are frequently depicted in bondage, reinforcing stereotypes of submissiveness. An "adult" video game entitled "Custer's Revenge" allows players to vicariously rape Native American women in a variety of scenes.[64]

Incest is also depicted in pornography. Sexual violence and discipline are linked together in a *Playboy* ad showing a teenage girl nude except for black stockings, chained to her bed with legs spread. The caption reads "How one family solved its discipline problem."[65]

It is all the more frightening, then, to learn that the combined circulation of the top six "adult" magazines (*Penthouse, Playboy, Hustler, Gallery, Oui,* and *Chic*) is 10,385,000.[66] When counting pass-along readership this number grows to approximately 52,000,000.[67] This still does not account for numerous smaller and underground publications. The circulation of just *Playboy* and *Penthouse* combined is twice that of *Newsweek* and *Time* combined.

The pornography industry is larger than the entire commercial movie and record industries, and 50 to 60 percent of sales in video stores is made up of pornography.[68] The annual box office receipts for pornographic films total $500 million per year.[69]

The production of pornography is violent in itself. Much pornography is manufactured and sold in underground markets, and pornography has been linked to child abduction and torture.[70] Domestic child abuse is linked with the production of amateur pornography.[71] Adult women are really physically and sexually abused in the production of pornography.[72] Linda Lovelace was treated virtually like a slave by her "manager" Chuck Traynor, and was threatened with death when refusing to have sex with a dog.[73] Even when it does not escalate to killing as in "snuff" movies, the production of pornography frequently involves sadistic humiliation, bondage, and torture of women.

Like all abuse, pornography—including mainstream visual imagery of violence against women—is spiritual sadism, because it empties women of their souls. Far from being the "mild" end of the spectrum of violence against women, it is the ultimate rendering of women into Its. It is not surprising, then, to discover explicitly religious themes in pornography. Jane Caputi and Diana Russell describe an issue of a superhero comic book series, "Green Arrow," in which a near-naked prostitute is tortured and crucified. The December 1984 *Penthouse* included a series of images of women being tortured with subtle religious imagery under the heading "Sakura: the haiku moment."[74] The text read:

> *waves of emotion, bursts of possibility, sun-bright and night-dark, a sea of mystery surging overspilling from the clear glimpse of the thing told, the thing seen. From pictures, magic.*

This caption appears over a woman's naked buttocks and splayed legs bound with rope. Her face and upper torso are completely hidden from view. This, a woman, is "the thing seen." Melissa Farley, a psychotherapist who organized a national protest against *Penthouse* together with activist Nikki Craft, describes this collection as follows:

The December 1984 Penthouse *contained nine images of Asian women tied up with heavy rope, bound tightly with ropes cutting into their ankles, wrists, labias, and buttocks. Two of the images show women bound and hanging from trees, heads lolling forward, apparently dead. Another woman is masked, trussed up, and lying on a floor, appearing dead. In another image from this issue, an adolescent girl is proffered by an older female to the camera/pornographer/ consumer/misogynist. The younger girl is bound harshly with heavy ropes around her neck, around her torso, which cut painfully into her labia. She has no pubic hair, so she looks quite young. The lack of pubic hair also permits the viewer to see precisely how the rope cuts tightly into her genitals. Her hands appear to be tied behind her back. The older woman, collaborator with the camera, herself has only a sheet draped around her, but with her hands on the young woman's shoulders, she seems to be pushing the resisting younger woman slightly, in deference/sacrifice. . . . Throughout these murderous images are sprinkled "artsy" haiku quotes that exude dominance and subordination.*[75]

Two months after this issue appeared on newsstands, an orphaned eight-year-old girl, Jean Kar-Har Fewel, was kidnapped, raped, and murdered in North Carolina, with ropes around her neck, attached to a tree.[76]

The pornographer elevates himself to the level of a sadistic god and invites his male viewers/readers to join him in his fantasies of domination. The more the woman is humiliated, the greater his power. In the pornographer's fantasy, the woman wants to be dominated—it is inherent in her very nature.[77] His will is her sole delight. Andrea Dworkin explains the religious significance of this perversion, using the widely acclaimed pornographic novel *Story of O* as an example: "O does more than offer herself; she is herself the offering. To offer herself would be prosaic Christian self-sacrifice, but as the offering she is the vehicle of the miraculous—she incorporates the divine." Dworkin distinguishes this from true mystical sacrifice, naming it possession. "Possession, rightly defined, is the perversion of the mystic experience; it is by its very nature demonic because its goal is power, its means are violence and oppression. It spills the blood of its victim and in doing so estranges itself from life-giving union." O's lover thinks that she gives herself freely, but if she did not, he would take her anyway. Their relationship is the incarnation of demonic possession:

Thus he would possess her as a god possesses his creatures, whom he lays hold of in the guise of a monster or bird, of an invisible spirit or a state of ecstasy. He did not wish to leave her. The more he surrendered her, the more he would hold her dear. . . . Since she loved him, she could not help loving whatever derived from him.[78]

O is the ultimate portrayal of a woman as It. Reduced to a nameless (and, as the story progresses, even faceless) O, a zero, an empty void, she is the image of woman completely devoid of soul.

Holding this and thousands of other images of It-Everywoman in their minds, real men rape, mutilate, and murder real women in the desperate illusion of achieving godlike power. They demonize themselves instead, and the God of love and justice weeps.

Toward a New Definition of Pornography

Pornography is often commonly understood as material that is too sexy for the general public, including minors, to see. A movie may be rated "R" for showing "full frontal nudity," and yet there is a great deal of violence shown in movies rated "PG," not to mention degrading and stereotypical images of women. This definition teaches children that sexuality is obscene, while degradation, objectification, and violence are acceptable. The U.S. Attorney General's Commission on Pornography determined that "slasher" films shown in general theaters, in which a great deal of violence is linked with sex, are more harmful in terms of reinforcing or increasing the incidence of sexual assault— although the sex acts are less explicit than in so-called pornographic films. "None of us has the least doubt that sexual violence is harmful, and that general acceptance of the view that 'no' means 'yes' is a consequence of the most serious proportions."[79]

Pornography is not obscene because it is too sexual.[80] Again, the issue is power and not sex. Pornography *is* obscene, not because it is too revealing of naked bodies and of sexual acts, but because it distorts those acts by dehumanizing them. Pornography is not obscene because it is too erotic, but because it is dehumanizing. *Eros* is love that includes physical passion but also includes the whole person, body and soul together. *Eros* is that life force that reaches out toward the other for intimacy, mutual creativity, and exchange.[81] The erotic is, in the words of the late African American Lesbian poet and activist writer Audre Lorde, "a measure between the beginnings of our sense of self, and the chaos of our strongest feelings."[82] In contrast, pornography "is a direct denial of the power of the erotic, for it represents the suppression of true feeling. Pornography emphasizes sensation without feeling."[83] The erotic is relational, empathic, whole, spirited and imaginative. It is real. Pornography is episodic, performance-oriented, fragmented, standardized, and addictive.[84] The root word *porno* has nothing to do with love—it means female captive.[85]

Pornography is obscene precisely because, as Susan Griffin says, its aim is to deny and even murder the soul of those portrayed in it—by *de*eroticizing them, robbing them of their deepest life-giving and life-seeking energy.[86]

A more useful definition is offered by Andrea Dworkin and Catharine MacKinnon, as:

> *graphic sexually explicit subordination of women through pictures and/or words that also includes one or more of the following: (i) women are presented dehumanized as sexual objects, things, or commodities; or (ii) women are presented as sexual objects who enjoy pain or humiliation; or (iii) women are presented as sexual objects who experience sexual pleasure in being raped; or (iv) women are presented as sexual objects tied up or cut up or mutilated or bruised or physically hurt; or (v)*

women are presented in postures or positions of sexual submission, servility, or display; or (vi) women's body parts—including but not limited to vaginas, breasts, or buttocks—are exhibited such that women are reduced to those parts; or (vii) women are presented as whores by nature; or (viii) women are presented being penetrated by animals; or (ix) women are presented in scenes of degradation, injury, torture, shown as filthy or inferior, bleeding, bruised, or hurt in a context that makes these conditions sexual.[87]

By this definition, much mainstream advertising, literature, art, and media qualifies as pornography. We do not recognize it as such, simply because it is so pervasive that we have become numb to its effects on us. The fact that these ideas have been around since the early 1970s and the feminist slogan "this objectifies women" is now almost a cliche does not obviate the need to continue raising these concerns. Griffin points out: "In pornography even when a real woman poses for the camera, she does not pose as herself. Rather, she performs. *She plays the part of an object*"[88] (emphasis mine). And this is no less true for much of mainstream advertising than for "adults only" materials. Images of women in the media have not improved in two decades—if anything, the threshold level of violence and objectification that is socially tolerable for mass media representations of women has been lowered.

Conclusion

Pornography, sexual harassment, domestic violence, sexual assault and rape, sexual abuse of children, clergy sexual abuse of parishioners, and ritual abuse all exist within this mythology of denial and hatred of the body, nature, and mortality, and all are enacted as a means of enforcing control and power. The repetitive, obsessive nature of the acts points to the impossibility of such control. Woman's power (and here I mean her authentic power-within), her life-energy, her real complexity continue to break through the stereotypes and to defy the misogynist myths pervading the culture at large. And so, in a downward spiral, these powers must be ever more forcefully repressed by patriarchal consciousness. Woman-subduing imagery turns uglier, more grotesque, more degrading, and more overtly sadistic. Acts of violence against women escalate. The more woman's power is suppressed, or relegated to what C.G. Jung called the "Shadow"[89] (unacknowledged and disavowed aspects of the Self), the more monstrous it seems in the patriarchal collective psyche, until it generates nightmares, neurotic symptoms, and, at last, psychoses. Violence and violent imagery escalate because the more tightly men's culture, via its individual perpetrators, tries to slam the lid down on the facts of bodily need, feeling, and the inevitability of death, the more monstrous and threatening these needs become—requiring more violent and more desperate measures to contain them.

FORMS OF VIOLENCE
AGAINST WOMEN

Sexual Harassment

His speech was smoother than butter, yet war was in his heart.

—Psalm 55:21

Dr. Maureen Longworth tells the story of the first time, as a new medical resident, she had to give a complete physical to a male patient. When she began examining his genitals, he said, "Shouldn't I be doing that to you?" In medical school, male colleagues would make lewd comments in her presence about female cadavers and also suggested that they practice their GYN techniques on her. She would find used condoms and bloody rubber gloves tucked into her personal belongings. She was terribly embarrassed, but when she finally told one of her professors, he told her to be a sport and just put up with it as "hazing." Nothing was done to stop the men's behavior.[1]

In an apartment complex in Fairfield, California, thirteen women and their twenty-five children brought a lawsuit in federal district court under Title VIII, the Fair Housing Act, against their landlord James Skinner.[2] He would use his master key to enter their apartments while they were sleeping or showering. He grabbed their breasts or genitals in public. Economic abuse was tied to sexual harassment. When women were unable to pay rent, he asked them to make up the payment by posing in lingerie. He went through their mail and withheld welfare checks and threatened to report them for fraud if they received small monetary gifts from family. He also threatened children with eviction and showed them his gun collection. When one of the women changed her locks, he demanded the new key, and local police told her that legally she had to comply or face eviction. Later, he entered her apartment while she slept. She awoke to find him leaning over her in his undershorts with his pants around his knees. She screamed and pushed him out. He threatened, "I'll get you for this." She was evicted a month later.

The case eventually settled for an aggregate (including damages, court costs, and attorney fees) of over $1.5 million—the largest sum ever awarded in the history of the U.S. Fair Housing Act. During the course of their case, Skinner was incarcerated for raping two women at the same apartment complex. With a grant from their attorneys, Leslie Levy and Amy Oppenheimer, the women founded a nonprofit group called WRATH (Women Refusing to

Accept Tenant Harassment) to advocate for women who find themselves victims in sexual harassment in housing.[3]

Katy Lyle was an honor student at a high school in Duluth, Minnesota.[4] She learned through the grapevine that the walls of the boys' bathroom were covered with sexually explicit comments about her, as vulgar as "Katy Lyle f--ks dogs," and "Katy Lyle is a dick-sucking, brother-f--king whore." As time went on, there was a "Katy stall," which included her phone number. Boys approached her in the halls, saying "Do me," and her family received numerous obscene phone calls. Katy and her parents complained sixteen times to the principal, but no action was taken for eighteen months. Her brother finally tried to sandpaper the writing off the bathroom walls, while the school officials took an attitude of "boys will be boys." Katy finally filed a charge of sexual harassment with the Minnesota Department of Human Rights, claiming that the school's lack of response created a hostile educational environment, and received a $15,000 settlement for mental anguish and suffering. However, the retaliation went on through high school, even following her to college. In November 1991, "Katy Lyle is a slut" was written in a bathroom stall at the University of Minnesota in Duluth where she was a student. She knew it was written by someone who was angry about the cash settlement in high school. After her brother talked to him, frightening new graffiti appeared: "It's not over yet."[5]

Margaret[6] was pressured by her boss, the head of a large and prestigious advertising agency in New York City, to go out on dates. He talked about the incredible tension of working side by side with her while desiring her so much. He finally persuaded her to sleep with him, and a few weeks later, gave her an unusually large promotion in responsibility and pay. Later, when she began to feel uncomfortable with the situation and questioned its propriety, he broke off their "relationship" in a rage. Soon afterward, she found herself moved laterally to a job with the same pay but less responsibility and less opportunity for advancement. Then her hours were cut back for "budgetary reasons," and finally she was laid off. She was the only employee laid off, in spite of her seniority and her excellent work record. When she consulted an attorney at considerable cost, he told her that because she had agreed to go out on the dates and to have sex with him, and because it was her boss and not herself who technically ended the relationship, she did not have a good enough case to press charges on the grounds of sexual harassment.

My own experiences, like most women's, have spanned my adult life. When I worked as a secretary during the summers while I was in graduate school, I was leered at repeatedly by a boss who also said on one occasion, "I like the way the sun shines through your dress!" When I told him, publicly, in front of the rest of the secretarial pool, "Please don't ever speak to me that way again," I was not supported by the other "girls." I was a summer temp. I could leave. They depended on their jobs for a living. For the rest of the summer I was treated as an outsider.

On another occasion, my whole graduate department went to the meeting of our academic society because it was being held in our city. There was an annual dance, and everyone danced with each other. One married professor held me very close so that I could feel him getting aroused. I tried in as lighthearted a way as I could to get loose, by saying, "My, you're dancing awfully close, aren't you?" He pressed closer and murmured, "What's wrong with that?"

Another former professor and mentor from my college days ran into me at that same conference. I said hello and talked to him about a paper I was writing on a topic I knew was of interest to him. He called the next week and asked me to come see him in his office and bring him the paper, which I did. He then proposed that he bring it back to me at my apartment to save me the inconvenience of going over there a second time. He could review it with me in more detail in person, he said. He also said that he was sorry if he'd seemed flustered when he saw me at the conference, but he had been "knocked out" by how beautiful I was, and he had "forgotten" what an attractive woman I was. I left feeling confused and mystified by what seemed both an apology and a come-on at the same time. I became increasingly nervous about the upcoming meeting at my apartment and finally called him and asked to meet at a library. He pressed me, and because I was too embarrassed to talk about my discomfort at the sexual aspect of what was happening, I told him my apartment was being fumigated for roaches that week (a pretty common occurrence in my neighborhood)!

In my college violin class, the professor was notorious for touching women's breasts "accidentally." We all had experiences of his sliding his hand along our breast as he "adjusted the bow position." He also brushed up against women's breasts in the crowded school elevator. Finally, my best friend said to him, very loudly in the elevator, "Mr. S _____ , do you realize that you just touched my breast?" He blustered and coughed and got out at the next stop. But he didn't stop doing it—except with us.

I also had an apartment manager who never "did" anything that I could prove, but who leered at me and created a general climate of unease. I began to be afraid because he had a master key to my apartment. Finally, after spending one weekend away, I came back to find a dead bat under my pillow, even though all the windows were shut and locked. (Roaches were commonplace in Boston's Back Bay, but not bats!) After that, I had a deadbolt installed on the inside of the door, even though it was technically against my lease. I soon found another living situation and moved out.

These experiences do not diminish with age. A colleague in ministry drew me aside not long ago, stood very close to me—in my "personal space"—and said, "I'm intrigued with all the work you're doing on the issue of clergy sexuality." Male parishioners have repeatedly pulled me close to them during the greetings of peace or the coffee hour and kissed me very uncomfortably on the lips. Another colleague recently said in front of a senior male colleague that he regretted missing an upcoming meeting that I would be chairing—because of my leadership? Yes, but especially because I was so cute. I was acutely embarrassed and angry, and wrote him a letter. Fortunately, in this instance, he wrote back an eloquent and gracious apology, and has been a model of appropriateness and collegial friendship ever since.

I consider my own experiences of sexual harassment to be relatively mild. I have not had condoms shoved into my briefcase or the word "whore" scrawled on my office door, as did one college professor at Oklahoma State University.[7] Dr. Glenna Matthews spoke at the conference at Laney College about her experience of harassment while working as the sole professor of social science at Oklahoma State. She said in an interview, "Most of my male colleagues were not hostile or abusive. But I became the lightning rod for every man who did feel that way toward women. Many didn't have credentials that were as good as mine, so they used sexual innuendo to put me in my place."[8]

I personally have not been threatened, either overtly or covertly, with the loss of my job or educational opportunities unless I slept with someone. Even so, the accumulated effects of even such "mild" experiences, year after year, create a constant, dull feeling of unease. Combined with routine harassment on the street by construction workers and men drinking beer in doorways, and with body contact on buses and subways that feels more than accidental, and with displays of *Hustler* and *Penthouse* at the gas station minimarket, and with posters of nude women over the cash register at the auto mechanic's shop, it is easy to begin feeling paranoid. A shell goes up. As young women grow up, we become wiser, tougher, and more immune to all but the most blatant forms of harassment. But this is life in a war zone. We learn, at best, to dodge the bullets or stay out of range as much as possible, but we can't stop them from coming at us.

Although it is often considered one of the "milder" forms of violence against women, because it does not generally result in visible bruises or wounds, sexual harassment must be considered a serious form of violence. In it are found all the themes of power and betrayal of trust that characterize all violence against women. It is also much more serious than it seems, because, although it is more elusive and more difficult (at times) for victims to prove, and may not cause physical pain (although prolonged harassment can often cause stress-related illness, as in the case of Anita Hill), it has long-term and devastating consequences, both economic and psychological, for victims. It is probably more prevalent than any other form of violence against women. And while not nearly all men harass women, nearly all women have been sexually harassed, although it is so commonplace that many women don't realize that their experiences constitute harassment. They blame their feelings of unease and confusion on themselves. After nearly every workshop I give on this subject in the context of the church, some woman comes up to me and says, "Let me tell you about something that happened to me" ten, twenty, thirty years ago. "I never realized that was harassment, but oh, my God, it was, wasn't it?"

Legal definitions of sexual harassment center on the workplace and, in some states, also apply to schools. In addition, many institutions have their own sexual harassment policies, usually worded closely to language found in the law. Sexual harassment also occurs, of course, in church settings, and when the offender is a pastor or pastoral counselor, there are additional aspects of betrayal of a sacred trust and exploitation of vulnerable parishioners and clients. This issue, together with other forms of sexual exploitation by helping professionals, will be covered more fully in chapter 7.

Definition of Sexual Harassment

Under Title VII (Section 703) of the 1964 federal Civil Rights Act, sexual harassment is legally defined as a form of sex discrimination that is an unlawful employment practice. The Title VII definition is as follows:

> *Unwelcome sexual advances, requests for sexual favors, and other verbal or physical conduct of a sexual nature constitute sexual harassment when:*
>
> *1) submission to such conduct is made either explicitly or implicitly a term or condition of an individual's employment*
>
> *2) submission to or rejection of such conduct by an individual is used as the basis for employment decisions affecting such individual; [or]*
>
> *3) such conduct has the purpose or effect of unreasonably interfering with an individual's work performance or creating an intimidating, hostile, or offensive working environment.*[9]

The first two criteria of the Title VII definition constitute what is known as "quid pro quo" harassment, in which the woman's sexual compliance is made a condition of a manager's or supervisor's decision to hire or fire, or used to make other employment decisions such as pay, promotion, or job assignment.

The third criterion, which is more difficult to prove, is "condition of work"[10] or, based on the language of the law, "hostile environment" harassment. In this category, the harassment either directly or indirectly creates an atmosphere that the woman finds difficult to tolerate, and often has the effect of driving her away from an economic and vocational opportunity. If she does manage to tolerate it, in the interests of keeping her job, this often is taken as proof of her consent.

Sexual harassment also goes beyond what is covered by law. It particularly goes beyond definitions that view harassment only as something perpetrated by one in power (a boss or teacher) against one in lesser power (an employee or student), or only in the workplace. Sexual harassment is about male power and female disempowerment. It is not only a matter of bosses and teachers exploiting the vulnerability of their employees and students, although this is commonplace and has particularly threatening consequences for women's economic survival and advancement. But sexual harassment is just as frequently carried out by men against women peers and even supervisors and teachers. As ethicist Carol Robb puts it, harassment can be directed "up" as well as "down."[11] An example of this "contra-power" harassment is the harassment of women professors by male students, in the form of obscene phone calls, hostile messages, lewd drawings or sexual propositions in evaluations, or a message on the blackboard suggesting that she would enjoy an act of sexual violence of a lethal nature.[12]

Women know that harassment occurs up, down, and sideways. Sexual harassment occurs on the streets, in the subways, and every place women dare to move freely in society.

The question is often raised in workshops, "Well, doesn't it go both ways? Don't women also harass men?" The simple answer is yes. However, both the incidence and impact are very different. While, technically, a woman could say and do some of the same things that men do to women, and while this could be embarrassing for a man, the actual occurrence of such behavior is much less common than male-to-female harassment. But more to the point, because of the relative inequality of power and privilege between women and men, and, as well, the social context of so much other violence against women, harassment by a woman against a man rarely carries the same implicit threatening quality that harassment by a man against a woman often does. Sexual harassment against women cannot be understood apart from the deeper context of the prevalence of sexual violence against women more generally.

Why does sexual harassment against women happen? What Peter Rutter has written concerning sexual exploitation of women by men in the helping professions also applies more generally to situations of sexual harassment:

> A great deal of trouble men have confronting sexual misconduct revolves around their failure to recognize how conveniently they shift among different aspects of their myth of the feminine. Between their wish that women remain deferential to masculine power, their occasional rage at women for not supplying them with nurturing on demand, and their fear and idealization of feminine power, there can be little room for honest self-examination.[13]

As discussed at length in chapter 2, women are viewed in patriarchal mythology as a sexual servant class for men. Men are surrounded by images of women as visual property. Men's "locker room" talk about women's bodies, and competitions and braggadocio about their own sexual conquests, seem to spill easily into group forms of harassment of women.

But there is a more insidious systemic reason as well: harassment keeps women in their place. It creates an environment of stress, insecurity, and fear that reduces all a woman's identity, role, and worth to her sexuality alone. It erodes her confidence, her initiative, and even her health, with direct consequences for her ability to work competitively and well.[14] As such, sexual harassment becomes an effective tool of social control and economic oppression. There is no other form of violence against women, except perhaps domestic violence, which functions so immediately and directly to constrain women's economic independence and social freedom.

Racism further complicates sexual harassment. For example, MacKinnon has written, "Black women's reports of sexual harassment by white male superiors reflect a sense of impunity that resounds of slavery and colonization. . . . Apparently, sexual harassment can be both a sexist way to express racism and a racist way to express sexism."[15] While working as a corrections officer in Arizona, an African American woman, Yolanda Stingley, was subjected to racial epithets including "watermelon eater," "naphead," "nigger," "spearchucker," "token," and was poked twice with a plastic fork by a coworker who told her he was "checking to see if the meat was done."[16] Women of color may feel doubly vulnerable to job loss and economic harm, and may also feel their credibility to be more at stake. Racism also affects the outcomes for perpetrators—on the one hand, allegations may be more readily believed concerning a man of color and more severely punished; on the other hand, he may successfully claim that the charges are false based on racism targeted against him.

Finally, sexual harassment is not only a form of violence in itself, but bound up as it is with the whole spectrum of male violence against women and the ever-present threat of rape, it constitutes a major threat both to her economic well-being and to her personal safety at the most intimate level. This wider understanding of the far-ranging consequences of sexual harassment against women provides the foundation for a more comprehensive definition, which goes beyond the provisions of the current law:

Sexual harassment [against women] is any action occurring whereby women are treated as objects of the male sexual prerogative.[17]

Categories of Harassment

There are many forms of sexual harassment against women:

— Intentional individual harassment of a number of women (coworkers, tenants, employees, students, etc.).

— Pseudo-romantic individual harassment of one or a few "selected" women. It is very difficult and frightening for women to try to discern whether such unwanted romantic attention will escalate into stalking or assaultive behavior.

— Intentional group harassment of women; here a "wolf pack" mentality operates, and peer pressure among the men loosens inhibitions and heightens the intensity of the harassing behavior beyond what some might do as individuals. This is not confined to the stereotype of construction workers whistling and shouting catcalls at women on the street—which is prevalent, psychologically damaging, and constricts women's freedom of movement.[18] It also pertains to offices and factory floors and other workplaces, and to work-related parties and conferences. The message is, "You do not belong here, except as a sexual object." Again, there is a fine line between verbal harassment and actual unwanted touching and assault, as the U.S. Navy's "Tailhook" incident demonstrated. Women wonder if "gang harassment" will escalate into gang rape.

— Unintentional/unenlightened harassment of women which nevertheless creates an offensive, hostile, or intimidating atmosphere; in such cases
the individual man does not necessarily realize—(at least consciously—that
what he is doing is upsetting to the woman or women who must come into
his environment.)For example, storekeepers display pornographic materials
near the cash register, workers keep sexualized photographs of women on
display in their work areas, tell lewd jokes in the women's presence, or play
music that contains explicit sexual language or describes violence against
women. The offense is often compounded when this is pointed out. The man,
rather than apologizing, often defends his "right" to continue his behavior,
sometimes in a hostile and belligerent manner. Even if the original intent was
not malicious, this staunch resistance after the fact is funded in patriarchal
privilege.

— Harassment with threats directly affecting the woman's economic or
educational condition; the classic "quid pro quo" harassment, either as a
bribe ("If you do what I ask, you will be promoted"), or as a threat ("Do what
I ask or you will be demoted/fired"). This is common enough that women
have even faced being battered at home after receiving a promotion because,
as in one report, the batterer assumed that his wife "put out."[19]

— Paraphilic harassment; these are acts that are recognized clinically as
symptomatic of disorders, and the women victims are usually nonconsenting
strangers.[20] This category includes voyeurism ("peeping"), exhibitionism
(suddenly exposing one's genitals to a stranger, for example, subway
"flashing")—a paraphilia occurring only in males and almost always targeting
a female victim—and frotteurism (rubbing genitals against a nonconsenting
stranger, or fondling her breasts or genitals, usually accomplished in a
crowded place such as a busy sidewalk or bus). Generally these compulsive
behaviors do not escalate to more violent acts but they are extremely frightening and threatening to most women, especially because of the fear of rape as
well as the sense of violation and disgust they produce.

— Harassment as a prelude to more serious violent acts, including assault,
rape, murder, and even mass murder. In fact, instilling fear, through harassing
phone calls, stalking, verbal threats (in person or by mail), or other means, is
one of the early warning signals for physical violence in the workplace. While
employees will often believe that it's "just harassment," experts on workplace
violence take such behavior seriously as an important indicator that the perpetrator should be stopped before he commits further violence.[21] Stalking can
lead to violence and even to murder. Some stalkers are deluded with fantasies
of being loved by the victim,[22] while others are seeking revenge after their victims have refused or ended relationships. Again, power plays a role, since
often those targeted are perceived as having power over the stalker or a
superior status: a teacher, doctor, or employer. Stalking has only recently
been recognized as a crime. The first stalking law was passed in California in

1990[23] in the wake of a corporate massacre committed by a former employee, the culmination of his stalking of a coworker.

Because no woman knows whether any form of sexual harassment will or will not escalate into one of the latter two categories, harassment always has the potential for seriously frightening women. Men who actually have little more on their minds than relieving sexual tension with a little "dirty joke" are often baffled to be told that this behavior is inappropriate, partly because they do not recognize the more threatening context within which women *experience* their behavior. But given the context of so many other forms of violence against women, a woman may always wonder, "Who knows how far *this* man might go? Who knows if it's harmless or not?"

This is precisely the reasoning behind the relatively recent "reasonable woman" judicial standard for assessing the validity of sexual harassment claims in court, and it gives the lie to arguments that gender equality would mean women could tell sexual jokes as easily as men; or that clergywomen, teachers, or other women in authority roles cannot truly be harassed by male parishioners, students, or employees because the power of their role cancels their gender vulnerability. In a landmark case in 1991, *Ellison vs. Brady,* two nominally conservative, male federal appellate court judges established the "reasonable woman" standard, with the following historic statement:

> We believe that in evaluating the severity and pervasiveness of sexual harassment, we should focus on the perspective of the victim. If we only examined whether a reasonable person would engage in allegedly harassing conduct, we would run the risk of reinforcing the prevailing level of discrimination. Harassers could continue to harass merely because a particular discriminatory practice was common, and victims of harassment would have no remedy.
>
> We therefore prefer to analyze harassment from the victim's perspective. A complete understanding of the victim's view requires, among other things, an analysis of the different perspectives of men and women. Conduct that many men consider unobjectionable may offend many women.
>
> We realize that there is a broad range of viewpoints among women as a group, but we believe that many women share common concerns which men do not necessarily share. [Here a citation is made that includes reference to the societal context "where rape and sex-related violence have reached unprecedented levels, and a vast pornography industry creates continuous images of sexual coercion, objectification and violence.] For example, because women are disproportionately victims of rape and sexual assault, women have a stronger incentive to be concerned with sexual behavior. Women who are victims of mild forms of sexual harassment may understandably worry whether a harasser's conduct is merely a prelude to violent sexual assault. Men, who are rarely victims of sexual assault, may view sexual conduct in a vacuum without a full appreciation of the social setting or the underlying threat of violence that a woman may perceive. . . .
>
> We adopt the perspective of a reasonable woman primarily because we believe that a sex-blind reasonable person standard tends to be male-biased and tends to

systematically ignore the experiences of women. The reasonable woman standard does not establish a higher level of protection for women than men. Instead, a gender-conscious examination of sexual harassment enables women to participate in the workplace on an equal footing with men. By acknowledging and not trivializing the effects of sexual harassment on reasonable women, courts can work towards ensuring that neither men nor women will have to "run a gauntlet of sexual abuse in return for the privilege of being allowed to work and make a living."[24]

Even when the harassment is no more than the level of verbal offense, women feel degraded and are often traumatized by the behavior—especially when it appears not to be just a one-time occurrence. At the very least, the message is that no matter how competent or talented the woman, no matter what her skills, and no matter how collegial and appropriate her own behavior, all that really is being noticed is her sexuality. This has a long-term demoralizing effect for women when we receive this message over and over so that it erodes our professional identity and self-confidence as well as the hope of finding and keeping meaningful and fulfilling work.

Reporting

Why do some women refrain from trying to stop or report harassment? Often women fear retaliation even when no explicit threats have been made. At the very least, women fear being made to appear oversensitive, foolish for having "misconstrued" the man's intent, or "man-hating." As with rape, women blame themselves and wonder if they somehow spoke or dressed provocatively, or otherwise "asked for it."

Another reason is that, in many instances, the woman genuinely cares for the offender, a situation that Catharine MacKinnon describes as "a murky area where power and caring converge."[25] She writes:

Although the woman may, in fact, be and feel coerced in the sexual involvement in some instances of sexual harassment, she may not be entirely without regard for, or free from caring about, the perpetrator. Further investigation of what might be called "coerced caring," or, in the most complex cases, an "if this is sex, I must be in love" syndrome, is vital. It is becoming increasingly recognized that feelings of caring are not the only or even a direct cause of sexual desires in either sex. In light of this, it cannot be assumed that if the woman cares about the man, the sex is not coerced. The difficulties of conceptualization and proof, however, are enormous.[26]

Another deterrent to reporting is that, most often, in attempts to assess the truth of what happened, the focus becomes the man's intent, and, as a corollary, the woman's credibility. When someone rolls a man sleeping on a park bench for his wallet, or holds someone up at a bank teller window, questions aren't raised about the emotional state of the victim, or the robber's intent. "Gee, I'm sorry, I didn't *mean* to take your wallet." The only question asked is whether the criminal behavior occurred or not. But in sexual harassment cases, the woman's state of mind, how she interpreted what happened, and the man's intent are all debated.

"I believe Anita" became the rallying cry for thousands of frustrated women in the fall of 1991, when Anita Hill's allegations of sexual harassment against Supreme Court Justice nominee Clarence Thomas exposed her, and by proxy all victims of sexual harassment, to a vitriolic campaign to discredit her and destroy her reputation. His intentions and her motives were the focus for most of the hearings. On the surface, who could have been more credible? And yet her gender in and of itself outweighed her professional achievement and an impressive array of evidence (including convincing details, documentation of stress-related illness, and a successful polygraph test). Ethicist Karen Lebacqz has written of the hearings:

> In short, one would be hard-pressed to find a more credible witness than Anita Hill. Her background, her clarity about what happened, her ability to provide specifics, the cogency of her story . . . her lack of motive for lying, her dignity in the face of painful questions, and her setting as a woman in a male-dominated institution all bode well for her credibility as a witness. Nonetheless, Anita Hill never stood a chance. Here's why:
>
> 1) The privacy within which sexual harassment happens ensures that her testimony cannot be corroborated.
>
> 2) She was not offered a trial by her peers. The Senate that "judged" the evidence was composed entirely of powerful, prominent men, many of whom are publicly known to have a history of inappropriate or highly questionable sexual conduct, and who therefore could not possibly be "impartial" in the face of the evidence. Consider how differently Anita Hill's testimony might have been received by a panel composed entirely of women, especially African-American women, who have been in the work place for ten or more years.
>
> 3) She presented her evidence in a climate of disrespect for women's voices and concerns. This climate was created in part by the very Senate panel that heard Anita Hill's testimony. This panel had previously allowed Thomas not to answer questions regarding abortion or other topics most central to women's concerns.
>
> But it was created in part by a larger cultural legacy of discounting women's voices. . . .
>
> . . . the general climate in which we live remains one in which a man's "word" is his honor, while a woman's honor remains lodged in what she does with her genitals. We do not picture a woman saying, "I give you my word of honor." This phrase is reserved for men.[27]

Lebacqz goes on to point out that a woman's word is not believed to be trustworthy, particularly in matters of sexuality: "So long as 'no' means 'maybe' and 'maybe' might mean 'yes,' women will never stand a chance." Given this analysis, can any woman win in a contest of "he said—she said"?

Women are also caught in a catch-22 of being intimidated out of reporting, and then being blamed for not reporting sooner. Failure to report the harassment earlier was one of many charges leveled at Anita Hill. The logic of this argument goes: If you didn't report it, even if some sexual behavior was going on, you must have been consenting. Lynn Wehrli refutes this:

> That women "go along" with sexual harassment, the assumption is that they must like it, and it is not really harassment at all. This constitutes little more than a simplistic denial of all we know about the ways in which socialization and economic dependence foster submissiveness and override free choice. . . . Those women who are able to speak out about sexual harassment use terms such as "humiliating," "intimidating," "frightening," "financially damaging," "embarrassing," "nerve-wracking," "awful," and "frustrating" to describe it. These words are hardly those used to describe a situation which one "likes."[28]

To quote Catharine MacKinnon, "That women 'go along' is partly a male perception and partly correct, a male-enforced reality."[29]

Prevention and Intervention

As with rape and domestic violence, there is nothing that predisposes a woman to becoming a victim, unless it is perhaps simply leaving her house. And even there, she may be subject to obscene telephone calls or harassment by her building manager or a neighbor. If a woman interacts with men at all, in any situation, she is at risk.

It is also a myth that if a woman simply learns to "let it roll off her back," ignores it, or responds in a joking manner, these techniques will necessarily defuse the harassment and make it stop. Often by ignoring it or responding in a joking way, the man will perceive these responses as permission to continue and even to go further. One study found that 76 percent of ignored advances escalated.[30]

My own first response to inappropriate and unwanted sexual jokes or comments is usually a mixture of confusion, disbelief, and embarrassment, and I often try to joke it off. But my experience has been that this is not effective as a deterrent, and eventually, as awkward and anxiety-producing as it may feel, if the behavior is repeated, I have firmly to request the person to stop. I have also learned that the most effective way to do this is in writing, which has the further advantage of establishing documentation for myself should the situation escalate.

The following are some general guidelines for dealing with harassment:[31]

1. Admit a problem exists, and recognize sexual harassment for what it is—unwanted sexual behavior or language. Don't ignore it—75 percent of the time, sexual harassment problems get worse when ignored.[32] Document all incidents with times, dates, places. Keep a log. Also keep any notes, drawings, or other materials that the harasser may have sent you. If offensive items are attached to your door, your books, your belongings, and so forth, try to take a picture of them. You may or may not want to produce all this documentation, but it is better to have it. Don't destroy anything out of anger or disgust—you might need it later.[33]

2. Reduce your own isolation as much as possible, remembering that isolation increases your vulnerability. Notice any possible witnesses who might be able to corroborate your story and discuss the situation with them. Secrecy

is likely to be more in the interests of the perpetrator—share your experience with others you trust. Possibly a pattern of repeat offenses will emerge that will add to all the victims' credibility.

3. If you feel safe in doing so, calmly tell the person you don't like the behavior. (An expert on sexual harassment, Susan Webb, suggests using "I" statements such as "*When* you call me 'honey'/touch me/tell jokes, etc. I *feel* upset/embarrassed/angry/offended, etc. *because* I want to be taken seriously/ want respect, etc." Name the behavior clearly, and make honest, direct statements—without apologetic or qualifying language. Back this up with body language that is strong and conveys self-respect. Use the broken record technique by acknowledging the person's response and then repeating your "I" statement. You do not need to be "reasoned," joked, or cajoled out of your original "I" statement.[34] You may want to ask a peer to go with you as both support person and witness.

4. If you do not want to confront the harasser in person for any reason, or if the harassment has happened more than once already, strongly consider putting your complaint to him in writing, documenting the incidents and clearly stating that you want the behavior to stop. Keep a copy.

5. If the behavior does not stop, or if you consider it very serious from the beginning, go immediately to a person in authority in the organization with as much documentation as you have.

6. Activate the formal sexual harassment or grievance procedure of the organization. If you have not already done so, this is a good time to get an initial legal consultation from an attorney. Company procedures are still often not fair, and harassers frequently enter the process with attorneys at their sides. It is important to enter the procedure prepared.

7. If the organization does not have a policy, does not respond helpfully, or protects or defends the harasser, consult an attorney regarding your rights to a legal remedy. Sexual harassment does not need to be tolerated.

While we do need to empower women to respond more assertively to incidents of sexual harassment as they happen, and to educate women about their rights, all this is still in the realm of teaching women how to "dodge the bullet." How can this problem be stopped? Are there any successful means of prevention and education?

Probably the two most effective means of stopping sexual harassment are to insist upon stronger laws and institutional policies, stronger enforcement of existing laws and institutional policies, and better mechanisms for allowing victims access to the policies. Clearer definitions of harassment need to be included in laws and policies, specifying that certain behaviors constitute harassment, period. In the legal system, this is often accomplished through the precedents established by prior cases, but in many institutions, such as schools, there is little consensus as to what specifically constitutes harassment. For this reason, better definitions are needed, and then the focus of investigations can be on whether certain behaviors occurred or not, and *not* on what either the victim or the harasser *thought* was going on at the time.[35]

A good policy should at minimum include:[36]

• a statement of the organization or church's understanding that harassment is wrong, and that it should be a safe place for all who work/study/worship there

• a statement of the importance of the problem

• a definition of sexual harassment, including a definition of what constitutes retaliation following an allegation

• examples of behavior that constitutes sexual harassment

• access to the procedure for making complaints, and safeguards for the complainant's safety, preferably including a panel or team of sensitive, trained advocates or ombudspersons to assist and support complainants in following through the procedure; advocates may also be in place to advise the accused and those in a position of authority to adjudicate the complaint[37]

• clear organizational procedures for processing the complaint

• disciplinary procedure in cases where harassment is found to have occurred, with clear consequences for the offender

• a statement to be signed by all employees/students/volunteers, etc., that they have read and understand the policy.

An equally important aspect of prevention is education. No policy will be effective unless it exists within a climate of support and belief of victims. Workshops and forums in which members of a church or organization have an opportunity to share their own ideas and concerns, receive information about the issue of sexual harassment, and study the organization's own policy are an important prerequisite for an effective policy. Workshops and forums should include many examples of unacceptable behaviors and case studies for discussion, especially around more subtle or complex situations. Stereotypical reactions such as "Oh, that's ridiculous!" or "You're telling me that giving a compliment is harassment?" need to be confronted. Often having others respond from experience about why certain behaviors feel like harassment from the point of view of the one receiving the harassment can begin to loosen people's assumptions.[38]

Larger questions of prevention reach beyond individual organizations and institutions to society. A need exists for education especially targeting youth. By the time they reach adulthood, many girls have already been harassed at a very young age in school. When they try to complain, they or their parents are frequently met by school authorities saying, "Boys will be boys," resulting in early conditioning of girls to believe that there is no point in complaining. New cases and rulings are now addressing school harassment of very young girls.[39]

It has been suggested that certain very direct techniques are successful and leave a strong impression on the boys, such as reverse role plays, where girls form two lines and the boys walk between them and are subjected to wolf whistles, comments about their bodies and clothing, and other behaviors that the girls have had done to them. Some may consider such methods too confrontational, even abusive. Training exercises like the one described in chapter 2 also effectively sensitize teens of both genders to issues of sexism, racism, and how oppression is learned without anybody meaning to hurt anybody else.[40]

Churches in particular can be active in disseminating information about resources for victims, hosting educational programs, organizing material assistance for agencies that offer prevention and intervention (for example, local YWCA chapters and women's resource centers). Perhaps most important of all, the churches can offer a moral example by developing proactive policies *before* any complaint arises and handling complaints that do arise in a manner that honors the dignity of victims, hears and does not try to minimize or cover up their suffering, and grants them the credibility that society so often denies.[41]

Theological Considerations

Sexual harassment strikes at the core of a person's dignity and self-esteem, precisely because it is sexual. Like pornography, it invades the deepest boundaries of a woman's spiritual self. Sexual harassment is also a spiritual assault because it erodes and attacks the dignity, identity, and worth of the victim.

No one should have to live in a war zone. A policy approved by the 1989 Churchwide Assembly of the Evangelical Lutheran Church in America affirms the role of the church as a safe place:

> *Whereas, all persons were created by God in the divine image, and human sexuality is a gracious gift of God;*
>
> *Whereas, our baptism into the family of God calls us to stand firmly and pastorally against all forms of abuse and to respect and empower our brothers and sisters in Christ;*
>
> *Whereas sexual violence of many kinds is widespread in our society (including sexual harassment on the job, rape and sexual assault, incest, and child sexual abuse); and experts estimate that two-fifths of working women experience sexual harassment, two-fifths of all American women experience one or more incidents of sexual assault, and one-third of American children experience sexual abuse before the age of 18; and*
>
> *Whereas, sexual harassment and sexual abuse betray God's creation, inflict grievous suffering on the victims and rend the fabric of the whole community of the people of God; therefore be it*
>
> *Resolved that the Evangelical Lutheran Church in America commit itself to work to make our church a safe place for all persons by working to eliminate these abuses; and be it further*
>
> *Resolved, that the ELCA will not tolerate any forms of sexual abuse or harassment by any of its personnel; and be it further*
>
> *Resolved, that each congregation commit itself to become a safe place by working to:*
>
> *a) provide an atmosphere where sexual abuse can be discussed with the freedom and compassion of the gospel, and where specific acts of ministry be encouraged;*
>
> *b) engage in education and prevention of all forms of sexual abuse and harassment;*
>
> *c) provide pastoral care for survivors and referrals for treatment of offenders;*

d) create policies and procedures that assist and support the members of the congregation and its leadership to cope in healing and redemptive ways with these abuses; and

e) manifest its concern for problems of this kind in its community, e.g., families, schools, and workplaces."[42]

The Baptismal Covenant in the Episcopal Book of Common Prayer calls all the baptized to "strive for justice and peace among all people, and *respect the dignity of every human being.*"[43] The Westminster Shorter Catechism of the Presbyterian tradition also states: "The Seventh Commandment requireth the preservation of our own and our neighbor's chastity, in heart, speech, and behavior."[44] The Council on Women and the Church of the United Presbyterian Church USA writes:

> *Though this is not the language to which we are accustomed today, we can discern in this statement a concern of people for the integrity of the other person, an integrity that is violated in sexual harassment. Certainly that concern for the integrity of the other person is expressed in the Sermon on the Mount as a part of Jesus' commentary upon the meaning of the seventh commandment (Matt. 5:27-28). Here as well as in his teaching regarding divorce Jesus was resisting the tendency of men to exercise dominance and compulsion in relation to women and was making room for women to come into fuller personhood, into their full humanity.*[45]

Sexual harassment is experienced by victims as war in the hearts of men, even though their speech may be "smoother than butter" (Ps. 55:21). If we are to preach the gospel of peace, this is not only a matter between nations, but also within our own communities and within the corporate conduct of the church itself.

O afflicted one, storm-tossed, and not comforted,
I am about to set your stones in antimony,
and lay your foundations with sapphires.
I will make your pinnacles of rubies,
your gates of jewels,
and all your wall of precious stones . . .
In righteousness you shall be established;
you shall be far from oppression, for you shall not fear;
and from terror, for it shall not come near you.
If anyone stirs up strife,
it is not from me;
whoever stirs up strife with you
shall fall because of you. . . .
No weapon that is fashioned against you shall prosper,
and you shall confute every tongue that rises against you in judgment.
This is the heritage of the servants of the LORD
and their vindication from me, says the LORD.

(Isa. 54:11-12, 14-15, 17)

CHAPTER FOUR

Rape

But he would not listen to her; and being stronger than she, he forced her and lay with her.

—Tamar's story, 2 Samuel 13:14

Recently, while on jury duty, I sat through the questioning of over twenty-five potential jurors for a case involving three counts of rape. The judge would always ask: "Have you, or any member of your family or a close friend, ever been the victim of a crime, including sexual assault?"

"Yes, my sister was raped when she was thirteen. . . ."

"I have a close friend who right now is dealing with the emotional problems she has because she was raped as a child. . . ."

"Yes, my mother was raped when she was in her twenties, but she doesn't ever talk about it, really. . . ."

"I was raped when I was eighteen. . . ."

"I have a cousin who was raped just last month. . . ."

"I was raped a few years ago. . . ."

"Yes, I was raped. . . ."

The judge: "Did you report this to the police?"

"Yes." . . .

To another juror: "Was anyone arrested?"

"No." . . .

And another: "Did they ever find the alleged perpetrator?"

"No." . . .

Again: "Did the police arrest anyone?"

"Yes. There were three of them."

"Were these men ever prosecuted?"

"No. The district attorney said there wasn't enough evidence." . . .

And again: "Was anyone arrested?"

"Yes. A man who lived down the street from me."

"Was he prosecuted?"

"Yes."

"What happened?"

"He was acquitted. The D.A. said that the jury couldn't find him guilty 'beyond a reasonable doubt.' "

We rarely talk about rape, certainly not in social settings, and rarely in public—yet here were twenty-five strangers, revealing under oath how rape had touched their lives. The impact was staggering. Here was the living truth of statistics we usually read and wince about and set aside, a social truth that is usually covered over by silence, reticence, and denial.

The statistics on rape are astounding: one out of three women will be raped in her lifetime in this country. Boys and men are also raped by other boys and men. About one out of five or six boys is sexually assaulted before the age of eighteen, and one out of fifteen to twenty men are raped within their lifetimes. There is also evidence that rape is increasing (beyond what might be accounted for by increased reporting).[1] Rapes continue to go unreported in as many as 50 to 90 percent of cases, making rape the most underreported crime in America.[2] Reasons for not reporting include lack of counseling and advocacy services, lack of public education about acquaintance rape, absence of laws protecting confidentiality and disclosure of the rape victims' names to the press. But even more compelling, the reality that relatively few rapes are successfully prosecuted and even fewer cases end in a prison sentence inhibits women from reporting. This is perhaps the major reason women do not report: They fear that they will be put through a terrible ordeal where they themselves feel they are on trial, only to end up fearing the violent retaliation of an enraged perpetrator who continues to roam free. In fact, no suspect is even apprehended in a majority of cases, and of those, only one-fifth to one-half go to trial, and only approximately 10 percent of *those* are convicted. Nor do all convictions, particularly on a "first offense," result in incarceration. Studies only confirm what women have suspected for decades: that justice will not serve them or protect them from their rapists.[3]

Even these horrifying statistics are a pale shadow of the reality of rape in the lives of women. As juror after juror told stories of rape, of rapists getting away without being arrested, of rapists not being prosecuted or found guilty, it became horrifyingly clear that fear of rape is simply a part of the fabric of everyday life for women. Almost every woman knows someone to whom it has happened. Every woman thinks about it. It is like background noise in every woman's life—static that interferes with her movements, her choices, her freedom.

We think about rape daily. We think about it when we park our cars, when we get into an elevator with a strange man, when we walk from our driveways to our front doors. We think about it when we buy extra locks for our apartment doors, install alarms on our windows, choose apartments and houses nearer to street lights. My daughter's two babysitters, sisters aged seventeen and eleven, carry self-defense keychains in the shape of cat's ears that can be aimed at the eyes of an attacker. Other women carry mace, whistles, hairspray.

But precautions about walking at night and weapons for self-defense cover only about half the situations in which rapes occur. Many rapes occur during the daytime. Rapes are more likely to occur in a woman's home than on the street. And rapes are three to four times more likely to be carried out by acquaintances than by strangers. Rapes are committed by friends. Rapes are committed by husbands.[5]

And rape changes lives forever. Rape survivor Ruth Schmidt writes:

> Although all these [social, political and theological] issues are important, personal experience is the only adequate window through which to view the reality of rape. It is difficult for many to imagine how one's life changes after living through an experience of terror. I cannot imagine how my life might have been had I not been raped. I have little connection to my life prior to the rape. Rape forced me to start over. In a very disturbing way I experienced the trauma of being torn from the womb and immediately recognizing that even while clothed I am naked, even in a family I am alone, even speaking I am silenced and even living I am dying.[6]

Rape has severe aftereffects: Rape victims are three times more likely than nonvictims of crime to suffer major depression, four times more likely to have contemplated suicide, and thirteen times more likely to have made a suicide attempt, and also significantly more likely to have more drug and alcohol problems than the general population.[7]

What Is Rape?

The traditional legal definition of rape hinges on the issue of consent. Rape is "unlawful sexual intercourse with a female without her consent."[8] This definition is quite narrow. Rape by physical force is in reality a subset of rape, in which physical force or threat of force is used. Date or acquaintance rape may involve other, less overtly violent forms of coercion. The issue of vaginal penetration, traditionally assumed in "carnal knowledge," does not encompass other forms of sexual battery that do not involve penetration: flashing, voyeurism, and other acts with varying degrees of physical invasion. Michigan state law, which has become a model for reform in a number of states, identifies four degrees of sexual assault, which broadens the definition of sexual assault to include penetration of any bodily orifice with any part of a person's body or any object, and intentional touching of the victim's genital area, groin, inner thigh, buttocks, or breasts (either with skin contact or through clothing). Further, the presence of a weapon, two or more assailants, or incapacitation of the victim (whether unconscious, mentally disabled, drugged, etc.) constitute an "aggravated" sexual assault. This type of law does not require penetration of a vagina by a penis, a definition that is more dependent on a male/assailant perspective than women's experience.[9] Nicholas Groth, an expert in the psychology of male rapists, writes, "All nonconsenting sexual acts are assaults."[10]

Marital rape has only recently been recognized in some states as a crime comparable to other rapes. In twenty-nine states it is a lesser offense, and in two states it is still not a crime at all.[11]

What the law cannot, by its nature, describe is that rape is the forcible entry into the most private, most vulnerable, and, arguably most sacred parts of the human body, and, as such, it is a spiritual crime as well as a physical one. In one of the first, groundbreaking descriptions of women's reality of rape, early in the formation of the antirape movement in the early 1970s, Susan Griffin wrote:

> Rape is an act of aggression in which the victim is denied her self-determination. It is an act of violence, which, if not actually followed by beatings or murder, nevertheless always carries with it the threat of death. And finally, rape is a form of mass terrorism, for the victims of rape are chosen indiscriminately, but the propagandists for male supremacy broadcast that it is women who cause rape by being unchaste or in the wrong place at the wrong time—in essence, by behaving as though they were free.[12]

Perhaps the most succinct definition was given by Andrew Medea and Kathleen Thompson, in another book early in the rape crisis movement: "Rape is all the hatred, contempt and oppression of women in this society concentrated into one act."[13]

Rape comes from the Latin word *rapere*, "to steal." This etymological root reveals the prevailing view of rape from earliest centuries—as a crime against property. Sexual assault, as in the story of Tamar, becomes a theft of another man's possession, rather than a violation of a woman's sovereign jurisdiction over her own body. Whether as a callous and utilitarian means to claiming a woman as a wife, retaliation or theft committed against a neighbor, or one of the spoils of war, rape has been practiced worldwide as men's prerogative—with the claims of another man upon a particular woman's body as the only possible deterrent.

In a number of ancient civilizations, rape was punishable by death (for example, see Deut. 22:23-29).[14] If the woman "did not cry out," she was also stoned (Deut. 22:23-24). The exception was in the case of the rape of a virgin. Then the rapist was required to marry the victim and pay her father three times her original marriage price (in Deut. 22:29, fifty shekels of silver). In addition, the girl's father was in some civilizations allowed a "rape of retribution," which legally permitted him to rape the ravisher's wife or sister. Many centuries later, while rape was viewed as illegal among upper classes, it was still considered the prerogative of a landed aristocrat to have sex with his servant girls and women—and especially to enjoy the privilege of deflowering them on the eve of their wedding. This *droit du seigneur* (master's right) became the subject of an entire opera by Mozart, *The Marriage of Figaro*, based on a play by the eighteenth-century playwright Beaumarchais. The dread of rape and the angry protest of the serving class against tyranny of the aristocracy lie at the heart of this seemingly lighthearted comedy of manners, which is now often seen—erroneously—as more charming than political.

The intertwining of class privilege with the privilege to rape is clearly demonstrated in early English law, which set different standards for punishment and compensation for rape depending on the relative social positions of perpetrator and victim. For example, a man "who lay with a maiden belonging (not married) to the King" had to pay fifty shillings for the rape, but if she was a "grinding slave" the amount was cut in half. On the other side of the equation, if a slave dared to rape a commoner's serving maid, he was castrated, and if he dared to rape anyone above that rank he was killed. It was legally impossible for a king or bishop to rape anyone. One word said in their own behalf would automatically clear them of all charges. If a priest was accused of rape or any other misdeed, he could take an oath while wearing his vestments and swear before an altar that the charges were untrue. He would then be cleared of all wrongdoing.[15]

Neither can rape be separated from racism.[16] Black slave women were routinely raped by white slave owners and by their black overseers as well. The narratives of slave women are filled with stories of rape and sexual violence.[17] Angela Davis wrote:

> As females, slave women were inherently vulnerable to all forms of sexual coercion. If the most violent punishments of men consisted in floggings and mutilations, most women were flogged and mutilated, as well as raped. Rape, in fact, was an uncamouflaged expression of the slaveholder's economic mastery and the over-seer's control over Black women as workers.[18]

Long after the Emancipation Proclamation, the rape of a white woman by a black man was a capital offense, when the maximum sentence for a white man who committed the same crime was only twenty years. African American researcher Darlene Clark Hine asks: What are the psychological consequences for entire generations of women living under the constant threat of rape?[19]

Racism also distorted justice for the accused. Rape charges against black men served a dual purpose of enforcing white men's ownership of women, both white and black, and of a "systematic weapon of terror" against black men.[20] To this day, the vast proportion of men arrested and convicted for rape are black, with no social evidence to support a disproportionate conviction rate.

Rape is also intertwined with other human rights violations, directly linking political repression, machismo, and torture of prisoners.[21] Rape is listed by Amnesty International and other human rights organizations as a common form of torture throughout the world. The recent rape of women in Bosnia is a clear example of rape as an act of political violence, domination, conquest, and hatred. This is but one moment in a history of rape that is centuries old. Rape of indigenous women was a routine part of the colonization of the Americas by the Spaniards and other Europeans, long before the wave of political violence in Latin America, which began in the middle of this century and which made use of rape to intimidate and silence the population.[22] Wherever in the world the most repressive dictatorships exist, racial oppression, genocide, and rape go hand in hand. South Africa has the highest incidence of rape in the world, with a much higher percentage in the black community than in the white, and possibly the highest level of silence: only one in thirty women reports rape to the authorities, and there is very little social support. "People never really talk about rape. Many of them don't report the incident to the police because they are ridiculed. Not only that, but they fear the police."[23]

Myths Surrounding Rape

Myth #1: Rape is an impulsive act, beyond the rapist's control.

This is a variation on the myth that men's sexual drives are uncontrollable once aroused, and that men are victims of their own biology. Statistics have shown that rape is more often than not premeditated: 90 percent in the case of group rape; 83 percent involving two perpetrators; and 58 percent involving a single perpetrator.[24] Thirty-five percent of male students in one study reported hypothetically that they would be likely to rape if guaranteed that they would not be caught or punished.[25]

Alcohol also does not cause rape, although it may be a disinhibitor. In one study, men who believed that they had drunk alcohol were equally aroused by violent rape pornography as men who had drunk. (A control group who did not drink were less aroused.) This implies a social placebo effect for alcohol as a disinhibitor as much as any physiological factor.[26]

Myth #2: Sex appeal is of primary importance in selecting targets. Beautiful young women are more likely to be raped.

In reality, women of all ages from infants to the elderly are raped. Stereotypical beauty or attractiveness is not relevant. Women in their nineties and infants as young as six months have been victims of rape.[27] A man assaults someone who is accessible and vulnerable.

Myth #3: Rape is an act of sexual passion.

Studies of rapists have shown sexual gratification as secondary or absent. Nicholas Groth writes, "Rape is never the result simply of sexual arousal that has no other opportunity for gratification."[28] Primary motives include power, domination, revenge, hatred of women, and desire for humiliation. Rape is an act of aggression and intimidation accomplished by sexual means. Groth, in describing his clinical work with sex offenders, told *Newsweek* magazine, "We look at rape as the sexual expression of aggression, rather than as the aggressive expression of sexuality."[29] Groth has developed a threefold typology of rapists: those who use sexual aggression to discharge anger by degrading and humiliating their victims; those who rape in order to compensate for feelings of powerlessness by overpowering a victim in the area of her greatest vulnerability; and those whom he labels as sadistic, deriving erotic gratification from sexual domination and torture. Even in this third category, the anger and power motives are primary, but in this case they become eroticized.[30] In his landmark book *Men Who Rape: The Psychology of the Offender*, Groth writes:

> Rape is a pseudosexual act, a pattern of sexual behavior that is concerned much
> more with status, hostility, control, and dominance than with sensual pleasure or

sexual satisfaction. It is sexual behavior in the primary service of non-sexual needs.[31]

Gang rape adds the dimensions of peer pressure, baiting, and group psychology to create a pack mentality in which individuals' inhibitions against committing crimes are loosened. Sixty-two percent of multiple-offender rapes are committed by young men under twenty-one, compared to 20 percent of single-offender rapes.[32]

Myth #4: No woman can be raped against her will.

This is expressed by the crude joke, "You can't thread a moving needle," and is used especially against women who do not fight back and in cases of date or acquaintance rapes. In many cases, fear is so immobilizing that a perpetrator does not need to use extreme force to accomplish the rape. This does not constitute an invitation on the victim's part. This myth gained official sanction as early as 500 B.C.E. in the writings of Herodotus, the so-called Father of History: "Abducting young women is not, indeed, a lawful act, but it is stupid after the event to make a fuss about it. The only sensible thing is to take no notice; for it is obvious that no young woman allows herself to be abducted if she does not wish to be." This is perhaps the purest statement of blaming the victim on record.[33]

One survivor bravely confronted this myth during her questioning by a police officer after she was raped. The officer gave her his billy club and asked her to insert it in the styrofoam cup he was holding. While holding the cup, he moved it back and forth quickly, trying to make the point that if she had struggled she could not have been penetrated. The woman responded by hitting the officer on the arm with the club, causing him to drop the cup. She then inserted the club into the cup.[34]

Myth #5: Women secretly want to be raped.

"She asked for it." Women do not want to be raped. While some women as well as men do fantasize about rape, and may even enjoy a mock sexual struggle, this does not equate with the terrifying reality of actual rape. In fantasy, the person fantasizing is still in complete control of what happens. In actual rape, she is completely out of control—dominated, humiliated, and often caused excruciating physical pain.

The moment of a woman's "no" is the turning point between seduction and sexual play on the one hand, and violation, fear, and pain on the other. There is no better illustration of this than the character Sarah Tobias, portrayed by Jodie Foster in the movie *The Accused*. Based on an actual incident of gang rape on a pool table in "Big Dan's" Bar in New Bedford, Massachusetts, in March 1983,[35] Sarah at first dances and flirts with one of the men. The viewer is set up to believe that here is an obvious case of a young woman who dressed and behaved in a way that was intended to invite sex. However, a dramatic change occurs. When she says she's had enough and wants to go home, he begins to force her. Egged on by their buddies at the bar, several of the men eventually take turns holding her down and forcibly raping her. There is no mistaking this for romance, seduction, or mixed communication. Again and again, she cries "no" and struggles. In a matter of seconds, what had seemed like flirtatious play is transformed into a prolonged episode of terror and violence. Jodie Foster's genius is to show how a woman's exercise of freedom—including sexual freedom—is turned *against her will* into a brutal violation. Later it is Sarah Tobias's struggle to prove that the exercise of sexual freedom did not warrant such a violation, and in the movie we are allowed to see how this becomes heroic.

Myth #6: If you're going to be raped, you might as well lie back and enjoy it.

Of course, the double bind created by this saying is: If a woman appears or pretends to cooperate with the rape, it is used as evidence that she was consenting and no rape occurred. Susan Brownmiller identifies this pseudo-consent as part of the rapist's own fantasy: "to make a woman a willing participant in her own defeat is half the battle. . . . It is a belief in the supreme rightness of male power."[36]

The cultural bias against women's using physical force, even in self-defense, ends up contributing to the further oppression of women. A corollary myth to "lie back and enjoy it" is the myth that attempts at self-defense will result in being killed. This belief deters many women from successfully defending themselves. However, studies have shown that self-defense often helps women in a number of ways. In a study of ninety-four women survivors of sexual assault (forty-three of whom were raped, and fifty-one of whom avoided rape although they were attacked), Pauline Bart and Patricia O'Brien at the University of Chicago concluded that the immediate use of physical force, especially when combined with other defensive strategies (yelling, screaming, fleeing, using deceptive maneuvers) was the best deterrent, although they emphasized that *no* strategy guaranteed that rape would be avoided. Fleeing was the best single deterrent when only one strategy was used.[37] They contend that women's socialization not to fight physically and not to play contact sports renders them much more vulnerable to rape. While no defensive strategy succeeded in avoiding rape 100 percent of the time, the use of *no* strategies resulted in *no* avoidance of rape in five out of five cases. The use of force, contrary to the prevailing myth, does not lead to greater injury once a woman is attacked. On the contrary, victims who did not fight back often sustained greater injuries.[38] Bart and O'Brien declare that women being advised to try to avoid rape through passive resistance or talking and thus "humanizing" the relationship are being misled in what amounts to yet another form of social control.

Some of their detailed conclusions, many of which have been replicated by Sarah E. Ullman at Brandeis University, included:

Acting "like a lady" is more likely to result in rape than in avoiding its occurrence;

the women whose primary concern lay in avoiding death or mutilation have been less likely to avoid rape than those who had a gut reaction of rage and were primarily determined not to be raped.

. . . raped women who used physical strategies were less likely to be depressed than raped women who did not. . . . They are less likely to blame themselves . . . , more likely to gain strength from the belief that they did everything they could in that situation.

We are told that if we fight back, if we physically resist, we will pay the price through severe injury or death. This admonition is not supported by our findings.

Women who fought back sustained the following kinds of injuries: bruises and bite marks on the neck, soreness for a few days, strained muscles, bruises and minor cuts, more serious cuts, back injury and aching the next morning.

Women who stopped their rapes did not respond differently to their assailant whether or not they knew him—except that they were more likely to yell or scream when the assailant was a stranger.

Even when there was some indication of a weapon, 44% of the women avoided being raped.[39]

Py Bateman, one of the founders of the women's self-defense movement, wrote of her own experience of defending herself in a prolonged rape attack:

We have always stressed determination as important, and it was determination that kept me fighting—and thinking—when he didn't give up, when he escalated the violence. Another factor, one that we didn't know so much about, was biology. I never felt any pain while I was fighting. Not even when I cut my hand grabbing the knife by the blade. My consciousness was dominated by the determination to come out alive and my plans for how to do that.[40]

None of this discussion should be interpreted as blaming women for being raped if they did not fight back. Encouragement to use physical resistance is an important self-defense message for women prior to being raped. It is *not* useful after the fact, when it may carry the implication, "If you had fought back you wouldn't have been raped." There are many factors to be considered in the decision whether to resist physically. In some cases, although not probably in the majority, the rapist may be further stimulated by a victim's resistance. Women must use their judgment.[41] In many rapes in which the woman's life is threatened, staying alive is the best resistance, regardless of the strategy used to do so. The final answer to the myth of "lie back and enjoy it" is that, while it may be debated whether rape is sex or not for the assailant, it is *never* sex for the victim. It is violence, and violence is not enjoyable.[42]

Myth #7: Women cry "rape" to get revenge.

This myth has biblical sanction in the story of Potiphar's wife (Gen. 39). Seventeenth-century jurist Matthew Hale wrote: "Rape is an accusation easily to be made and hard to be proved, and harder to be defended by the party accused, though never so innocent."[43] Statistically, however, this myth is hard to defend. As with battering, as few as one in ten rapes is reported to the police.[44] False accusations of rape do not statistically exceed any other crime (approximately 2 percent).[45]

Myth #8: The myth of the black rapist.

The stereotype of the black man raping the white woman was seared into the popular imagination in 1915 in D. W. Griffith's monumentally racist propaganda film *The Birth of a Nation*. In this movie—the first feature-length film telling a cohesive story and thus intended as a heroic milestone for the director—the fragile, doll-like Lillian Gish is saved from a black man's rape by the Ku Klux Klan.

Facts tell a different story. The vast majority of rapes are same-race crimes.[46] The one exception to this is that Asian women are slightly more likely to be raped by white men.[47] This reality is distorted by media attention to black-on-white crimes and relative ignoring of white or black-on-black crimes. It is also distorted by the fact that men of color are disproportionately convicted and jailed for assault—although only a small percentage of male assailants are men of color, they are 48 percent of those convicted and 80 percent of those jailed for assault.[48]

While black men are not more likely to be rapists, black women are significantly more likely than white women to be victims,[49] and they are subjected to more violent attacks.[50] Black women and other women of color are sometimes more vulnerable for reasons of lack of community awareness of the problem, the necessity of working undesirable hours, high utilization of public transportation, and residences located in high-crime neighborhoods with inadequate police protection. Several of these reasons are because of the economic inequalities in the lives of women of color and pertain to all poor and working-class women to some degree. Women of color also face a dilemma in reporting, because of justifiable mistrust of racist law enforcement and public agencies, unwillingness to subject themselves to racist disbelief and blame, and reluctance combined with social pressure against exposing a brother to arrest or incarceration.

Myth #9: Most women are raped at night by a stranger in a desolate place.

In reality, statistics show that sexual assaults occur over one-third of the time at home, and one-third occur during the day.[51] And contrary to the myth of the stranger, 50 to 78 percent of rapes are committed by someone known to the victim. As many as 46 percent of rapes are committed by family members (husbands, ex-husbands, fathers, stepfathers, and other relatives).[52]

Myth #10: Only women are raped.

For its crime reporting program, the FBI conforms to the traditional definition of forcible rape as "carnal knowledge of a female forcibly or against her will,"[53] so certain national crime statistics cannot indicate the prevalence of sexual assaults against men and boys. Sociological studies generally show that one out of four girls is raped, and one out of five or six boys, before the age of eighteen. Over age eighteen, one of every three women is raped, and one out of fifteen to twenty men is raped (by other men).[54] Twelve to 14 percent of the sexual assaults treated at the San Francisco Rape Treatment Center in 1992 were suffered by men, both straight and gay.[55] While the focus of this book is on violence against women, it is important not to ignore the fact of male victims' pain and terror. Men, too, become victims of male violence.[56]

Rape in the Language of the Mystics

> Batter my heart, three-person'd God; for you
> As yet but knocke, breathe, shine, and seeke to mend;
> That I may rise, and stand, o'erthrow mee, 'and bend
> Your force, to breake, blowe, burn and make me new.
> I, like an usurpt towne, to'another due,
> Labour to admit you, but Oh, to no end,
> Reason your viceroy in mee, mee should defend,
> But is ca'tiv'd, and proves weake or untrue.
> Yet dearely'I love you,'and would be loved faine,
> But am betroth'd unto your enemie;
> Divorce me,'untie, or breake that knot againe,
> Take me to you, imprison mee, for I
> Except you'enthrall mee, never shall be free,
> Nor ever chast, escept you ravish me.[57]

A rape fantasy takes on a profound and transcendent glow in the words of John Donne, seventeenth-century poet-mystic. The imagery of sexual assault is used as a powerful metaphor for being overshadowed and transformed by the presence of the divine. But this raises a number of questions. First, could such imagery ever be used quite so rapturously by a woman? Or is the relative absence of fear of literal rape necessary for such romanticization of it?

The imagery of sexual surrender as a spiritual metaphor is not unique to John Donne. Compare his seemingly fearless desire for being ravished by God to the words of St. Teresa of Avila:

> The Lord wanted me while in this state to see sometimes the following vision: I saw close to me toward my left side an angel in bodily form. . . . I saw in his hands a large golden dart and at the end of the iron tip there appeared to be a little fire. It seemed to me this angel plunged the dart several times into my heart and that it reached deep within me. When he drew it out, I thought he was carrying off with him the deepest part of me and he left me all on fire with great love of God.

Here we have similar sexual imagery, of being overwhelmed, even impaled by divine shafts of love. Teresa does not use language of violence: "batter" and "ravish." Her imagery is ambiguous between enjoyment and suffering, but perhaps seems more relational and voluntary: "the pain was so great that I screamed aloud, but simultaneously felt such infinite sweetness that I wished the pain to last eternally. It was the sweetest caressing of the soul by God."[58]

We may also ask, has Teresa's experience itself been transmitted well, or has it been used at the service of the patriarchal myth of women's enjoyment of rape? Perhaps the most famous image of Teresa is the statue by the Renaissance sculptor Bernini. In it, God is concretized in the form of a youthful angel—presumably male, but having androgynous characteristics—whose expression is both smiling and vacant, plunging a spear into the heart of a swooning figure of Teresa. Art historian Kenneth Clark has written, "The *Ecstasy of St. Teresa* is one of the most deeply moving works in European art. Bernini's gift of sympathetic imagination . . . no doubt enhanced by his practice of St. Ignatius's spiritual exercises—is used to convey the rarest and most precious of all emotional states, that of religious ecstasy."[59] Is Bernini faithfully depicting Teresa's own authentic experience of inner rapture, or is there an element of pornography that is perhaps inevitable in the translation of one woman's interior, mystical experience into the concrete medium of marble sculpted by a male master? Would it even be possible for Bernini, embedded as he was in the assumptions of his time and culture, to separate out an image of female ecstatic surrender from supposed ecstatic enjoyment of rape?

The use of rape is not exclusive to the religious imagery of Christianity. Rape stories abound in Greek and Roman mythology, and have been retained in the artistic imagination of our own Western culture. Gustav Klimt's painting of the rape of Danae seems on the surface to be a sensitive and loving portrayal of female sexual ecstasy. Danae reclines on her back, nude, with a look of sleepy fulfillment on her face, as a shower of golden light pours down between her legs.[60] Yet once again, the question must be raised, why *this* image of ecstasy? And where are the myths and images of male surrender and male ecstasy in being overpowered and sexually overtaken?

John Donne is unusual in this regard—it is himself of whom he says, "Batter my heart, O God," and "ravish me." And yet this poem is clearly not a desire for literally being raped. It is the overpowering of the soul, which itself carries socialized connotations of the feminine (the *anima*). Here again, a masculine voice presumes to speak universally of the human quality of spiritual surrender. And while such surrender may in fact be at the heart of all human experience, male and female, such a romanticization of rape belies the pain and horror of the actual experience—an experience in which any redemptive quality is questionable.

Even contemporary psychologists utilizing mythology to illuminate the deeper aspects of the human psyche may differ according to gender in their retelling of stories of rape. Jungian writer and therapist Naomi Ruth Lowinsky, drawing on quotations from the Greek poet Homer,[61] retells the myth of the rape of Kore/Persephone, which was the heart of the Eleusinian mystery cult:

> In the myth, Kore, the adolescent daughter of Demeter, goddess of the grain, is picking flowers in a meadow with her friends. She is drawn to a particularly beautiful flower, a narcissus. As she picks it up, the earth opens up and Hades, Lord of the Underworld, seizes her and carries her, crying and protesting, into the realm of the

shades. When her mother, the "awesome goddess with her beautiful hair," realizes
that her daughter has disappeared:

> a sharp pain seized her heart
> With her lovely hands
> she tore the headdress
> on her immortal hair
> she threw off
> the dark covering
> on her shoulders
> and she shot out,
> like a bird,
> over dry land
> and sea
> searching.

*The goddess goes into so deep a state of mourning that her beauty fades and she
looks like "an old woman . . . beyond childbearing, beyond the gifts of Aphrodite."
In her rage and grief she causes the earth not to take seed, the "white barley" to fall
"uselessly upon the earth." So angry and full of grief was she that "she would have
wiped out the whole race of talking men" if Zeus had not interceded, ordering
Hades to return his bride so that her mother could see her "with her own eyes."*[62]

This is a full rendering of the pain and anguish of both mother and daughter, without minimization or qualification. Lowinsky goes on to use this myth
as an argument for reclaiming and restoring honor to the depth and mystery
of the mother-daughter connection: "Imagine, if you can, a society of men
and women so permeated with the inner meaning of the female mysteries that
they would hold in silence the secrets of life that were revealed to them. Imagine women and men sharing the rage and grief of the mother whose daughter
has been seized by the lord of the underworld."[63]

Jungian analyst Jean Shinoda Bolen similarly emphasizes the pain and grief
of mother and daughter. She adds that in one version of the myth Demeter
herself is raped by Poseidon while searching for Persephone. Bolen highlights
Demeter's outrage at Zeus's betrayal:

*Helios, God of the Sun . . . told them that Hades had kidnapped Persephone and
taken her to the underworld to be his unwilling bride. Furthermore, he said that the
abduction and rape of Persephone had been sanctioned by Zeus. He told Demeter to
stop weeping and accept what had happened; Hades was after all "not an unworthy
son-in-law." Demeter refused his advice. She now felt outrage and betrayal by Zeus
as well as grief. She withdrew from Mt. Olympus. . . .*"[64]

Bolen compares Demeter's maternal persistence even in the face of danger to
the *Madres de la Plaza de Mayo*, the mothers who confronted the authorities
in Argentina to demand the return of their sons and daughters who had been
"disappeared" by the state police.

In contrast, another Jungian writer, Thomas Moore, makes use of the same story, not focusing on the anguish of the victim and her mother, but finding a psychological argument supporting Zeus's complicity:

> From the Demeter point of view, the abduction into depth is an outrageous viola-
> tion. But we know, from the complicity of Zeus, that it is also a necessity. If Zeus
> approves, then whatever is happening is truly the will of God. It is in the nature
> of things to be drawn to the very experience that will spoil our innocence, transform
> our lives, and give us necessary complexity and depth.[65] (emphasis mine)

He further goes on to characterize Demeter's actions as "neurotic activities."[66]

It can be argued, of course, that this is taking these mythological stories of rape too literally, and that the use of rape as metaphor and deep truth cannot be confused with women's actual experience. Moore, for example, is making the valid point that we must all descend into depth, which involves a loss of innocence and an initiation through danger, in order to move toward fuller life. But again, to focus on the validity of the male gods' larger purposes sacrifices the female victim's experience, erasing her voice just as Tamar's was silenced, and draws us once again to read these stories and myths of rape through the universalism of a patriarchal lens. Are we to read myths of rape as metaphors and abstractions because that is how masculinist history has read them? Or, as women, are we called to challenge these myths as inappropriate expressions of spiritual development, because we know too well that rape is *not* a matter of glorious surrender, and that only one who does not fear rape could ever really glorify it? Are these metaphors and abstractions not, in fact, more subtle propaganda for the myth of women's enjoyment of rape? Isn't the spiritualization of rape through myth and male mystical imagery one of the deepest forms of denial of women's actual experience of rape and horror and violation?

There is one central truth revealed by the prevalence of rape in mythology and even in the language of the mystics: Rape is not just a matter of the body, but of the soul. The feminist saying, "Rape is power and not sex," is true in the sense that the goal of the rapist is not primarily sexual pleasure but domination. And, paradoxically, it is the sexual nature of the act that renders it most powerful and most violating—at the level of soul itself.

Rape is a violation of the most private territories of the body and, as such, is a violation of soul. Nor is it enough to call these territories simply "private"—our "private parts" are connected with procreation and birth as well as sexual ecstasy, and because of this they are not only private but sacred. The mind-body split of our culture, reinforced vehemently by Christian theology and tradition, denies the sacredness of the body. And yet, a very young child who has not yet been immersed in this confusing separation of body and mind, body and spirit, knows that her bodily integrity represents the boundaries of her Self. And there is a part of each of us into adulthood who knows that truth as well. The violation, then, of the most private parts of the body— the parts connected with procreation, birth, and sexual pleasure—constitutes a violation of nothing less than one's spiritual core of being. It is the sexual nature of the violation that makes it so profoundly a crime against the spirit.

There is one way in which rape as a metaphor does, admittedly, speak to a deep aspect of the human condition and the human spiritual journey. I say this cautiously, because to claim that rape has an allegorical message transcending gender experience can all too easily reinforce patriarchal universalizing of male reality and male rape fantasy as normative for behavior. It is instructive, however, to make the distinction between mystical-mythological rape imagery as *surrender* as opposed to *submission*.

John Donne and Teresa of Avila, however patriarchally conditioned their use of rape as metaphor, are pointing to an act of voluntary and chosen giving up of the confines of one's own limited ego consciousness and surrendering to the larger life of God which is loving and good. The result is ecstasy, not trauma. Here in the mystical imagination, the fantasized loss of control is encapsulated safely within the voluntary choice the mystic has made to enter into this state of being taken over.

Psychologist Mary Tennes distinguishes between submission and surrender, and points to the implications of this distinction for feminist psychology:

> *Submission, on the one hand, entails a relinquishment of our authentic and necessary self-expression. The giving over in submission is to the powerful and willful other for whom we become an object rather than a subject. Submission is motivated by the fear that unless we sacrifice our own subjectivity and abide by the other's will, we will be abandoned, hurt, or violated; the fear of losing or being harmed by the other takes precedence over the fear of losing ourselves. . . .*
>
> *Surrender, on the other hand, involves relinquishing control in a way that propels development forward. The "giving over" in surrender is not to the terms or perspectives of another, but rather to the possibility that our developmental requirements are outside of our control. Contrary to submission, which requires a forfeiture of our most essential selfhood, surrender involves a yielding to what we are "meant to be," an alignment with ourselves and with the direction of our self-realization. Implicit in the concept of surrender is the experience of a force beyond our conscious intent which motivates and guides our growth and healing. Jungians call this the Self (with a capital S) as distinct from the ego, and note that the ego must eventually realize its subordinate position to the Self in order for the individuation process to evolve. . . . This process can, like submission, be experienced as a loss of self. But the loss is one that expands and enlivens us, rather than one that causes our sense of self to be diminished. . . .*
>
> *I would argue that because the consolidation of the female self has been so influenced by the demand to submit and the refusal to do so, many women resist the process of surrender, thereby curtailing essential developmental possibilities.*[67]

Seen in this light, surrender is the relinquishing of conscious control by the ego, to let in the fullness of the soul's wisdom. It is "not my will but Thine," opening the confines of consciousness to an ecstatic flooding of divinity. In reading Teresa or John Donne, we cannot confuse inner experience with outer, or concretize what is being expressed in allegorical language. We cannot eliminate images of surrender from the mystic-mythological realm, because they represent a deeper truth about where the soul must go to stay alive and move on its journey.

Christ's own surrender on the cross may be seen as paradigmatic for this part of the soul's journey. Feminist theologians Joanne Carlson Brown, Rebecca Parker, and Rita Nakashima Brock, among others, have argued that the cross represents "an abusive theology that glorifies suffering."[68] They rightly identify that Christ's suffering as it is understood in St. Anselm's classic theory of the atonement (in which Christ is believed to have died for all of humanity's sins in order to satisfy God's requirement for justice while preserving God's desire to be loving and merciful) sets forth a paradigm of a divine child abuse.[69] This view casts Jesus' death as submission rather than surrender.

It is possible, however, to understand Jesus' sacrifice as one of surrender, a voluntary action taken in the face of political and religious injustice, in fidelity to his own faith and principles—rather than as an act of submission, which would have been to the secular forces of oppression that sought to silence his message of justice, his proclaiming of the immanence of God's Realm. Even in their critique, Brown and Parker approach this interpretation: "Jesus chose to live a life in opposition to unjust, oppressive cultures. Jesus did not choose the cross but chose integrity and faithfulness, refusing to change course because of threat."[70] Some victims of rape and abuse have found hope in the crucifixion in the sense that, through his experience of suffering, Jesus stands in solidarity with their suffering and there is no suffering that is unknown to God.

Brown and Parker assert that suffering is never redemptive and can never be redeemed. "The cross is a sign of tragedy. God's grief is revealed there and everywhere and every time life is thwarted by violence. God's grief is as ultimate as God's love. Every tragedy eternally remains and is eternally mourned. Eternally the murdered scream. Betrayal. Eternally God sings kaddish for the world."[71] Christ's surrender to the cross, however, is not redemptive because of his suffering, but because of his choice to remain faithful even in the face of death. And it was that choice, and not the suffering, that was vindicated by the resurrection. God does not cause suffering, but stands in solidarity with those who suffer. This has been a central understanding of Latin American Liberation theology.[72] Survivors of violence can find strength in both sides of the crucifixion/resurrection mystery—the knowledge that God stands with them and sings kaddish for their agony, and at the same time vindicates them with the resurrection gifts of healing, transformation, and new life.[73]

The feminist critique of atonement theory and the glorification of suffering may be applied to the mystical-mythological images of rape in the writings of Christian contemplatives. Is Brown's, Parker's, and Brock's assertion that suffering is never redemptive and can never be redeemed a confusion of inner and outer realities, a splitting off and rejection of necessary imagery that represents a deeper picture of the ego's surrender to God—or is it a necessary warning that torture can never be a useful symbol?

There are no easy answers to this question. Rape must not be glorified, and there is no doubt that rape imagery is drawn from a patriarchally contaminated history of domination and torture of women. What can be said is that both real and imagined rape participate in the realm of soul, and it is precisely this conjunction of sexual violence with the sacredness of the body that makes the *allegory* of rape so powerful in the mystic imagination and the *reality* of rape so heinous.

Pastoral Response

Over the next few weeks after the rape when I spoke of anything at all, it was about this attack; but more usually I kept it to myself. Within a week I gradually received the nonverbal cues that it was time to stop mentioning it. . . . There seemed to be no further need for your attention or solicitude. True to form, I had continued my usual stance of maturity and calm. Now you should know, because next time it might be more serious: though my routines and words signaled, "I'm all right," I was lying through my teeth.[74]

A pastor may be confronted with the news that a parishioner has very recently been raped. At this time, crisis skills are needed. However, there are often others, particularly trained rape crisis specialists, who are available to assist in the immediate aftermath of the assault. A pastor's sensitivity and knowledgeability are perhaps even more essential as time passes and family and community crisis resources begin to diminish.

Rape crisis workers commonly refer to a "rape trauma syndrome,"[75] in which there are several stages of recovery that can last as long as several years even with support and intervention. In one version, the first is the acute or "impact stage,"[76] which lasts from several weeks to several months. This stage includes disorganization and disruption of normal coping mechanisms, shock, fear (including fear of retaliation), anxiety, withdrawal, crying, unexpected outbursts, self-blame, intrusive reliving of the events of the rape, and other classic post-traumatic symptoms such as nightmares, sleep problems, startle responses and hypervigilance, and physical symptoms such as nausea and headaches. Anyone in recovery from alcohol or drugs may experience setbacks in the recovery process. What the survivor "knows" intellectually may be far beyond what she can allow herself to feel emotionally. She needs permission and validation for all her feelings, without hint of blame or shame. She is likely to be certain that the pastor either won't believe her or will blame her. The pastor must let her know that he or she is proud of her for coming in and knows how hard it must be. In this stage, a victim needs calm, matter-of-fact, reliable pastoral presence, and reassurance that all of her reactions, both emotional and physical, are normal.

In the second "recoil" or "pseudo-adjustment stage,"[77] lasting from several months to several years, the victim appears outwardly to be coping well and to have adjusted. Her life is pulled together again and normal activities are resumed. Symptoms may diminish, although many may remain, often more hidden to observers. Fear may be managed but not yet worked through. It is in this period that it becomes important to check in with the victims, remind them that it's OK not to feel completely pulled together, and to invite them to continue to talk. The victim may be trying very hard to appear "just fine," and may need the pastor to take the initiative. She may need reassurances that the pastor is not bored, annoyed, frightened, or put off by the victim's continued preoccupation with the rape or any of her feelings, ranging from anger to confusion to sadness.

The final "integration"[78] or "reorganization"[79] stage is the stage at which the assault is put into some personal sense of perspective, however the individual woman defines it, and most symptoms are gone. Still, the victim may experience brief periods of depression and may have occasional setbacks. This phase may even initially resemble the first phase, as emotions are now being fully felt. The assault of a friend, a big rape story in the media, a graphic scene in a movie, or seeing the assailant can all re-evoke the terror and anger of her own rape. Another attack, or related incidents including sexual harassment and seemingly milder forms of personal or sexual violation, can trigger post-traumatic symptoms at any time. Normal developmental changes and major stresses throughout her life can trigger assault-related emotions. These after-effects are permanent in most women. It is important in this stage for the pastor to recognize and celebrate that the woman has passed over from "victim" to "survivor" and has regained a sense of her own power. Much of the work of this stage has been compared to the process patients go through in coming to terms with death and dying.[80] It is also important to validate the lasting effects of the assault, and once again to provide reassurance that some residual effects will be lifelong and are a normal part of the healing process itself.

The most important response to a variety of victims' reactions is *acknowledgment*.[81] In the immediate aftermath of a rape, a victim may respond with feelings of extreme powerless and helplessness—particularly in connection with feeling she was almost killed. She may present a composed, silent reaction, or respond by screaming, crying, giggling, or shaking. She may respond toward helping professionals and significant others with hostility, denial, shock, self-blame, or embarrassment. It is important for a pastor or counselor to allow the victim to be as she is and not urge her somehow to respond differently—for example, to think she should be "talking it out" if she needs to be quiet, or to be angry when she is mainly feeling fear and grief. A pastor may find it frustrating if she is in denial, and may be too frightened or angry or embarrassed to ask important questions. If the pastor is also a survivor of rape or another form of violence, the victim's own emotions may trigger the pastor's own helplessness, fear, or rage. If this is not recognized and processed *apart from the victim*, it is likely to be projected onto her situation. This actually distances the pastor from the victim, because the pastor is seeing him- or herself rather than being fully present to the victim.

Conclusion: Biblical and Theological Resources

I am an uncomfortable person. To know me is to know that we live in a society where rape is permitted, where women live as second-class citizens denied rights that so many men take for granted, to know an uncomfortable feeling of "all is not right" in this life. To know me is to know an anger which is ice blue, to know that women are vulnerable as a sex, to know that hatred is not simply a concept of philosophy, but a painful reality. Women are raped out of hatred. Women hate out of the reality of rape. To know me certainly is not to love me. And to love me is to risk incredible frustration and painful rejection. For I live first and foremost as a survivor of rape, as a spokesperson of inequality, as an angry, angry woman.

Listen to my anger. I have been taken in darkness.

"All that came to be had life in Him and that life was the light of men, a light that shines in the darkness, a light that darkness could not overpower." I do not know that light. "Sin began with a woman and thanks to her we all must die." I do not know that sin.

Listen to my anger, for it cries out from everywhere and nowhere. It lives in the headlines, in the news broadcasts, on the movie screens, in magazines, in the hollow eyes of our daughters, sisters and mothers, and in the lost lives of those of us who don't survive.

See my anger, it is abundant. It is glaring, it is blinding, it is plastered on billboards, it hangs in store windows, it is drawn on the covers of books.

Touch my anger. It is damp from tears. It is hot from smoldering. It is heavy and difficult to carry. Taste my anger, it is bitter. Smell my anger, it is rancid, it is filled with sweat from a heaving man forcing himself upon me and into me.

Understand my anger, for you have brought it upon me. "Happy are those who are persecuted in the cause of right; theirs is the kingdom of heaven." I do not know this heaven.[82]

A rape survivor in the immediate aftermath of the crisis needs support, belief, and nonintrusive caring. But as time goes on, and she reaches out to the church specifically for what it—and no social worker, therapist, or crisis advocate—can give her, she needs spiritual sustenance, a fortified sense of justice, and hope. The last thing she needs is platitudes, even in biblical form.

Rape victims do not need to hear how their suffering is blessed, how they share in Christ's suffering, or how the rapist is troubled and needs forgiveness. They do not need premature cheerfulness or encouragement. Rape survivors do need hope, a hope that is grounded in righteous anger and a zeal for truth. They need to hear that God affirms them in all their wholeness, anger, shame, bitterness, and all.

Some women are helped by scriptural assurances. There are two cautions with this. First, that Scripture should not be imposed on a survivor, but offered at the woman's request. Second, it is not helpful to be literal and concrete. Assurances such as "God keeps you safe" are not necessarily true at a literal, physical level. A survivor will hear this as false and revictimizing. However, at a deeper and less concrete level, many biblical passages are particularly appropriate to share with rape victims:[83]

For Fortitude and Hope

2 Cor. 4:6-18—"In our affliction, we are not crushed; we are persecuted, but not forsaken; struck down, but not destroyed."

James 1:2-6—Faith faces trials and endures.

Many psalms, including Psalm 143—"Answer me now, Lord! Rescue me, Lord, as you have promised; in your goodness save me from my troubles."

Remind her of the strength and courage that brought her this far and helped her to survive. Celebrate each decision she makes, and remind her that God stands with her through it all.

Naming Evil

Luke 18:1-8—The parable of the unjust judge. One woman insists upon justice and the need to name evil.

To Address Fear

Isaiah 44:1-2 and 51:12-13; Psalms 31, 44, 91, 94. Even the writers of Scripture knew fear. Validate her experience that God did not protect her literally, physically from the rape. God cannot interfere with humanity in that way, but God does grant a peace that no human being can take away, the "peace that passes all understanding." God is not an external avenger, but brings continual healing and courage from within.

Her own power can be validated also: Acts 1:8—"When the Holy Spirit comes upon you, you will be filled with power."

Abandonment

Matt. 27:45-46—Even Jesus cried out on the cross: "My God, my God, why did you abandon me?"

Rom. 8:35-39—There is nothing in all creation that will ever be able to separate us from the love of God.

Psalm 27:9-14—"My father and mother may abandon me, but the Lord will take care of me."

Guilt

Rom. 8:1-2; John 3:17-18; Ps. 103:11-13; Luke 5:20; 1 John 1:9 are all passages about God's forgiveness. It is important to stress that the survivor's assault is not her fault or her sin. Some survivors, however, will ask for forgiveness, and after counseling them that the rape was *not* their fault, it may be healing to pronounce absolution for whatever is still troubling their own conscience about it.

Shame

1 John 3:1-3—Everyone who has this hope in Christ is pure; Rom. 12:2—We are transformed by God inwardly; 2 Cor. 5:17—If anyone is in

Christ, she is a new creation; and Rom. 8:16-17—Because we are God's children, we possess the blessings God keeps for us. For the Christian survivor, messages about who she is in Christ may be helpful to counteract her fears that she is "damaged goods," or that what happened to her is too horrifying for anyone ever to love her or come close to her again. (Again, messages about her basic goodness in creation are also important)

Depression and Suffering

Here the message of Scripture is that healing takes time, and that neither God nor the church expects her to be cheerful or to get on with her life as if nothing happened. Scriptures about the cyclical nature of life are helpful: Eccles. 3:1-8—There is a time to break down, to weep, and to mourn as well as to build up, to laugh, and to dance. Rom. 5:3-5—Trouble produces endurance and ultimately hope—but these things take time.

Anger

There are many expressions of righteous anger in the Bible. Job (7:11), Jeremiah (chap. 15), and even Jesus (Matt. 21:12-13) were angry. It is not necessary for the survivor to swallow or hide her anger in order to be a good Christian. She may even feel angry with God, and this must be understood and validated. Passages like Eph. 4:26-27—"Do not stay angry all day"—need to be understood in terms of the long-term, cyclical nature of the healing process. Eventually, perhaps, some of her anger may be released. But this is not ever a requirement that the church lays on her.

To Affirm Her Goodness

Gen. 1:1-2:2—Remind the survivor that God created the world and declared it good, and that she is a part of this goodness.

1) scripture requested!

2)

Battering

Give ear to my prayer, O God; and hide not thyself from my supplication!
My heart is in anguish within me,
the terrors of death have fallen upon me,
Fear and trembling come upon me,
  and horror overwhelms me.
And I say, "O that I had wings like a dove!
  I would fly away and be at rest;
yea I would wander afar,
  I would lodge in the wilderness,
I would haste to find me a shelter from the ranging wind and tempest . . .
It is not an enemy who taunts me—then I could bear it;
it is not an adversary who deals insolently with me—then I could hide from him.
But it is you, my equal,
  my companion, my familiar friend,
We used to hold sweet converse together;
  within God's house we walked in fellowship . . .
My companion stretched out his hand against his friends,
  he violated his covenant.
His speech was smoother than butter,
  yet war was in his heart;
his words were softer than oil,
  yet they were drawn swords.

—Psalm 55, selected verses

I first heard of Eleanor's story[1] from Alice, a public defender who was soon to represent Eleanor at a sentencing hearing in county Superior Court. Fearing that a jury would not believe her story, Eleanor, a shy and soft-spoken African American bus driver, had pleaded guilty to a reduced charge of second-degree murder. This was against Alice's advice. Alice thought that Eleanor's case was strong and they could win. But Eleanor was not willing to face a jury trial with charges of first-degree murder. She was not willing to risk being found guilty and spending all of her children's growing-up years in prison. Now Alice was hoping that at least the sentence could be mitigated, and was asking me to give expert testimony to help the judge understand the reasons Eleanor had felt threatened and afraid—frightened enough by one of her husband's assaults, that she had tried to defend herself and had accidentally killed him.

Alice and Eleanor came to my office at the battered women's shelter, and Eleanor quietly and haltingly told her story. Eleanor had been married to Bob for eight years. During their first year of marriage, Bob had become verbally abusive, calling her a slut and a whore, falsely and obsessively accusing her of having affairs, disappearing for nights at a time in retaliation for her supposed infidelity, and finally one night, after months of haranguing, punching her in the arms, face, and stomach until she passed out. After that, he had said that he'd "come to his senses" and apologized. Eleanor became more withdrawn and jumpy after that, but she felt that the worst was over and believed that her love would help heal him and their troubled relationship. Bob did not beat her again for several years, but the stream of verbal abuse continued. Now, due to her nervousness around him, he began to tell her she was mentally disturbed, a judgment she sometimes came to share. He also made veiled threats. In one instance, he brought a large industrial hose made of very hard rubber into their bedroom and laid it at the foot of the bed. When she asked what it was for, he said it was to whip burglars.

Bob also did sexual things that Eleanor felt were abusive, but she did not dare complain. He would grab her at any time of the day or night, throw her down wherever they happened to be, and force her to have intercourse, all the while grinning and saying, "Don't you like it, babe? I know you want it!" She believed that it was her duty as a wife to comply with his sexual demands, and she also was afraid that if she ever refused, he would go back to accusing her of having a lover. She feared his disappearing again and then coming back and beating her.

On the day in question, Bob and Eleanor had been arguing. He wanted the milk that was in the refrigerator, and Eleanor had asked him to save it for the children for supper. Bob suddenly towered over her in a rage, holding the full milk carton high in the air. "You don't want me to waste milk?" he shouted, and started to pour it around the kitchen, splashing the walls and the ceiling. Eleanor started to cry. He then backed her up against the sink and started to hit her on the head with the sharp corner of the milk carton. He grabbed for her throat with his other hand. Eleanor felt behind her on the kitchen counter in a panic. She was terrified that this time he would kill her. In her terror, she thought maybe she could distract or disable him just long enough so that she could get out of the house and run to the neighbors' for help. Her hand found a knife, and she stuck him in the thigh.

Bob fell to the floor, shouting and bleeding profusely. Just at that moment, the children came home and banged on the glass sliding door that opened into the kitchen. When they saw their father, they began to scream and cry. Eleanor was distraught. She led the children to the neighbors', tried to calm them down, and called 911. The ambulance came, and then the police were called. Bob was unconscious when the police arrived, and blood was all over the floor. Eleanor was crying, and when the paramedics said to the police, "He's not going to make it—too much blood loss," she cried, "Oh, my God, I killed him!" Eleanor was arrested on the spot. In an effort simply to disable her attacker, Eleanor had unknowingly stabbed him in the femoral artery, and he had quickly bled to death.

The hearing took just an afternoon. The judge had been prepared to give Eleanor the maximum sentence because, he said, "When there's blood on the floor, someone has to pay." But after hearing the testimony, he told me that he now understood Eleanor's fear as justifiable, and he gave her a much reduced sentence: time served, and six months in a minimum-security work program.[2] Eleanor was able to see her children and able to leave the women's facility to work every day. But tragedy continued to pursue her. As a secondary consequence, Eleanor lost her job. She had been a county bus driver, and because she was now on record as a convicted felon, she was told that she was no longer eligible to work for the county, and was fired.

The Facts about Battering

All too often, battering leads to death—most often, the death of the woman, and sometimes, as in Eleanor's case, the death of the batterer himself. Some 2,000 to 4,000 women are beaten to death every year.[3] One-third of homicides of women are committed by a husband or intimate partner, compared to just 4 percent of homicides of men.[4] Estimates ranging from 79.3 to 90 percent of women incarcerated for homicide[5] killed their batterers, and many of them were denied self-defense as an argument in court, either because they could not prove that there was a threat sufficient to warrant using deadly force, or because the threat was escalating over time but there was no imminent attack in the moment the woman killed the batterer.[6] For many offenses, women and men receive the same sentences, but for offenses traditionally considered "masculine," including murder, women tend to receive heavier sentences.[7] Many battered women's advocates are now involved in a movement to gain clemency for women who were convicted and are currently still serving time for killing their batterers.[8]

What is battering? Although there is much more general awareness now about this epidemic problem, battering, or domestic violence, continues, perhaps even increases, and misconceptions still abound. Battering is still commonly seen as a problem of stress and poor communications, a problem within the embattled couple, in which one or both partners are abusive when tempers flare. But battering is both more simple and more difficult than that.

Battering is abusive behavior that *intimidates and controls the battered partner, for the purpose of establishing and maintaining authority.* Again, as with other forms of violence against women, battering is a matter of power, and its aim is not primarily to discharge anger or stress, but to assert ownership and enforce control. This is the simple reality, the simple truth that a battered woman lives day by day—the walking on eggshells, the fear of "catching it" if she

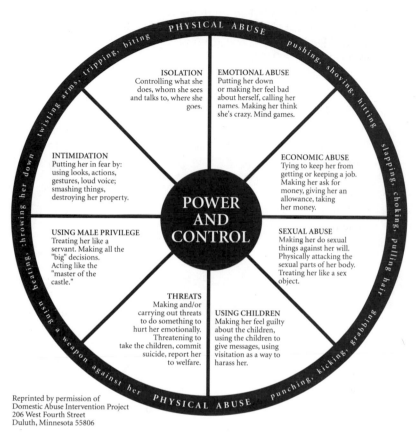

Figure 5.1   Power and Control Wheel

Reprinted by permission of
Domestic Abuse Intervention Project
206 West Fourth Street
Duluth, Minnesota 55806

"steps out of line," the increasing regimentation and restriction of her life in attempts to please her abusive partner, placate him, and avoid being hurt again.

But it is also difficult—difficult to explain, difficult to confront, difficult to change. From the outside looking in, it is tempting to analyze a battering relationship in any number of complicated, sophisticated psychological ways. It appears as if the couple is locked in a closed system in which both partners refuse help, refuse to let in the light of day. But it is the violence, the intimidation and control, that are the padlock, and not any other internal factor in the woman's psychology, or some mysterious symbiosis between them. It is the violence that keeps the system shut tight, and only an interruption of the cycle of domination and control can begin to break it open.

A useful tool for understanding the dynamics of a violent relationship is the now classic "Power and Control Wheel"[9] (Fig. 5.1). The wheel shows the variety of abusive behaviors that a battered woman may be experiencing,

ABUSE IN RELATIONSHIPS IS: Any pattern of behavior by one person that causes another person to do something they do not want to do, prevents them from doing something they want to do or causes them to be afraid. Abuse can be verbal, physical, sexual, emotional, economic, social or psychological.
COOPERATIVE RELATIONSHIPS ARE:

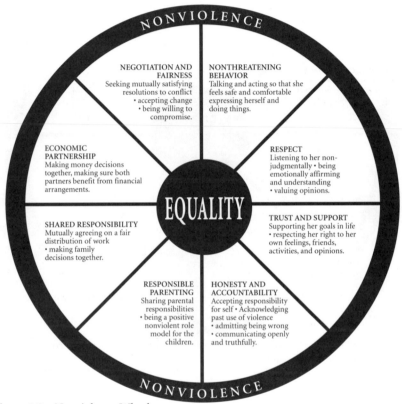

NONVIOLENCE

NEGOTIATION AND FAIRNESS
Seeking mutually satisfying resolutions to conflict • accepting change • being willing to compromise.

NONTHREATENING BEHAVIOR
Talking and acting so that she feels safe and comfortable expressing herself and doing things.

ECONOMIC PARTNERSHIP
Making money decisions together, making sure both partners benefit from financial arrangements.

RESPECT
Listening to her non-judgmentally • being emotionally affirming and understanding • valuing opinions.

EQUALITY

SHARED RESPONSIBILITY
Mutually agreeing on a fair distribution of work • making family decisions together.

TRUST AND SUPPORT
Supporting her goals in life • respecting her right to her own feelings, friends, activities, and opinions.

RESPONSIBLE PARENTING
Sharing parental responsibilities • being a positive nonviolent role model for the children.

HONESTY AND ACCOUNTABILITY
Accepting responsibility for self • Acknowledging past use of violence • admitting being wrong • communicating openly and truthfully.

NONVIOLENCE

Figure 5.2   Nonviolence Wheel

encircled and hemmed in by the all-encompassing motive and effect of domination and control. A very useful counterpart, a "Nonviolence Wheel,"[10] has also been developed more recently to highlight the healthy features of cooperative relationships and contrast these to the abusive relationships depicted in the Power and Control Wheel (Fig. 5.2). Sometimes a woman will come to a battered women's agency, still uncertain whether she is "really a battered woman." The wheel is a useful tool in helping her to see that what has been happening in her relationship is unacceptable and dangerous, and that the physical violence is part of a larger picture of intimidation and domination.

A checklist of characteristics of an abusive relationship can also help a battered woman to identify how unhealthy, controlling, and unsafe her

Is Your Relationship Healthy and Nonabusive?

Has your spouse, ex-spouse, lover, or date repeatedly:

1. Withheld approval, appreciation, or affection?
   ☐ Yes ☐ No

2. Ignored your feelings?
   ☐ Yes ☐ No

3. Ridiculed your most valued beliefs?
   ☐ Yes ☐ No

4. Criticized you, called you names, shouted at you?
   ☐ Yes   No

5. Humiliated you in private or in public?
   ☐ Yes ☐ No

6. Insisted you dress the way he/she wants?
   ☐ Yes ☐ No

7. Insulted you in front of your friends or family?
   ☐ Yes ☐ No

8. Been jealous about imagined affairs?
   ☐ Yes ☐ No

9. Controlled what you do, who you see, or where you go?
   ☐ Yes ☐ No

10. Punched, shoved, slapped, bit, kicked, choked, hit you, or thrown objects at you?
    ☐ Yes ☐ No

If you answered "yes" to any of these questions, you may want to contact your local battered women's agency.

Figure 5.3   Is Your Relationship Healthy?

relationship is. A sample is shown in Figure 5.3: "Is Your Relationship Healthy?"[11]

Battering exists on a spectrum from verbal abuse to death, and in almost all cases the violence escalates over time if there is no intervention. On the seemingly more "mild" end of the spectrum, there is already danger. Women report verbal abuse, name calling, and constant put-downs. The continual criticism and verbal harassment wears the woman down, like water dripping on a stone. It erodes her self-esteem and her sense of self-worth, and creates an artificial dependency in which she believes that she would not be able to do anything in her life without her partner. It sets the stage for further violence and control. Verbal abuse easily escalates into threats. Verbal threats often escalate into threatening actions. Harming pets, destroying furniture or other property, stealing the woman's personal belongings, or slashing or pouring bleach on her clothes not only carry the destructiveness of the actions themselves, but also serve as threats: Do what I say, or it will be you next time.

Isolation serves to reinforce the batterer's domination and the woman's entrapment. Batterers will slowly undermine women's relationships with family and friends. Battered women hear and sometimes try out of concern for the batterer to accept such statements as "He was making eyes at you, and I don't want you to talk to him," or "Your family never liked me—I don't want us to spend so much time with them," or even "Why do you spend time with her? You're too good for her."

Some women do not identify themselves as battered because they have never been hit. But they have been shoved, dragged, or pushed up against a wall. They have been locked in or locked out. This is battering.

Many, many women, of course, *have* been hit, punched, slapped, and beaten. In the State of California, criminal law activists convinced the Bureau of Criminal Statistics to count fists and feet as deadly "personal weapons," because so many women are killed, not only by knives and guns, but by punching, choking, kicking, and being thrown down stairs, through a window, or across a room. Women are also bludgeoned with hammers, two-by-fours, and chairs. They are slashed with broken bottles and scissors. And, yes, they are stabbed with knives and shot with hunting rifles and handguns. In short, battered women live their lives in a war zone, enduring from uneasy truce to uneasy truce. They are prisoners of war as any captured soldier, except that no one knows to look for them, and often no one will believe their stories if they tell.

In a majority of cases—though, importantly, not all—there is a now fairly well-known "cycle of violence," as first described by pioneering psychologist and battered women's advocate Lenore Walker[12] (Fig. 5.4). Walker built this theory on evidence that a battering relationship typically moves through a tension-building phase, in which the woman experiences "walking on eggshells" and tries a variety of strategies to avoid or defer a violent incident; the acute phase, in which the batterer inflicts severe harm over a period usually ranging from two to twenty-four hours (but in some cases stretching to a week or more); and finally, an unreliable respite phase of kindness and contrite, loving behavior. This is sometimes referred to as the "honeymoon" phase, but for the battered woman it is no honeymoon. At best, it is a shaky reprieve within a context of coercion, threat, restricted options, and injury.[13] The cycle repeats in spiral fashion, with the tension-building phases becoming longer, the violent incident becoming more dangerous, and the respite phases becoming shorter or nonexistent.[14] A tension-building phase may extend even over years as threats, intimidation, and isolation serve to maintain the batterer's domination.[15]

There is a trap here for clergy and others who would help. Often a woman will initially break silence about abuse in the aftermath of a particularly frightening beating. But when the pastor follows up, he or she is told that

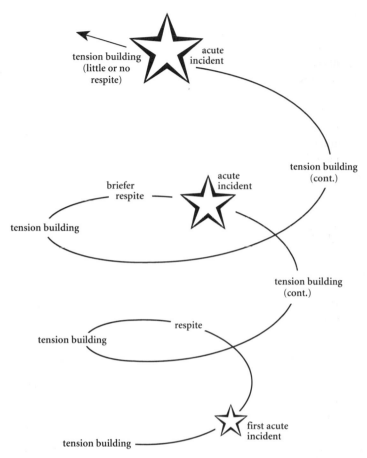

tension building
(little or no
respite)

acute
incident

tension building
(cont.)

briefer
respite

acute
incident

tension building

tension building
(cont.)

respite

tension building

first acute
incident

tension building

Figure 5.4   Cycle of Violence (Author's Visual Interpretation)

everything has been worked out now, they will be seeing a counselor, the husband has repented, and not to worry. Occasionally the batterer will even come
to the pastor for confession and absolution. It is important to recognize that
this is likely to be part of the respite phase of the cycle, and not to be drawn
unwittingly into collusion with the abuse. Marie Fortune has written clearly
about the difference between this kind of glib pseudo-repentance and the true,
hard-work, long-term repentance of turning one's life and behavior completely around.[16] Quick and sudden reassurances on the part of either the
victim or the batterer that all is now OK should always be cause for concern,
not relief. Both partners need to be educated about the cycle of violence and
urged—separately—to get appropriate help.

The cycle of violence is also an important factor in women's ability to leave
an abusive relationship. While the respite phase is the period in the cycle

during which it is probably safest for a woman to leave the relationship (although at no time is this completely safe), it is sadly the time she is least likely to go. Leaving or threatening to leave is often the occasion for the worst violence in the relationship, and many women are killed just as they are trying to leave or have recently left.[17] Women report time after time that their batterers have threatened, "If you ever try to leave me, I'll hunt you down no matter where you are, and I'll kill you." Sometimes this threat is accompanied by the insanely paradoxical statement, "That's how much I love you." This is the ultimate assertion of ownership, because a women's threat to leave is heard by the man as treason against his property rights.

Shelters almost always are set up at confidential locations for just this reason. Anyone who has worked at a shelter for any length of time knows the dread of the knock on the door in the middle of the night by an enraged batterer looking for his partner. We have all heard the rare but terrifying stories of shelters whose security was breached, and residents or shelter workers hurt, even killed.[18] We have all fielded calls from men who are sure their wives are staying with us—whether this is the case or not. Those of us who have worked at shelters long enough have also felt the grief and despair of losing a client—not only because women return to their batterers, but because their batterers stalk them, find them, and, in the worst cases, murder them.

How prevalent is battering? The FBI estimates that one out of four American women will be physically battered by an intimate partner at some time in her life. The California attorney general, in agreement with Dr. Lenore Walker, estimates twice that many, i.e., half of all women, will experience at least one violent incident in an intimate relationship.[19] Prevalence studies conducted in specific settings such as hospital emergency rooms, family service agencies, and other public institutions generally show a figure of about 28 percent. This is staggering. To get a clear mental picture of these statistics, sit on a bus, or in a large meeting or conference, or in church, and count off: one, two, three, *four*, one, two, three, *four*. At least this many women are statistically likely to have been battered or to have battering in their futures.

One question often arises in workshops at this point: What about battered men? It is probably important to separate out physical from emotional battering. Physical battering is much easier to measure, and prevalence studies consistently show that 95 to 98 percent of battered spouses are women. In the rare instances where the battered spouse is a man, it is often the case that the man is elderly, sick, or disabled, and the power imbalance in the relationship weighs in on the woman's side in an unusual reversal of the societal norm. What is important is that, regardless of gender, battering remains a matter of power and control.

In the area of emotional battering, it is sometimes said that women are more often verbally abusive than men. While it is certainly true that verbal abuse can be terrible, and it would be naive to assert that women are incapable of meanness and mental cruelty, this picture of the nagging or cruel wife needs to be reexamined, first in the light of stereotyping, and then also in the light of the societal power dynamics that exist beyond the boundaries of the couple's own relationship. While it is certainly true that a woman can verbally badger and insult an intimate partner, the level of intimidation possible is far less than that which accompanies the same verbal abuse from a man. A man is much more likely to be able to back up put-downs and threats with physical force, and men are more socialized by far than women to use force to resolve conflict. Men also have options to get out of the relationship more easily and with fewer negative consequences. This is not to assert that divorce or the break-up of an intimate relationship is ever painless for either men or women. But to a very unequal degree men have the economic means, and the social support system, decisively to draw the line and leave. Studies have shown that after divorce a man's income and standard of living is likely to go up, while a woman's is likely to go down. And while women are socialized to stay in relationships at all costs, to "stand by your man," men are socialized not to take any guff from anyone. More will be said below about why women stay in abusive relationships. As for men, it is likely that they will either find ways to reassert their control through physical retaliation to squelch the verbal abuse, engage in a mutual battle of cruel words and passive-aggressive retaliation, or try to ignore the woman and—because they have the relative freedom to do so—partially or totally absent themselves from the emotionally abusive environment.

Women who do verbally abuse generally do so out of a stance of powerlessness, not power. In the absence of real authority and sense of self-worth, the women sometimes do resort to the tactics of the oppressed: manipulation, hypercriticism, and nagging. The stereotype of the carping, henpecking wife all too often feeds into the myth that somehow a woman deserved to be battered. Our language abounds with words for the nagging spouse: harpy, shrew, virago, termagant, bitch, all gender-specific to women, with no counterpart specific to men. These terms, especially those drawn from mythology, carry the weight of being eternal truths about women, which both women and men internalize as beliefs. While these behaviors are certainly destructive, and especially poisonous when applied to children, it is the whole power-over/power-under dynamic of the relationship that needs to be changed. Blaming women for nagging does not address the root causes of social powerlessness and personally ingrained feelings of inferiority.[20]

Myths and Stereotypes about Battered Women

A number of persistent myths and stereotypes about battered women can influence women's ability to extricate themselves from violent situations and also can unconsciously hinder our capacity to help them. Some of these have been touched on already. These myths are so ingrained in our culture that, even after years of working directly with battered women in shelters and agencies, domestic violence advocates still need to confront their own tendencies to slip back into one or another of these misconceptions about survivors of abuse. Openly exploring the myths is the first step toward stopping the abuse.

Myth #1: "I would never be a battered woman."

There are many variations on this myth—that battering only happens to poor women, or black or Hispanic or Native American women, or women without a college education. White women, "nice" women in upper-middle-class families, professional women, women in "nice" suburban homes don't get battered. It doesn't take very long working on a domestic violence hotline to lose this myth. I have answered hotline calls from women doctors, lawyers, psychologists, and nurses, women professors and the wives of professors, women living in affluent communities and quiet suburbs known for being "free of crime." Women who, the myth would say, "ought to know better." Women who treat battered women in their own professional work.

One variation on this myth is that battering doesn't happen in church families. Parishioners may genuinely believe "the people in this parish are nice, upstanding, law-abiding people. I can't believe it could happen to one of us!" Because no woman has ever approached the pastor with a complaint of violence at home, the pastor then believes that it's not happening. The truth is, most battered women have sensitive antennas and are not as likely to tell someone who is not ready to believe them.

There is no one group of women who are more likely to be battered than any other. Domestic violence cuts across all lines of education, class, color, sexual orientation,[21] and religion. The frightening truth is—especially for women—that *any woman can be battered*. The sheer prevalence of battering statistically suggests this. This leads to . . .

Myth #2: Battering is rare and is only done by a few sociopathically violent men.

If, as described above, somewhere from one-fourth to one-half the women in this country—upwards of sixty million women—will be battered in the course of their lifetimes, then this is clearly a widespread social problem and not a bizarre or rare crime. The State of California registers over 180,000 calls to police by battered women each year. When this figure is multiplied by the average number of incidents that are not reported, this means nearly two million battering incidents each year in one state alone. More will be said about the profile of the typical batterer below, but statistics alone indicate that battering is not only not rare, but terrifyingly commonplace, and that batterers are no more or less sociopathic than all men in society. This is equally true within and outside the church. Even ministers sometimes are batterers.[22]

Myth #3: She deserved it/provoked it.

This has been touched on above. Battered women themselves believe powerfully in this myth and are doubly convinced of it because it is what their batterers tell them by way of excuse. "If you were more responsible . . . if you would keep the kids quiet when I come home . . . if you could ever be on time

. . . etc., etc., I wouldn't have to hit you to teach you a lesson . . . I wouldn't lose my temper that way. . . . "

Victim-blaming also takes more sophisticated forms. Shelter workers and others in the grassroots battered women's movement have long criticized the psychotherapeutic community for subtly perpetuating models that blame women for violence against them.[23] This can take several forms. The most traditional form of woman-blaming comes in viewing battering as a symptom of her own mental illness or emotional problems. Battered women have been mistakenly diagnosed for behaving in ways that may have been their only alternatives for surviving life-threatening violence by their partners, including: masochism,[24] borderline personality disorder, paranoid, even schizophrenic,[25] or (thankfully eliminated from DSM-IV) "self-defeating personality disorder."[26]

A much more appropriate diagnosis for the problems a woman may be experiencing is Post-Traumatic Stress Disorder (PTSD), under which Lenore Walker assigns her "Battered Woman Syndrome."[27] This diagnosis is based not on any assumption of prior emotional disturbance before she was battered, but on the after-effects of living with constant terror. In this view, battered women's so-called symptoms are similar to those of survivors of war, out of whose experience after the Vietnam War PTSD was identified.[28]

Another clinical approach that can be subtly used to place blame on the victim is the family systems approach.[29] As an alternative to classical psychoanalytic approaches, family systems theory was actually a liberating approach when it was first put forward, because it presented the idea that the person identified by the family as being "sick" might actually be the family scapegoat, or at least be "carrying" or "acting out" unspoken issues of other family members. This person was understood to be the "identified patient,"[30] and it was often the wife or an adolescent or child who bore this role. The systems view was liberating in that it required the apparently more "normal" or "healthy" family members to acknowledge their own roles in the family pathology and participate in making changes in order for the therapy to succeed. However, this view can backfire miserably for a victim of abuse. When it comes to physical or sexual violence, the perpetrator must take full responsibility for the abuse. All too often, from a systems perspective, the battered partner is seen to be contributing to the dysfunction in the family system, and the battering is only seen as a symptom of this dysfunction, to which she herself is viewed as coresponsible.

Finally, a third popular trend in therapy, borrowing from chemical dependency treatment, examines relationship dynamics in terms of "codependency"[31] or "women who love too much."[32] Battered women find much of value in the self-help books in this category and in support groups based on them, because the view is clearly one of claiming a healthy life for oneself and extricating oneself from destructive relationships. However, there is still a subtle form of victim-blaming inherent in this trend, namely, that the focus is still on what the victim should or could do to change, rather than on the perpetrator's responsibility.[33] Robin Norwood, author of *Women Who Love Too Much*, directly adapts a disease model from the recovery movement to describe women in destructive relationships as having a "relationship addiction."[34] She defines this as "a progressive and ultimately fatal disease process,"[35] and states that women afflicted with this addiction will "choose dangerous men and dangerous situations"[36] in order to produce an adrenaline rush, and that they will provoke violence through "clinging, placating, nagging and pleading."[37]

The adaptation of an addiction/codependency model applied to battered women becomes especially complicated when alcohol or drug abuse is actually present. A major pitfall of many social work and community mental health counseling approaches is that they often blame the chemical or the addiction for the violence, whereas alcohol and drugs are usually the perpetrator's excuse for the violence and not the cause.[38]

The bottom line, which is never doubted in the case of stranger assault but nearly always is forgotten in the case of domestic violence, is: No one asks, causes, or deserves to be assaulted or abused. To believe that a woman deserved or provoked a man to violence is to confuse violence with anger. Anger is legitimate, even necessary and healthy in a relationship. Violence is not.

There is, finally, a particularly subtle enactment of the myth that she caused or provoked the violence, which is set in motion by the perpetrator but made to appear the other way around. On occasion, a batterer will taunt and provoke a woman to lash out at him in reaction. She may slap him or hit him. He then restrains her with his greater physical strength and proceeds to beat her with a great deal of force. Later, she believes that because she hit first, it was all her fault, and if she were to report it, he would simply claim self-defense or mutual battering. This can be particularly difficult to sort out in cases of lesbian or gay male battering. Especially in these relationships, it is important to survey the entire pattern of who is intimidating and controlling whom, who defers to whom, who has *and uses* greater physical strength, and who is frightened, and not simply to evaluate the abuse quantitatively on the number of blows. Again, this is not to excuse any violence, but to remember that battering is behavior for the purposes of intimation and control, an assertion of authority. It is not simply a matter of temper or poor communications.

Myth #4: She's masochistic/she's into "S & M."

Masochism, the "M" of "S & M," is a (highly controversial)[39] term in clinical psychology, referring specifically to a sexual disorder. "Sexual masochism" is defined in DSM-IV as "recurrent, intense, sexual urges and sexually arousing fantasies, over a period of at least six months, or behaviors involving the act (real, not simulated) of being humiliated, beaten, bound, or otherwise made to suffer. The fantasies, sexual urges, or behaviors cause clinically significant distress or impairment in social, occupational, or other important areas of functioning."[40] It has nothing to do with battered women per se.

Sexual sadism, the "S" of "S & M," is the corresponding disorder in which the "psychological or physical suffering (including humiliation) of the victim is sexually exciting."[41]

"S & M," or sado-masochism, is therefore a term referring to sexual activity that involves humiliation, bondage, and physical pain. Sometimes this is described as a pursuit of pleasure heightened by the stimulation of fear or pain itself. It has also been described as being a way of working through issues of power, dominance, and submission.[42] Perhaps especially because of my work with battered women, I have grave misgivings about this activity as ever being acceptable. I seriously doubt whether any relationship can ever be safe and equal enough in power to make authentic consent to violence possible.

Nevertheless, S & M is *at best* a *mutually consensual* sexual activity practiced by some people. Battered women unequivocally do *not* invite, nor do they consent to the violence that is perpetrated upon them, even though their batterers may claim that they do.

Myth #5: If it was so bad, she could just leave.

Perhaps the most commonly asked question is, "Why do battered women stay?" People unfamiliar with the dynamics of an abusive relationship find it difficult to believe that anyone would tolerate violence. This is often regarded, not only by the uninformed public, but also by certain experts and clinicians, as a sign of weakness and identification with the role of victim. However, in my experience, women often remain committed to violent relationships precisely because of their strength.[43] Their belief in their own capacity to change, heal, or renegotiate the violence-torn relationship, compounded by societal expectations of marital and family unity, often creates a dangerous but persistent illusion that with just a little more effort on their parts, the violence will end. The idea that battered women "stay" is, in itself, an oversimplification of most women's experience. Many battered women do not stay in a frozen and passive state, but more commonly engage in a dynamic process of "stay-leave-return."[44] This is an active process, in which the leave-takings, however temporary, are intended to signal how seriously the woman takes the violence, and returning to the relationship is aimed toward renegotiating a violence-free relationship.[45]

Over time—often a great deal of time, and much longer than anyone trying to help her may be able or willing to understand—a battered woman's thoughts do turn toward leaving the relationship permanently. It is important for observers and helpers to understand that this final decision comes with a great deal of sacrifice, in terms of her emotional investment, her investment of effort often spanning many years in the relationship, and also often in terms of the economic and material realities of the life they have built together. Most of all, her hopes and dreams, invested in this partner, must be sacrificed or transferred to another possible future relationship or relationships.

These dreams and investments are reinforced by societal expectations and realities. The most frequently mentioned external constraint on women's ability to leave a violent partner is economic. Sometimes this is a function of the batterer's isolation tactics, reinforced by traditional expectations about a woman's place being at home with the children, in which a husband refuses to let his wife work outside the home. Long absence from the working world, combined with her batterer's verbal assaults on her confidence, may make her doubt whether she could find a job to support herself and her children. Many battered women who first seek assistance from a shelter or agency in permanently leaving their batterers feel overwhelmed by the prospect of finding an apartment, applying for assistance, searching for work, and then locating appropriate, safe child care—to be accomplished all at once, and often secretly or while in hiding from her batterer.

Another reason why women stay is the societally conditioned belief that "love conquers all." The battered woman may believe the promises made during the "respite" phase of the cycle of violence. She often still loves or at least cares for the man she first fell in love with. She feels she should stand by him, believe in him, and help him change. Few women, especially early on in the violent relationship, want to give up on a partner who in other ways has been important to them, even apparently loving and caring. Then, as months and years go on, this initial hope is replaced by the time and emotional investment in the relationship which she does not want to discard. Starting all over seems a grim prospect, especially when one's hope is already so worn down. Rather than view the relationship as hopeless, the woman may try to separate the "good man I married" from the man who batters her. Often, she accomplishes this by viewing his violence as a sickness, one for which she should be able to help him find a cure. In this way, she may come to feel responsible for healing or changing him.

Pressured by public and religious norms, she may believe it is her moral duty as a woman to stand by him at all costs. If she is Christian, she may believe that it is un-Christian not to forgive him again and again, and that she must continue to "turn the other cheek."[46] For a woman with children, there is also often a deep moral struggle between her own need to feel safe, and what she—and society— may view as her children's right to be with their father—or his right to be with them. Her own needs are low on the list of priorities, beneath her belief in families staying together, fathers and children being close, and a profound socially conditioned ideal of family unity. Sometimes influenced by her own minimization and denial about how much she is hurting, she may not as easily see that her children are also being harmed by witnessing this violence. She may not even see as clearly as she should that the children themselves are being emotionally and perhaps physically abused by her husband.

The attitudes of family, friends, counselors, and pastors all have a critical impact on how much the societal reinforcements for a woman's staying with her batterer will hold sway. Rather than pointing out her supposed weakness in capitulating to the batterer, they can point out the enormity of the pressures she is experiencing and help her to name them. They can also mobilize her strength and hope toward the many concrete tasks of designing her own safety and freedom and that of her children, rather than pouring it into a relationship that is only likely to end in tragedy.

I am aware that this view is somewhat different from a currently prevailing understanding of battered women as lacking self-esteem. Many battered women and their advocates do subscribe to a belief that a woman is unable to leave the violent relationship because her self-esteem has been so beaten down by the violence and the verbal abuse that she has come to believe she deserved the beatings. She fears that no one else would ever want her, that she will be alone for the rest of her life. She may fear that, in addition to what her partner has told her about all the things that are wrong with her, she is now further "damaged goods" because of the abuse, and no one would ever love her again. She may believe that it is possible that the "devil she knows" is truly better than the "devil she doesn't know"—hope has failed and there are no better alternatives. She stays because it is easier than to contemplate the overwhelming task of reconstructing her life from ground zero.

She may come to believe that if only she were a better wife, her husband would not beat her. This is terribly compounded if she has, in fact, done things in the relationship that went against her own internal moral code—for example, if she believes she was "bitchy," or shouted too much, or if, out of loneliness and despair, she had an affair. She sides with her partner's abuse as just punishment for her own sense of wrongdoing. She cannot forgive herself and believes she has caused the abuse. She even comes to believe, at least some of the time, that it is for her own good.

In my experience, this is not incompatible with an understanding that a woman stays because of a core strength. She acts, repeatedly, out of strength and a core conviction that she can and should be able to remedy the relationship in which she has invested. She often blames herself for failing to renegotiate a nonviolent relationship, because deep down inside, she believes that she should be able to change it, either by changing herself or modulating or controlling his behavior. Because, in reality, she cannot bring about these changes, she may experience a deepening sense of guilt, frustration, and depression as the relationship wears on.

This depression can be demobilizing and may look to outside observers like a passive acceptance of a victim role. Lenore Walker has made the connection between the psychosocial learning theory of "learned helplessness" and the question of why women stay in battering relationships. Researchers have found that victims of repeated, random trauma are essentially reprogrammed by their repeated experience of helplessness to believe that they do not have the normal human capacity to control or influence their environment. Whereas people who are subjected to one-time traumas, such as fires, plane crashes, or hurricanes, mobilize quickly to rebuild their own lives or to help others, human beings respond to repeated trauma by becoming passive and convinced that they cannot do anything to help themselves.[47]

The more a woman tries to stop or control the battering herself by trying to adapt her own behavior to please her partner or by attempting to reason with him or help him change, and (inevitably) *fails* in her attempts, the more the learning is reinforced in her that she can do nothing to change the situation. Although he may give pseudo-reasons for his abuse (the dinner wasn't cooked, the house wasn't quiet enough, etc.), and she may consciously believe them, the unconscious learning is that the violence is random and chronic, and that the threat of further harm is pervasive. Over time, her ability to mobilize her own defenses is eroded and her capacity for hope is numbed. This is important for those who would help her to realize she has options—she may in fact resist outside efforts to free her, because she has become programmed to stay in the prison of the abuse. This does not mean that she does not "want" to be free of the violence, but concrete plans for action no longer seem believable to her. This strikes at the heart of the theological task—journeying through despair and rebuilding hope are not philosophical luxuries, but necessary precursors to any liberating change.

The application of this theory of learned helplessness to battered women is being challenged by some in the battered women's movement who point out that the theory casts women as "quintessential victims."[48] Researchers Dobash and Dobash object that the theory of learned helplessness and Walker's cycle of violence may be used as a new orthodoxy to pigeonhole women into a static pattern, when in fact women are making active and conscious choices in a dynamic process. The "stay-leave-return"[49] pattern of many women begins as an active, not passive, process. I believe that the mounting frustration and despair that are described by the theory are accurate and have much more to do with a woman's conviction that she *should* be able to save the relationship, out of a position of strength, than any stance of weakness. Perhaps "learned hopelessness" is a more accurate term and one that not incidentally names the theological dimension of her plight.

This is where shame, embarrassment, and failure enter the picture and further prevent women from leaving. To leave is to admit defeat, and this defeat is in the area in which women are most expected to excel—the area of relationships and care. It is ironic and tragic that a person who is beaten by an intimate partner will feel ashamed, but that same person would not hesitate to report or discuss being held up by a stranger on the street. This shame is a function of externally conditioned and reinforced social stigma and public unresponsiveness, combined with internalized values of women as nurturing, patient, and ever-faithful, no matter how they are abused. Shame breeds secrecy, and that secrecy becomes the receptacle for more and more abuse.

Finally, perhaps the most compelling reason why women stay is *fear*. She has been told that if she tries to leave, he'll make sure she never sees her kids again. Or, worse, he'll kill her, and if she does manage to escape temporarily, he'll track her down wherever she is and kill her. Enough batterers carry through these threats that women are justified in feeling terrified when they hear them.

Many of the factors described above also relate to why women so seldom report battering to the police (usually only one in ten incidents are reported), and why they are so reluctant to follow through with prosecutions or other legal options. Minimization and denial set in soon after a battering incident, making it seem less significant than the crisis it truly was at the time. Loneliness, doubt, low self-esteem, and brainwashing to believe it was her own fault begin to take over once the worst injury is past. A battered woman also has fears, often justified by past experience, that the police or the justice system won't believe her or won't treat the battering seriously. If police respond inadequately, for example, by just walking the man around the block with a friendly admonition, or if the justice system simply gives the batterer a "slap on the wrist," it is tantamount to permission to continue battering. Economic factors enter into a woman's decision not to report as well: she fears that her partner will lose his job or lose valuable work time if he is held in jail. Finally, she is terrified of his retaliation. Almost every battered woman shrinks from the thought of jail time for her partner, because she knows that he will be released sooner rather than later, and upon his release, he is likely to make a beeline for her with intent to kill her. There are too many horror stories about women who were not warned of their batterer's impending release from prison, and because they were not warned, they were murdered.

Given all these realities, it is no wonder that women find it difficult to leave. Recently this question of why battered women stay has been challenged and turned upside-down: Once again, why is the focus on the woman? Why not ask the question, why do *batterers* stay? If they are so provoked, so angry, so miserable, why do they stay in a relationship that they feel drives them to violence?

Myth #6: Domestic violence is a private family matter. People should stay out of it, and it certainly doesn't belong in the courts.

First, without intervention, even if that intervention seems unwelcome, a battering relationship is at high risk for ending in the death of one or both partners. Couples do not just "work things out on their own." Our bias toward privacy, often a legal cornerstone for women's rights, in this case works against a woman's safety. Studies have shown that people who would intervene when witnessing a stranger assault, back off and refrain from getting involved when they perceive that the assailant is known to the victim.[50] And second, thanks to the hard work of battered women's advocates for two decades now, the legal biases against battered women, inherited from eighteenth-century English jurisprudence, are slowly being eroded, and laws against battering, stalking, and marital rape are increasingly being passed through state legislatures and enforced.

Profile of a Battered Woman

Are certain women predisposed to becoming victims? This question, again, assumes that there must be something wrong with women who are battered— before they even meet the batterer. But given the statistics, and the complicating factors involved in women's socialization to take responsibility for holding relationships together at all costs, it is safe to say that any woman can be battered. There may be particularly vulnerable times and situations, and it may be true that women who survived abuse in their childhood may be less clear about their own right to safety or about what constitutes a loving relationship. However, many battered women had nonabusive childhoods and were completely unprepared for the eventuality of violence in their adult relationships. This points to a need for primary prevention and reaching women at risk— even before the first physically violent incident occurs. Premarital counseling, Engaged Encounter, and other church-based interventions with couples early in their relationship can be helpful in outlining dynamics of healthy versus abusive relationships and in talking about the early indicators of abuse in terms of dynamics of power and control. Almost all violence occurs either before the marriage itself or before the birth of the first child.[51] The best indicator of potential violence is how the relationship has been in its first two years and how power and decision-making are shared or not shared.

Most interventions begin after violence has occurred. Once a woman has been battered, certain common traits may emerge relating to the psychological burden of survival in such a hostile environment. These traits need to be understood as outcomes of living daily with trauma, and not as pathological. They are similar to the responses of prisoners of war: diminished self-esteem; being anxious to please (if she's just perfect enough, maybe the beatings will stop); indecisiveness, inability to plan, inability to project into the future (violence has interrupted their life so often, planning seems futile); depression, even major clinical depression and suicidality—the results of despair, and rage that had to be buried because it was too unsafe to feel or express; flattened affect—the numbness of a survivor of atrocities; mood swings, being jumpy, nervous, irritable, or drifting off into daydreams—all classic traits of Post-Traumatic Stress Disorder seen also in war veterans; self-destructive acts, sometimes disguised in the form of drug or alcohol abuse, reckless driving, or eating disorders, or sometimes quite frank in the form of self-mutilation, cutting, slapping, biting, or self-starvation. In nearly all cases, battered women end up with problems with boundaries—although they may not have started out that way—because their sense of self has been so shattered. These boundary wounds may manifest themselves in swings between extremes of dependency and independence, blame of others versus self-blame, outward expressions of anger versus self-destructiveness, wishes for revenge versus wishes to rescue the abuser; and questions of identity and meaning: "What's it all worth, anyway? And who really cares?"

Profile of a Batterer

While there is no identifiable set of predisposing traits for battered women, there are predisposing factors toward being a batterer. Not all batterers have every trait, but the more traits are present, the more likely the person is to resort to violence in intimate relationships.

While there is no single type that describes every batterer, most fall into one of two general categories: the sociopathic or antisocial batterer who has very limited self-control and is highly irritable and violent generally in all situations, including at home; and (more common) the more "classic" batterer who is violent only with his intimate partner and about half the time also with his children. It is this kind of batterer who is more difficult to spot, and who engenders the comment, "I can't believe that John would beat his wife. He's such a nice man and such a good, upstanding church member!" Therein lies, perhaps, his most dangerous qualities—his ordinariness, his niceness.

Still, looking beneath the surface, one is likely to find a number of traits common to batterers. First, he has an explosive temper, but one that is controlled enough to be limited only to a safe, private environment—with a wife or girlfriend. He is viewed by most people, even relatives, as a nice guy, gentle, even meek. Second, he suffers from low self-esteem, accompanied by an extreme need to control the people and things in his immediate environment. He may or may not be a "loser" in the world's terms, but he is always terribly afraid of being one. Another very common trait is possessiveness. Battered women often describe their batterers as pathologically jealous, imagining that they are having affairs, accusing them of being too sexy for wearing shorts in public in the summer, beating them for simply exchanging polite words with waiters or grocers. One batterer spread flour under all the windows and doors every day when he left for work to be sure that his wife wasn't escaping on some romantic adventure. Another called his wife from work every half-hour to be sure she was still at home.

Batterers generally have very strict traditional ideas about sex roles and a "woman's place." They are anxious to prove their own masculinity. One batterer routinely beat his wife during or after a visit from his brothers, who had ridiculed him since childhood for being the smallest of the four. Superbowl Sunday is also thought by some to be the heaviest day in the year for battering incidents—related not only to alcohol consumption, but to the vicarious identification with the violence on the television screen and the sense of license given to dominate others by use of force.[52] A man's failed dreams of masculine glory all too often result in the bullying and destruction of those within his reach who are weaker and who are least likely to retaliate.

Ironically, in light of these displays of frustrated machismo, batterers are more than usually dependent on their partners. They do not know how to have their emotional needs met by anyone besides their partners and cannot form friendships easily. They do not communicate well, particularly in the area of expressing feelings, and they are inhibited in asking for what they need. They tend to confuse intimacy with sex and mistakenly attempt to achieve intimacy through control, domination, and sexual activity (whether by consensual sex or rape). They believe on some primitive level that their very survival depends on making sure their spouse provides for every need, from clean socks to hot meals to a social environment necessary for their work or recreational routines. Their violence betrays their (unconscious) panic that if just one of these needs is not provided adequately by this partner/parent, they will die.

There is controversy concerning whether witnessing abuse in childhood "causes" men to batter. This is known as the "intergenerational cycle of violence." There is some evidence that batterers are more likely to have witnessed their fathers beat their mothers or to have been beaten themselves as children. However, many boys grow up in violent households to become loving and nonviolent husbands and fathers, repudiating the violence of their pasts. And similarly, not all batterers grew up in violent homes. All too often this is used as an excuse for violent behavior in adulthood. It should also be noted that witnessing or experiencing violence in childhood does not necessarily predispose girls either to be batterers or to be battered.

Finally, batterers have a very difficult time accepting responsibility for their own negative behavior. They seek to place blame outside themselves and generally minimize and deny violent acts that they have committed. Whether this is understood as narcissism or as deeply ingrained shame that leads to defensiveness, externalized blaming, and fear of responsibility, it is the factor that, combined with the battered partner's *over*-responsibility and self-blame, tends to keep the reality and magnitude of the abuse hidden, even from the consciousness of the partners themselves much of the time.

Pastoral Response

Battered women are more likely to turn to clergy than to any other resource.[53] Traditionally, the clergy's responses have ranged from uninformed to harmful.[54] However, there is some evidence that with education and support, this picture is slowly changing.[55]

What can clergy and religious professionals do, specifically, to help women and their families break the deadly cycle of domestic violence?

First, *recognize the signs*. Be alert that battering probably occurs in families in your congregation. If statistics hold true, one-fourth to one-half of the women in the parish have been or will be battered at least once in an intimate relationship. Common indicators of abuse include women who seem "accident-prone," or seem to have far more bruises and injuries than one would expect. Common explanations are falling down the stairs, walking into a door, being injured getting out of a car, etc. Strokes in young women may also be an indicator of abuse, caused by blows to the head or damage to neck arteries due to strangulation. Anxiety or anxiety-related health problems such as ulcers, headaches, or other symptoms are also common. More subtle indicators include hypervigilance and "startle response," daydreaming, an unusually isolated lifestyle or inability to come out to church for weekend or evening activities. A battered woman may make oblique references to her partner's "anger" or "temper" in the fleeting hope that a sensitive helping professional will read between the lines. When with her partner in public, she may defer to him or be unusually quiet around him for fear of saying something for which she will be punished later. She is generally very protective of him with others, particularly those in authority. At the same time, the abuser may be verbally abusive in subtle or obvious ways, may make attempts to impugn her reputation or her sanity to the pastor, may show signs of unwarranted jealousy, or may engage in a custody war with the woman and even kidnap the children. If a woman seems to be frequently leaving and then returning to her home or relationship, battering should be suspected. Battering should always be considered as one possibility when there is any suicide attempt.

Once battering is suspected, when it is safe and the batterer is not present, *ask the question*: Is someone hurting you? Are things happening in your home/relationship that are making it hard for you? If she indicates that this is so, ask even more directly: Is your partner physically hurting you? It has never been my experience that a woman was upset or "put off" by such a question. In cases where I was wrong, it was shrugged off easily, and usually some other kind of revelation was made that was equally important. But in most cases, it opened the door to real support for the woman, sometimes for the first time.

Talk about the violence straightforwardly and don't be afraid to ask. Do not refrain from asking what is really happening out of a mistaken notion of respecting her privacy or not embarrassing her. If she is being battered, she needs an opportunity to disclose in order to break the silence that perpetuates the abuse. It is also possible that a pastor will refrain from asking because he or she really doesn't want to know. The details may be too painful—or the consequences, for example, of knowing that a senior and respected parishioner is battering his wife may be too overwhelming. On the other hand, a pastor may be too personally interested in the details of a parishioner's intimate life. It is important to ask all questions from a centered and calm place, motivated by a genuine interest in what is best for the parishioner.

(1) *Believe her.* You may be the first person to whom she has disclosed. She may be expecting you to defend her batterer, to tell her what a nice man he is, and to disbelieve. Let her know that you trust her and that you believe her story. Let her know that she is not alone. Share some of the statistics with her. Let her know that there are others who have gone through similar things, and steer her in their direction (a support group run by a local shelter, or perhaps another woman in the congregation who went through similar experiences and has indicated a willingness to help others).

(2) *Remember her safety first at all times.* Remember that any intervention you suggest to her may have consequences for her safety.[56] Making appointments with you outside of her regular schedule, making phone calls that may appear on a telephone bill at the end of the month, receiving a call from you at home—in fact, *any* exercise of freedom on her part or sign that she is breaking her customary isolation may arouse the batterer's suspicion and cause him to escalate his violence. Respect her intuition at all times about what is safe for her, and remember to raise the issue periodically even if she does not.

Recognize that she may be minimizing the danger of the situation. Let her know that violence that continues unchecked is extremely dangerous and may end in the death of one or both partners. In cases where you believe the danger to be acute, you must warn her of this and let her know that one of you needs to call the police. Under no circumstances should you share what she has told you with the batterer.

(3) *Let her know this is not her fault.* Battered women will find many ways to blame themselves and exonerate their batterers. Too often the clergy have reinforced this pattern. Even in print, one author exhorts clergy:

> *Pray with the battered woman. At this point she will have little or a very damaged faith. Let her depend on yours. Ask God to bring her a sense of peace and to give her wisdom in* knowing how to avoid conflict at this time. *Give her a gentle hug.* She needs to feel a man gently embrace her who is not her husband. *Asking God to change herself is the first step.* She needs to become aware of what words, actions, or other activities of hers are provocative. What kind of stress is she putting on her husband *(emphasis mine).*[57]

This advice is not only dangerous and victim-blaming, but also borders on abusive revictimization of the woman in the guise of the gentle embraces of a man who is not her husband.

The battered woman needs to be empowered with information about the cycle of violence—if it pertains to her situation, about the many ways in which battered women in general take the responsibility for the violence and believe—dangerously and erroneously—that they can control it or stop it. She needs to know that she is a victim of a crime, and that it is neither her fault nor a sin. Responsibility lies with the person who chooses to cross the line and use physical violence, regardless of the supposed provocation.

(4) *Share with her the myths and stereotypes about battered women and the information you have learned.* Women often recognize themselves and their own beliefs in the myths and stereotypes outlined above. Some, although not all, battered women will also recognize the cycle of violence as describing their situation and may identify with the theory of learned helplessness. Let her decide for herself what of the theory fits and doesn't fit for her, but in any case sharing knowledge is sharing power. Suggesting readings, especially those written specifically for women currently in battering situations,

is also very helpful for some women—for example, Ginny NiCarthy's *Getting Free*, a workbook for getting out of an abusive situation, and Marie Fortune's very concise and helpful *Keeping the Faith*, which addresses Christian battered women's theological and moral concerns. (Bear in mind that she may need to figure out a way to obtain books without arousing the batterer's suspicion. Don't just assume she can take such books home with her.)

(5) *Refer her to expert, specialized help.* Let her know there are others who can help her and who have expertise on this issue that exceeds your own. You do not need to bear the burden of helping her by yourself. Pastors provide crucial and sustaining spiritual support. Battered women's agencies and shelters are uniquely equipped to provide the logistical supports she needs, especially in the crisis stage of an acute battering incident or a decision to leave her batterer. Even if she does not seem likely to use these resources immediately, be sure she knows where to find their telephone number, and familiarize yourself with what services they offer so that you can introduce them to her.

(6) *Respect her right to self-determination.* Do not press her into action, but respect her process and her sense of what is safe. Give her options and resources, but do not insist. Similarly, in spiritual matters, offer support but do not press her to forgive, to preserve a relationship, or simply to pray. Let her know that exploring all her options, including shelter, legal services, police, and counseling services is compatible with—even indispensable to—living faithfully with God's plan for her. Also reassure her that whatever she decides to do or not do at this time, you will be there for her. You will not abandon her or judge her choice.

By the same token, do not be overactive in the situation or try to rescue her. Pastors should not try to do the work that battered women's shelters are set up to do. It is far better to refer and then support the work done through that referral. Giving advice may merely substitute one dependency (on the pastor) for another (on the batterer). Except in the case of acute, imminent danger, when you believe the police must be called, let all decisions and actions rest entirely with her. Then support her actions. Even when the police should be called, help her if at all possible to do this herself, so that the authority for the action remains with her. Helping her identify her own options and respecting her self-determination are the most helpful ways to empower her.

(7) *Do not use a couple counseling format.* It is unsafe.[58] This format is very familiar for some pastors, but it is necessary to realize that this is not just an issue of poor communication or lack of intimacy. Couple counseling also may convey the message, however unintentionally, that the preservation of the relationship is more important than the safety of the woman and other family members. In some cases, Christian marriage counseling holds as its explicit purpose to "save the marriage." Both partners may have been taught that divorce is sinful and unbiblical and expect the church to value the marriage over all else. It is important to remember, and to share with the family and the

congregation, that it was the introduction of violence into the marriage, and not the divorce per se that broke the covenant between the couple.[59] Once violence enters into a relationship, the relative equality and peership necessary for any successful couples' mediation has been destroyed. Violence has injected intimidation and control into the relationship, and it is not safe for the battered partner to speak freely in a couple's setting. Whatever she says can be used against her later and can actually increase the likelihood of further violence. Combined with the illusion of security sometimes generated during a respite phase, and the couple's minimization and denial, they may both ask for couple counseling, but it should always be avoided. Refer separately.

(8) *Regarding help for the batterer, let him know that you stand ready to support him with referrals to batterers' programs to help him stop his violence, but let him know that violence is wrong, period.* As difficult as it may be in the face of his convincing denials and explanations, let him know that he needs specialized help and that what has happened is not OK. It is precisely because you care about him that you want him to get the kind of help he really needs—and you are not the one equipped to do it! More details about discerning appropriate agencies and programs for referral will be given in chapter 10.

(9) *Let the congregation know that it's OK to talk about abuse.* By mentioning domestic violence in sermons and in newsletter articles, and posting informative brochures and posters from local battered women's agencies on the bulletin board and in the tract rack, you are sending a message that it's OK to discuss what is happening without being shamed or disbelieved. There is an increasing number of excellent church-related resources for battered women available as well, in the form of posters, brochures, tracts, and congregational study guides.[60] Battered women have strong survival skills and finely tuned antennae. They do not disclose abuse lightly, because they know the extreme risks involved, but they are longing for a truly safe place to share their fear and pain and to begin working their way toward a safer and happier life.

(10) *Assure the battered woman of God's love, and help her build a spiritual support community.* There are certain messages that the church can uniquely give: You are loved by God. You do not deserve to be abused. You are not alone. This is not your "cross" to bear—God wants wholeness and abundance of life for all people. God does not cause or desire our suffering: God suffers with us when we suffer, and God is moving in your life to bring you liberation and joy.[61] No, you don't have to feel pressure to forgive him now. True forgiveness needs genuine repentance and justice to occur first. Perhaps the Holy Spirit was moving in you to bring you this far, to tell your story and to seek help. Do not give up hope—you deserve freedom and joy.

And you are not alone! Not only is God with you, but I am here for you, and there are people here in this congregation who are sensitive and supportive, and who will help you if you want. Would you like their names? We also have a women's support group on Wednesday nights. There is child care. Do you think you can safely come out to that meeting? How can I help you to take the steps you feel you want to take now? Please know that I stand ready to assist you.

Conclusion

Battered women are not crazy or deserving of their abuse or few in number. Battered women are in your congregation, maybe even in your family. Battered women deserve wholeness, freedom, and support. An educated and sensitive clergyperson can mean the difference between a battered woman's inability to escape the trap of violence in her life and her having the strength and courage and conviction to create a new life for herself and her children. She may never be completely free of fear, but she can walk tall with the certainty that God loves her and that she deserves the fullness of life that God wills for all God's precious children.

> The thief comes only to steal and kill
> and destroy; I came that they may
> have life, and have it abundantly.
> —John 10:10

Clergy Sexual Abuse

Katya[1] shakes her head and tears well up in her eyes as she asks, "How could I have been so stupid? How could I have been taken in by him like that?" Several years ago Katya's children were growing up, and she was a lay volunteer with her church youth group. Noticing her talent with the teenagers, the pastor, Sam, suggested that she become a member of the parish staff and worked with the church council to create a paid youth director position for Katya. She was ecstatic. All her years of experience were being validated for the first time—she was a professional now! She grew in the job, read voraciously, received more training, and considered going to graduate school for an education or psychology degree.

But all this was short-circuited. The pastor began to ask her to lunch and to spend more and more time with her discussing her work with the youth and more philosophical questions about the future of the church. Finally, one day at lunch, he sat next to her instead of across from her. With his knee brushing hers, he reached over and took her hand. "Katya," he said, "I'm going to take a big risk here. I think you're feeling some of the same feelings that I am. Am I right?" He looked into her eyes. Her own eyes filled with tears. Her own husband Bob had not shown this much interest in her in years. His work kept him on the road a great deal, and although she loved him, there was not much sexual attraction. There never had been. They had dated in high school and married in college. It was what everyone had expected, and they were "in love," but Katya had never felt real sexual desire before. Now there was an attractive man, learned, gentle, sensitive—even *holy*, who was encouraging her talents, seriously listening to her ideas, and he was gazing into her eyes and telling her he was in love with her. It was like a novel.

They went to her home that afternoon and touched and kissed. They didn't make love—he said it wouldn't be right since they were both married, and she felt the same way. But they began to talk freely with each other about their love and about when the timing would be right for a deeper sexual involvement. They even saw his therapist once to talk about their growing romance. The therapist encouraged them to be honest with their spouses and to begin planning their divorces so that they could express their love more openly. Katya had grave reservations, however, because she did not want to break up her family and still loved her husband.

Finally, Katya's husband came home and announced that his company wanted to transfer them out of state. Katya agonized over what to do. She felt she could not say anything to Bob about her feelings for Sam, and although she would miss Sam terribly, she passively fell in with the plans to move. She went into a deep depression and often found herself weeping silently in church. The day the moving van arrived, Sam called and asked to see her. Her heart leaped, and she wondered if he had come up with a last minute plan for them to be together. He came to the house while Bob was out. "I can't stay," he told her, "I just want you to know that I've told my wife everything. We never should have gotten involved, and I hope you understand that we can never see each other again. Please don't try to contact me." Katya was shattered. She moved to her new home in a fog of desperation and misery. She blamed herself for everything and wondered what she had done wrong. She abandoned her plans for graduate school and questioned whether she could even go to church again. Everything reminded her painfully of Sam, and she no longer trusted any minister.

Peg was going through a divorce. Her abusive husband kidnapped both children in the course of a scheduled Christmas visit and took them out of state. Peg was wild with grief, desperate to get her children back, and afraid for their well-being. As she shared more and more of her feelings with her pastor, Rick, he began to hug her and hold her to comfort her.

"Come closer," he said. "You've been trying so hard to hold it all together for your kids, to be brave and strong. But you have a little girl inside of *you* that needs to be taken care of, too." Peg told me, "It is my recollection that I was working as secretary and work was done and he locked the door. He didn't ask if I wanted to make love; . . . he said that he loved me, pulling me close, and specifically said, 'It is you who must set the boundaries in our relationship.' Being needy, gut level desiring touch, I began our physical session (after months of his touching my hair, stroking my shoulders and back, holding me). We had sex in his office. I shall never forget his comments about my setting the limits—after months of his determining I had none."

In a first draft of this chapter, I had written, misremembering, that Rick had put a blanket on the floor. Peg corrected me: "Reading your version did bring up shame. It sounded so much more romantic than it was. It's funny how your saying he put a blanket on the floor touched me. That phrase sounded so caring . . . as there never was a blanket."

Peg saw Rick sexually for a number of years, even agreeing to visit him when he moved hundreds of miles away. Rick swore her to secrecy, because "the parish just wouldn't understand." The secrecy wore her down, and she began to confront him about getting married. Her divorce had been finalized long ago, and her children were back with her. Why couldn't they make their relationship public?

Rick became more remote and finally ended the relationship. Soon after, he married another parishioner in his new congregation. Years later, Peg finally told a women's group at her church what had happened and found out that several other women had been similarly drawn into sexual relationships with Rick when they were going through crises in their own lives.

A Long-Held Secret

Despite an increased awareness of other forms of violence against women, only a few works have addressed the issue of pastors' sexual abuse of parishioners. Most of these frame the problem as a psychosocial one rather than placing it squarely in the spectrum of power abuse. Important exceptions are Marie Fortune's *Is Nothing Sacred? When Sex Invades the Pastoral Relationship*[2] and Peter Rutter's *Sex in the Forbidden Zone: When Men in Power—Therapists, Doctors, Clergy, Teachers, and Others—Betray Women's Trust.*[3]

My own observations of this particular topic come from working since 1989 as a consultant and group facilitator for survivors of clergy exploitation. I have consulted in more than one hundred cases of clergy sexual abuse, both with victims and with denominational executives. This is also a form of violence with which I have had personal experience. In my consultations, I have witnessed the lasting devastation and anguish that these women have experienced, some for many years. Through this work, the many parallels between male pastoral sexual abuse and incest and wife- or partner-battering have become increasingly clear to me. Such parallels are particularly apt, because the church is so often portrayed as family.

Clergy sexual abuse—defined as clergy engaging in sexual or romantic relationships with their parishioners or counselees—is much more prevalent than is commonly supposed. Some estimates even exceed the 5 to 13–percent figure ascribed to male psychotherapists.[4] Preliminary statistics indicate that somewhere from one out of eight to one out of three clergy have crossed sexual boundaries with their parishioners.[5] Of all extramarital contact self-reported by clergy in one study, over two-thirds was with a counselee, staff member, lay leader/teacher, or other congregant.[6] Thirty-one percent of clergy in the same study reported that they experienced *no* consequences for extra-marital contact, and only 4 percent said their churches ever found out about what they had done.[7] Over 76 percent of clergy in another study reported knowing of a minister who had sexual intercourse with a parishioner.[8] These are staggering figures, and there is no indication that any one religion or denomination is more prone to such sexual misconduct than any other.

The abuse often is seen by parishioners and denominational executives as something else—a problem with alcohol, for example, or an emotional or relationship problem of the pastor or the parishioner, or a parish conflict. A single pastor relating intimately with a single parishioner is typically seen as an acceptable and even time-honored practice. I argue, however, that such intimate relating is always a boundary violation and that it is always the pastor's ethical responsibility to maintain appropriate boundaries.[9]

As with rape, a pastor's sexual or romantic involvement with a parishioner is not primarily a matter of sex or sexuality but of power and control. For this reason, I have called it clergy sexual abuse[10] rather than a private matter of sexual activity between consenting adults. Even when adultery is involved, unfaithfulness is not the primary issue. I have found that a majority of ministers who enter into romantic or sexual relationships with parishioners do so primarily because there is an imbalance of power between them at the onset, and because they need to reinforce and heighten the intensity of that power dynamic. This need is driven by internal forces and is reinforced by societally conditioned expectations that women will function as a nurturing, sexual servant class to support men's external achievement.

As Marie Fortune has outlined in *Is Nothing Sacred?*, there can be no authentic consent in a relationship with such unequal power. No matter how egalitarian a pastor's style of ministry, he carries an authority as pastor that cannot be set aside. I have deliberately used the term "he" here, because my experience and that of others in the field indicate that the vast preponderance of cases involve male clergy.[11] Also, the power imbalance is much more clearly tipped by societal reinforcement in the male clergyman's direction. It is possible for a male parishioner, particularly one with special financial or organizational clout—a church council member, for example—to harass a woman minister. This abuse also occurs between pastors and parishioners of the same sex. In such cases, the same power dynamics also pertain, further complicated by internalized homophobia and additional pressures and fears on the victim not to disclose or report.

The clergy role carries a great deal of power in and of itself, and one of the most insidious aspects of that power is the role of "man of God." In some sense the minister carries ultimate spiritual authority, particularly in the eyes of a trusting parishioner who looks to him for spiritual guidance and support. But the male minister possesses other forms of power stacked beneath it: As a man, he carries the power society confers upon men and socializes them to hold over women, often in the guise of being for their own good, as protectors. He is often physically stronger and more imposing. He may also be an employer. He may also assume a teaching or mentor role, which encourages her to listen to his advice and correction and sets her up for a particularly virulent form of psychological abuse. Often, he also functions as her counselor, with all the transference inherent in such a relationship. The parallels to incest within the church "family" are clear and hold similar devastating consequences.

Because of this power, just as in the relationship between therapist and client, there needs to be a commonly accepted ethical code—yet to be established—that ministers must not ever get involved with parishioners, and must avoid as much as possible getting into the area of dual relationships.[12] This is admittedly sometimes difficult in the parish context—the minister is set up as friend, pastor, religious/spiritual advisor and pastoral counselor, administrator and CEO, and even employer for many of the same people—and at the same time is the parish's employee.[13] Nevertheless, the pastor must remain aware that dual relationships—even friendships—can easily become exploitative or inappropriately intimate. While dual relationships are often difficult to avoid, pastors should be trained to be conscious of the potential for harm, and to understand that they hold the ethical responsibility as professionals for keeping the boundary intact. From the perspective of working with victims, I must at this point insist on an absolute taboo against sexual or romantic relating with parishioners, because the potential for devastating harm is too great. More will be said below about single clergy dating.

What Is the Harm Done?

Harm done to victims may be framed in terms of the opportunities ministers have for positive life-giving, healing work, and how these opportunities are destroyed by violation of sexual boundaries:

1. In our counseling role, clergy have an opportunity to heal and strengthen fractured boundaries; many parishioners are suffering from childhood abuse and bring this need. It is deeply damaging for him to initiate a sexual relationship and exploit this vulnerability for his own needs and fantasies. Even if a parishioner appears to be taking the initiative, and/or acts out sexually, the minister should recognize this as a clear cry for help. The last thing he should do is read it as a valid invitation. In the ideal, the pastoral relationship can and should be a sacred trust, a covenantal place of safety and nurture where a parishioner can come with the deepest wounds and vulnerabilities, and even act out sexually, and through appropriate modeling of boundaries and healthy response, the pastor can begin to empower her to heal those wounds. The harm when this is exploited is no less than a violation of sacred space, which further ruptures and destroys the woman's boundaries, devastating her sense of self and her mental health. What every therapist knows (or ought to) about this should also be required training for every pastor.

Moreover, no one is without wounds. No matter how professional, how well educated, how polished in appearance, every parishioner has vulnerabilities. If the church is truly to touch our inner lives at the deepest places, then it must be a consecrated place of safety in which people can bring their fragility, their wounds, to be anointed with assurances of God's grace. In order to be truly ministered to by the church's ministers, people must feel free to bring their whole selves, including their vulnerabilities, without fear of violation, exploitation, or re-abuse.

2. In our authority role, pastors have an opportunity to be role models of appropriate uses of power and authority. As clergy, we can emphasize power-in-community, leavened with responsible power-for, rather than a power-over process model in the parish. The harm done by sexual relationships, with all the clandestine qualities attached, is to reinforce a traditional male power-over

dynamic, and to breed a closed, destructively hierarchical parish model. Such a parish dynamic personally reinforces the victim's socialization to lesser power and meaning, while it more generally erodes the confidence and leadership of the entire congregation.

3. Through our pastoral role, clergy have opportunities to encourage, validate, and uplift the gifts and talents of our parishioners. When a pastor focuses on the woman's sexuality, her other gifts and competencies begin to be devalued. Frequently the very talents that attracted him to her in the first place become discounted by him once the sexual relationship begins.

4. Finally, when a pastor violates a parishioner's boundaries, he is stealing from her the appropriate, powerful, and sustaining relationship of spiritual guidance and support that the church has represented to her. Particularly because of the threats to her own reputation, he is robbing her of an important arena for her creativity and contributions (although he will frequently encourage and exploit these for his own ends while he can). Many women report in the aftermath of this abuse that they not only lost their own parish community, but their trust was so violated that they felt they could not go back to church anywhere.

Who Loses?

Both pastor and victim lose. Their families lose. And the church loses. But the woman victim loses the most and, sadly, as things still stand in most denominations, the pastor loses the least. Typically, once such a relationship or multiple relationships are uncovered, he gets a slap on the wrist and is referred to counseling, often with a great deal of sympathy. The parish is left to cope with feelings of betrayal and rage, which are often directed at the woman as seductress. The pastor's family is left to cope with their anger at his betrayal, often dealt with by minimization and denial, and blame of the parishioner. His wife is sometimes also caught in a power dynamic in their own relationship, which has her feeling confused, abused, and fearful. The family of the woman is often broken up and the burden of blame placed on her. She loses her reputation, her parish, sometimes her job, and sometimes her whole life in the community—especially in a small town or in a small community within a community.

In the past, the best she could usually expect from her denominational leaders was sympathy, but no real justice—that is, no real action taken against the pastor to prevent him from doing it again, and no real recognition of the seriousness of his violation. At worst, she could expect disbelief or blame. This is changing slowly with education, but still in the vast majority of cases, justice is at best partial.

The Case against Clergy Dating Parishioners

One of the greatest areas of resistance in the church, especially among clergy, to an absolute proscription against romantic involvement with parishioners, is the issue of single clergy dating single parishioners. Seminarians genuinely wonder if they will ever find a partner who shares their religious beliefs and practices if they cannot seek her within the parish. Veteran clergy also wonder what this means for colleagues who married parishioners, following time-honored practice—are they now to be condemned?

The decision of some regional church bodies to implement a qualified standard that permits clergy dating under some circumstances is usually motivated by a genuine and caring desire to be pastoral to clergy. In particular, the case is often cited of clergy who had married parishioners in the past, and for whom the arrangement seems to have worked out very well. Passing new codes and standards seemed judgmental toward these senior colleagues. But there is another way of approaching this issue with compassion, without judgment on such long-standing marital relationships. That is to say, we are in the midst of a paradigm shift that is wrenching for everybody. (It is already being thrust upon us by changing laws—for example, sex with parishioners is a felony in Minnesota and Wisconsin.) Just as sex roles have been changing, including our ideas about marriage as a more equal partnership, so is our understanding of all professional roles—not just those of clergy. It is not necessary or appropriate to condemn anyone who operated under the old paradigm when it worked and when no complaint is being brought. But we know differently now, times *have* changed, and we need to act on what we know now, especially when we turn our gaze toward policy-making and the prevention of future harm.

Because my working definition of pastor-parishioner romantic involvement is that it is not primarily about sex, but about abuse of power and misuse of the professional role, I am concerned about the growing trend in denominational policies of making allowances for single clergy dating single parishioners.[14] Ethicist Karen Lebacqz and pastor and former denominational executive Ronald G. Barton have tried to solve this dilemma by identifying a separate category of clergy, the "normal neurotic," for whom it may be difficult and fraught with dangers, but for whom it may not be ethically wrong to date certain persons in the parish who are single, mature, healthy, and not terribly vulnerable.[15] They elaborate safeguards to minimize the possibility of exploitation, in particular, not allowing the relationship to be clandestine, and finding the parishioner another pastor.

However, in my view this still sidesteps the central issue of the imbalance of power and the vulnerability, by definition, of every parishioner without exception. Several points are to be considered:

1. The standard of conduct needs to be firm, so that the burden of proof for any exception needs to be on the pastor, as the professional. Otherwise, it is still up to the victim to prove that it was abuse. Many survivors say while still involved in the situation that they *are* mature, capable, and willing participants. Often the woman's presenting issues for counseling after the relationship has ended, sometimes years later, are depression, anxiety, inability to trust or form relationships, loss of faith, or just a vague sense of "why can't I

seem to get over this?"[16] Only in therapy does she come to realize that the relationship with her pastor was, in fact, exploitive. Then she has to face proving it.

No matter how apparently mutually consenting the relationship, it is important to remember that *as soon as any form of romantic relationship has begun, the parishioner has already lost her pastor.*

2. There are implications here for what we know now about professional self-care. I have often heard single pastors ask, "But where else will I ever meet somebody if not in my parish? I work sixty to seventy hours a week, and everyone I know, my whole social life, is with the congregation." My response to this is that we, as clergy, need to learn to limit our urge to be ever-present and ever-available, and we need to cultivate a social and personal life beyond the parish—for our own health!

3. Who is to be the arbiter of who is mature and able to enter into a relationship with a pastor, and who isn't? Who is "too vulnerable" and who isn't? Is it really enough to draw the line at whether pastoral counseling is officially occurring? We should all be encouraged in our faith journeys to bring our deepest wounds—which we all do have, however competent and accomplished and mature we are—to the church, via its clergy (among other avenues) for healing and growth. Every parishioner is vulnerable and should be able to find a completely safe environment in which to heal. Every pastor-parishioner romantic relationship is, on these grounds, potentially incestuous on a deep, unconscious level.

4. There is in many denominations a desire to be more egalitarian with parishioners. As a feminist, and a respecter of group process, I agree that the foremost duty of clergy should always be to empower and equip the laity for leadership and ministry. However, empowering the laity for shared leadership does not mean divesting the clergy of their own role and unique power. The numinous role of the minister—particularly in his or her sacramental role—should preclude dating any parishioner. One cannot publicly and ritually mediate Christ, mediate the divine, for someone, for example, in the public celebration of the Eucharist, and be his or her lover at the same time.

5. The prognosis for such relationships is extremely poor. Those relationships that do not dissolve tend to perpetuate a power-over dynamic, and the parishioner remains vulnerable to exploitation within the relationship.[17]

6. Finally, I am concerned, again out of my experience in consulting on specific cases, about what the consequences are for the community.[18] What does it mean to single out one parishioner for special love and intimacy? What does it say to others not chosen? What factions begin to be set up, pro and con, or aligning with one partner or the other? And what if the relationship breaks down? It is rare for the pastor to be the one to leave the parish if one party must leave. The potential for divisiveness, for people leaving hurt and angry, and for loss of trust and loss of community for the woman is

tremendous. It cannot but harm the minister's own ministry in that place, and possibly for generations after him (or her).

For all these reasons, while we may be tempted to create loopholes in our ethics policies from a desire to be pastoral to everybody, including the clergy, we need a strong, unqualified standard—because especially from the perspective of victims, the potential for harm is otherwise too great.

Are Certain Women Predisposed to Becoming Victims?

There is no one type of woman predisposed to victimization by clergy. As in battered women's work, we know from experience that, contrary to prevailing myths and stereotypes, because of the way all of us, women and men, are socialized, any woman can be abused. There are, however, some generally learned susceptibilities that incline women to overlook, forgive, and tolerate a pastor's sexual exploitation:

(1) socialization to be polite, nonconfrontational, accepting of men's behavior;

(2) training and desire to heal men's wounds—offending clergy often present themselves to women as needing their special love and healing;

(3) submissiveness as a Christian value, especially ingrained in church women;

(4) self-identity defined for women by society as primarily sexual in function.

Particular life situations can add to a woman's vulnerability, and many clergy perpetrators have an uncanny knack—some women call it almost telepathic in intensity—for zeroing in on women with these vulnerabilities (partly because the intimate details are being shared with them in counseling):

(1) divorce, marital conflict, or abuse;

(2) a husband who shows indifference or is frequently absent—the pastor's interest in her as a person can be very affirming;

(3) a time of career confusion—his encouragement is very important to her;

(4) decade passages (especially at midlife or older)—a powerful man who validates her attractiveness is affirmation for which she hungers;

(5) a new, young, or problem child—he makes her feel like a person in her own right again, not just an overburdened mother;

(6) particular dedication to the church—this includes lay ministers, people very active on church committees, employees, and seminary interns. This makes the potential embarrassment or loss if she confronts him or says no very difficult to deal with;

(7) a personal history of family boundary violations—sexual, physical, or psychological—which makes it harder for her to have clarity about what is inappropriate on his part;

(8) particular power differentials such as a large age difference, or if he has particular prominence in the community or denomination.

In short, just about any life change or growth that brings a woman in to talk with her pastor can then be exploited as a gateway to satisfying his own power needs at her expense.

Profile of Clergy Abusers

A number of explanations are now being put forth for clergy crossing sexual boundaries with parishioners. Two typologies have been proposed that are becoming increasingly well known. Marie Fortune has described sexual abusers on a continuum between two types: "the wanderer," who "wanders across" boundaries, and the "predator," who seeks out victims deliberately and is lacking in conscience.[19] A sixfold typology based on extensive work in the field of clinical assessment and rehabilitation of offenders (including therapists and other professionals as well as clergy) has been developed by Gary Schoener: uninformed/naive, healthy or mildly neurotic, severely neurotic and/or socially isolated, impulsive character disorders, sociopathic or narcissistic character disorder.[20]

Such typologies have both advantages and disadvantages. They are useful because they give descriptive examples of clergy offenders that resonate well with the experience of victims and congregations. They bring more nuance and complexity into the work of understanding clergy who cross sexual boundaries. The disadvantage of typologies is that they can sometimes be misused by offenders to minimize, protect, and redefine their behavior in the most favorable light, by convincing others in authority that they fall on the "less serious" end of the typological spectrum.[21] The tendency to minimize often joins with the tendency of church leaders to see things in the most immediately forgiving and optimistic way available. Born out of an authentic desire to care for offenders, the culture of the church still predominantly wants to view the majority of offenders as "wanderers," or "naive," or "mildly neurotic." In fact, at least half of offenders fall on the side of the spectrum of more serious woundedness, resulting professional impairment, and poor prognosis for rehabilitation.[22] The church's culture of optimism too often leads church officials to view many offenders incorrectly as belonging to "wanderer" or "neurotic" categories, where they are given inappropriate latitude for supposed rehabilitation and rapid reinstatement. The pastor's remorse and contrition, assurances that he is in personal therapy, or a proposal for supervision and limitation of duties are frequently then seen as sufficient for reinstatement. While this demonstrates compassion for offenders, it very often results in a trivialization of victims' complaints and the generation of more victims in years to come.

For this reason, it may also be useful to understand clergy professional misconduct in terms of contributing factors, the more of which are present, the greater the likelihood that abuse has occurred or will occur in the future.[23] The advantage of this approach could be that it values the complexity and individuality of cases. The danger is that these factors might be used as excuses. Neither a typological model nor a model of multiple factors is intended to excuse behavior or to remove responsibility from the minister who crosses a professional boundary. Only with this caution in mind, a model of contributing factors might include: (1) educational gaps, (2) situational stresses, (3) characterological factors resulting from core woundedness in many clergy.

Education

The training of seminarians in professional ethics has been woefully lacking in most ministers' educations. Only recently has the issue of professional boundaries been included in clergy training in most institutions, or in books for clergy.[24] Most mentions of sexual ethics have focused exclusively on sexual morality, not power and responsibility. In some cases, training has emphasized overcoming temptation and learning to resist feminine wiles.[25]

Lack of training has been, in some cases, compounded by confusion in recent decades about sexual norms. Many clergy practicing today either received their initial training or passed through continuing education experiences during the late 1960s and early 1970s, when the helping professions in general were in a state of flux and experimentation. The clergy profession was giving increasing attention to the field of psychotherapy just at a time when the more abstinent methodology of psychoanalysis was being challenged on both professional and more popular fronts. The development of encounter groups, transactional analysis and group marathons, sex therapy, as well as vehement debates among psychotherapists about the possibility of touching clients (and more)[26] filtered into popular literature and had a formative influence on many clergy. Especially in liberal mainline denominations, these discussions gave tacit permission, and even supplied a rationale, for loosening traditional standards of sexual morality in the practice of ministry. Most of these discussions were focused on the freeing effects of shedding repressive sexual norms. Issues of the clergy's own power and professional responsibility were missed.

Situational Factors

One situational factor, and the one most often cited as the cause of clergy sexual misconduct, is clergy stress. In particular, marital discord, workaholism, social isolation, loneliness, and lack of significant relationships, or loss of a parent or child, are cited as pushing vulnerable clergy over the edge into misconduct. Burnout and overcommitment to work are frequently mentioned in connection with clergy dysfunction,[27] although some are beginning to question whether stress is being overrated.[28]

Certain other external factors may serve as disinhibitors for misconduct. The absence of supervision and accountability within the church setting, and the minister's unique access to vulnerable parishioners, including visits to their homes and bedsides, are also situational factors.

Alcohol is sometimes cited in cases of misconduct. As in cases of rape or domestic violence, it is important to recognize that drinking is not the cause of the abuse, although it is often used as the excuse. The common myth, often held by the wife and by the parish and the denomination, is: "Once he admits and deals with his alcohol problem, the sexual misconduct will stop." This can lead to unproductive treatment plans for the abuser, because the power dynamic of the abuse is deep-seated and independent of any substance abuse. It is more accurate to see alcohol as a disinhibitor—the clergyperson must already want to cross the boundary and feel on some level an entitlement to do so.

There is another situational factor as well, which is less often cited. An institutional culture of subordination and devaluation of women's experience, combined with a tolerance for sexual harassment and patriarchal sexual prerogative, also creates a powerful, if largely unspoken, situational factor. The relative social powerlessness of women to define their own boundaries and protest boundary invasions creates a climate where sexual abuse can thrive unspoken and unseen.[29] To the extent that the institution fails to convey or enforce a message that sexual abuse will have consequences, offenders will read an opposite message of tacit permission.

Wounded Clergy

Educational and situational factors alone do not explain clergy misconduct. While nearly all clergy are affected by at least some of these external factors, still approximately 80 to 90 percent of clergy do not cross sexual boundaries with parishioners. Internal factors, then, must also be considered.

The factor with the most predictive power for clergy sexual abuse is the woundedness of clergy. A number of mental health problems have been cited in cases of clergy abuse, from chronic depression and dependency, compulsive/addictive personality, narcissism, "borderline" personality, to sociopathy and, in rare instances, psychosis. Some studies even suggest that the clergy profession may attract individuals at risk.[30]

And yet, even with this range of problems, not all neurotic or even disturbed clergy cross sexual boundaries, although they may be at greater risk. For this reason, I also see a strong thread of narcissistic problems running through the entire range of clergy offenders.[31] Narcissism has its origin in the first years of life, and is therefore very difficult to heal.[32] It impairs a minister's professional judgment in a way that puts him particularly at risk for crossing boundaries, because it damages his capacity for empathy and causes him to seek gratification of his own needs first, regardless of the cost to others. Even a "wanderer" or "neurotic" pastor may show narcissistic wounding through manipulative behaviors, externalization of blame, and a tendency to use others especially in times of stress to meet personal needs.

Narcissism begins with early childhood wounding—sometimes quite subtle—in which the normal grandiosity of the very small child is crushed, leaving a great hole to be filled. A great deal of unconscious defendedness, like scar tissue, conceals the core wound and often results in behavior which in turn victimizes others. Wants are seen through a distorted lens as needs. The narcissistically wounded professional tends to conceal his insecurities and cravings for attention under a behavioral style of specialness—a style often condoned and even reinforced by the clergy role. At the mild end of the narcissism spectrum, a particular priest may become impatient because he does not feel he should have to stand in line at the bank. At the extreme end is sociopathic behavior—an inability to feel empathy resulting in an absence of conscience. Because manipulation and the projection of a star image are common to narcissistically wounded people, empathy and conscience are often convincingly feigned. But at the core of the person's soul is overwhelming despair, emptiness, and fear. For this reason, there is often great difficulty establishing appropriate intimate relationships and friendships with male peers—often resulting in a "Lone Ranger" style of ministry as well.[33] Other people are used compulsively and heedlessly in a desperate attempt to keep the demons of worthlessness at bay.

The narcissistic clergy's personal craving for recognition combines explosively with the power of the clergy role and a social climate of masculine privilege. This helps to explain why clergy sexual abuse is, at its foundation, an abuse of power and not sex.

Why Don't Women Stop It or Report It?

A woman will often neither stop nor report clergy sexual abuse, for several reasons.

First, she probably feels responsible. But, as Marie Fortune has written, even if a woman initiated the sexual contact herself out of her own need or vulnerability, it is the pastor's responsibility, just like a therapist's, to maintain the appropriate boundary. It was not her fault. Even if she didn't, society blames women for attracting men—why rape survivors usually feel that they are the ones on trial. This is further compounded by myths and stereotypes portraying all male pastors as innocent "sitting ducks" for the seductive wiles of female parishioners. The woman parishioner carries society's brand as the instigator of all sexual entanglements, still a prevalent theme in today's pastoral professional literature.[34] This is reinforced by a long woman-blaming tradition of romantic fiction portraying the virile but naive young pastor being preyed upon by sex-starved divorcees and overbearing wives.[35]

Victim-blaming, however, can also take the more sophisticated guise of clinical diagnoses of women, ranging from masochism and self-defeating personality disorder to "codependency," borderline personality, and woman-blaming-once-removed by blaming the perpetrator's mother for poor bonding and causing his narcissistic wounds! All such strategies serve to divert attention from the appropriate focus: holding the abuser accountable for the abuse.

Second, the woman may fail to stop or report abuse because initially she feels validated by it on some level. It's flattering; it makes her feel special. At vulnerable times especially, this is compelling. Third, over time, her self-esteem is seriously battered down by this relationship, especially when, as often happens, his initial encouragement and validation give way to discounting and criticism. Fourth, once the sexual relationship is begun, the perpetrator will commonly engage in deliberately confusing behavior, or "crazy-making." Women have consistently reported extreme highs and lows in the relationship and an on-again, off-again quality. Promises of marriage are proffered and then withdrawn.

Fifth, she is sworn, with a religious intensity, to secrecy. "The parish would never understand our kind of love." Sometimes, in the worst cases, this opens the door for multiple relationships with several parishioners at once.

The woman doesn't want to hurt his career. She loves him and believes he needs her. The good times make the bad times worth it—the good times are the "real him." She may be unwilling to hurt his wife and family or the church's reputation. Both his wife and the congregation would be quick to blame her as the source of their pain for bringing the truth to light, rather than placing the blame on the one who caused the abuse in the first place.

Finally, a woman may fail to stop or report abuse out of fear. Once a certain determination to think about leaving has taken hold in her, it is fear that keeps her stuck: fear (often realistic) that no one will believe her side when it's her word against his; fear (often realistic) that she will be the one held responsible; fear (often realistic) of losing her attachment to that church, as well as sometimes the community in which she lives, her personal reputation, and, if she is employed there, her own professional reputation; and even fear of his retaliation—sometimes within the sphere of personal and church life, but also sometimes toward the end there are actual instances of physical violence, rape, or threats of violence by these men, and the women have reason to fear them. Perhaps most chilling and most unique to clergy abuse is the fear of violation or retaliation on the spiritual level. This became increasingly clear to me in work with the survivors' group. It is difficult for a nonsurvivor to comprehend the sheer terror that accompanies this form of abuse. But often because of the image of charismatic spiritual power that these men have asserted and fostered, there can be a terror akin actually to being cursed or damned. Sometimes this kind of threat is almost made explicitly by the abuser, treading dangerously close to the realm of ritualistic abuse. Its power is clearly demonic in nature and intensity—victims fear that their very souls will be stolen.

The Clergy Nightmare: False Allegations

This is always a very real fear, and some conscientious clergy may feel overly constrained in their pastoral relationships by the new sexual ethics policies that are emerging, for fear of false allegations or of having genuine warmth and concern misconstrued as a sexual advance. However, most denominational executives and professional counselors working with cases of abuse will state that, in their experience, victims are so frightened and ashamed that they are much more likely to minimize and deny their experience than to inflate it or make false accusations. Cases of disturbed individuals making false charges are rare.[36] The fear among clergy is often fueled by false "information": for example, the myth of the predatory female who, especially if scorned, will turn and cry rape; the sensationalism surrounding rare cases of false accusation; and especially the rampant denial about real cases—including perpetrator-colleagues' convincing retellings of what occurred—which are then dismissed as false allegations by entire communities.

There is no doubt that false allegations can be devastating both to clergy and to congregations. And of course, if a minister is concerned about this issue with a specific parishioner, it is well to err on the side of caution to maintain extra vigilance about boundaries—emotional, physical, and psychological[37]—and to make careful use of good supervision/consultation. It is helpful to clergy worried about this to keep two things in mind: first, that any woman who actually approaches her pastor sexually is sending a signal for help and needs appropriate and compassionate support and limits; second, that, given the severe scrutiny to which even legitimate complaints are subjected, false allegations are extremely unlikely to stand.

Helping the Survivor

As with other forms of abuse described in previous chapters, the most important messages are: "I believe you," "I am so sorry—in the name of the church that I love and serve—that this happened to you," and "No matter what sense of responsibility you feel, it is always the clergyperson's responsibility as a professional to maintain the boundaries—it is not your fault." Validate her feelings, which may include rage, fear, grief, guilt, and shame. Be alert to threats from the abuser—even threats of physical violence have been known to occur once the survivor decides to make a report. Help her think through an action plan should retaliation begin to emerge. Do not offer forgiveness unless she asks you for it, and even then let her know that she has done nothing wrong.

Assist her in finding an advocate within the denominational system who can accompany her through the process if she chooses to report. Reporting is not a light matter. Perhaps the most important conviction a survivor needs to carry with her into any formal proceeding is that she is deciding to report for her own sense of integrity, and not because she needs or expects the institution to respond perfectly (it won't), or the abusing clergyperson to "see the light," repent, and change (rare).[38]

Prevention and Intervention with Clergy
Prevention

The discussion above of factors contributing to clergy misconduct has implications for prevention and intervention. Most prevention programs currently being implemented tend to focus on improving education and remedying situational problems. This is very important work indeed. Some prevention education focuses mainly on avoiding legal liability or on learning a set of safety rules (such as never closing the door while providing pastoral care—of course, for the safety and confidentiality of the parishioner, one must be able to provide privacy!). Knowing safeguards is important.[39] However, the most effective education emphasizes not solely *what* clergy can do, but *how* they are to think about themselves, their strengths and weaknesses, their role as clergy, and issues of gender, power, and authority.

One diocesan committee framed preventive measures in the helpful terms of "habits of mind": cultivating a habit of self-questioning, recognition of danger signals, and a framework of containment, peer supervision, and checks and balances for accountability.[40] Clergy need to acknowledge and accept rather than suppress personal feelings, including a calm awareness that sexual feelings will sometimes develop,[41] but, importantly, they must then be able to distinguish between feelings and behavior and take responsibility for acting appropriately.[42] Clergy should be prepared for this. William Hulme writes:

> *Charles Rassieur in his book,* The Problem Clergymen Don't Talk About *(1976), quotes a pastor in regard to a woman counselee, "Hey, she turns me on! I wonder what's going to happen now?" (p. 71). Anybody who has to wonder about this is ill prepared for any vocation in which responsibility is expected. This is a question that needs to be faced and resolved when one accepts the call to be ordained. It is a question of identity. If you know who you are, you will not wonder what will happen when you become turned on by another with whom you are involved in a ministerial function. You will know.*[43]

Clergy also need to know what forms of pastoral counseling are beyond their training and professional experience, and have clarity about when to refer parishioners for psychotherapy.[44]

Yet even this good training is not sufficient. If woundedness of clergy is the most predictive factor for abuse, then programs for clergy wellness, beginning at the seminary level, are crucial. Further, if a majority of offenders are troubled by characterological problems stemming from narcissistic wounding, even clergy wellness programs will not be able to prevent abuse in many instances. This reality raises the need for much greater vigilance at the threshold of ministry, including more rigorous testing and screening of candidates for ministry. Both seminaries and denominational commissions on ministry need to empower themselves to recognize the early warning signs and to counsel at-risk candidates away from the helping professions, toward more appropriate work.

Intervention

1. *At the outset, if there is a presenting problem of alcohol, family disruption, or financial impropriety, or a parish dynamic of secrecy and closed or chaotic process, it is important to be alert to possible sexual abuse.* A typical indicator of abuse in a parish is multilayered confidentiality, a lot of gossip, and just a few people in an inner circle "in the know." A healthy parish dynamic, in contrast,

would be one where process is transparent, there are few or no intentional secrets, and business is conducted openly.

2. *Where there is one kind of boundary violation, expect to find others.* For example, sexual abuse of parishioners often goes hand in hand with unethical personnel practices, lying, and financial abuses.

3. *Once sexual abuse has been identified, expect minimization and denial, expect to be diverted onto issues of alcohol abuse or extreme stress, and don't lose sight of the power pattern that is really operative and needs to remain the focus of treatment.* To join in minimizing his responsibility is inadvertently to reinforce his behavior.

Treatment programs that explain the underlying problem of clergy offenders solely as "sexual addiction"[45] are not appropriate. The term "sexual addiction" misleadingly frames the clergyperson's misconduct in terms of a physiological disease, like alcoholism, which may further distance him from taking responsibility for his behavior. The sexual misconduct and exploitation of power will not stop until it is dealt with directly as such. A purely addiction-model treatment will not address a male power addiction, because the dependency model does not delve deeply enough into confronting the root societal forces that keep male power over women in place and name it normal.

4. *Give an unequivocal message that all sexual or romantic relating with parishioners is wrong.* Educate him about why it is wrong and about the socialization that has harmfully made it seem acceptable. All young men are socialized to some degree to see women as prey, sexual seductresses who will say no and mean yes. Help him to see how this has harmed his ability to relate to women and thus harmed his ministry—and his life.

5. *Avoid collusion.*[46] What does a clergyperson do upon finding out that one of his or her colleagues is abusing a parishioner or parishioners? Depending on the denomination's polity, perhaps the best route is to go to one's bishop or equivalent judicatory officer for pastoral advice, and let him or her handle the matter. Confronting the abusing clergyperson first is not necessarily the best choice of action, unless one feels quite safe doing so. Beyond one's own personal safety, it is absolutely necessary to respect strictly the safety of the victim. It is important to share the policies and procedures of the denomination with her, if such policies exist, and let her know how to access the complaint procedures, if any. If she has reported the abuse to you and has asked you to keep it in confidence, it is possible to ask her permission to share it with the bishop or other executive or designated person. If she says no, keep supporting her process, but respect her wishes and follow her own instincts about what is safest for her—knowing that she may fear reprisals. If she has not reported, but you have found out another way, you might take it to the bishop for advice. However, in all cases, the victim's safety must come first.

The best safeguard against collusion is remembering to whom we owe our first loyalty—to the victims, both present and future.

The Development of Policy: An Institutional Mandate

The church needs a new ethical code that accurately names and recognizes the prevalence of the problem. Many new policies and procedures are being developed now, as churches are increasingly facing the reality of clergy sexual abuse—and are being called to legal, financial, and, most of all, moral responsibility for professional clergy who minister in the name of Christ. Many models are now available,[47] with the understanding that this is a pioneering time and many new policies and procedures are only now being tested as more women are being given the institutional message that it may be safe to come forward with their stories.

At minimum, denominational policies should include:[48]

(1) recognition of the prevalence of the problem and the need for a policy, including theological rationale;

(2) justice rather than only sympathy for victims—including clear policies and procedures for the support of victims and mechanisms for restitution. Having victim advocates or ombudspersons in place is often the best mechanism for offering appropriate, confidential support;

(3) reeducation/resocialization, rather than just sympathy, much less collusion, for the perpetrator. State-of-the-art assessment by a specialist with expertise in professional misconduct and treatment for those deemed treatable should be assigned by the denomination. The denomination should have appropriate referrals established prior to any complaint. In conjunction with this treatment, the local church and denominational office has an *ongoing responsibility* for monitoring that treatment process rather than simply referring and "being done with it," and, as Marie Fortune has advocated, for establishing clear consequences;

(4) clear consequences, which include accurate public naming of the problem, some form of censure or suspension with the goal of preventing harm to others, required evaluation during and at the conclusion of treatment, and appropriate restitution to victims;[49]

(5) a clear standard of behaviors in each judicatory body of each denomination with a clear disciplinary process that holds the pastor responsible for *all* sexual boundary violations. (In most states, it will be essential that denominations take the initiative to adopt such policies. In most states, attempts to legislate pastoral professional ethics, similar to laws regulating professional behavior of therapists and medical practitioners, have been blocked by church lobbies on the grounds of separation of church and state.);

(6) an established program for investigation, processing, and healing for congregations in which abuse has occurred,[50] and specialized training for

interim clergy and "after pastors" whose job it will be to help a congregation heal from betrayal;

(7) an established program of prevention and education about the root causes of male violence and power against women, and a commitment to a vision of equality.[51]

Conclusion

In conclusion, nothing less than a total paradigm shift is needed, from treating the problem as one only of sexual morality, emotional instability, or addiction, to addressing the power dynamics of these mostly hidden abuses. Only when this begins to happen, and the church removes its rose-colored lenses of denial and collusion, can the church community be a safe place of authentic power, healing, and proclamation for both women and men.

Child Sexual Abuse

Try to find out what is pleasing to the Lord. Take no part in the unfruitful works of darkness, but instead expose them. For it is shameful even to mention what such people do secretly; but everything exposed by the light becomes visible, for everything that becomes visible is light.

—Eph. 5:10-14

In hiding places they murder the innocent.

—Ps. 10:8b

For nothing is hidden that will not be disclosed, nor is anything secret that will not become known and come to light. Then pay attention to how you listen.

—Luke 8:17-18a

This chapter is about secrets. Secrets from the family. Secrets from the community and society. Secrets from the self. At the heart of child sexual abuse is the dynamic of secrecy and theft.

Myla's Story[1]

On a warm summer evening, Myla was sitting at my house. We were planning a training session on sexual abuse of children, and she began to tell me more of her own story. Myla is an adult survivor of severe childhood physical and sexual abuse, but she remembers very little. Her memories have come to her as dreams and images and "weird half-memories, like what led up to a particular rape but not the rape itself." What she has been able to piece together through therapy and self-reflection begins to make a coherent story, but this is not at all how the information seems to her and not how she tells it. She can only talk about it at all by circling around the details, taking long digressions like mental pauses for breath, and by reminding me to remind her of what she was just talking about. Her speech is calm, cool, detached as she talks of her abuse. It is as if she were telling someone else's story, a long time ago and very far away. The emotion, she tells me, will come later, while she journals or draws, or when she hears someone else's story. Her empathy is finely tuned, and she will weep with sorrow at another's tragedy, but she cannot weep for herself except in very rare, protected moments. It is too terrifying to tell the story and to feel at the same time.

Myla is the daughter of a famous professor and a depressed, alcoholic mother who Myla now knows was molested repeatedly herself as a child by Myla's grandfather. Myla knows she was first hit before age five but cannot remember when it started. Her first sexual abuse memory is from age five, and it continued until at least age thirteen or fourteen—her last rape memory, "which consists of the room, which was what I must have been focusing on, and not really what happened to my body."

From what she has been able to piece together, Myla's father treated her like a special protégée by day and raped her by night. As an only child, Myla was made to feel special by her father, who fostered an intellectual bond with her that deliberately excluded her mother. When her mother had to go away on business, her father said it was their "special time," when they would be rebellious and naughty together—ordering pizza, staying up late, letting her try beer and cigarettes. They became coconspirators against her mother, who was cast as the strict and unloving parent. He was the parent to be emulated, the one who was brilliant, clever, fun.

The sexual abuse seemed to occur separately from these times. The good times were wonderful, superlative; the bad times were furtive, designed to be forgotten. Anyone's perception that anything was unusual or "off" was squelched as overreacting or imagining things. Her father regularly walked around the house in the nude, and no one was allowed to question. Her father carried on affairs and saw prostitutes, and even brought home a sexually transmitted disease to her mother, but this was all hushed up and suppressed. Although she was his special protégée, Myla also remembers being terrified of her father, his criticisms, his sarcasm, his verbal cruelty. He maintained an absolute psychological control over the household.

Myla's memory is doubly confused because her father gave her drugs when he wanted to abuse her sexually. The sleepy, confused state brought on by the drugs returns with the memories of the abuse. She has repeated dreams about being chased, pinned down, and strangled by her father, but not of the actual rape itself. She has a conscious memory of being nine years old and wondering why her vagina was so sore and chafed, but having no memory of the abuse even then. She remembers asking herself in bewilderment, "How did this happen? It really hurts."

Myla only began to remember that she was sexually abused when she was sexually assaulted in her apartment at the age of twenty. During the attack, she "flashed" to a different situation, a darkened room, being pinned down and being afraid.

She had known her family had problems for a long time, but this opened a different level of pain. When she told her parents about the assault, rather than showing sympathy, her father got up and left the room. Myla says that at that moment she knew that something was really wrong with his reactions, and then the memories began to come. As she recovered from the trauma of the assault in her apartment, images and feelings from her childhood came up as if released from deeper inside.

Her symptoms, which she always suspected meant she was crazy, began to make sense. She had panic attacks, slept always with the light on, kept a Tazer gun, and propped furniture against the door at night. She was unable to concentrate in school. During her panic attacks it felt as if everything was sinister, even the furniture. She had a heightened sensitivity to any movement in her peripheral vision and felt that at any moment she would be taken by surprise and attacked.

As she learned about child sexual abuse, she started naming her feelings as memories. She would read other survivors' stories and think, "That's me." She concludes her story by saying, "Other people go to horror movies to have fun being scared. I go to horror movies because that's what it was literally like growing up. They remind me how I feel inside, since most of the time I can't feel anything."

Most of the time now Myla feels strong, and through therapy, groups, and participating in advocacy for other survivors, she has regained a sense of authority and safety for her own life. Yet, in spite of some external corroboration for her memories, she can say, "On one level, there was a moment when it clicked, and I 'knew' that I was an incest survivor. And yet, in some ways I'm still deciding." This is something Myla was never supposed to know. The voice inside that says it really happened is getting stronger and stronger, but the taboo is always there: "Don't remember, don't know, don't feel, don't tell."

The Persistence of Secrecy

There is enormous resistance, even among the most well-intentioned, to believing victims' stories of childhood sexual abuse. On one level, perhaps, this is simple to explain: no one wants to face the horror and pain of victims' experiences, and particularly to accept the pervasiveness of sexual abuse. To face the truth is to realize it is happening everywhere, on our streets, in our schools and daycare centers, and in our homes. We do not want to be drawn into anyone's pain, especially children's pain. And perhaps this is explanation enough. There are some particular shadings to the denial of child sexual abuse, however, which deserve exploration.

First, in spite of a surface, public commitment to address the abuse of children which has grown since the 1970s when the federal Child Abuse Prevention and Treatment Act was passed by Congress and mandated reporting of child abuse was implemented in all fifty states, individual children are still afforded little credibility. Children are disenfranchised from nearly every decision, law, and policy that concerns them,[2] and all the more when they have a complaint that goes against the vested interests of powerful adults. Even in the private sphere, this unquestioned allegiance of adults to adult values and perceptions, or adocentrism,[3] infuses adults' relations with children. When faced with a contest of loyalty between a distressed child or angry adolescent, and an adult whose words seem mature and reasonable, even a sensitive and educated parent or other caretaker usually finds it difficult to stand with the child.

This would all be damaging enough to victims' credibility, if all victims readily told someone what was happening to them. But the myth of rarity of child sexual abuse is reinforced by the fact that most children do not and cannot tell—especially when the abuse is at the hands of a family member, teacher, or someone their parents know and respect. What adults expect as normal reactions to sexual abuse—physically resisting the abuse, kicking, screaming, telling someone right away, seeking help—are, in fact, atypical responses. The more normal response to victimization is what psychiatrist Roland Summit has named "Child Sexual Abuse Accommodation Syndrome,"[4] including secrecy, helplessness (akin to the learned helplessness described above in reference to battered women), entrapment and accommodation, and finally, delayed, unconvincing disclosure and retraction of complaints. Contrary to adult expectations and the current media alarm about mass hysteria and false reports, children rarely tell of their abuse, especially at the beginning.[5] Children are coerced into keeping the incest secret by the powerful threat of the breakup and annihilation of the family if they tell anyone. And children rarely resist physically, out of confusion, guilt, secrecy, and their own sense of powerlessness, dependency, and often love for the perpetrator.

Summit writes:

> The more normal the child is in her reactions, the more she will discredit herself. And the better she adapts to the experience, the more she will be condemned. . . . Children's normal reaction patterns defy popular, commonsense, and professional dogma about how children should behave in response to incestuous assault. And the unwillingness of key adults to accept the child's behavior leaves the children all the more trapped in a sense of total isolation and self-condemnation. The cycle of disbelief and rejection serves to maintain adult comfort and to reinforce child helplessness until the child learns to behave "normally" and to present the adult world with a credible account of her experience.[6]

Children do sometimes signal their terror and despair, but typically these communications are in a nonverbal mode that neither adults nor the children themselves can easily decode into conscious verbal expression. Trauma specialist Lenore Terr describes a typical reaction to trauma in children which she calls "post-traumatic play." In contradistinction to normal childplay, which she describes as bubbly, light-spirited, and changeable, and in which pretending moves the child away from her normal situation or identity,[7] post-traumatic play is obsessively repeated without changing (sometimes for years), grim, monotonous, and literal rather than metaphoric. Parents or other onlookers are likely to describe it as "weird" or worrisome. It has a furtive, forbidden quality. It may be an unconscious attempt to replay the trauma and "undo" the real experience, but this does not succeed. Rather than relieving stress or helping the child to work through the trauma, post-traumatic play tends to leave the child more frightened after playing than before. And it is, according to Terr, nearly literal communication about the nature of the child's traumatic experience: "Post-traumatic play is probably the best clue one ever gets to the nature of a childhood trauma—that is, if one doesn't get to see the traumatic event itself. This play, when it comes, is absolutely literal. It may reflect a child's compensatory wishes, too. But it will recreate the child's trauma the way a theatrical production recreates a certain mood or a history book recreates a specific happening."[8]

As adults, we tend retrospectively to project our adult capacity for perspective and cognition onto children and adolescents. Most adults, unless severely impaired developmentally by their own childhood traumas or numbed by ongoing abuse, know that there are better and worse situations, are capable—at least some of the time—of distinguishing good relationships from bad, and can view the world from another person's perspective and then modify their own judgments about what is happening to them. Children, on the other hand, particularly prior to adolescence, developmentally *cannot imagine* another reality, another worldview than that of their parents. The parents literally define what is real and what is not. If a perpetrator says, "This never happened," or "This is for your own good," or "You asked for it"—and there is no other adult in the environment where the abuse is happening who can perceive the abuse and intervene—a child has no developmental capacity even to think that life could be otherwise. Once a child reaches adolescence and begins to develop the capacity to view the parents' attitudes and behaviors more relatively, anything she says to accuse her perpetrator can be dismissed as adolescent rebellion or craziness.

Children's credibility is further diminished because adults want corroboration. Questions are raised: "Where is the proof? Did anyone hear or see anything amiss in the classroom? Where was the mother? Surely if incest had occurred, she would have known!" But perpetrators are adept at keeping secrets and leaving no traces. The question of mother-blaming is especially raised in the context of incest in the home. If the incest is determined to be false, the child is blamed. If the incest is determined to be true, the mother is blamed for not adequately protecting her child, for being a "collusive mother."[9] In neither of these scenarios is the perpetrator held fully accountable.

There are many reasons why mothers and other adults in an incest family do not and *cannot* perceive that abuse is occurring. The stealth and paranoid self-protection of the perpetrator must be taken into account first, rather than (as is more typical) seeking answers in the pathology of women (as codependent, collusive, enabling, distant, frigid, etc.). It is not valid to assume that most mothers are aware of abuse, or even that they are "unconscious abettors."[10] Indicators that become obvious in hindsight are not at all obvious before abuse is revealed. Women may sometimes feel something is "off" or notice an intense or "special" relationship between their husbands and one or more of the children. But it is a tremendous leap for a woman to make from such observations to assume or even to question that the man she married and whom she trusts (or feels she ought to trust) would molest their child. She is more likely to doubt her own perceptions and to doubt her child than to doubt her husband.[11] This is reinforced by society's labeling of women as irrational and men as reasonable, which women then internalize and turn against themselves and their children. A heritage of thousands of years of normalized violence against women and male prerogative may also be combined with the mother's own very specific history of abuse.

Many women's perceptions of abuse may, in fact, be impaired because of their own experiences of childhood victimization, resulting in repression, inability to distinguish normal from abnormal physical affection to recognize the signs of abuse of their own children, especially at the hands of someone they love. As any mother knows, mother is omniscient in the imagination of a toddler or small child. The younger the child, the more absolute the belief that mother sees all and knows all—and can fix every hurt. Unconscious vestiges of this belief can last into adolescence and beyond. It is not necessarily due to the psychological impairment of the mother, but just as possibly due to the cleverness of the perpetrator in hiding his crimes, that mother genuinely does not see the abuse. However, from the child's point of view this is experienced as betrayal: mother's "eyes in the back of her head" should have seen. This understandable but impossible expectation of mothers by children adds to the blame already heaped upon mothers by the culture for the abuse of their children at the hands of others.

Another myth has added to the difficulties of bringing family sexual abuse to light: the myth of the molesting stranger. Much prevention aimed at educating children still revolves around the image of "child molesters" as evil, twisted strangers who seize unsuspecting children from behind bushes or lure them into cars and abandoned buildings with candy. Of course, this does happen, and children need to be taught in an age-appropriate, nonalarmist manner to avoid strangers, just as they are taught other safety rules. However, the public preoccupation with keeping children safe from strangers can obscure the fact that the overwhelming majority of sexual abuse (89 percent in one landmark study)[12] is actually committed by someone close to the child— a relative or acquaintance of the family.[13]

There is overwhelming evidence that the public, and even educated professionals, profess to want to know the truth, but that, in fact, they do not want to know. In the absence of a social climate that supports the truth of sexual abuse, the pressure to ignore or misdiagnose is enormous. Suzanne Sgroi, a physician who specializes in the diagnosis and treatment of sexually abused children, has written:

> Why is sexual molestation of children the last frontier in child abuse? And what are the major obstacles to identifying the sexually abused child? In practical terms, the answers are lack of recognition of the phenomenon, failure to obtain adequate medical corroboration of the event, and reluctance to report. If one accepts the

premise that it is impossible to protect the child victim of sexual molestation unless we know that he exists, these obstacles take on major importance. Each is rooted in ignorance and taboo and must be considered accordingly. Recognition of sexual molestation in a child is entirely dependent on the individual's inherent willingness to entertain the possibility that the condition may exist.[14]

Finally, the climate of secrecy of sexual abuse is perpetuated, perhaps most insidiously, by the reality that a sexually abused child is forced, for reasons of psychic and even physical survival—entirely unconsciously—to keep the secret of the abuse from herself. A child is psychologically unable to conceive of a parent on whom she depends for love, nurture, and life itself, being bad. An unconscious psychological mechanism is activated, called splitting, in which the child splits off the parent's bad actions from the image of the good parent which she needs so desperately for her identity and survival. The price the abused child pays for survival is nothing less than an internal division of the structure of her personality, what Sandor Ferenczi nearly fifty years ago called "the atomization" of the self.[15]

Leonard Shengold describes this internal process as follows:

> *If the very parent who abuses and is experienced as bad must be turned to for relief of the distress that the parent has caused, then the child must, out of desperate need, register the parent—delusionally—as good. Only the mental image of a good parent can help the child deal with the terrifying intensity of fear and rage which is the effect of the tormenting experience. The alternative—the maintenance of the overwhelming stimulation and the bad parental image—means annihilation of identity, of the feeling of the self. So the bad has to be registered as good. This is a mind-splitting or a mind-fragmenting operation. In order to survive, these children must keep in some compartment of their minds the delusion of good parents and the delusive promise that all the terror and pain and hate will be transformed into love.[16]*

The younger the child at the time of onset of abuse and the greater the dependency, the deeper this split and the more delusional its intensity. "The earlier the trauma and deprivation, the more likely the child will be overwhelmed and the more extensive the damage."[17] Remaining feelings of badness are then assumed by the child onto herself in the form of guilt and self-blame:

> *The absolute need for good mothering [sic] makes the child believe in the promise that her parents and "dear, kind God" [quoting Dostoyevski] will be good and rescue her, and to believe that she must be bad. The moral facts get confused along with the realistic ones—the child can take on the guilt for what the parents do, guilt that the righteous, God quoting parents may not even feel (or may not feel for long.) Ferenczi writes of what happens after a sexual attack on a child: "Moreover, the harsh behaviour of the adult partner tormented and made angry by his remorse renders the child still more conscious of his own guilt and still more ashamed. Almost always the perpetrator behaves as though nothing had happened, and consoles himself with the thought: 'Oh, it is only a child, he [sic] does not know anything, he will forget it all.' Not infrequently after such events, the seducer becomes over-moralistic or religious and endeavours to save the soul of the child by severity."[18]*

This leads to a discussion of the final, most compelling aspect of secrecy—that, as part of the splitting mechanism, the child splits off conscious knowledge of the abuse and, all at the level of unconscious process, the abuse becomes a secret from the child herself. Repression (the process by which the conscious mind forgets what happened) and dissociation (a comprehensive term for a number of processes by which the conscious mind absents itself from the abuse scene) are protective functions that help the child to survive what otherwise might overwhelm her to the point of psychic or even physical annihilation. But they serve to protect so well that the secret is also protected. Not only the victim, but also the perpetrator and anyone who might be able to help are shielded from the truth and its consequences. (More will be said about the mechanisms of repression and dissociation below.)

Shengold has described child abuse and deprivation as nothing less than "soul murder."[19] A classical psychoanalyst, he defines "soul" in nonreligious terms as "sense of identity,"[20] "primary identity,"[21] and "psychological structure and functioning."[22] However, the nineteenth-century German judge who, he says, first used the term in connection with the imprisonment of a child fully intended a more theological meaning:

> . . . it is the iniquity perpetrated against . . . his spiritual nature which presents the most revolting aspect of the crime committed against him . . . such an attempt must be a highly criminal invasion of man's [sic] most sacred and most peculiar property—the freedom and destiny of his soul. . . . Inasmuch as all the earlier part of [Kaspar's] life was thus taken from him, he may be said to have been the subject of a partial soul-murder (emphasis mine).[23]

Thus, healing, if the restoring of the whole person is to take place, is a priestly work, involving nothing less than the anointing and revival of a crushed spirit, the reconsecration of a violated sacred temple.

Prevalence of Child Sexual Abuse and the Myth of Rarity

While as recently as the early 1970s sexual abuse of children was considered extremely rare, perhaps only one to five cases per one million people,[24] current statistics indicate that from one in five to one in three girls, and one in sixteen to one in eleven boys are physically sexually abused by the age of eighteen.[25] When factoring in nonphysical sexual abuse, the figures may rise to more than one-half of all girls.[26] One in six girls are victims of abusive incestuous contact.[27]

Not surprisingly, given the pervasiveness of violence against women and the climate of misogyny already described, girls are victims of sexual abuse about three times more often than boys, and the vast majority of abuse (81 to 95 percent)[28] is committed by men against girls.[29] This is in no way meant to excuse or minimize the sexual abuse of boys, but rather to show the connection between this form of violence and the rest of the continuum of violence against women.[30] Sexual violence against children, regardless of gender, is yet another band on the spectrum of patriarchal abuse of power. And, regardless of the gender of either the victim or the abuser, the abuse of power and a tacit cultural acceptance of objectification and power over others as a right to ownership and control over another's boundaries is the acting out of patriarchal norms and of (dys)relationship.

The myth of rarity no doubt is reinforced by the sheer horror of the prevalence statistics. We recoil at the magnitude of the truth. The myth of rarity, until very recently, carried the imprimatur of the psychiatric profession, going all the way back to Freud.[31] After hearing numerous stories of paternal incest from his women patients, Freud at first formulated a groundbreaking theory to explain female hysteria. In 1896 in his "seduction theory" he acknowledged that his women patients had been, in the language of the late nineteenth century, "seduced" by their fathers, with long-lasting psychological consequences.[32] However, Freud was unable to withstand his own denial and disbelief that the good bourgeois men who sent their daughters to him for cure of their hysterical symptoms could be secret child molesters. Over the next thirty years, this internal pressure of disbelief united with the opprobrium of his own professional peers, and in 1924 he recanted, replacing his seduction theory with the Oedipal theory—in short, a theory that these women were driven by internal sexual impulses and fantasies to make it all up.[33]

Psychiatrists, especially those with psychoanalytic backgrounds, consequently followed Freud in believing that their patients were expressing repressed wishes—constituting seven decades of professional denial of women's reality. This professional predisposition to view patients' stories of sexual contact with fathers or father figures as fantasized wish fulfillment combined with patients' own uncertainty, shame, and amnestic memory loss to convince them that it was they themselves who were crazy, and to collude with the perpetrators' denial and self-justification.

Judith Herman has also pointed out that, without a sociopolitical context for hearing the truth, it cannot survive. Concerning Freud, she writes:

> Freud's subsequent retreat from the study of psychological trauma has come to be viewed as a matter of scandal. His recantation has been vilified as an act of personal cowardice. Yet to engage in this kind of ad hominem attack seems like a curious relic of Freud's own era, in which advances in knowledge were understood as Promethean acts of solitary male genius. No matter how cogent his arguments or how valid his observations, Freud's discovery could not gain acceptance in the absence of a political and social context that would support the investigation of hysteria, wherever it might lead. Such a context had never existed in Vienna and was fast disappearing in France. Freud's rival Janet, who never abandoned his traumatic theory of hysteria and who never retreated from his hysterical patients, lived to see his works forgotten and his ideas neglected.[34]

Perhaps it is the church's role to begin to function as a community of resistance to the prevailing socio-political forces of denial and repression. If one commitment of the church is to be faithful witnesses to the truth, then perhaps we in the church can create a countervailing atmosphere of courage and openness to hearing survivors' realities.

Definition(s)

Defining sexual abuse might seem fairly clear-cut in the case of minors. Young children are now taught in prevention programs in schools and on educational television to recognize and say "no" to sexual (and physical) abuse, by understanding that there are three kinds of touch: good touch, necessary touch, and bad touch. Good touch is appropriate physical affection—the lick of a puppy, the "high five" clap on the hand, a spirited wrestle with a friend, the loving and caring hug or kiss of a parent or sibling or friend. Necessary touch is when someone who is responsible for caring for the child (a parent or other family member, child-care provider, or medical professional) touches her to change a diaper or bathe her, or appropriately administers a needed medical procedure. Bad touch is unwanted and unnecessary touch, and children are taught in good prevention programs that their bodies belong to them and they have a right to say no to any kiss, hug, tickle, or other touch that they don't like—even (or perhaps especially) from family members.

Any physical sexual contact with a minor—that is, someone under the age of eighteen—constitutes abuse, regardless of consent or even invitation by the minor. Even apparently consensual sexual activity with a minor constitutes statutory rape in all fifty states in the United States. These laws acknowledge the (often enormous) imbalance of power and responsibility between an adult and a minor and make it clear that it is the *adult's* responsibility to know and maintain this boundary.

Some have argued that there is no intrinsic harm in an adult having sexual contact with a child. Partly as an outgrowth of the so-called sexual revolution, there is a small but vigorous political movement advocating for adult-child sex under the label of a "sex positive" philosophy. Sado-masochistic practices are also included under the "sex positive" umbrella. In Diana Russell's words, "these groups commonly rationalize their self-interested desires to have sex with children by pleading the cause of children's rights to have sex with whomever they please."[35]

There are many arguments against this self-serving reasoning. Much—though not all—sexual abuse is physically injurious to children's bodies, particularly small children. The psychological damage caused by sexually intrusive acts (whether physical or not)—the shattering of a sense of safety and even a sense of self—are seen in hundreds of thousands[36] of cases in therapists' offices. Finally, as discussed in chapter 7 above, there is the compelling ethical argument that nonabusive sexual activity requires consent, and a child cannot give authentic consent. Researcher David Finkelhor makes a clear argument that consent requires a knowledge of what the person is consenting to and true freedom to say yes or no—neither of which pertains to children.[37] In a court of law, motive, intent, or consent are not considered—only whether or not the sexual contact occurred.

Defining sexual abuse is not always so simple, however. Sexual abusers often know enough of laws and of cultural taboos to disguise their behaviors, tricking or confusing their children into thinking that nothing bad really happened—even children who have been through prevention programs. Telling good touch or necessary touch from bad is not always easy for children. Sexual abuse can include devious sexual touching in the guise of necessary touch: while bathing or diapering a small child, for example, or continuing to bathe a child who is old enough to bathe him- or herself. Sexual abuse can also include apparently acceptable affectionate touching, such as backrubs or tickling or hugging and kissing—when it is unwanted and when it invades the child's right to say no. Some displays of affection may be intrusive but not sexually motivated, which is already enough to give the child a message that her body is not her own. But many times this touching is even worse, serving a covert sexual need of the parent. This sexual gratification of the parent at the child's expense is something the child almost always intuits but cannot find the words to articulate, even to herself, much less to the parent. And even if she could and did confront the parent with her sense of what was really happening—as some adults who were molested as children eventually choose to do—the parent's response would likely be shocked denial and anger at the child for "thinking such a thing."

Sexual abuse can be even more subtle. It can include no touching at all. More obvious forms include masturbating in front of the child, or coaxing or forcing her to watch adults have sex. Sexual abuse may include taking photographs with sexual content or overtones, or looking at sexually explicit pictures, movies, or other materials with the child. It can include talking about sex to derive pleasure, not merely to convey educational information—or making the child one's confidant in sexual matters, burdening him or her with details inappropriate to his or her age, and in any case inappropriately treating the child as a peer or even as a parent—the "parentified child." It may include inappropriate staring, "undressing with the eyes," or "accidentally" opening the door to the bathroom or bedroom while the child is undressed. It may include unnecessary and intrusive medical interventions, for example, enemas or other pseudomedical practices revolving around the child's toileting. It may even be expressed as hypervigilance about an older child's dating—constantly criticizing her for looking too sexy or for behaving too seductively with boys. Overprotectiveness becomes a mask for sexual possessiveness and jealousy.

Force may or may not be a factor in sexual abuse at all. While molestation may conjure images of a father or mother forcing unwanted sexual acts on a child with threats and physical violence, more sexual abuse actually is accomplished through deception, persuasion, rationalization, and the exploitation of the closeness of the relationship and the child's overwhelming need to please and care for the parent or other close trusted adult. At the root of this power of persuasion is at first the child's instinctual need for the parent's care in order to survive, and in later years, his or her conditioning to believe that this is simply how the world is. The helplessness of minors is reinforced in our society by their almost total lack of legal and political voice and a cultural assumption—now fading, but dying hard—that adults are more trustworthy and believable than children, and that respect for elders means obedience in all things. Even a parent's well-meaning insistence that a child "give grandpa a kiss" when the child doesn't want to takes the first step down a road of teaching the child that her boundaries are not important, and that physical affection is not something about which she gets to decide for herself.

All these considerations show that sexual abuse is a complex and often very hidden phenomenon—not only hidden behind closed doors, but hidden even from the understanding of the victims themselves, and covered over as well in the conscious minds of the perpetrators with a veneer of denial and self-justification.

Defining *incestuous* abuse is even more problematic. Experts disagree regarding the closeness of familial relationship and the age difference necessary to distinguish between mutual, consensual sexual experimentation and incestuous sexual exploitation. All unwanted sexual contact is understood as abusive, whether there is an age difference or not, and incest is also considered abuse where there is an age difference of five years or more.[38]

Generally, there is also now the understanding that it is necessary to go beyond literalistic interpretations of people's blood ties to an understanding of emotional and psychological family bonds. If one person is in a parental or older sibling *role* with another person, this is more compelling psychologically than the actual biological relationship between the persons involved. Drawing the circle this way helps also to explain how people in foster families, in Big Brother/Big Sister programs, teachers, coaches, and clergy are in a position of high trust, and when this trust is exploited sexually, the dynamic is one of incest, with all the psychological intensity and damage incest entails. Perhaps the best definition of incest is one given in a 1992 special report by *Lear's* magazine: "[Incest is] any sexual abuse of a child by a relative or other person in a position of trust and authority over the child. It is the violation of the child where he or she lives—literally and metaphorically. A child molested by a stranger can run home for help and comfort. A victim of incest cannot."[39]

In summary, sexual abuse is a complex and largely secret phenomenon, but its prevalence is sickeningly overwhelming. It is, in its broadest definition, the violation of a child's boundaries by an adult, accomplished by the power of physical strength, authority, or closeness of relationship, for the adult's own sexual gratification at the expense of any care or concern for the child.

Consequences of Abuse/Recognizing a History of Sexual Abuse

How is it possible to know if sexual abuse happened to someone?

This is a difficult question, because the aftereffects of childhood sexual abuse sometimes include very severe difficulties in relating and in general functioning, and yet the cause of these difficulties can remain unknown for years, even decades.

Sexual abuse wounds every victim to the core and leaves lasting scars that may heal with time and proper care, but that never fade away completely, and that permanently shape the person's experience of the world. While it may be too much to say that every sexual abuse survivor's capacity to trust is permanently impaired, it is certain that sexual abuse does permanently affect her or his *way* of trusting others (which can include too much or too little), the nuances and quality of that trust, and the relative alacrity with which a survivor can reach a place of trust in any relationship.

Survivors often experience aspects of post-traumatic stress, including depression, nightmares, and other sleep problems, vague feelings of anxiety and dread, a constant sense of being on guard, difficulties with trust and intimacy, uncontrolled outbursts of temper, problems with sexual relating and with forming healthy relationships in general. Although other forms of violence against women can also produce sometimes quite severe post-traumatic stress reactions, childhood sexual abuse is far more likely to be completely hidden— not only from a helping professional, but from the survivor herself in the form of repression and dissociation.

Repression is the psychological mechanism by which information is consigned to "back drawers" in a person's memory banks, where it generally is removed from conscious thought. It is not forgotten, strictly speaking, because it is still encoded—in some form, whether verbal, visual, physical, symbolic, etc.—somewhere in the person's brain. It is not lost, merely "filed away."

Repression is not pathological. Everyone represses, partly to clear away unneeded or trivial information. The two main kinds of information that are repressed are the trivial and the traumatic.[40] Sexual abuse, especially incestuous abuse, is particularly susceptible to profound memory repression, however, because it is reinforced by the secrecy and denial in the family in which it occurs and by societal disbelief.

Repression can be so total, especially in cases of more severe abuse, that it is sometimes possible for a survivor to have no conscious memories of abuse at all. Memories may emerge only in deeply symbolic, and thereby screened, dreams, or vague but nonspecific feelings of unease or fear. Memories that have "gone underground" may also manifest in physical symptoms (e.g., migraines, ulcers), eating disorders, or a variety of anxiety disorders without obvious connections to any history of abuse. Some memories are encoded in the body in the form of unexplainable physical sensations, aversions to certain kinds of touch, or manifested in muscle tension and features of posture.

Related to repression of memories is *dissociation*, which initially occurs during the traumatic incident itself and then stays with the memory of the event, as if wrapped around it. Dissociation is an altered state of consciousness in which the entire person is not fully aware of or present to the events in his or her immediate environment, "the separation of a mental, emotional, or physiological experience from the mainstream of consciousness."[41] Just as everyone represses memories, so also everyone dissociates. It is a normal phenomenon of the human mind.

Dissociation exists on a spectrum that includes a number of quite common states of consciousness.[42] For example, some mild dissociative states that are completely normal can include feeling "beside yourself" with joy or distress, being in markedly different roles, or allowing different behaviors to emerge in different environments (for example, the different states we feel when we are at work, at parties, or quietly alone), and the states induced in deep prayer and meditation, guided visualizations, and guided imagery tapes—which are, in fact, mild forms of hypnotic trance. Sleepwalking, "zoning out," missing one's exit on the freeway ("highway hypnosis"), and mystical experiences constitute slightly deeper forms of dissociation.

In response to trauma, dissociation is a way in which the mind helps the person to "go away" and cushions the impact of the pain, both physical and emotional. The more severe the trauma, and the earlier in life it occurs, the more profound the dissociation.[43] All trauma probably involves at least some dissociation. Deeper forms of dissociation range from amnesia (total memory loss of a certain period of time), having a sensation of not being real or watching oneself from a distance, behaving for a period of time in unusual ways and then having no memory of it, and, at its deepest, partial or full multiple personality phenomena—in which one or more partially or fully formed "alter" personalities take turns controlling the activities and consciousness of the body. Much more will be said about this end of the spectrum in chapter 8, since multiple personality is usually associated with severe forms of abuse and torture.

It is important to understand repression and dissociation as positive, even life-saving mental processes that allowed the child to survive her abuse, physically and emotionally. In the words of Renee Fredrickson, an expert on repressed memory of sexual abuse, to survivors:

> Your mind has played a trick on you, but it is a trick to help you rather than hurt you. When you were abused you were too young and too fragile to retain the memory, or you may have undergone torment too appalling to handle it in any other way. You needed your strength for play, for learning, for seeking and holding on to whatever love you could find in your world. So your wonderful, powerful mind hid some or all of the abuse from you until you were strong enough to face it.[44]

Once memories are repressed and traumatic events are dissociated from the person's conscious experience, they are difficult to retrieve. Generally, memories only begin to emerge when a person feels safe—often not before middle age. Memories sometimes only emerge in the context of a caring, non-judgmental relationship (whether with a partner or spouse, a friend, or a therapist). The wisdom of the *totality* of a person's mind, which is far greater than the little ego-consciousness that generally manages our day-to-day awareness, also serves as a powerful gatekeeper for repressed and dissociated trauma. A traumatic memory generally will not surface into ego conscious-ness until this wisdom, or Self, judges that the person is ready for it.

And then it will come out. For just as repression and dissociation served a protective function while the person was being abused, truth needs to come to light eventually for full healing and wholeness to occur. This emergence of truth is instrumental not only in personal healing of victims, but also in the healing of society. Judith Herman writes:

> The ordinary response to atrocities is to banish them from consciousness. Certain violations of the social compact are too terrible to utter aloud: this is the meaning of the word unspeakable. Atrocities, however, refuse to be buried. Equally as powerful as the desire to deny atrocities is the conviction that denial does not work. Folk wisdom is filled with ghosts who refuse to rest in their graves until their stories are told. Murder will out. Remembering and telling the truth about terrible events are prerequisites both for the restoration of the social order and for the healing of in-dividual victims.[45]

Because memory loss is so pervasive with sexual abuse, and because trau-matic memory is not necessarily encoded with the clarity of usual visual or verbal recall, survivors even with fairly clear memories still often vacillate be-tween acceptance that they were molested and sometimes complete denial. Society's own ambivalence about the recent recognition of the pervasiveness of child sexual abuse reinforces individual victims' doubts with skepticism and backlash.[46] The truth almost certainly lies somewhere between the idea that *every* vague image, dream, or fantasy of abuse experienced by a person should be counted as literal evidence, and the long-standing skeptical viewpoint that vague memories should be considered suspect and counterfeit.

The very nature of traumatic memory, and the way the protective mecha-nisms of repression and dissociation work, mean that, paradoxically, the most authentic presentations of abuse histories will appear inauthentic to the un-informed. In a technical book for clinicians treating adults molested as chil-dren, psychologist John Briere has written:

> . . . the clinician may be left with the question "How do I know what happened, and what didn't?" Some therapists have dealt with this ambiguity by constructing an internal list of what they believe to be truisms regarding abuse, and then com-paring the client's presentation to this list. Among these "truths" are the notions that (a) abuse disclosures should be accompanied by intense negative affect—the client should cry or show some other evidence of obvious psychological pain, (b) the story should be consistent—there should be no major gaps in the recounting, and

the major points should be consistent from disclosure to disclosure, and (c) the client should appear authentic—there should be no hidden agendas.

Unfortunately, . . . these litmus tests for abuse are quite likely to be invalid. Molestation disclosures often occur during dissociation, when the client is unconsciously detaching herself from the feelings that accompany replaying an abuse memory. This coping technique may result in either little visible emotional response (affective blunting) or "inappropriate" responses such as laughter, inordinate casualness, or intellectualization. Secondly, the survivor's unconscious attempts to deal with the painful affect surrounding victimization experiences may have generated periods of amnesia or confusion regarding the specifics of the abuse and may be associated with conflicting memories and perceptions (including mixed flashbacks to more than one victimization episode). The client's continuing attempt to "not know" about the abuse (and thus render it nonexistent) may unfortunately be all too successful in the short term, producing questions in the therapist's mind regarding the truth of the disclosure. Finally, sexual abuse often results in disturbed interpersonal functioning, and thus the client's behavior in therapy (an intensely interpersonal process) is likely to include some "gamesy," adversarial, or dysfunctional components.[47]

Given the demonstrated prevalence of sexual abuse, the known mechanisms of repression and dissociation as a response to trauma, and the amply documented phenomenon of societal denial, it is still safe to say that fabricated accusations of sexual abuse are rare—from 2 to 8 percent, according to researchers.[48] Whether certain memories are literal enough to constitute provable historic fact, or whether they are symbolic, composite (in which several events are collapsed into a single memory), or screen memories (in which an image of an event stands in for the actual event), is not resolved. However, if anything, screen memories usually represent events in less severe form than the actual horror of the trauma that was experienced. No matter how symbolic, any type of memory of abuse still indicates that injury occurred, and the more confused or disguised the memory, the more likely that the abuse was severe.

False retractions of complaints are much more common than false reports.[49] In fact, retraction is named explicitly by Roland Summit as a predictable part of Child Sexual Abuse Accommodation Syndrome. This is the "normal" course.[50] Given the combined pressures of internalized doubt, confusion, and dissociation, threat of retaliation by perpetrators, and a social climate of disbelief, it is a wonder that any survivor either remembers or reports.

And some survivors never do "get" memories. In the words of Ellen Bass and Laura Davis, authors of the widely recognized book *The Courage to Heal: a Guide for Women Survivors of Child Sexual Abuse*, "If you don't remember your abuse, you are not alone. Many women don't have memories, and some never get memories. This doesn't mean they weren't abused."[51] This quotation has become controversial, and I do not dispute the claim that there are (in a small minority) therapists who may seem to be "jumping on an abuse bandwagon," or "looking for sexual abuse behind every tree." The appropriate stance of the therapist working with clients who may have been abused is one of neutrality and openness to the client's reality—not bringing an agenda to the work, not looking for abuse. This allows the client's own experience to emerge naturally according to the dictates of her own inner process. However, the notion that a large number of clients are somehow being coerced into producing incest memories is untenable and is mostly a product of societal denial and backlash.[52]

In the case of very early childhood abuse, there is, in fact, evidence that no narrative memory even exists in the brain, in the sense that most adults remember events including a beginning, a middle, and an end. Because the brain is not fully developed, traumatic events happening to children prior to age twenty-eight to thirty-six months simply cannot be recorded in a way that would produce full verbal recall.[53] Spot memories, behavioral memories—that is, memories expressed through changes in play, fears, or observable personality changes—and symbolic or metaphorical memories are characteristic of very young children. And repeated or variable traumatic events—characteristic of abuse—are less fully remembered than single events. Much is still unknown in the field of memory research, but the absence of narrative recall does not, in and of itself, mean an absence of abuse.

Without eliciting or pushing for memories, most counselors will, in fact, find many, many clients spontaneously uncovering memories and images of abuse. This process is usually accompanied by intense suffering, doubt, and fear—but it is necessary for eventual healing. Briere writes: "As thorny an issue as the above [question of truth] may be, most specialists in the area of sexual abuse agree that only a very small proportion of people who describe sexual abuse experiences 'make them up.' . . . Far more likely is the reverse scenario: A therapist is told of a client's sexual abuse experiences and, for a variety of personal and social reasons disbelieves them."[54] Clients themselves are far more likely to minimize and deny their own abuse experiences than to fabricate or exaggerate them.[55] The psychic pain experienced by adult survivors of childhood sexual abuse is evidence enough: something happened. In the words of one therapist, "Nobody puts herself through this for no reason."

Aftereffects as Indicators of Sexual Abuse

Because repression and dissociation are such common features in the aftermath of sexual abuse, naming common aftereffects has become much more important in identifying this form of abuse than perhaps any other. Recent research shows certain aftereffects to be common among survivors of childhood sexual abuse. This is not a checklist that "proves" sexual abuse, and many of the items may be signs of other disturbances as well. However, the more items a person struggling with suspected sexual abuse identifies as part of her experience, the clearer the message that something traumatic may have occurred. Many of these may be well disguised beneath a well-adapted performing social or "false self."[56]

Common aftereffects can be grouped into several categories: fears and anxieties; numbing and dissociative reactions; physical symptoms; emotional symptoms; lack of self-care, unconsciously self-destructive behavior and outright self-injury; and difficulties in interpersonal relationships (including sexual difficulties).[57]

Fears and anxieties:
- fear of being alone in the dark
- sleep disturbances: nightmares and recurring dreams, especially of being pursued or violated, waking frightened at the same time every night, a sense that someone is in the bedroom, waking up feeling suffocated or choking sensations
- panic attacks, extreme anxiety
- certain other strong unexplainable fears—commonly of basements, closets, or certain household objects
- inability to trust reality, a fear that the rug will be pulled out and beneath the surface of so-called reality, some horror will reveal itself.

Lack of self-care, self-destructive behavior, and self-injury:
- alienation from the body—not feeling at home in the body or taking good care of the body; manipulating body size to avoid sexual attention
- neglecting teeth, avoiding the dentist, feeling the mouth is disgusting
- eating disorders, such as inability to eat, bingeing, fasting, inducing vomiting, compulsive dieting, or unexplainable aversion to certain foods
- excessive use of alcohol or drugs (including prescription medications)
- compulsive gambling, workaholism, other compulsive behaviors
- high risk taking oscillating with inability to take risks
- self-injury, such as interfering with the healing of wounds, picking, being "accident-prone," and self-mutilation[58]
- suicidal thoughts, attempts.

Physical symptoms:
- physical symptoms including gastrointestinal problems, headaches, joint pain, persistent vaginitis, or other gynecological disorders
- a tendency to "somaticize" or unconsciously displace stress and emotional pain onto the body in the form of physical pain
- pain during intercourse (which may not have a physiological cause, or which may, in fact, be a result of injury from the abuse)

Emotional symptoms:
- depression
- bouts of rage or physically attacking partner or child
- extreme mood swings, unstable emotional reactions

Numbing and dissociative reactions:
- frequently using sleep, books, or television as an escape
- "spacing out," "zoning out," losing one's sense of time, numbness, out-of-body experiences
- having holes in childhood memory

- blackouts, dizziness, confusion, fatigue
- "spacing out" during sex
- a transient or recurring sense of being unreal, or everyone else being unreal
- experiencing strange or violent pictures flashing through the mind; intrusive memories or "flashbacks"

Difficulties in interpersonal relationships:

- general relationship issues: inability to maintain intimate relationships, being either too clingy or too distant, repeatedly testing people, experiencing constant drama, expecting to be left or taken advantage of, finding it very difficult to trust; being hypervigilant and controlling;
- sexual issues: aversion to certain or all kinds of sexual touch, pain during intercourse, inability to have an orgasm, preoccupation with sex, compulsive masturbation, fantasies of abuse during sex, compulsive sexual behavior, needing always to take the initiative or never, frequent "impersonal" sexual contacts with many partners but inability to have sex in an intimate relationship, prostitution or other work in the sex trade, other forms of sexual acting out;
- problems with self-esteem: feeling crazy, different, dirty, or unreal—what one expert calls "negative specialness,"[59] a secret sense of badness (which caused her abuser to be unable to restrain himself); perfectionism; being "other-directed," oriented more toward pleasing or satisfying others than self, basing self-worth on performance; extremely low self-esteem, self-hatred, contempt, or loathing, which may or may not be cloaked in a superficial grandiosity or brittle self-justification;
- inability to recognize inappropriate behavior toward oneself, intrusion, violation, or danger.[60]

Readers of this book may be raising the chilling question for themselves: "Did it happen to me?" Clergy and other helping professionals, as well as general readers, should pay attention to this disturbing question, since there is some evidence that we have disproportionately high histories of sexual as well as physical and emotional abuse.[61] The implications for seminary education and the training of helping professionals are striking, particularly concerning the primary need for healing of wounded would-be healers.[62] This will be considered further in chapter 9. If you are finding that this chapter is stirring and disturbing deep places inside of you, continue reading with the utmost gentleness and care for yourself, and consider the importance of exploring these feelings more deeply with a therapist.

Profile of Perpetrators

In general, perpetrators may seem warm and loving but lack a critical dimension of empathy for their victim(s). In some cases—though not perhaps as overwhelmingly as is commonly thought—perpetrators were abused themselves as children[63]—they cannot even begin to imagine what their victims might be thinking or feeling about the abuse, at least not until they can feel for their own childhood pain. And they have buried this for a long time in order to survive. The abuse they inflict on others is a compulsive, often grim reenactment of what happened to them, and while it may bring momentary physical pleasure, there is no true warmth or pleasure of a mutual, intimate relationship. Whatever pleasure they imagine in the victim is a projection. The myth is often that they themselves have been seduced by the child, but in truth sexual abuse has nothing to do with seduction. It is the result of a striking lack of normal human compassion, a part of them that was hidden away or killed by their own abuser years, even decades, before.

The vast majority—approximately 93 percent—of perpetrators against both girls and boys are men.[64] This deserves notice, because popular literature about offenders often falsely represents information about male and female offenders as if they were much more equivalent in number, and because we are socially conditioned to imagine an equality that does not exist, thus colluding with the abusive reality.[65] While more cases of abuse by women have recently came to light, this is still proportionate to the number of all types of cases that are emerging from long-held secrecy.[66] Existing prevalence figures for female perpetrators are also sometimes inflated by listing both mother and father as perpetrators if the father was the active offender and the mother was perceived to have "permitted acts to occur," even though she did not actively abuse the child herself.[67]

Perpetrators of sexual abuse, as of rape and domestic violence, do not generally look like monsters, nor are they usually society's "losers." They are often upstanding, successful in their work, prominent in the affairs of their community, and highly respected members, even leaders, of their church. Under the veneer of respectability, however, they are wounded users of others.

As with other forms of violence described in this book, it is perhaps most important to remember that the sexual abuse is, to use David Finkelhor's word, "alloyed" with issues of power, dominance, and aggression. Nicholas Groth has asserted that "distorted expression of identification and affiliation needs, power and control issues, and hostile and aggressive impulses, rather than sexuality, were the underlying issue in pedophilia."[68] There is no question that this is a form of abuse that has a sexual component, and that perpetrators experience erotic attraction for children or adolescents to varying degrees. It is my opinion that the sexualization of children is not separable from the issue of power and control, particularly given the sexualization of children in the society and the equation of male sexuality with aggression and dominance. Nothing displays dominance more compulsively or more thoroughly than a sexual violation, because it strikes at the soul of the child.

Within these broader understandings about the dynamics of perpetrators and their victims, current studies are beginning to identify various categories of offenders.[69] It is beyond the scope of this book to offer clinically detailed descriptions. However, some generalizations can be made as to types. In the case of male perpetrators, some achieve sexual gratification exclusively from sexual behavior with minors (although they may appear to have sexual relationships with adults). These are true pedophiles, about 95 percent of whom are men according to clinical research, and for whom a prognosis for rehabilitation is very poor. Many are drawn exclusively to younger children or exclusively to adolescents. Some pedophiles are only attracted sexually to children in their own families, over whom they feel a sense of entitlement and control. Other pedophiles may molest children indiscriminately whenever the opportunity arises, whether in or out of the family, and may in fact *seek out* employment or volunteer positions that will bring them close to young people. This poses a very frightening threat to churches because of the many arenas involving children and youth, from Sunday school and youth groups, to church-run daycare centers and private schools.

Other male perpetrators are not pedophiles, strictly speaking, because they can achieve sexual gratification from adult relationships. Nevertheless, they also use children for their own sexual gratification, sometimes as a substitute for an appropriate adult partner, and in some cases because they identify unconsciously with the younger person's developmental stage as if he or she were a peer, and lose sight of their own responsibility and biological maturity.[70]

In almost all cases, male perpetrators deny and minimize their responsibility. Some refuse to admit to allegations, even after a court conviction. Others admit to committing at least some of the acts alleged but deny responsibility. Like rapists, they blame the victim, saying that she was too sexy, or that she never said no, or that she really wanted it.

In any case, experts are very guarded about clinical prognosis for offenders, because the wounds are so deep, and the denial—or the compulsions—are so ingrained. These factors, combined with the tacit societal condoning of sexualized violence, do not bode well for prospects of rehabilitation of offenders.

A Note about Female Perpetrators

The small percentage of women perpetrators seems to follow a different pattern from the men. In a St. Paul study,[71] women abusers were identified as teacher-lovers (socially sanctioned as the "older woman" sexually initiating an adolescent in films such as the *Summer of '42*); experimenter/exploiters who were brought up in such strict, repressive households that they used babysitting situations as opportunities for sexual experimentation; "predisposed" offenders who were themselves severely abused as children, never learned the distinction between abuse and appropriate affection, and then repeat the pattern with their own siblings or children; and male-coerced women, who abused children because forced to do so by abusive husbands or partners. Only 5 percent of women offenders in this study were true pedophiles, and those had experienced severe sexual abuse from the age of two onward. Sexual abuse by women perpetrators is often less overtly violent or coercive than by men, often enacted in the guise of normal maternal activities such as bathing or dressing,[72] providing medical treatment, or comforting a child. The St. Paul study indicates that women abusers take responsibility much more readily, are capable of empathy for their victims, and experience shame and conflicted emotions about what they did.

Again, because of popular misconceptions, it is important to remember that only a small percentage of perpetrators—approximately 7 percent—are women. The question of female perpetrators, however, does raise interesting questions beyond the issue of prevalence. The pervasive misogyny of society is a two-edged sword. It sends a message of entitlement and self-justification to male perpetrators. It sends a message to girls that they want and deserve the abuse they get. But it may also send a message that if women abuse boys, and especially if they abuse girls, it is less important, because whatever women do is less important. As long as child care is considered women's domain, covert abuse by women can go unrecognized or unseen under the pretense of diapering, bathing, dressing, or providing medical care. And as long as stereotypes maintain that women are less violent, then violent abuses by women will be even more readily denied and disbelieved. While patriarchy sets the stage in general for more abuse of girls and women of every kind at the hands of men, and conditions men to view women as objects for their gratification rather than fellow human beings worthy of empathy and care, it is important to acknowledge the particular complexity of sexual abuse. In the arena of sexual abuse of children, the power dynamics of patriarchy pertain but may at times go beyond generalizations about the gender of perpetrators and victims.

bell hooks writes compellingly from the perspective of a black woman activist, committed to feminism but critical of the many white middle-class assumptions in the feminist movement of the 1960s into the present. One of these assumptions, already challenged by the recognition of lesbian battering, was that only men were violent or coercive. Her critique may be particularly relevant to the issue of child sexual abuse:

> The social hierarchy in white supremacist, capitalist patriarchy is one in which theoretically men are the powerful, women the powerless; adults the powerful, children the powerless; white people the powerful, black people and other non white peoples the powerless. In a given situation, whichever party is in power is likely to use coercive authority to maintain that power if it is challenged or threatened. Although most women clearly do not use abuse and battery to control and dominate men (even though a small minority of women batter men) they may employ abusive measures to maintain authority in interactions with groups over whom they exercise power. . . . While it in no way diminishes the severity of the problem of male violence against women to emphasize that women are likely to use coercive authority when they are in power positions, recognizing this reminds us that women, like men, must work to unlearn socialization that teaches us it is acceptable to maintain power by coercion or force. By concentrating solely on ending male violence against women, feminist activists may overlook the severity of the problem.

They may encourage women to resist male coercive domination without encouraging them to oppose all forms of coercive domination.[73]

It is important to hold both realities together—that the vast majority of sexual abusers of children are men, *and* that the complexities of power and socialization must be considered in all cases of sexual abuse regardless of the specific gender of the perpetrator.

Pastoral Response

It is a general maxim of this book that clergy and other religious professionals and church leaders should work collaboratively with the talent and expertise available in their communities and refer survivors of violence to appropriate professionals and agencies. This is nowhere more true than in the case of survivors of sexual abuse. A survivor of childhood sexual abuse and incest needs—and deserves—the support of an appropriately credentialed professional therapist with solid training and experience in the field of sexual abuse. Not all therapists are experienced in this area, and only a few clergy who also have psychotherapeutic credentials are truly qualified actually to "treat" sexual abuse survivors.

On the other hand, clergy and religious leaders can do a great deal to support the recovery of sexual abuse survivors, as an adjunct to therapy. The spiritual wounds of sexual abuse are deep, as deep as the most secret, protected core of the person, as deep as her soul. The survivor's understanding of her own worth, her experience of the world, her expectations of people's goodness or badness, and her most basic beliefs about God are all touched and shaped—or misshapen—by the abuse she suffered as a child. She may have a fractured or confused sense of boundaries and may have very limited ability to protect herself from certain kinds of emotional, physical, or sexual damage as an adult. She may consciously or unconsciously expect the pastor to abuse her as her perpetrator did.

By modeling appropriate boundaries and maintaining them under stress and when tested, the clergyperson already goes a long way toward the healing of wounded boundaries in a parishioner with a history of sexual abuse. By remaining alert to the possibility that, simply based on statistics, a large number of parishioners may be survivors, the pastor becomes open to hearing stories of pain and believing rather than discounting them. By being prepared for the rage and the shame that can be unleashed by the recovery of memories, the pastor can be a resource for simply listening and thereby modeling a crucial message: "I, your pastor (and by extension your church, and by extension your God), am not destroyed by any of what you are feeling. Your feelings are valid, and you have a right to them. You are not crazy. You are worthy and lovable. It is good that you are here on the planet." And by consistently, firmly, and lovingly giving the message that the abuse was not the victim's fault, no matter what she thought or felt or did, the pastor can begin to unravel the years of shame and self-blame that the victim has been carrying.

Often, abusers use religious, even biblical justifications for the abuse. The pastor can help by naming such misuses of Scripture and pseudo-Christian morality as blasphemous, and giving an authoritative moral voice to shore up that part of the survivor's consciousness that recognizes that what was done to her was wrong.

Finally, the role of pastor or lay counselor brings something unique into the caring relationship that is not the usual domain of psychotherapy, support groups, and other forms of care: an authoritative religious voice that affirms that God, "unto whom all hearts are open and from whom no secrets are hid,"[74] loves the survivor, hates the abuse, stands beside her in her terror and her doubt, and is continually stirring the waters of healing within her soul.

"My frame was not hidden from you, when I was being made in secret, intricately woven in the depths of the earth" (Ps. 139:15). If secrecy is at the heart of the evil of sexual abuse, then the act of reminding a survivor that there are no secrets too deep to be hidden from God's healing power is a sacramental act. Nothing is unknown to God, even if it is unknown to the survivor. God's healing can reach the most shrouded places in the soul, even if the survivor's consciousness cannot find its way there to know everything that happened to her. Just as Jesus chased the moneychangers from the temple, the pastor and the survivor together do the work of cleansing the violated temple of soul and body. Healing and justice are united in this sacrament of exposing the secrets and bringing the truth to light.

> Rise up, O LORD; O God, lift up your hand;
>   do not forget the oppressed.
> Why do the wicked renounce God,
>   and say in their hearts, "You will not call us to account"?
>
> But you do see! Indeed you note trouble and grief,
>   that you may take it into your hands;
> the helpless commit themselves to you;
>   you have been the helper of the orphan. . . .
>
> O LORD, you will hear the desire of the meek;
>   you will strengthen their heart, you will incline your ear
> to do justice for the orphan and the oppressed,
>   so that those from earth may strike terror no more.
>   (Ps. 10:12-14,17-18)

Ritualistic Abuse

Listen to me and feed back my wisdom
Let me hear that it is my own
That I am the one who knows me best
That I am the one who owns my soul
That it was never lost
Just dismembered
and hidden in the myriad fragments
I was forced to secret it in
Help me to remember it, and know it's Mine
so that I may truly heal.

—Caryn Stardancer[1]

This chapter is about courage and the miraculous capacity of the human mind to endure in the face of shattering evil. It is about the experience of dwelling day after day, even year after year, in the valley of the shadow of death. It is about outlasting intimate experiences of terror and about the strength of the soul. It is about the incarnation of Love through sheer survival. It is about God's presence wracked by torture. It is about the crucifixion. Even more, it is about resurrection.

The first time I met a victim of ritualistic abuse was when Christine[2] and her children came to stay at the battered women's shelter. At first, her story seemed tragically typical. Her partner had beaten her and stabbed her. She was distraught but determined to leave and change her life. She had been referred by another shelter because they felt their location was too close to where her batterer lived, and she would be safer with us. He would be less likely to look for her twenty miles away.

On the second night she was with us, I got a telephone call at home at 11:00. Jan, one of the shelter counselors, was on the line, sounding panicked and asking for advice. She had been closing the midweek support group with a guided visualization exercise. Christine had got an uncharacteristic look on her face, jumped up, and run into the bathroom and locked herself in. Jan and I both feared that Christine might be trying to hurt herself. While we talked, another shelter counselor continued to talk to Christine, and finally she was calm enough to come out and go safely to her room to sleep. She had not cut herself, and when asked why she had gone in there, she seemed confused and unable to explain her own behavior. Shaken, the next day we all had a conference. "She looked at me with a look I'll never forget!" said Jan, shaking her head. "I was terrified. It was like she was somebody else." After further conversation, I began to suspect that Christine might have multiple personalities. When I suggested it, a group shiver provided some intuitive inner confirmation for all of us. None of us had the kind of clinical experience to deal with what was then called "multiple personality disorder," and we felt a chill of awe and fear about the unknown into which we had been plunged unawares by Christine's arrival. We still had no idea how much more we would be facing.

We called the local hospital at the suggestion of a therapist, but they told us that because Christine could easily pass a mental status test (she knew her name, the date, the last two presidents of the United States, etc.), there was nothing they could do for her. We then called Jim,[3] a local Episcopal priest who I knew had unusually in-depth experience with ritual abuse survivors in his parish, and asked if he would be willing to come and talk to Christine and give us a sense, from his expertise, of what was going on. Jim talked with Christine at some length and, at the end of their interview, confirmed our fears. Christine had "switched" personalities several times in his presence. At the sight of his clerical collar, her internal world had scrambled for a response. Some aspects of her panicked, others cried "Rescue me!" A personality identifying as a satanic alter emerged to threaten him and vowed that she would soon return to the cult. We were stunned. How could this be? We felt plunged into a world of unreality.

We also had some immediate ethical dilemmas. Jim pointed out that Christine had signed all the confidentiality and safety agreements. But what would happen when Christine wasn't there? Would one or more of her alter personalities—that is, other personalities that resided within Christine—emerge and compromise the safety of the other residents? At the very least, because our house was not staffed twenty-four hours a day, we should refer her to a shelter that was, where Christine and her children could be monitored continually. Before we were able to make a referral, in fact, one of Christine's alters did emerge, throwing open a second-story window and shouting down to the street below, jeopardizing the confidential location of the shelter.

Christine's story, as much as we know of it, may have ended tragically. We referred her to another shelter and later learned that she had violated their safety rules so seriously that she ended up being asked to leave after just a weekend. Shelter workers there reported that Christine felt she had no choice but to return home—where in all likelihood she and her children would once again be exposed to the satanic cult and be vulnerable to the most terrifying forms of psychological and physical abuse and torture we had ever encountered in our work. We had kept her safe the longest of any shelter she visited, and she was with us for only two weeks. We felt a sense of shame and despair that we could not figure out any better solution, and that so few resources seemed to exist at that time.

This failure prompted me to attend a conference on ritual abuse two months later.[4] It was a terrifying, destabilizing experience. An exhibit of survivors' artwork was especially powerful and shocking in its graphic depictions of horrors involving infants and small children, images so perverted and so brutal that I felt frozen inside just looking at them.[5] I thought after so many years of hearing the stories of battered women and seeing their bloody faces and bruised arms and legs that I was unshockable. During my travels to El Salvador to work with church people there, I had been exposed to the photographs of tortured, mutilated bodies—men, women, and children "disappeared" and murdered by the right-wing death squads—that were displayed on the walls of the Non-Governmental Human Rights Commission. But nothing had prepared me for the images I saw in this exhibit.

The faces of the children in the pictures especially horrified and riveted me. As Dr. Lenore Terr wrote of her experience of viewing a photograph of a five-year-old client taken during the course of her sexual abuse and seized by the police later in their investigation:

I look. First I am arrested by the baby's face. I cannot take my eyes off her eyes and mouth. The most incredible mixture of emotions—of terror, distress, pain, curiosity, seriousness, and, yes, excitement—has infused the features of that baby. There is no way, I feel, that an actor could simulate a look like this. I have never before seen such a look.[6]

The horror of the conference was heightened by the pain-filled, almost unearthly stories of multiple personality that emerged during the course of the day.[7] Survivors and therapists testified to some survivors' having more than two hundred alter personalities (or personality fragments),[8] some of whom were babies and young children, others were teenagers, others wise inner helpers, and others satanic personalities (some persecutory, others feigning satanic allegiance in order to help the person resist and survive).[9]

Some said their original or core personality had died, killed by the extreme abuse they suffered during infancy. There was no "original" personality left. Others said their core was sleeping, or hiding. Some had integrated, having undergone a process in therapy in which their separate personalities had been reunited. Others had not yet done so, and still others declined ever to do so.

Therapists testified that multiple personality is much more prevalent than the psychiatric community ever believed, and often is misdiagnosed for years. They seemed to be saying that nearly anyone could have multiple personalities, and probably everyone knows someone who does—or even *is* one who does. And if there is any sexual abuse history, any dissociation present, then there might be a ritual abuse history as well. (I now believe that to be an oversimplification that implies an inflated occurrence of actual ritual abuse.[10] However, the initial impact of even entertaining such a possibility is shattering.)

After a two-hour car drive home from the conference I called my former therapist and asked to come in. How could I cope with this information? I felt frightened, destabilized. If such horror could really exist, not only in a war zone like El Salvador, but in our own backyards, and especially if it could exist *largely unrecognized*, the implications were enormous. Identity, trust, reality itself were shaken. This must be how it felt for Holocaust survivors, for whom reality was shattered, sometimes in a moment. The rug was pulled out. One day a survivor's cultured and esteemed family was eating a chicken dinner on a beautiful table, in a room with a chandelier and an Oriental carpet. The next day they were herded onto the trains, their arms tattooed. They were separated, they were crowded into camps, and so many of them were slaughtered. This was Germany! This was only a few decades ago! These were my professors at Boston University and at Harvard, and the parents and grandparents of many of my childhood friends. Two Holocaust survivors lived two doors down in my "nice" suburban neighborhood. I remember their stories, and it becomes harder to trust that today's "reality" will last. Unspeakable horror really happens.

Much later I learned that this reaction of mine to my first encounter with ritualistic abuse was the common response, called "backlash" by those who work closely with ritual abuse survivors. As my own therapist said at the time, "How could you *not* feel destabilized? It's nearly beyond human imagination. You're not going crazy. Your response is the sign of health. In fact, I'd be worried if you *didn't* have a reaction!" This is the reassurance I offer to the readers of this chapter. First exposure to this issue is terrifying indeed.

The Little We Know: The Emerging Field of Ritual Abuse Intervention

What is ritualistic abuse? First and foremost, it is torture. One of the best resources on ritual abuse, a report of the Ritual Abuse Task Force of the Los Angeles County Commission for Women, defines ritual abuse as:

> *a brutal form of abuse of children, adolescents, and adults, consisting of physical, sexual, and psychological abuse, and involving the use of rituals. Ritual does not necessarily mean satanic. However most survivors state that they were ritually abused as part of satanic worship for the purpose of indoctrinating them into satanic beliefs and practices. Ritual abuse rarely consists of a single episode. It usually involves repeated abuse over an extended period of time.*[11]

Like all the other forms of violence described in this book, it is my hypothesis that the major purpose of the abuse is to achieve domination and control over the victims, using the most extreme and sometimes sophisticated forms of terrorism, bizarre brutality, and brainwashing techniques.[12] Ritual elements are combined with other techniques of indoctrination, including sleep deprivation, starvation, and drugs, to break down the mind and spirit of the victims and reform them into obedient members—and sometimes force them to perpetrate against other victims, "dangling them on the edge of sanity and/or life by placing them in a situation where they were forced to harm another or be harmed."[13] The Los Angeles Ritual Abuse Task Force reports: "Both during and after the abuse, most victims are in a state of terror, mind control, and dissociation in which disclosure is exceedingly difficult."[14] Rituals are also used systematically to enforce silence and to convince victims of the omnipresence and omnipotence of their abusers. Believing that their abusers are everywhere, and that no one can be trusted, victims refuse to tell anyone who might be able to help them. Eventually, through internal processes of numbing and dissociation, victims finally are unable to tell even themselves the full extent of their experience of torture. As difficult as it is for a victim of nonritualistic sexual abuse to disclose and to be believed, this is compounded for victims of ritual abuse with multiple personalities. The lack of credibility granted generally to reports of child sexual abuse is compounded by a professional denial of multiple personalities as a genuine phenomenon.[15] All these effects serve to obliterate the victim's free will and attempt to destroy all natural connection to God and one's own life-giving spiritual core. This is blasphemy—such an intentional attack against the core of a person is an implicit sacrilege against God.

Satanic ritual abuse in particular is also explicitly blasphemous. Satanic rituals also serve the purpose of indoctrination into the cult's belief system, which usually includes the grandiose aim of gaining a near-cosmic level of power and control through manipulation of demonic forces and spirits. In intentional satanic cults, the belief system is one in which good is bad, bad is good, and most ritual elements actually derive from the deliberate inversion or gross perversion of Christian liturgical practices (for example, ritually crucifying victims upside-down, or using words from the Christian Eucharist while torturing or sacrificing victims on an altar, or using real flesh and blood in a satanic "communion"). However, similar effects are achieved by ritual cults that actually identify themselves as Christian or as belonging to other religions, or certain atheistic or quasi-political cults. Abusive rituals also have the effect of extreme intimidation and threat of death—not only physical death, which would be terrifying enough, but the damning extinguishing of the soul itself for eternity, especially if cult leaders and rules are disobeyed or their secrets revealed. The extreme and fantastic qualities of ritual aspects of this abuse, tragically, make it seem so unbelievable that the victim's credibility is weakened and criminal prosecution is rendered very difficult. Indeed, stories from victims of mind control, infiltration by cult members of highly respected institutions—including day care centers, public schools, and churches—often lead helping professionals to make diagnoses of paranoid delusional disorders rather than believing, protecting, and initiating a process for justice for the victims.

Examples of psychological, physical, and sexual abuse are extremely upsetting, and I write this with great compassion for the reader, who is no doubt becoming increasingly uneasy and disturbed by this material. Some specific cases[16] have included threats or actual acts of mutilation of the victim; killing of animals in victims' presence as an example of what might happen to them; telling victims that their parents are members of the cult (in cases where they truly are not) so that reporting seems futile; confinement in cages, closets, basements, wells, or coffins, and telling victims they are being left there to die; being hung upside-down in a hole with a dead body or the mutilated parts of an animal or human being; being confined with snakes, insects, or rodents, or being tricked into believing that frightening animals are present; forced smearing or ingestion of urine, feces, or semen; forced nudity and participation in the production of pornography;[17] subjection to mind-altering drugs; rituals like "magical surgery" in which a child is drugged, cut open, and told that a devil's heart or a bomb programmed to explode if they tell anyone of the abuse is planted inside them; programming/mind control that plants detailed instructions to commit extreme self-injury or suicide rather than leave the cult or remember or disclose cult activities; being forced to mutilate or kill others, particularly children, even one's own children, or to participate in cannibalism. Rituals specifically for the purpose of bonding the victim to the group include a mock marriage to one or more members of the cult, birthing rituals in which victims are "born" into the cult out of the body of a dead animal or even human corpse, and ritual "deflowering" in which a very small child is penetrated with a ritual object— or, in the most extreme case depicted by one survivor's drawing, with the severed limb of a murdered infant. Physical abuse can include forms of torture that are not easily detected even by medical examiners, including near-drowning, withholding food and water, sleep deprivation, being hung, electric shock, and pins or "shots" inserted between digits, under fingernails, or in genital areas. More detectable examples, often in cases where the entire family is involved in the cult and escape or reporting are much more difficult, include beatings, tattoos and burns, starvation, and mutilation. Sexual abuse in ritual contexts involves forcing victims into the extremes of sexual perversion, including forced sexual contact with animals, infants, and children, dead or dying people, and penetration with knives and guns or ritual objects such as wands, knives, and crucifixes. The primary purposes of ritual sexual abuse are total dominance over the victim and heightening of personal powers, as well as sexual gratification or enjoyment of the ritual itself. While it is the premise of this book that *all* abuse, including sexual abuse by pedophiles, serves an unconscious purpose of power and control, ritualistic sexual abuse is overt and extreme in its goal of complete domination and annihilation of the victim's will.

The Connection of Ritual Abuse with Multiple Personality

Extreme, sadistic abuse is now generally understood as the most likely antecedent of "Dissociative Identity Disorder"[18] (formerly called "Multiple Personality Disorder"[19]), hereinafter referred to as "DID."[20] Researchers have determined that a child is most likely to develop multiple personality states when several factors are present: She has a natural, inborn capacity to dissociate, often above-average intelligence and creativity, and these native traits are combined with "exposure to severe, overwhelming traumata such as frequent, unpredictable and inconsistently alternating abuse and love."[21] Severe, repeated sexual abuse, extremes of sadism, and bizarre forms of abuse are more common in the histories of psychiatric patients diagnosed with DID than in other abuse survivors.[22] The more extreme and bizarre the abuse, and the younger the child at the onset of the abuse, the greater the tendency to develop a dissociative disorder, including the possible formation of multiple personalities.[23] The violence, terror, and confusion are too extreme for the human mind, especially the mind of a child, to withstand. The psyche splits off a personality state that holds the experience and memory of a particular horror or abuse. With further abuse, identity and consciousness may continue to split and split again. This is the case not only with ritual abuse, but with other forms of extreme physical and sexual abuse as well. Dissociation is probably the most common psychological response to severe trauma, whether in the extreme form of multiple personality, or in milder forms of trance—for example, seemingly seeing oneself float above a scene in which one is in shock or in pain, or having flashbacks of a traumatic incident. The younger the child, the more flooding, terrifying, and inexplicable any abuse will seem. She simply does not have the cognitive capacity or the perspective to understand what is happening to her. Dissociation is mobilized as nature's defense when the alternative to dissociation may be insanity or death.

Dissociative Identity Disorder is defined in DSM-IV:

> The essential feature of Dissociative Identity Disorder is the presence of two or more distinctive identities or personality states that recurrently take control of behavior. There is an inability to recall important personal information, the extent of which is too great to be explained by ordinary forgetfulness.[24]

The number of distinct identities can range from two to over one hundred, with roughly half of reported cases having ten or fewer.[25] Different personality states are likely to see themselves as having different appearances. They may have talents unique to them, different dialects, even speak languages unknown to each other. They may have different physical characteristics, including different eyesight, allergies, rashes, or even chronic diseases that do not appear in all the personality states.[26]

Personality states are almost always a variety of ages and sometimes are different genders as well.[27] Commonly there is a host personality who may be "out" or in executive control of the body the greatest amount of time. The host is often the personality state that first presents in therapy for a common range of symptoms including depression, anxiety, sexual problems, and headaches. Hosts often have no idea there are other alters and are frightened by a diagnosis of DID/MPD.

Infant, child, and adolescent personality states are often present, holding traumatic experience frozen in time from the original abuse. There may be a variety of protectors, including some who seem quite fierce, performing the role of bodyguard. The function of other protectors often is to intervene when another alter becomes self-destructive. Because of the frequency of sexual abuse, there may also be extremely sexually active or even prostitute alters (often very opposite in character to the host, and sometimes leaving her to come to in the midst of frightening or potentially dangerous situations). Suicidal personalities are common, both because of depression from the abuse and, in the case of ritual abuse survivors, because of suicidal programming from the cult. Abilities of alters range from physically disabled and autistic personalities to personalities (often fragments) with unusual talents and skills. Substance abusing alters are common as one method for dulling pain.

There is a growing awareness that many cases have in common the existence of a benevolent wise personality, or Inner Self Helper,[28] who allies with the survivor's helping professionals to guide the therapy[29] and protect the survivor. Survivors sometimes perceive these personalities as external to the rest of their system, more like a true guardian angel or emissary of healing and wisdom from God.

Satanic ritual abuse survivors often have, in addition, a layer of satanic alters. Some may be persecutory or perpetrator alters who are aligned with the cult or carry internalized representations of the abusers. These are most likely to inflict punitive harm on the survivor's body, and they may represent grave physical danger to the survivor and to others. Others may be posturing in order to appease the perpetrators as a survival mechanism and are not usually a danger to the survivor or others.[30] In either case, these are not external demonic forces and do not warrant attempts to exorcise them. The question of exorcism and deliverances will be discussed further below.

An original or core personality, defined as the "identity which developed just after birth and split off the first new personality in order to help the body survive a severe stress,"[31] is usually not the host personality.[32] The core most often emerges late in therapy, after what survivors often describe as having been put to sleep or sent far away. The emergence of the core can be a joyful and profound spiritual experience for survivors.[33]

Personalities often do not know of the existence of others, or at least all the others, although this amnestic wall between personalities often begins to break down in therapy. Indeed, one goal of many therapeutic approaches is to help the different personality states become closer and more cooperative. The process of therapy generally moves through four stages:[34] (1) initial work to erode amnestic barriers and help the distinct personality states become aware of each other; (2) establishing communication and cooperation among personalities; (3) replacing dividedness with agreement to work together; and (4) work toward what is variously called fusion, unification, or integration.

The final goal of most therapies is integration, a process or a state in which all identities are rejoined into a single state of consciousness—often accomplished with the aid of hypnosis, although this is no longer considered necessary by some practitioners. Integration can be experienced as frightening or ecstatic, even as a series of deaths, as each personality surrenders and merges into a larger whole. Ideally, it represents an increasingly firm self-understanding that all the split-off parts of the self still belong to and constitute a single "I."[35]

Integration is now being challenged by some survivors and their therapists, aiming instead toward better teamwork and respect among personalities who nevertheless choose to remain distinct.[36] "Internal group therapy," originated by David Caul, has been successfully employed to address conflicts among alters in the personality system, often as a means of addressing impasses in therapy.[37] However, integration is still generally viewed as a natural by-product of sound therapy in which inner conflicts are resolved and the survivor is committed to intense self-examination.[38]

To anyone unfamiliar with the phenomenon of dissociative identity disorder (DID), it can seem alien and frightening, although in fact it is a natural potentiality of the human psyche and one that serves in a healthy way to protect survival. For centuries, DID was known but little acknowledged. Except for a brief surge of interest coinciding with a general psychiatric interest in hysteria and hypnosis between 1880 and 1920,[39] only in recent years has the psychiatric community recognized it as genuine, and even when acknowledging it as a possibility, most therapists until recently believed that they would never see it in their own practices.

As recently as 1980, the American Psychiatric Association's Diagnostic and Statistical Manual of Mental Disorders, 3rd ed. (DSM-III), which served as the primary diagnostic manual for all or nearly all American therapists, reported, "The disorder is apparently extremely rare." In the 3rd edition revised (DSM-III-R), published in 1987, this was changed to read: "Recent reports suggest that this disorder is not nearly so rare as it has commonly been thought to be."[40] The current (fourth) edition (DSM-IV) reflects continuing debate among clinicians up to the present moment about the prevalence of DID, demonstrating the complexity of diagnosis of disorders involving trauma, memory, and dissociation: "The sharp rise in reported cases of Dissociative Identity Disorder in the United States in recent years has been subject to very different interpretations. Some believe that the greater awareness of the diagnosis among mental health professionals has resulted in the identification of cases that were previously undiagnosed. In contrast, others believe that the syndrome has been overdiagnosed in individuals who are highly suscep- tible."[41] On average, most persons suffering from DID are not accurately di- agnosed for six to seven years.[42]

For years, Multiple Personality was thought of by the general public in terms of two best-sellers, which were also made into movies: *The Three Faces of Eve* and *Sybil*. However, these cases were not necessarily typical and have created some false impressions. Multiple personalities are not always as distinct—nor as limited in number—as described particularly in *The Three Faces of Eve*. People diagnosed with DID may or may not be severely impaired at work or in all aspects of relationship.[43] Nor are all as artistically inclined as Sybil and Eve, although a great many are. The actual switching from one per- sonality state to another may not be nearly as dramatic as in the books. In fact, many people with multiple personalities, although suffering deeply at some level, may be spouses, parents, or workers, who appear to be doing as well as the next person. In fact, one reason why DID/MPD was so rarely diagnosed until recent growth in awareness by therapists was that it was so often *mis*- diagnosed, or only partially diagnosed, as something else—most commonly "borderline personality," or sometimes in extreme cases as schizophrenia be- cause of complaints of hearing the voices of others in their heads.[44] Depres- sion is also a common diagnosis, when suicidality emerges. It has even been shown that certain cases of alcoholic blackouts actually represented a dual di- agnosis of alcohol addiction and multiple personality.[45] Switching can be subtle, and different identities are adept at "tag-teaming"[46] in a seamless way in order to function in the world. Dramatic accounts of major amnestic epi- sodes in which people disappear for days and "wake up" to find themselves in strange surroundings, or stories of discovering strange and uncharacteristic clothing in their wardrobe, may not occur in all cases, although a person with multiple personality states is likely to have more subtle experiences of losing time or "spacing out."

Losing time is one of the key signs of multiple personalities.[47] The experi- ence of time in general is more fluid in persons experiencing multiple person- alities, not only because of the discontinuities caused by switching, but also because of the sometimes quite intense and dreamlike flashbacks to past events. There is not a solid sense of "now."[48]

I believe strongly that it is important to see the original formation of mul- tiple personality states as a strength and not an illness, although it may well be a coping mechanism that has outlived its usefulness and is now causing prob- lems, even very serious problems. To understand this, and to "depathologize" DID, it is necessary to understand the genesis of multiple personality states in the pain and abuse suffered by the originally unified child. It is now quite gen- erally accepted that the dissociative splitting that creates a new personality is a defense against extreme pain or terror. Rather than dying or dissolving into insanity, the mind splits the pain and horror into a compartment and seals it there. For this reason, almost every personality had a "birth" in terror. He or she came into being to handle a new stress or trauma that the original personality and other personalities could not withstand. This is surely a miracle of human resiliency and deserves tremendous respect.

The amnestic walls built between personality states are precisely to protect each other from memories too horrifying to bear. Several personalities or fragments may separately contain parts of a single abuse memory in the areas of behavior (what happened), affect (emotional feeling), sensation (physical feeling), and knowledge (cognitive perception of the experience).[49] There are varying degrees of permeability between these barriers.[50] Depending on how many personalities or fragments may exist, there may be a quite complex systemic structure in which certain identities group together into similar "families" and can be graphically represented in a format similar to a family tree.[51] Once personalities emerge in treatment, it is also common for some to come forward, while yet more "layers" of personalities lie deeper beneath to be discovered only as healing progresses.[52]

In place of a view of DID/MPD as a disorder or sickness, it is perhaps useful to view it as a process rather than a static condition. It is a process, perhaps inherent in *every* human mind, for entering into a trance state to survive trauma. Someone with DID has become unconsciously adept at entering into this state and creating new identities to cope with pain and stress.

Dissociation identity disorder also can be seen as existing on the outer end of an otherwise quite normal spectrum of diversity within a single healthy self. We all have distinct and quite different aspects of ourselves, personality or ego states that come to the fore in different environments or contexts. Some of these can even seem inconsistent or contradictory, especially depending on how limiting or narrow the social context in which one finds oneself. Role expectations relegate certain traits into shadow and others into high relief, depending on the context. Clergy are very familiar with the sense that many aspects of their personalities—their sexuality, their humor, their irreverence, their own sinfulness and doubt—are barely tolerated in certain church contexts, while among their social friends these aspects of their personalities may be welcomed and even encouraged. No one is monolithic. But for a person with DID, these differing aspects become split off from awareness, and boundaries are erected that prohibit the fluid, conscious flow that most of us accomplish as automatically as breathing, from one feeling-state or memory or behavior to a different one.

It is precisely because this process *is* so natural in one sense and so continuous with the construction of every human personality in all its diversity that it may not be recognized for a long time. And it is because the process of creating alter personalities is so life-*supporting* that it is so difficult to unlearn when dangers are no longer present, and the switching becomes disruptive rather than helpful.[53] Integration or greater cooperation among personalities is likely to be necessary to help the person become more fully present and grounded in reality—but this cannot be forced, and the history of abuse and manipulation will make it very hard for the personalities themselves to see the wisdom in this. It is crucial to recognize the process as the hard-won miracle of life that it is.

The process of healing itself is often experienced by the survivor as highly threatening. Generally it involves remembering, and sometimes actually reexperiencing in vivid sensory detail (called "abreaction")[54] the repressed tortures and terrors that were sealed into personality compartments *for a good reason*. This requires gentleness and a great deal of time—both in terms of intensive numbers of hours and long years. It is a process that should always be guided by a trained clinical therapist, although it can and should be supported by pastors and pastoral caregivers.

Can psychotherapy actually make multiplicity worse, even encourage or create more personalities? This accusation is sometimes made by skeptics in order to discredit the whole phenomenon of dissociative identity disorder as therapists' confabulation. In general, the answer is no, but it is true that deep therapy with any survivors of abuse, particularly therapy in which abreaction work is done—that is, where memories are brought up, relived, and in some sense discharged through catharsis—is highly stressful. For a client whose coping mechanism by habit has been to split off and create new alters to bear pain and deal with stress, it is not unreasonable to suppose that, at least initially, more personalities could emerge.[55] However, not to attempt to do the work of healing would be absurd. The goal of therapy is always to facilitate healing and wholeness and empowerment, and this work needs to be validated by the survivor's entire network of support.

Ritual Abuse: The Ultimate Abuse of Power

Why include this chapter in a book on violence against women, when men and boys as well as women and girls are ritually victimized? Clearly, ritual abuse, as well as incest and child sexual abuse, have large numbers of male victims—likely far more than is statistically the case in marital battering or rape. Nevertheless, there is a link to the larger culture of male violence against women. Not only is it apparently the case that in a large majority of cults (both satanic and nonsatanic or quasi-Christian), top leadership positions are held by men.[56] But, further, if the issue of violence against women in our society is one of control, dominance, and power as power-over, then there is nowhere in our society a more extreme manifestation of this abusive form of power as brutal domination. If power-over is the model of success in "normal" societal interactions, then ritual abuse is not completely disconnected from this social norm. Why are people ever drawn to becoming such brutal perpetrators (if they are not brainwashed into it by the cult itself)? There is no other answer possible than to realize that some are drawn to such perverted activities in a twisted attempt to garner as much power-over as possible, even attempting to gain supernatural powers for oneself through some occult beliefs about torture and murder—for example, a belief common in many satanic cults that one may assimilate the powers of another by releasing their blood, killing them, or literally eating them.[57]

While such behavior must on one level be viewed as sociopathic or psychotic, it is more complicated still than the individual murderer or even the serial killer lost in his obsessions or delusions. There is a tremendously powerful group psychology that pertains in such cult violence. What can be the group chemistry among people, some of whom may have dissociative identity disorder themselves and are literally split off from their capacity for intimacy, empathy, even their capacity for humanity? Isn't it outside of the realm of human experience?

How common is this terrifying phenomenon? There are no clear-cut answers to this question. Actual evidence of satanic cult activity is rare. The case of the bodies discovered in connection with a satanic cult in Matamoros, Mexico, is unusual for the amount of graphic ritualistic evidence left behind, but this may be attributed to the likelihood that Matamoros was not an intergenerational cult, but rather a "crudely organized drug-running cult with low-level dabblers,"[58] and therefore less meticulously organized. Survivors of highly organized satanic cults, which are often intergenerational, claim that the very secrecy and paranoia of cult leaders means that scrupulous measures are taken to leave no evidence of cult activities in any location where the cult has conducted rituals. Alternatively, satanic cults find such remote and isolated locations to perform their rites, that, especially combined with the general climate of disbelief, no one makes the effort to discover their encampments. The problem of lack of physical evidence is intrinsic to the extremely secretive nature and ideology of the cults.[59]

Even experts cannot agree on the actual prevalence of ritual abuse. Perhaps all we can say at this point is: there is something there. Some survivors do, in fact, find corroboration and physical evidence.[60] Richard Kluft, an internationally recognized expert on multiple personality disorder, has said he cannot confidently assert the extent of the true reality of ritual abuse.[61] Is it the client's reality? Yes, and it must be deeply honored as such. Do recovered memories of satanic rituals constitute *forensic* evidence in a court of law? A great deal is still unknown about the mechanism of memory recovery, especially how a small, preverbal child interprets what he or she is experiencing. Is ritual abuse a "bandwagon"? Is it a fantastic story that is circulating especially among sexual abuse survivors at the level of urban legend? What could be more ultimately horrifying to a trusting, helpless infant than the betrayal of its tenderest, most vulnerable sexual boundaries by a parent—by the one who is Godlike to the infant in power to care and protect, and who abuses that Godlike trust to seek his or her own gratification? Is it such a far stretch of the imagination to remember and interpret such abuse later in life as satanic, especially if it was particularly cruel and violent—physically, sexually, or emotionally?

What is probably fair to say, absent further research, is that ritual abuse does exist, although probably somewhat less than a vocal minority of activists might insist, and much more than the public or professional imagination would like to believe. It is also safe to accept that survivors' reality *always* represents severe trauma, whether one can ever ascertain the precise historical facts. Survivors are due the utmost respect for their tenacity and valor in the face of an experience of what must have been unspeakable evil.

Pastoral Response

Two principles are paramount in ministry with survivors of ritual abuse: *cooperation* with clinical professional(s), and the importance of *community*.

Clergy are not equipped and *must not* try to "go it alone" in healing work with survivors of this kind of extreme trauma. As much as this is true for other forms of abuse, it becomes even more critical in ministering to survivors of ritual abuse. From the survivor's point of view, cooperation between her pastor and her therapist send a powerful message that the church and her therapy work are not at odds or in competition with each other, but united and compatible.[62] From the pastor's point of view, the severity and terror of ritual abuse cannot leave the pastor unaffected. A pastor must have knowledgeable, professional support. Professional help is needed in understanding and appropriately ministering within the context of almost inevitable dissociative effects of some kind. Substance abuse is often seen as an attempt to dull the terror or pain of the abuse, requiring professional treatment. In addition, there are some immediate dangers, necessitating a team approach: survivors may be preprogrammed to become suicidal if they tell anyone, perhaps especially if they reveal secrets of a satanic cult to a Christian clergyperson or "priest." Persecutory alters may threaten actual physical harm to the survivor or even to the pastoral helper.

On the other hand, clergy need not turn a survivor over to a therapist referral and avoid further contact. Clergy can contribute a great deal to the healing process, and because of their intimacy with the realm of spirituality, their training, and their role as religious professionals, they can bring a different and needed authority of reassurance and spiritual healing to the survivor's recovery process.[63]

Some ritual abuse is a distortion of Christian belief and practice—for example, some survivors have reported belonging to so-called Christian cults where members were deprived of sleep or food, or subjected to physical punishment such as flagellation or extremely prolonged periods of kneeling, all "in the name of Jesus." In satanic abuse, Christian symbols and practices—baptism, a sacramental meal of bread and wine, anointing, and the cross itself—are deliberately perverted or turned upside down in an intentional identification with the opposite of all that Christianity understands as good. Because Satanism is so negatively dependent upon Christian symbolism and rituals, it can be said, in the words of one survivor: "Without Christianity, there could not be Satanism."[64] Satanism is also not synonymous with witch-craft.[65] It is the enactment or incarnation of evil *as* evil is understood in Christian tradition, and this is often accomplished by distorting and perverting powerful Christian symbols and rites. The Christian Eucharist is intentionally perverted by Satanists, sometimes using chalices stolen from churches, with real blood sacrifices and the forced eating of real flesh and blood.

Whether the ritual abuse is identified as Christian or as anti-Christian/ satanic, a ministry of inclusion into a loving and genuine Christian community and a pastor's strong words of assurance, cleansing from past abominations, and healing can do much to reverse much of the destructive programming of the abuse, and to begin to release the survivor toward true freedom and spiritual wholeness.

Responding to requests for religious affiliation can, in and of itself, begin this process of healing.[66] Having the strength and the personal base of support to hear out a survivor's story of terror and pain—often in many different voices, because different memories are sometimes encapsulated in different alters' separate experiences—is also healing in itself. As with any abuse survivor, but even more so with ritual abuse survivors, trust is low and secrecy and fear are high. Boundaries must be observed especially carefully and set-ups and tests for untrustworthiness expected as a matter of course.[67] A calm, firm, and consistent presence in the survivor's life who also takes seriously her spiritual concerns and has deep and genuine empathy for her religious and spiritual pain and questioning is of tremendous value to her healing process. As a pastoral representative of the church, the message given just by listening is that nothing is beyond the pale, nothing is outside God's own capacity to hear, to care, and to mend.

Scripture can also be a powerful tool of assurance and healing. Survivors have reported how reciting the Twenty-third Psalm got them through times of terror—particularly the affirmation "Yea, though I walk through the valley of the shadow of death, thou art with me; thy rod and thy staff, they comfort me." Similar passages of God's presence in the midst of terror and peril are life-giving to survivors; for example, in the Hebrew Bible, the prophet Elijah encounters God in the "still, small voice" following raging wind, earthquake, and fire. He is not abandoned by God. On the contrary, he is given a new mission. In the Gospel of Matthew, the disciples are terrified in the middle of a violent storm while out in their boat. Jesus comes walking to them across the Sea of Galilee, invites Peter to come to him, rescues him when his faith falters, and finally calms the wind itself. Stories like these give the survivor an assurance that no terror or danger is outside God's capacity to come near, to comfort, and to save.

In addition to the care of a pastor and a therapist, community becomes essential in a survivor's healing. Ritual abuse survivors have often been told that they are too tied to the cult and/or their terrible experiences, or are too violated and sullied, ever to be accepted and loved by any other community. They are often caused to believe that they are marked and set apart, beyond the redemption that might be possible for other "normal" human beings. For this reason, the context of a community where care and justice are valued and enacted, and where they are assured again and again that no one is outside of God's salvation, becomes essential for healing.

I am aware that increasing numbers of pastors and congregations now find themselves ministering with survivors of ritual abuse. To give one example, I am acquainted with a small, mainline Protestant church that has begun and maintained for many years an extraordinary ministry with ritual abuse survivors.

The senior minister gently observes people coming and going from the back row. He knows that ritual abuse survivors can tolerate any kind of ritual only in gentle, small doses. The Eucharist in particular is so disturbing, and has so many resonances to satanic rituals, that survivors often have to get up quietly and leave. He and some members of the congregation are aware of their painful journey. They give them the space they need and honor their own sense of timing and participation.

Many things can be "triggers" for horrifying memories—a red rose, a black robe, a candle. The congregation is flexible, and offending objects are sometimes removed. This is taken up as a pastoral issue between the minister and the survivor and worked through in a caring, mutual way. "The way we've always done it" and people's sense of liturgical propriety frequently give way to sensitivity, compassion, and patience.

The essence of this healing and care is that it takes place in the context of community. While it was the minister alone who was contacted initially by the first survivor, and it was he who first faced and wrestled with all the terror and disbelief, it was both he and, as appropriate, members of the congregation together, who educated themselves and created a loving and welcoming place for healing to take place. At any point, he or they might have said no. "No, this can't be happening. No, this can't be real. No, we're not ready for this. Please don't disturb us with your stories and your upsetting and perplexing behaviors." But they said, instead, "You are precious in God's sight. Not all ritual is evil. If you are longing to find God again, to be able to worship again, we will try to help make that possible." It is a sign of hope that this particular parish is becoming less and less unusual for its openness and knowledgeable responsiveness.

Over time, the process becomes lighter and easier. There is ordinary friendship, ordinary church business, even ordinary bickering and socializing in the midst of the sense of unreality and horror. Humor allows many a meeting to move forward that would otherwise be mired in pain. In helping to plan a special memorial service for ritual abuse survivors at a local hospital,[68] I became more intimately acquainted with this community and was amazed by the brilliant, sardonic humor that abounds in survivor culture. Ritual abuse and multiplicity are taken very seriously, but the pain is not idolized or held so sacred that nothing can touch it. Pain is exploded not only by deep psychotherapy and healing ritual, but also by laughter and conviviality.

Some Words about Ritual Healing for Ritual Abuse Survivors

Specialized ritual is often thought of as one of the first remedies for survivors of extreme abuse. This impulse should be resisted. It is my belief that efforts at healing through ritual can do more harm than good if not grounded first in the solid pastoral relationship and context of Christian community described above. Specialized ritual, even Christian-based ritual planned and conducted by faithful and caring church members, can easily deteriorate into a technique or a quick fix that bypasses deeper elements essential in a survivor's recovery.[69]

The two central sacraments of the Christian tradition, Baptism and Eucharist, are in and of themselves, arguably, the most powerful rituals for healing.[70] Specialized rituals that are set apart risk conveying the message once again that the survivor cannot be fully a part of the Christian community without making extraordinary or special efforts. Baptism and Eucharist assure the survivor that she is, like every other member of the community, adopted by God and heir to God's Realm of love and justice.

Baptism, as the public initiation into the community of the church, assures the survivor of inclusivity, cleansing, and grace. It is the entrance into a new community founded on the principles of love and justice rather than on their perversion and inversion. What has been turned upside down in the survivor's spiritual life by satanic practice and belief, or distorted beyond recognition by pseudo-Christian abuse, is now touched with the possibility of being set right again.

Baptism should never be pressed on a survivor, thereby replicating the kind of forced ritual participation of her abuser(s). It should be at the survivor's request and with in-depth pastoral care and education to mitigate any impression that this is simply one more magical rite on the order of the ones she has previously endured in her abuse. Each step of the baptism ritual should be carefully explained in advance, since "pseudo-baptisms" are frequently performed in cults, incorporating terrifying ritual elements.[71] Baptism should be done publicly, preferably during the regular Sunday worship service (and on a day designated traditionally for baptisms in liturgical traditions where this is observed). Public baptism as part of the regularly gathered community reinforces the central meaning of baptism as welcoming the survivor into the whole community of faith and helps to reverse patterns of abusive pseudo-sacraments carried out in secrecy and an atmosphere of terror and coercion.[72]

The Eucharist is similarly powerful in the healing of ritual abuse survivors. James Ward, an Episcopal priest, has written:

> The Holy Eucharist, while very provocative and disturbing for survivors who have been forced to eat human flesh and drink human blood, is, precisely because it is so laden with recollection and meaning, a powerful means of putting right the reversal and perversion which they have undergone. Since the damage has been done to the victim's self, or to the One (God) represented by the self, the healing will be at some point or on some level "spiritual" and the great religious traditions can provide irreplaceable resources.[73]

Again, careful preparation and explanation in advance are necessary. In the Eucharist, the community of faith established by baptism is gathered to reaffirm this promise of restoration, to join in solidarity with all who suffer, and to share in Christ's promise of the Realm of God in which such evil and injustice is banished forever.

Other types of rituals are potentially very problematic. In particular, exorcisms and deliverances, while sometimes thought of first—both by pastors and by survivors themselves—are, usually, at best ineffective and at worst actually harmful or even dangerous to the survivor's recovery process. "Spiritual warfare,"[74] in which demons are ritually cast out or satanic alters are purged, is more likely to drive such personalities or fragments deeper underground in the survivor's psyche than actually to heal or relieve her of them.[75] Furthermore, as has been pointed out previously, some so-called satanic alters may actually be helpers and should be engaged rather than driven away.[76] Exorcism continues to give the message that some parts of the survivor's psyche truly are beyond the pale, and the only remedy is to cast them out. It is my view that no part is beyond connection with the Self or outside the reach of God. It is precisely the embracing of all the parts that brings healing and wholeness to the survivor.

As an alternative to exorcism, when survivors are actively requesting the spiritual intervention of a priest or pastor in dealing with their satanic alters, clergy—in concert with the survivor's therapist, and not before this relationship is established—may participate in a discussion or "confrontation" in which an alter who is identified as persecutory, frightening, or satanic is invited to come out and enter into dialogue.[77] The approach must be calm, unintimidated, caring, and empathic toward all parts of the survivor's personality system. The frightening alter needs to be acknowledged and empathically understood as also being an "unfree sufferer in pain."[78] The religious language and beliefs of the survivor must be respected and appreciated. In this way, the alter may possibly begin to feel safe enough to let down his or her threatening posturing and to reveal the meanings, experiences, or feelings that govern his or her existence. This approach, contrary to exorcism or deliverance, enlists the support of the frightening alter(s), initially by appealing to their own self-interest—relief from pain and continuing bondage by the abuser(s)—and over time, transforming the alter(s)' perspective toward cooperation and investment in greater wholeness and peace for the entire system. There is no magic fix in such an approach, and it may be more time-consuming, more painstaking, and far less dramatic than an exorcism. However, the rewards are likely to be deeper and more lasting.

Admittedly, this discussion begs the question of objective evil as a force and the possibility of an actual intruding evil entity possessing part of a person or personality system from the outside. If such objective evil exists as a force, it is outside the scope of my expertise.[79] What is important to remember in ministry with multiple personalities is that it should never be assumed that persecutory or satanic alters are true manifestations of demonic possession. Such a possibility should only be considered as a last resort, with the expert consultation of a therapist experienced in working with dissociative identity disorder, and with as much concurrence from the host and dominant personality system as possible.[80] It is also advisable that such a procedure take place in the context of an established, trusting relationship, and not by a priest or exorcist who is brought in solely for that purpose.

Survivors may also request anointing for healing and/or protection. One of my own former parishioners was hospitalized because of a serious suicidal gesture made by one of her four alters. While the full extent of her abuse is only beginning to be uncovered, one of her alters is now remembering certain ritualized tortures, including being hung in a closet with a dead animal. When I made a pastoral visit to the hospital to bring communion and to anoint for healing—as I would in any visit to a hospitalized parishioner—I took care to ask how each of the alters was doing and to offer anointing to each of them individually. She said that one anointing for all would be OK, that they all could hear everything and participate together, but that acknowledgment mattered a great deal to her. I called each of them by name in the anointing.[81] In another case, a pastor was asked by a survivor and her therapist to anoint and then rename an alter who had engaged in mutilating behavior. This effected a positive transformation in the alter, and the self-destructive behaviors ceased.[82]

Finally, ritual healing may also take the form of an actual worship service, or part of a service, dedicated to the healing and remembrance of ritual abuse survivors and those who died. Again, this should be a step that grows organically from the relationships of persons in community, at the request of survivors themselves, and not offered out of context. Survivors must take the lead in planning. With these cautions understood, my experience of the two memorial services for survivors in which I participated was powerful, and the services did appear to facilitate healing for many who attended. But the healing power of such services is not without qualification, and any effort to do such work must be undertaken with the utmost caution and sensitivity.

Planning for any such event cannot be carried out without the complete involvement of survivors at every step.

One of the services was held at a church, and the second service, a year later, was held at survivors' requests in a hospital meeting room because it was more neutral. Dates were chosen carefully to avoid satanic holidays. There are a number of common triggers to avoid, which means doing without some of the usual appurtenances of worship: participants were asked not to wear robes as vestments (especially black robes), but only clergy collars with street clothes. Incense, chalices, and flowers, especially red roses, were avoided. Candles were used only with care and with pastoral explanations. We did have a paschal candle at the entrance of the worship space in the hospital—and this was controversial. Symbols that helped facilitate healing included the use of water, green leaves, yellow chrysanthemums, and fabrics of earth tones, white, green, yellow, blue, and gold. Note that these are intended only as examples. Anything can be a trigger, and it is important in this regard to work from a consensus of the survivor community who are gathered to plan worship.

The services included careful introduction and invitation to participants to explain what was planned and to invite participation only at whatever level was comfortable for each person present; readings from Scripture and sharing by survivors; prayers and expressions of justice, healing, and peace; a litany of remembrance; a closing ritual, and a final benediction. (Because it was an interfaith service, and also because at that time a number of survivors found the eucharistic symbolism too upsetting, there was not a Eucharist.)

In a service like this, survivors may participate in the prayers in many voices. A young woman clutches a teddy bear and sobs in the voice of a two-year-old in fear and pain. Another woman offers a prayer for the babies she was programmed to birth and then sacrifice. The congregation shares in the horror and lets the healing stories come out.

An especially moving ritual was used to close both services, called an "Act of Committal into the Arms of a Loving God." Participants were invited to come forward and take pink rose petals from a bowl, and in memory of those who had died, to scatter them in a large basin of water, while observing silence. Occasionally alters may actually be continuing expressions of victims who have not survived.[83] The "Committal" can provide an opportunity for release of this burden and the energy it took to maintain that alter in the personality system.[84]

James Ward has outlined seven important general guidelines for healing rituals.[85] First, healing ritual invokes, engages, and confirms the goodness of God, of Creation, and of the human soul and body. Second, healing rituals must be voluntary. While this is true for all rituals of healing and remembrance for any kind of abuse, this is especially necessary with survivors who were forced to participate in abusive rituals of torture. Participants are free to leave, and/or to participate at whatever level they choose. This not only ensures safety, but effects healing by reversing the experience of forcible participation. Third, healing rituals are experienced in an open context of supportive relationship:

> God uses people to heal people. Participants need to overcome the anonymity of the ritual life of the community to develop loving and caring relationships which go beyond it. Anonymity as it is practiced in twelve-step programs is a very important part of the healing process. At some point, however, this anonymity becomes a barrier to integration in the everyday world. Developing relationships with non-survivors which involve mutual sharing and support helps the religious ceremonies to be more effective instruments of healing.[86]

Fourth, nothing is secret or hidden, unlike the survivor's experience of abuse in a climate of secrecy and theft. Fifth, healing rituals present an affirmation of life and a vision of unity and integrity—hope is affirmed in the possibility of a positive future, that "God's promised reign of justice and peace is made manifestly present" at the eucharistic table. Both the unity of the community, and of God who is embraced as three-in-one, are powerful symbols to the survivor with multiple personalities of the possibility of unity in diversity.[87] Multiplicity and wholeness are held together.

Finally, ritual can provide and perform a model for healing. "Christian ritual is healing because it rehearses and re-enacts our culture's central story of liberation. This story in both its Jewish and Christian forms involves a baby who survives the infanticidal designs of an evil king and grows up to be called and empowered as liberator of God's oppressed people."[88] Even Jesus' own experience of ritual torture on the cross offers survivors faith in an immanent God to whom nothing in their experience, however terrible, is unknown or unhealed. Resurrection is, for all of us, but especially perhaps for a survivor of ritual abuse, the symbol of promise and transformation even out of the most extreme torture and the designs of human evil.

Finally, Ward writes, "Healing rituals also strengthen the survivor's capacity to function in society."[89] Survivors are invited by their baptism to be full participants in the life and mission of the church. In this model, pain is not idolized and survivors are not held in a patronizing way as only wounded persons and victims to be cared for or tolerated. Like Elijah, after withstanding the ordeals of human persecution, raging windstorm, earthquake, and fire, survivors are not only visited by God in the still, small voice of sheer silence and peace, but are given a mission. This, too, becomes empowerment for healing and new life.

Conclusion

Healing can and does happen, but not usually without reliving terror and extreme pain. The ministers and communities who choose to say yes to these survivors, and to welcome them fully into their midst, are inviting an experience of challenge, even horror, perhaps, but also wonder and personal transformation for themselves as well as for the survivors. Being with survivors is faith-challenging. Their questions necessarily interrupt our assumptions and break into our security about our faith and what we thought we rationally knew to be true. To know a person with multiple personalities is to enter a twilight zone of formerly unimagined questions about the meaning of personality, identity, even soul, but also to become acquainted with the creativity and ingenuity of the human mind for survival. Ritual abuse survivors are perhaps the most extremely wounded, the most fragile, and at the same time some of the most courageous and tough survivors I have ever known. No one is capable of empathy for the crucified Christ more than they. They have known the experience of being lacerated on the jagged outer edges of reality and sanity and have somehow resisted and endured. To break bread with them, to enter into their world with them, is perhaps the most extraordinary journey anyone or any community can ever experience. They are living, breathing signs of the resurrection.

> I am the earthly host
> the humble ghost
> walls and corners
> of flesh and blood
> home now to those orphaned
> by the wayward course of my life.
>
> roof of stars,
> grass between my toes,
> yet the comforting
> floor of dirt beneath my feet
> seems always just beyond my footfall
> and my eyes,
> ever glancing upward for the shelter I seek there,
> become night blind
> and bedazzled
> by the distant multitude of souls gone before me
> the reflection of my insignificant offering
> chilling my hearth
> my hand falters at the woodpile
> and the wind of infinity,
> stealing through the uncaulked cracks
> of my foundation
> or windows left ajar for the scent of Earth's reassurances,
> sends my boarders
> huddling together in fear of eviction
> the host now insufficient for her suppliants
> needing in turn
> to restore myself with their offerings
> and fill the communion cup
> once more.

Let us raise our voices to the rafters,
embrace one another
in a ring around life's heartflame
sheltering it,
our backs to the wind,
so that it blazes up for a bit
warming our hope
and illuminating our faces
so that we may see our purpose
in each other's eyes.

I am the earthly host
the humble ghost
walls and corners
of flesh and blood
home now to those rescued
along the returning path of our lives.
—Caryn Stardancer[90]

THE CHURCH'S RESPONSE

The Pastor as "Wounded Healer"

To the question "How Can I Help?" we now see the possibility of a deeper answer than we might once have expected. We can, of course, help through all that we do. But at the deepest level we help through who we are. We help, that is, by appreciating the connection between service and our own progress on the journey of awakening to a fuller sense of unity.[1]

Our Own Woundedness

Henri Nouwen, in *The Wounded Healer*, recounts a story from the Talmud, which he suggests as a parable for the wounded minister:

Rabbi Yoshua ben Levi came upon Elijah the prophet while he was standing at the entrance of Rabbi Simeron ben Yohai's cave. . . . He asked Elijah, "When will the Messiah come?"

Elijah replied, "Go and ask him yourself."

"Where is he?"

"Sitting at the gates of the city."

"How shall I know him?"

"He is sitting among the poor covered with wounds. The others unbind all their wounds at the same time and then bind them up again. But he unbinds one at a time and binds it up again, saying to himself: 'Perhaps I shall be needed: if so I must always be ready so as not to delay for a moment.'" (Taken from the tractate Sanhedrin)

The Messiah, the story tells us, is sitting among the poor, binding his wounds one at a time, waiting for the moment when he will be needed. So it is too with the minister. Since it is his [sic] task to make visible the first vestiges of liberation for others, he must bind his own wounds carefully in anticipation of the moment when he will be needed. He is called to be the wounded healer, the one who must look after his own wounds but at the same time be prepared to heal the wounds of others.[2]

We are all wounded. Many of us are drawn to the work of healing because we understand being wounded from inside the experience. We are our own science experiments. We study pain "out there" in an (often unconscious) effort to transmute pain "in here." Often we learn about helping others as a way of healing ourselves.[3] Freud's suggestion that a strong desire to help others is rooted in childhood pain has been echoed by numerous others, including Karl Menninger[4] and Alice Miller.[5] At a perhaps more conscious level,

women who have been raped or battered, and who have received much healing support in their lives, sometimes decide to volunteer at women's crisis
agencies so that they can pass on what they were given and share their strength
with other victims.

Whatever the motivation, and however conscious, being a "wounded
healer" has both advantages and perils. The advantages are perhaps obvious: a
greater capacity for empathy, having been through a similar trauma; an insid-
er's or veteran's knowledge of systems and resources. The perils sometimes lie
in having *too much* empathy of an emotional quality, which leads to over-
involvement, overidentification, and carrying too much of the helpee's pain
vicariously until exhaustion and burnout set in.

A helper's own past traumas, fears, grief, and personal rage are often triggered by survivors' stories. It is very important to avoid overidentification
with the survivor or assuming that her experience and subsequent reactions
and feelings will be the same because it sounds so familiar. Sometimes the
helpee's story touches us at places that are still raw, and we find ourselves in
the middle of our own post-traumatic reactions. The boundaries become
blurred and our own wounds bleed again.

Pastors who find themselves working with survivors of violence and abuse
are, like therapists, subject to additional strain in the form of "vicarious" or
"secondary" traumatization.[6] First observed by professionals working with
Holocaust survivors, Vietnam veterans, and Southeast Asian refugees, this
second-hand traumatization shares many of the symptoms of actual abuse, especially over time. The experience of horror is contagious. Helpers including
clergy and lay religious counselors should *expect* the feelings of being helpless,
overwhelmed, and "de-skilled"[7] as a regular part of the challenge of the work,
and to know that it is a normal reaction even for experts with long experience.

Because of the stresses and the effects of second-hand or reactivated traumatization in working with survivors of violence, which are the rule and not
the exception, the importance of naming, reflecting upon, and seeking ongoing support for healing of one's own wounds cannot be overemphasized. Like
the Messiah in the Talmud story, we cannot be binding up the wounds of
others when our own bandages are falling off and we are bleeding and in pain.
If we think it is heroic to ignore our own pain, we must remember that if we
bleed to death, we will not be there to help anyone ever again. By attending
compassionately to our own stories and binding up our own wounds, we have
more compassion and skill to offer another survivor.

Burnout

Classic burnout is a syndrome common among individuals doing intensive
"people work." It consists of emotional exhaustion, or "compassion fatigue,"
combined with a tendency to dehumanize those who are supposed to be
helped by the work, and a feeling of reduced personal accomplishment.[8]

Signs and symptoms of burnout include fatigue, isolation, withdrawal, cynicism or a blaming attitude toward those to be helped, self-preoccupation, and suspiciousness, paranoia, and rigidity in thinking. Burnout can result in physical symptoms, including sleep disorders, frequent colds and flus, frequent headaches, and gastrointestinal problems. It can also spill over into marital and family conflict and tensions and irritability in social relationships.[9]

People are at high risk for burnout, according to experts, from a combination of environmental factors and ways in which the individual helper's temperament intersects with those conditions.[10] There is some suggestion that environmental factors matter the most: "Psychologically, burnout . . . represents a response to an intolerable work situation."[11] This is very significant for working with survivors of violence, which is in and of itself highly disturbing and stressful. A chronic situation of too much to do and not enough time to do it, constantly being in demand, lack of input on decisions and policies, conflict among coworkers, and lack of good communication with people in supervisory roles are all risk factors for burnout[12]—and all are frequent characteristics of pastoral ministry!

Needless to say, some times are more difficult in ministry than others. The situation needs to be assessed on an ongoing basis: If environmental supports are not sufficient, or if other stress factors are too great, the pastor should weigh carefully what her or his helping role can realistically be and not try to take on too much—which can lead to letting the survivor down, or depending on the work with the survivor to meet the pastor's own intimacy needs. Both situations ultimately revictimize the survivor.

Burnout is more likely in a situation where the helper feels powerless. Having a sense of impact and control may be the most significant factor in burnout.[13] In this sense, it has a strong kinship with trauma itself. This can heighten the normal, expectable dynamic of vicarious traumatization from the work with the survivor and weaken the pastor's response-ability.

While environmental factors are important, some personal factors enter into the picture as well.[14] Rather than paint a picture of people more at risk, as if to blame them for burning out, it may be instructive and have preventive value to describe those at lower risk for burnout, based on the research. (Of course, some factors are things that can be changed, and some are not.) Demographic predictors for higher resistance to burnout include being older (the advantages of more experience and perspective, knowing that changes don't happen overnight), being married and having children (even if family life is stressful, it gives balance and work isn't everything), having postgraduate training (which presumably includes some preventive education about self-care and burnout), and being black (because researchers suggest that strength of community, an often more honest and even confrontational style of communication, and a realistic experience of problems and pain because of discrimination and sometimes poverty all lend perspective and healthy realism).

Personality characteristics and habitual patterns of responding to stress also make a difference. Being assertive, being able to set limits, patience, humor, political savvy, flexibility, and initiative all help to mitigate burnout.[15] Sadly, many pastors feel "trapped and hostile" in relation to the church, feelings that over time are destructive to effective ministry.[16] When such a chemistry mixes with the survivor's traumatic history, laden as it is with her own experience of entrapment, terror, and rage, a great deal of harm can be unconsciously revisited on the survivor. A pastor may project the feelings that resonate with trauma onto the survivor and then unconsciously live out his or her agenda through the survivor's struggles. If the pastor cannot bring this tendency to consciousness and deal with it apart from the survivor, the survivor will be used—and thereby revictimized.

Beyond the legitimate altruistic motivations, everyone has other needs that are met as well by doing helping work. The more conscious and the more in balance these other needs are, the less likely the helper is to burn out. If the helping is being done primarily to assuage a sense of badness or guilt, or to gain approval, affection, and admiration, then it is being done at the survivor's expense. And this replicates her experience of victimization—having her own needs, even her most central core of bodily and spiritual integrity, discounted and overwhelmed by the aims of her perpetrator.

Spirituality for Wounded Healers

Dorothy McRae-McMahon writes:

> As we take our stand in the river, we may well wonder what lies ahead for us each day and each year. In our hands lie the bread and the wine and the water of the grace of baptism. When these precious elements were placed in my hands on the day of my ordination, I wondered if I would ever be worthy of carrying them. But as I broke the bread and offered the wine, I realized that the life I held would never be dependent on me or the strength or worthiness of my hands. A presence was always there in once-offered grace and freedom; it was simply named by me and claimed in thanksgiving by the people of God.[17]

If isolation is the single greatest risk for burnout and destructiveness, then as faithful ministers, both clergy and lay, we are blessed with a resource beyond what the secular literature offers. We do not have to be alone. Not only can we build networks for personal support and professional growth—we have a promise from God that we are not abandoned.

"Listen! I am standing at the door, knocking; if you hear my voice and open the door, I will come in to you and eat with you, and you with me" (Rev. 3:20). The Statement of Faith of the United Church of Christ begins and ends with the affirmation, "We are not alone. Thanks be to God."

We do not need to be fully professed contemplatives ourselves to enter into the contemplative realm. Several of my friends and I all keep our own variations on a personal altar or "spiritual work table." We write the names of people we want to hold in prayer on pieces of paper and leave them on the altar as a way of reminding ourselves and consciously intending that they will be held in God's care even during moments when we cannot be consciously remembering them. One friend also tears stories of terror and violence out of the newspaper and leaves them on her altar, saying, "I know this is too much for me to deal with, but God can hold it."

Daily prayer, wordless meditation, and quiet time just spent in God's presence, or more formal practices like reading the Daily Office or saying Morning Prayer, Vespers, or Compline are not indulgences in our compacted schedules. They are the assurances of God's presence and the balance points of quiet in our day that keep us effective as healers and bearers of the Good News.

Spirituality also means witnessing to the truth. For example, the Oakland Coalition of Congregations holds a regular Wednesday noon prayer vigil on the site of a murder that has taken place that week. By vigiling together with members of the neighborhood affected, the message is that no violent death will go unnoticed—or unprayed for. It is at once a political action and a spiritual devotion.[18]

Staying Effective

1. Keep the learning process alive. Read up on the issues affecting the person you are helping.

2. Be aware of class, race, and other cultural differences. The only assumption possible is to be aware that the other person's context and possibly a whole set of assumptions may be different from yours, until real (not imagined, hoped-for, or theoretical) common ground has been established. Learn about cultural differences; do not pigeonhole or assume that general cultural traits will apply to the person sitting in front of you. When in doubt about how to help, ask.

3. Cultivate the difficult art of *empathic detachment*. "This is not my story." This isn't the same as being selfish, callous, hardened, or jaded. It is essential.[19]

In detached concern there is the recognition that, in different ways, both distance and closeness can help people deal with the emotional demands of the helping relationship. By being close and concerned the provider sees the recipient as a fellow human being (instead of an anonymous statistic), has a more sensitive understanding of the problems that person is facing, and is personally motivated to help. On the other hand, by being distant and detached the caregiver appraises the problems objectively (instead of being blinded by personal biases and feelings), implements solutions in an orderly and rational way, and is straightforward in assessing their success (or failure). Thus, detachment and concern complement each other. . . .[20]

4. Boundaries are good for everybody.

5. Practice self-care:

• Eat well, sleep, and exercise. A young man entering a yoga retreat center was surprised by the monk's first question: "What do you eat?"[21] Body and spirit are one. If this seems obvious, simplistic, and dispensable, consider this: Ignoring the body's needs is not separate from the denigration of the body that underlies sexism and misogyny.

• Take time: Allow for some spaciousness in your day and in your life. Don't overschedule. Allow preparation and decompression from all interpersonal work, especially crisis work. Schedule in "unscheduled time" and keep it as you would any other appointment. And take time off! Compulsive work, even at work one loves, may be the signal that there is an underlying depression or anxiety that one is keeping at bay by staying too busy. This compulsivity is often reinforced by the specialness that is placed on having a religious calling or doing altruistic work (paid or volunteer). Diane Fassel writes: " 'Doing' religion workaholically is an assault on the very spirituality the church promises. How can you teach 'life and life more abundant' when you are working yourself to death?"[22]

• Assertiveness and direct, honest communication prevents frustrations from building up and prevents a feeling of being trapped. Regardless of a helper's basic temperament, invaluable skills can be learned through classes, counseling, or other resources. Survivors especially need to consider that this may be an area of difficulty and explore getting some support and training in this area.

• Don't try to heal yourself through counselees. Seek appropriate support—therapy, spiritual direction, pastoral consultation, and friendships—and seek it in more than one place (i.e., don't depend on a spouse or friend to be the sole support and confidant).

• Cry. (Do it on your own time and not counselees'—but do it!) One seminarian, in response to a class exercise on dealing with pain and grief, wrote: "Crying into a doll or stuffed animal helps a lot. When I was little and got sent to my room, I used to cry on the big head of my Raggedy Ann doll and leave the tear marks on her cheeks instead of mine."

• *Pray* for those you counsel, for *yourself*, and for the *community*.

6. Take time for theological reflection, both alone and in your study group. What does this person's story mean to you? What beliefs does it challenge? What new meanings are to be found? How is your faith affected? Deepened? Disturbed?

7. Be collegial: In addition to personal support, it is essential to seek appropriate *professional* support. This is as true for volunteers and lay religious counselors as for clergy. Join or create a peer group that can function as a forum for confidential, supportive, mutual reflection, concern, and also redirection and critique as needed. Two excellent models for this are (1) peer-led study groups in which members take turns presenting "cases," just as therapists and medical professionals might do in a case consultation group, or (2) a group of peers who meet together under the guidance of a paid consultant, perhaps a therapist or senior pastoral counselor with specific expertise in trauma and violence against women, to take turns presenting cases as in a case

seminar. Both models are an opportunity for theological praxis-reflection. The goal of both kinds of group is not only personal support, but focused study of specific cases. It is not only up to the pastor involved with the particular abuse survivor to come up with all the ideas for helping that person. Common traps—from which *no one* is exempt!—can be avoided.

The isolation of victims can flow over into a parallel process in which caregivers, including clergy, can become increasingly isolated. Recognize this as a danger unconsciously inherent in the work and stay committed to breaking down isolation. Isolation can lead to feelings of specialness, lapses in boundaries, and reabuse of the very person you're trying to help.[23]

The importance of an individualized network in which you have the utmost confidence for referrals, consultations, and support for yourself can not be overemphasized. Have a dog-eared, well-thumbed rolodex file. Update it often. Know personally the people in local agencies to whom you refer. Do not give in to the temptation of taking care of everything yourself. Being a "lone ranger" not only can be ineffective, it can lead to becoming abusive, because isolation avoids accountability, as described in chapter 6 above.

8. Create community. The educated and supportive community is important not only for the healing of survivors, but for the effectiveness of the pastoral helpers as well. The true purpose of such a healing community is not the alleviation of pain per se, much less the glorifying of suffering, but the restoring of wholeness and holiness through liberation, the discovery of a new vision—again and again refining each new vision of justice that comes with ever-deepening understanding.

Nouwen writes:

> No minister can save anyone. He can only offer himself as a guide to fearful people. Yet, paradoxically, it is precisely in this guidance that the first signs of hope become visible. This is so because a shared pain is no longer paralyzing but mobilizing, when understood as a way to liberation. When we become aware that we do not have to escape our pains, but that we can mobilize them into a common search for life, those very pains are transformed from expressions of despair into signs of hope.
>
> Through this common search, hospitality becomes community. Hospitality becomes community as it creates a unity based on the shared confession of our basic brokenness and on a shared hope. This hope in turn leads us far beyond the boundaries of human togetherness to Him who calls His people away from the land of slavery to the land of freedom. It belongs to the central insight of the Judaeo-Christian tradition, that it is the call of God which forms the people of God.
>
> A Christian community is therefore a healing community not because wounds are cured and pains are alleviated, but because wounds and pains become openings or occasions for a new vision.[24]

Beyond all of these qualities, which still may seem more a prescription for things to study and skills to acquire, there is a quality of which Ram Dass and Paul Gorman speak, which perhaps counters against burnout more than any other: the quality of being the Witness. The Witness is the corrective for the compulsive doer in each of us. The Witness observes our inner mixed motives and ego gratifications, which seem to complicate and frustrate our service to others. Rather than suppressing them in shame or allowing them to overwhelm us with guilt, the Witness notes how these things interfere and allows them to exist, while good things get done almost miraculously in the process. Being in the mind of the Witness, we cease to measure our helping work by tangible results—an almost certain prescription for burnout in a seemingly endlessly troubled world. We balance that kind of measuring with observing simply how we are rather than what we are doing, and by holding ourselves in compassion as much as those we are trying to help. They write:

> If we persevere, our identification with the Witness grows while our attachment to being the doer seems to fall away. Quite remarkably, moreover, we also notice that while our identification as the doer is falling away, much is still being accomplished. We're still setting about our work, perhaps even more productively. It's just that we're not so personally identified with it any more. We see that in this state we're less likely to be frustrated, to feel rejected, to doubt ourselves, to burn out. "The sage does nothing, but nothing is left undone."—Lao Tsu[25]

Summary

There are no pat answers and prescriptions for combatting the second-hand trauma of helping victims of violence. Simple formulas for "stress reduction" often ring false because one person's stress is another person's stress reliever. Rest may not be as essential as balance: balance of mind, body, and spirit; balancing activities that drain with activities that recharge. It is important to know ourselves, to know whether we are recharged by time with people (extravert) or by solitary quiet (introvert), and also to know that for some of us, this is also changeable.

Finally, it is important to discover within ourselves the mind of the Witness, that inner observer who can release us from overidentification with our work or with our notions of success. "It's not always our efforts that burn us out; it's where the mind is standing in relation to them. The problem is not the work itself but the degree of our identification with it."[26] By having the mind of the Witness, we gain perspective and freedom. Through both prayer and collegiality we interrupt the isolation that destroys our ministry and revictimizes those we want most to help.

Conclusion

> In the beginner's mind, there are many possibilities. In the expert's, there are few.
> —Suzuki Roshi

Nothing can prepare any of us to be helpers in a true emergency, and yet, in another sense, everything prepares us. There is a point at which all we have learned and studied, all we have developed at the level of theory, give way to intuition—and the guidance of the Spirit. This is not to say that all learning and experience go out the window! On the contrary, this prepares us to act wisely and constructively. Our skills "kick in" almost as if on automatic pilot. I believe the Spirit uses all the knowledge and ability we have. But in moments of fear and urgency, our intuition in partnership with the Spirit may respond better than our conscious, careful intellect would ever predict. Perhaps above all this openness to being Spirit-led when the true emergency or crisis arises is the best protection against burnout, cynicism, and fatigue.

The greatest emergency in my life did not come in working with battered women, but in El Salvador. My husband and I were involved with a ministry of accompaniment with church leaders in El Salvador who had received death threats. The paramilitary death squads, who were known to be linked to police and military forces funded by our own government, were reluctant to harm North Americans. It would incur too much negative publicity. The only time military funding to El Salvador had been seriously questioned by the U.S. Congress was in the aftermath of the killing of four North American church-women. They were not willing to repeat that mistake. So we believed that Salvadorans in the company of North Americans were also less likely to be abducted to be tortured or murdered. A small group of us were spending ten days accompanying the Lutheran Bishop Medardo Gomez as he went on his pastoral missions into the countryside. On the particular day in question, we were celebrating the first anniversary of a repopulation village called Panchimilama—a village that had been joyfully and defiantly reclaimed by returning displaced persons after being driven out by government bombings a few years before. We hiked arduously down into the ravine in which the village was nestled, following the bishop who galloped easily down the steep path at breakneck speed with the help of his walking stick. The bishop baptized eight babies, and after the service of worship, there was an outdoor festival of speeches, music, and firecrackers. A dance was planned for that night. People were nervous because there had been reports that soldiers had been seen in the area, and it was not unknown for grenades to be thrown down into such ravines, or for such villages to be shelled at any time. Nevertheless, the celebration was grand and joyful.

Three of the five of us stayed that night for the dance, but my husband and I and two other North American women decided to go back out with the bishop before sundown. I wasn't feeling very well and was actually giving less thought in that moment to sticking with the bishop than I was to the real bed waiting miles away in the Lutheran guest house in the capital.

When we finally made it back up the trail to the roadside, we discovered that the van meeting us was not there. We waited for a long time, our hopes of getting out of the area before dark slowly dwindling away. Finally, the van came as the last red in the sky was fading to black. We were nervous about being stopped, nervous about the rumors of military in the area. We were unusually quiet, and the driver took us very fast over the bumpy, desolate rural road.

About halfway to San Salvador, our worst fears were realized. We spotted green uniforms behind the trees at the side of the road and knew an encampment was nearby. Still, we hoped to drive on past. A few moments later, our van was surrounded by soldiers. We were ordered out of the van at gunpoint. I hummed a hymn very softly on the way out of the van and then became frightened that it might somehow seem suspicious to the soldiers and stopped. I felt stupid and useless. The soldiers appeared to be very young—teenagers— and at least two of them seemed possibly to be high on drugs. Even the most absurd details seemed surreal in the moment: We prayed that the live chicken we were carrying in the back didn't squawk and startle them into shooting. The soldiers went through the van, looking through our knapsacks, rattling a box of tissues and asking what was in it. We had been warned not to carry books, although we probably did have a Bible along. The soldiers openly accused us of being with the guerrillas, and kept asking, "Where is the propaganda? Where is the communist propaganda?" My husband and the two women kept showing them our U.S. passports and explaining that we had been at a church service. I let them do most of the talking since their Spanish was much better, and I actually responded in English to questions to underscore the fact that some of us were North Americans. The soldiers kept looking at the passports and acting as if they didn't know what they were.

Through all this, I took up a place next to Bishop Gomez, my arm around his shoulders. Under my hand I could feel him trembling like a leaf, although his face was stern and impassive. He had been captured once before and had been tortured and interrogated. I remembered that and held on tighter. I looked at the guns that were trained on us and determined that I could at least get in the way. If they killed Medardo, they'd have to take a North American down too. I remember thinking how very small and narrow the muzzle of a machine gun was—I had imagined it somehow to be much bigger.

And then I looked up at the sky. The moon was full, with just a few clouds in the sky. Over the branches of the trees, it made a beautiful milky light. Still feeling Medardo's shoulders under my arm, I suddenly felt tremendous peace and calm. I didn't feel "safe" from the bullets of the soldiers, but I felt that whatever happened, it would be all right—that the Holy Spirit was with us. It was a moment filled with grace, the "peace that passes all understanding."

I remember very little after that. Somehow the soldiers decided to let us go, and we all piled back into the van. Somewhat later down the road we were stopped again, but that time we did not have to get out, and we made it back to the capital, quiet and shaken, but tremendously relieved to be alive.

I still don't know how much I helped in that situation and how much I hindered. I asked myself again and again if I did the right things (a common response). But I knew two things: first, that the outcome of that situation might well have been very different for Medardo had we not decided to go back with him in the van. If he had not had North Americans with him, he might well have been abducted that night.

Second, I had wondered and worried whether I would be level-headed in an emergency or whether I would fall to pieces. I had been in risky situations before, both in El Salvador and, years before, when I was operating a program for street people. But would I be reliable and helpful in a true emergency, a situation of terror? I still do not know if all my choices that night were the best ones. But I also know that I didn't fall to pieces.

I know enough about trauma to understand that much of what I experienced that night, and how I remember it now, was a function of the typical human response to trauma—the sense of time being frozen, the vividness of every visual image, the moon, the chickens, the barrels of the guns. The sense of calm was, in part, a function of dissociation. My feelings were suspended while my mind was alert and clear and focused on my task—to protect Medardo.

There was one very important feature, however, that distinguished the experience from pure trauma—the fact that I had chosen to be there, knowing full well that this scenario or some variation could happen. Because the situation was in some sense chosen and prepared for, we did not feel completely helpless and overwhelmed. It was the difference between involuntary suffering and voluntary risk. (Of course, had the situation gone on longer, had we been held in captivity, it is questionable how much this original sense of volition would have overcome the experience of trauma.) I was also in community. The power of being in a group, as opposed to being isolated, mitigated the experience of helplessness.

Is there a difference, in a moment of trauma, between the balm of a dissociative response and the benediction of the Holy Spirit? When I reflect on my experience in El Salvador, I find that I do not have to choose between viewing myself as being in a traumatic thinking state, which I certainly was, and viewing God's grace as active. My faith is that both were true and perhaps flowed together. Perhaps every battered woman, every molested child, is surrounded by the wings of the Spirit, which cushion the psychic blows and give her enough peace to "keep on keeping on," to survive.

In holding fast to Medardo, in surrendering myself to the decision to take my stand with him, I experienced calm in the midst of terror and the benediction of the Holy Spirit. I faithfully believe that this is available to us all, and that we can enter into the deeply wounded places of people's lives with the assurance that we are not alone. Grace gathers up all our skills, all our knowledge, all our experience, and blesses them with the added gifts of intuition and peace.

Ministry with Violent Men

This chapter is not about monsters. It is about ordinary men, but ordinary men who have learned that violence is necessary to their survival. They have come to believe that the only way to have the power of choice, action, and self-determination is to exert power over others. Whether they are rapists, batterers, or perpetrators of other forms of violence against women, they also believe at some level that it is *women* who are responsible for their well-being, satisfaction, and even survival, and that they must overpower women and establish and maintain authority and control in order to get their needs met. Beneath the surface in most of these men is a mixture of fear, hatred, and utter (unacknowledged) dependency on women.

The line between perpetrators of violence against women and other men is thin and indistinct. Paul Kivel, in his book for men entitled *Men's Work*, writes:

> When I began this work in 1979, there was a rape crisis movement, an antipornography movement, and a battered women's movement. The male activists supporting these movements fluctuated between believing that each kind of violence was a separate pathological category . . . and believing that all men contributed to the problem. . . . In theory we were supportive. In our lives, however, we were ambivalent. Sometimes we said we were completely different from the sleazy strangers in overcoats who lurked in the dark alleys. This is the type of man who rapes, we thought. At other times we blurred all distinctions and lumped men together as bad and oppressive. In either case, we distanced ourselves from men so we could feel less guilty about ourselves and more self-righteous and angry about them.
>
> In 1979 I thought I knew all about men and violence. But as I worked with incest offenders and batterers, as well as hundreds of men in workshops, it became harder for me to tell the men apart. The batterers and sexual offenders were not very different from the "ordinary" men we encountered in public workshops. Not only that, the ordinary men in our workshops turned out to be much more violent than I would ever have assumed. In other words, the offenders were extraordinarily ordinary by any standard I could devise, and the ordinary men were extraordinarily violent.[1]

All men are socialized, to greater or lesser degrees, about what it means to be men. Oakland Men's Project calls it the "Act Like a Man" Box (see Table 2).[2] Men are not only indoctrinated into the beliefs represented by the "Box,"

TABLE 2: ACT LIKE A MAN	
Men . . .	*Men are . . .*
yell at people	aggressive
have no emotions	responsible
get good grades	mean
stand up for themselves	bullies
don't cry	tough
don't make mistakes	angry
know about sex	successful
take care of people	strong
don't back down	in control
push people around	active
can take it	dominant over women

but they are boxed in by it. Its confining limits cut away parts of men's humanity and deprive them of the full human range of feeling, experience, and happiness, just as a corresponding "Act Like a Lady" box confines women.

All men receive this socialization but not all men develop the will or the capacity to cross the line of physical violence. This has become the subject of considerable debate among those who work with victims as well as with perpetrators. Characteristics of perpetrators of particular forms of violence against women have been discussed in the preceding chapters. One common characteristic, however, seems to be the externalizing of needs. Underneath the need to impose domination through physical and sexual violence and exploitation is most often a deeper need in the abuser's psyche: the need for security and a (largely unconscious) panicky sense of threat to his very survival.[3] A woman's independence, or lack of interest or ability to meet a man's emotional, physical, or sexual needs, may trigger a deep and infantile rage, which is then acted upon. A batterer, for example, is most likely to use violence when he perceives, correctly or incorrectly, that the woman has defied his authority or has denied him services.[4] Many men do not even go as far as using physical violence but nevertheless assert their authority in other abusive ways. Physical violence forces compliance from a woman when persuasion, silence, passivity, or seduction fail. Self-worth becomes confused in the violent man with being able to extract compliance from a woman (or child) who, he believes, should be servicing his needs. Men's socialization to appear strong and invulnerable paradoxically works against their ability to express legitimate needs and desires.

Men's socialization to suppress their feelings also results in a "funnel effect" in which all negative feelings tend to funnel into anger and rage. Sorrow, fear, loneliness, and anxiety are banished as unmanly, but anger and rage are encouraged and even held up as heroic by the culture. The impulse when confronted with any discomfort or problem, then, is to get it under control as quickly as possible. And all too often this means controlling a woman who, in the perpetrator's mind, comes to stand in for the solution to his need, whether that need is for sexual gratification, physical care, or emotional comfort.

Alcohol or drug abuse, a family history of childhood abuse or witnessing a father being abusive, exposure to large amounts of media violence, and peer pressure (as in the case of a gang rape) can all serve to disinhibit or normalize violence against women. Most violent offenders will characteristically use minimization ("I didn't hurt her that badly"), denial ("She's exaggerating/lying"), and externalization of blame ("She was coming on to me all night," "She bruises easily," "It's her—she knows how to push my buttons," or "If you knew how much pressure I'm under at work . . . ").[5] However, the root cause is always power, control, and domination as a defense against helplessness, pain, or need and a social system that teaches men that they have a right to maintain authority over women—especially "their" women.

Right and Wrong Kinds of Help

Differing theoretical understandings of why men violate women inevitably result in differing theories for how to stop male violence. These methods include efforts to reeducate and rehabilitate men focusing on behavioral self-management techniques, deeper psychotherapeutic attempts to heal childhood wounds presumed to be at the root of violent behavior, more politically-oriented group models that both support and confront in a tough-love style reminiscent of twelve-step meetings, and criminal justice solutions that provide maximum containment and monitoring.

These methods are successful to varying degrees, but the shocking truth is that most evidence points to *a very poor statistical prognosis for nearly all forms of male violence against women.*[6] When weighing safety of both past and future victims together with the likely outcomes of most forms of treatment, it is advisable in almost every case to develop a rehabilitation plan that includes some form of *containment* and monitoring as well as education and/or therapy. Whenever possible, it is essential that past victims be kept informed of the whereabouts and the progress of the offender—particularly if he has been jailed and is to be released. In cases of battering or other family violence where the perpetrator is allowed to remain with the partner or family, it is also essential to ask for participation by the victim(s) in the treatment plan of the offender, and for periodic reports on their own sense of safety and his progress. Similarly, counselors and group facilitators should be in close contact with probation officers or others involved with monitoring the offender's behavior. Though difficult, a balance can be achieved between appropriate confidentiality and close contact with authorities—these are not mutually exclusive.[7] Without this kind of monitoring and cross-checking, with both victims and other helping professionals, the typical minimization and denial of offenders can give counselors and group facilitators a dangerously unrealistic picture of the offender's actual progress and perpetuate serious risk for

women. And even with monitoring and cross-checking there is danger. Sometimes monitoring in and of itself can convey a false sense of safety to women.
Programs fail to make lasting change in perpetrators more often than not. The
only *absolutely* safe containment method is jail.

This is a difficult issue for church people. Clergy and religious professionals
usually have a view of human beings that is optimistic. Classical Christian doctrine teaches that no human being is beyond God's redemption: We are all sin-
ners, but our sins are redeemed by God's saving action in Jesus Christ, so,
although human beings are unworthy and undeserving by themselves, God's free
grace is poured out for the redemption of all who believe. More liberal theological
views may deemphasize the sinfulness of humanity, pointing to God's "original
blessing" of humanity in creation and expanding God's gift of grace to all, regardless of what they precisely believe. In either understanding, it is difficult for
modern Christians to take action to limit and contain a person on the basis of
what feels like a harsh, cold clinical assessment of "poor prognosis." Whether the
offender is a child sexual abuser, a clergyman who has sexually exploited a parishioner, or a batterer, to name just a few examples, a great deal of emotional
energy and material resources are poured into an effort to help him avoid containment. "What he needs is counseling. . . ." "What he needs is our understanding and forgiveness. . . ." "What he needs is our love. . . ."

In my view this trend presents two serious problems. First, while it is certainly true that perpetrators of violence against women need understanding,
this is often misused. The understanding needed is a critical and complete understanding of the nature and extent of his abuse and his history, not an expression of sympathy that helps him to excuse his behavior on the basis of his
own woundedness. Understanding should lead toward requiring full accountability for his actions and whatever rehabilitation is possible. Counseling also
needs to include more than a "tour of excuses," from alcohol and drugs to
childhood abuse. It needs to include taking full responsibility for the choices
he has now and a critical examination of the larger issues of men's socialization and tolerance for violence. This is most effectively done in groups of
peers (discussed more fully below). It must be done in conjunction with safety
monitoring and some form of containment. All too often, people in the
church end up recommending the wrong kind of help out of misplaced sympathy or a lack of understanding of the true benefits of the toughness needed
if any real reform is to take place.

Research has shown that arrest may be the most effective single deterrent to
the recurrence of abuse.[8] Concerning child sexual abusers, Roland Summit
has written:

> I believe there is a therapeutic benefit to criminal conviction for crimes against children,
> whether the crime is committed within the privacy of the family or on the street, and
> whether the child is four years old or fifteen. With conviction, the primary responsi-
> bility of the offender is clearly defined, bringing what Giaretto called "the hard edge of

society" against the man rather than the child. Conviction also challenges the power of the offender to act as if he is above the law and immune from the discomfort of the child. . . . For habitual child molesters, there is little optimism for treatment but all the more need for effective sentencing and societal controls.[9]

This is equally applicable for rapists, batterers, and other repeat violent offenders. External controls are both therapeutic and necessary.[10] Helping an offender to avoid legal consequences is not helping him.

Second, it is all too often the case that the church's sympathy and resources are mobilized for the abuser, while the pain, fear, and very serious safety needs of the victim(s) are downplayed or largely ignored. Something deep in our psyche as Christians derives more joy and satisfaction out of trying to redeem an offender than trying to protect and vindicate a victim. Of course there are the parables of the lost sheep and the prodigal son, and of course there is much rejoicing in heaven when someone lost is truly found. But there are also the immediate needs of the abused that must be balanced with this. Jesus' ministry was also one of healing the injured and bringing justice to the oppressed. The parable of the good Samaritan, which teaches the importance of caring—even extravagantly—for a victim of violence, surely stands beside the parable of the lost sheep in importance.

It is not only Christians who have a hard time standing with the victim rather than the perpetrator. We do not want to hear the truth spoken by victims. It breaks down our own denial that such things could happen to us or to our wives or daughters. Perpetrators speak the lies we want to hear: "It wasn't really as bad as she is making it out to be. . . . " "She really wanted it. . . . " "It's all in her mind. . . . " "It never happened. . . . "

All the foregoing chapters have clearly taken a stand with victims and set forth the dynamics of various kinds of abuse, as well as making an appropriate pastoral response to and with victims. This chapter, however, is about making a pastoral response *to* and *with the perpetrator*. How is this possible while also standing in solidarity with victims? It is my position that it is not helpful to an offender to sympathize or collude with his violence, or to be taken in by his minimization and denial. Nor is it honoring the moral complexity of the situation to merely say, "He's a victim, too, in his own way." Prior to any other pastoral response, the violence must be named and the perpetrator held responsible.

My belief is that beneath the surface of self-justification and compulsive arrangement of his life to make further violence possible, the offender wants to be stopped. What he needs and at the deepest level longs for is "holding," as the sensitive parent holds a very small child who is disintegrating and lashing out in temper. The holding called for in such an instance is not merely soothing, but strong and containing. The violent person, of whatever age, needs the security of a container stronger than himself to keep both him and the rest of the world safe from his uncontrollable destructiveness. Appropriate containment must precede any attempt at rehabilitation, because a person who cannot control his violence must first have the experience of being controlled from outside before he can eventually internalize and learn ways to control himself. Sadly, the evidence seems to point to an inability for many perpetrators ever to internalize this containment, possibly because they are too deeply damaged at too early an age.[11] The development window of opportunity has been closed by too much scar tissue, preventing the man from ever being fully repaired later in life.

Given the complexity of all these considerations, particularly the ever-present need for safety of both past and potential future victims, combined with the high level of manipulation and denial which is not only common but, indeed, predictable and *characteristic* in offenders, it is *unsafe and unethical* for pastors to undertake the rehabilitation counseling of offenders—except as an adjunct to other specialized offender treatment—unless the pastor him- or herself has such specialized training and is involved in an appropriate agency or clinical practice that specializes in treatment of offenders. The appropriate and very needed role for pastors is supportively to assess and refer men who are violent—and to report them to law enforcement or child protective services as soon as reportable offenses are discovered. Clergy can then provide ongoing support to reinforce the man's participation in an appropriate program.

How to Recognize an Appropriate Program to Help Men Who Abuse

The watchwords for pastoral intervention with men who violate women (and girls, boys, and other men) are *assess* and *refer*. This requires good skills not only in recognizing patterns of abuse (the assessment piece), but also in recognizing appropriate programs for offender treatment and reeducation.

Good programs for rehabilitation of offenders may use a variety of formats and a variety of theoretical perspectives (and corresponding jargon), but they have some things in common that are essential for effective treatment:

First, they should have a philosophy that places the safety of victims (both in the past and potentially in the future) as the first priority, and that acknowledges stopping violence as the primary goal. Other goals, such as personal healing of the offender, or repair of couple or family relationships, may or may not be included (or, in the case of couple or family reunification, even appropriate), but safety must at all times be the primary focus.

Safety automatically means certain limitations and exceptions to client confidentiality. As in all counseling programs, but particularly with a population of known offenders, the duty to warn potential victims of harm is of paramount ethical concern. Good programs should have:

• guidelines for assessing when the duty to protect or duty to warn any potential victim(s) arises;

• procedures for notifying the potential victim(s) (relevant in cases of familial or relationship violence) that threats of violence will be disclosed to them promptly, and for arranging appropriate means of contacting them if necessary (without implying that this procedure in and of itself will keep women safe);

- guidelines for police notification
- a policy addressing whether it is an ethical or legal necessity to advise clients that threats will be disclosed to the potential victim
- a repertoire of strategies that the counselor and/or the group can undertake to dissuade or prevent the threatened behavior (which is not a substitute for warning or taking protective action on behalf of the victims)
- guidelines for implementing the obligation to protect potential victims of dangerous clients other than providing a timely warning
- a review of the law of the state(s) where the program provides services to assure that internal procedures comply with the law
- a mechanism for review and approval of these procedures by local relevant women's agencies (e.g., battered women's shelter, rape crisis center, women's crisis support, etc.)[12]

Practitioners and agencies should also be asked about their intervention philosophy. The following are the basic minimum elements of a fully qualified program's philosophy:[13]

Program Philosophy:

- clearly defines violence (whether between strangers, acquaintances, or family members) as a crime
- holds the perpetrator accountable and requires that he take personal responsibility for his violence, both physical and emotional (for example, the violence is not blamed on the victim's behavior, dress, or supposed provocation, on peer pressure, work stress, a history of childhood abuse, or alcohol or drugs)
- in cases of violence within a relationship, stopping the abuse is the priority and major focus, not personal or relationship issues. Safety, not keeping a couple or family together, is the goal of treatment
- recognizes violence as an issue of power,[14] and understands that male violence against women, and the presumption of men's right to assert authority over them, are both learned and socially sanctioned[15]
- is committed to ending violence against women and, to that end, networks with local women's crisis agencies, is responsive to their concerns, and is engaged in community coalitions for violence prevention and relevant political action.

Intervention Strategies:

- Given the potential for lethality and recidivism, the victim's (and children's) safety must always be the first priority. Potentially dangerous interventions such as couple and/or family counseling for cases of intrafamilial or ongoing relationship violence are therefore excluded until the violent behavior has been demonstrably stopped (at least one to two years without offending).[16]
- The program teaches that violence is part of a pattern of coercive control that includes physical, emotional, sexual, and economic abuse. Addressing

this pattern of learned and socially sanctioned behaviors is the foundation of all program intervention.

• The program holds the perpetrator accountable for the violence—the perpetrator must accept the personal responsibility and consequence for that behavior and for changing it.

• Stopping the violence is the priority and major focus, not other personal or relationship issues, e.g., focusing on keeping a couple or family together or repairing family communication.

• The intake should include the abuser's family history, emphasizing the occurrence of violence, substance abuse history, other forms of violence and coercion used in the past, and an assessment of current level of dangerousness. Due to perpetrators' characteristic minimization and denial, sources other than the perpetrator should be consulted, including the victim(s), police, and probation.

• The initial intake may be the only time the perpetrator is seen, since the dropout rate in noncourt-mandated situations is high. For this reason, the initial intake should include information about what violence is and present beginning techniques for recognizing and stopping violence, such as "time-outs" for batterers (see below).

• One year of weekly sessions is minimal, and more should be made available through referrals if the program itself does not go beyond a year.

• Victim input and accountability to victims should be part of data-gathering, assessment, and ongoing treatment. In cases of relationship violence, the partner or family members should be contacted regularly to advise them of progress, to inquire about their perceptions of improvement or lack of improvement, and/or to warn them of potential increased danger at any time. The partner or family should be clearly informed that participation in a program does not guarantee that the abuser will be nonviolent, and should be given information about whom to call in case of recurring abuse and about resources in the community that they can turn to for assistance.

• Components of the program should include education about gender-role socialization, the nature of violence and the dynamics of abuse, and its consequences on both women and children, as well as "anger management"/ behavior modification techniques such as time-outs, relaxation, cognitive behavior modification techniques such as assertiveness and empathy training, anger management, and positive self-talk. Anger management programs by themselves do not create effective change.[17]

• A same-gender men's peer group model is recommended as the most effective treatment modality. Because violence is a learned and socially sanctioned response to anger and stress, the best method for change involves peer-group unlearning of violence, resocialization, and ongoing mutual support for nonrepetition of violent behavior. This peer support counteracts the pervasive societal pressure to behave violently.

• Referrals should be made to substance abuse programs for concurrent treatment, and clients should be required to attend the program substance-free.

• The program should have the right to determine an offender ineligible for treatment, and in the case of court-mandated counseling, the program should have the right and the responsibility to report noncompliance or nonimprovement and terminate the offender's participation in the program. The program should not collude with the perpetrator in helping him to avoid personal or legal consequences of his violence (up to and including incarceration).

• The offender and any partner or family member(s) should be informed about the limitations of the program, the process of treatment and rules of the program, the reporting policies of the program in the case of repeated violence or noncooperation, and rules and limitations of confidentiality.

• Staff training should include specific knowledge about forms of violence against women and children; the association of violence with sexism, racism, classism, heterosexism, and other power imbalances and systemic oppressions that promote violence; substance abuse issues; abuse dynamics; relevant laws and procedures of the legal system, especially where the program operates; and detailed, specific knowledge of their legal and ethical responsibilities to protect victims and potential victims, and to report child abuse, elder abuse, and dependent adult abuse.

• Provisions should be made for the treatment of monolingual, non-English-speaking perpetrators, and age-appropriate and culturally sensitive services for groups such as youth, the aging, gay men, lesbians, ethnic minorities, or any other groups that have particular needs relating to the program.

Regardless of theoretical orientation, good programs are committed to re-education. They recognize that violence is not a problem of "a few bad men over there," but a problem of all men and therefore all men's responsibility—although not all men use physical violence. Violence is a learned response, both through personal family of origin experiences and through the larger experiences of socialization to "act like a man." No man entirely escapes this socialization. Programs that focus *only* on the personal, intrapsychic dimensions of a man's violent behavior, or on specific behavioral techniques for managing anger and stress,[18] and do not address the larger social root causes of male violence, will not go far enough to help the man make lasting changes that can withstand the continual bombardment of society's messages of misogyny and emotionally constricting roles for men. For example, in batterers' treatment: "The use of anger control techniques with batterers is problematic when battering is framed exclusively as an anger problem, when the issues of dominance and control of women by men are ignored in treatment, and when practitioners fail to address societal reinforcements for battering."[19]

Good programs also scrupulously monitor themselves for collusion with perpetrators' defenses and self-justification. It is easy for male counselors, in spite of years of training and experience, to be pulled into minimization and denial with the conscious intent of building rapport, empathizing, or maintaining a counselor's unconditional positive regard. Some examples of subtle collusion include avoiding words like "batterer" or "offender," agreeing with offenders that the victim had a share in provoking the violence, or bending over backwards to regard their clients as victims also. Says Barbara Hart: "It is true that some batterers have been the victims of crime. Some were abused as children. Some are oppressed by racism. Some have experienced class prejudice. These injustices do not compel batterers to thereafter inflict violence upon their partners. But often they conclude that, having been wronged, this fact somehow pardons their own wrongful conduct toward partners."[20] She goes on to show how counselors identify and bond with this misconception of men as victims:

> *Pro-feminist men who feel deprived of a complete range of emotions by this patriarchal culture often identify this limitation as victimization, which to some corresponds to the oppression of women in a sexist society. In concluding that the oppressions are equivalent, they forget that they can choose* to learn new behaviors and ways to express emotions. Women cannot abandon the oppressions of sexism. . . .
>
> *Clearly pro-feminist men may be discriminated against for adopting anti-sexist politics and conduct. . . . But the poor treatment pro-feminist men receive is not victimization. It is punishment for class desertion, which may be avoided by publicly embracing class identity once again. And pro-feminist men can also choose how much power to give up. Changes can be private, discreet and related only to internal family matters—minimizing the risk that the system will penalize them for breaking ranks. Pro-feminist men can always disregard progressive practices, abandon pro-feminist identification and recapture male entitlement. . . .*
>
> *So when batterers repeatedly assert they are victimized, it is not surprising that many pro-feminist counselors begin to believe them, and to identify themselves as victims of retaliation by a sexist society. These feelings encourage alliances between batterers and pro-feminist men that minimize the batterers' responsibilities for their violence. Counselors must be aware of the ease with which these alliances can form and must help batterers understand that they are not victims of their battered partners.*[21]

Peer Group Format and "Time-outs"

A peer group format, by itself or in addition to individual counseling, is indicated as probably the most effective method of addressing issues of socialization and peer pressure, and providing a forum for both support and needed confrontation.[22] A clinical or therapeutic approach in and of itself can collude with male violence by overemphasizing individual pathology and avoiding the larger root causes of male violence that all men share to some degree.

The peer group format is especially helpful in moving through three phases of work:[23]

The first stage is stopping violent behavior. Groups join together in unlearning violence by recognizing the signs of impending abuse as well as minimization and denial, and then by learning concrete tactics for changing behavior. Men can help each other by identifying and confronting resistance and avoidance tactics in groups (much as in twelve-step groups). A facilitator serves to notice collusion with violence, to ensure that the agenda is not derailed, and together with more senior class members to point out avoidance strategies such as debating, sidetracking, rationalizing, or "batter-babbling"— justifying or even getting satisfaction from talking about their violence.

Men in groups at this stage can also encourage and support one another as they begin to learn strategies for keeping themselves safe (in batterers' programs, for example, learning about taking a "time-out"—see Table 3).

Reenactments are also used in some approaches: for example, where they came to identify a critical moment when they could have chosen not to use violence. Alternative actions can then be identified and rehearsed.[24] Such an approach keeps the responsibility for the violence squarely with the man, while supporting him in finding alternatives.

Once violence is controlled for a period of time, the men can enter a second phase of work, learning to replace aggression and acting out with genuine communication and nonviolent assertion of needs. Reeducation is necessary in this phase as well, to replace assumptions about having authority over women and expectations of receiving services from them with new assumptions of self-responsibility and self-care and the skills and capacities to reinforce these new assumptions. Men discover that they can provide care for themselves and each other. This phase of work involves learning intimacy with other men, thus relieving the unrealistic expectations that women will provide all of men's emotional and other needs.

A final phase of work, absent from many programs but extremely useful in solidifying the gains of the previous phases, is reaching out to the wider community and participating in community service and education. Here men train as advocates to assist in the work with new men in the program and also become committed to social change through public speaking, men's hotline work, and other educational work.[25]

This model also assumes male facilitation and leadership, in close cooperation with and with close monitoring by related women's agencies (for example, battered women's shelters for batterers' programs and rape crisis centers for rapists' programs).[26] There are concerns about the appropriateness of all-male facilitation versus a male-female cocounseling team. The risk involved with all-male facilitation is unwitting collusion, as described above.[27] The risk of male-female cofacilitation is "perpetuating the model of women as 'co-' "[28] or, in other words, perpetuating the stereotype of women as nurturing men and carrying the role of social and emotional coach, roles that men need to learn with each other.

There is another risk associated with female facilitation of offender programs. Sometimes, the reason for a woman facilitator is explained as helping the men to cultivate respect and empathy for women. The risk involved with this is perpetuating a myth of easy empathy for women. Sometimes programs

TABLE 3: A TOOL FOR BATTERERS: TAKING A TIME-OUT:[29]

A "time-out" or "cool-down" is essential in batterers' unlearning of violence, and potentially has applications to some other forms of male violence as well. It involves the following steps, which are simple to learn and can be practiced ahead of time:

1. Paying attention to warning signals of your violence. For many men, the emotion of anger is not easily identified, but physical signs may be noticed: heart pounding; tightness in arms, head, chest, or throat; breathing becoming more shallow; feeling ignored, abandoned, cornered, desperate. These are the warning signs. Learning about your own, individual warning signs allows you to recognize when you are about to be abusive.

2. State your need for a "time-out." As *soon* as you feel the warning sign begin, take a time-out. Tell your partner "I'm beginning to feel angry," "I'm going to take a time-out," "I'll be back and check in with you in _____ " (state the amount of time you feel you need in order to be able to be calmer, more objective, and able both to communicate your feelings and ideas and to listen to the other person's feelings and ideas).

3. As soon as you have said this, *leave.* Do not debate the time-out. Go for a walk or a run. You may also want to call someone who you believe will support your intention to remain nonviolent, or call a men's hotline. When you call someone, you are committing yourself to change in a new and powerful way. *Do not drive, drink alcohol, or take drugs* while you are doing a time-out. Remember that the purpose of taking the time-out is to calm down and clear your thoughts, *not* to punish your partner or strategize for when you return. Return when you said you would, or call and say you need another specified length of time.

4. After the time-out, you have three choices: (1) Drop it. You may discover during and after the time-out that you are no longer upset or concerned about what triggered your anger. (2) Put it on hold: You may need more time to think and talk with someone objective. Suggest putting the subject on hold for a specified amount of time. (3) Discuss the problem if you feel you can communicate nonviolently, and you are ready really to listen. *Remember: if you start to feel angry again, you can take another time-out.*

Note: It is a good idea to prepare with your partner for taking a time-out before you actually need to take one. If this technique comes as a surprise to her, it can feel like an abandonment or another form of manipulation or abuse. Explain the technique, indicate your commitment to using it in order to remain nonviolent, and practice so that when an angry moment comes it will not seem awkward or strange.

---

have even been proposed in which offenders, such as rapists, meet survivors in order to gain some perspective or to begin to understand how they feel. This seems of little clinical value to me in most cases, because the act of perpetrating is already so dissociated from any truly relational state with another person, that such a confrontation may be dramatic at the time but

will not get beneath the thick layer of denial and dissociation that a perpetrator experiences in the moment of abusing. If perpetrators were capable
of feeling such empathy as readily as to be changed by one encounter
with survivors, they would not perpetrate in the first place. It is difficult
even for nonoffenders, particularly men, to identify with victims—easier
to feel angry than terrified, strong than trapped, choosing than resisting, gaining rather than simply enduring.[30] It is easier to feel in control than controlled.

Barbara Hart writes:

> *Counseling must not undertake to engage batterers in empathy for battered women.*
> *It would take years of counseling and accountability for batterers to achieve empa-*
> *thy with the women they have violated. To suggest that empathy is easily achievable*
> totally trivializes the tyranny experienced by battered women. *Thus, although we*
> *believe it is important for counselors to empathize with battered women, it does not*
> *follow that a goal of batterer counseling or educational groups should be empathy*
> *by the batterer with the battered women or the individual woman he violated.*[31]
> (emphasis mine)

While I do believe that the goal of all long-term counseling is insight and a
greater capacity for empathy and care, this cannot be made a goal of early
treatment of offenders.

Finally, it is important to ask the length of time usually expected for
completion of treatment. Quick fixes are unacceptable. The work of unlearning violence, like unlearning racism or recovering from addiction, is a lifelong
process. Some programs have inevitably sprung up in the hopes of receiving
government contract funding and promising short-term results. Most serious
practitioners reject such claims. Six months to one year is the minimum just
for the first phase of stopping violent behaviors (although in the case of inpatient treatment models, as with sex offenders, not all of this time must be
spent in an inpatient setting and some can be accomplished through out-
patient follow-up). It is not unusual for responsible treatment models to go
for two years or longer.[32]

Men's Work

To summarize, it is men's work[33] to unlearn violence as a response to need,
to learn to acknowledge and express needs in healthy, nonviolent ways, and to
form relationships of intimacy and interdependence rather than dominance
and control.

> *Men understand violence and abuse. These were used to control us as boys, and as*
> *men we often rely on violence or the threat of it to control women, children and*
> *other men. Men also understand courage and resistance to violence. We've had to*
> *learn to stand up for ourselves and what we believe in and to act powerfully in the*
> *world. We can take responsibility for eliminating abuse—by stopping our own vio-*
> *lence, backing women as they fight for equality, and reaching out to other men.*

Remember, as a child, when you were first told to act like a man and keep your feelings to yourself? When you stopped being held and comforted? How about the first time you were hit? Or had to fight? And when did we learn that men should support, protect and control women—and they should provide us with sex, love, caring, meals and children in return?

What about the first time you felt strong and capable? Remember the respectful and intimate relationships with women and men that you have developed in your life?

We've all learned both hurtful and powerful parts of the male role. We have within us the strength and bravado, as well as the pain and confusion, of what we learned. And we can call on that strength to confront the pressures toward control and abuse in our lives right now. We have learned our role with and from other men. With other men we can change it. That is men's work.[34]

A Note about Court-Mandated Treatment

Voluntary treatment is often more effective with offenders of every type than court-mandated counseling because self-referral can signal the beginning of acceptance of responsibility. On the other hand, court-mandated counseling is more likely to hold a perpetrator in treatment for the needed length of time once his own sense of remorse or external pressures from a partner or family members have faded.

A danger exists in states where counseling is sentenced *in lieu of* going to trial ("pretrial diversion"). In such a case, the counseling itself is set up as an avoidance of consequences and may inadvertently collude with the perpetrator's minimization and denial. This does not bode well for the outcome of the work. One State Justice Institute study has suggested that brief-format, court-ordered treatment for domestic violence offenders, by itself, is significantly *less* effective in stopping reoffenses than treatment combined with other sanctions including intensive probation, incarceration (including weekend detention), community service, or other alternatives.[35] The author of the study, Adele Harrell, writes: "Courts need to be wary of allowing the promise of effective treatment to divert attention from the primary fact that a crime was committed—a crime for which the offender should be held accountable."[36] She also points out that by the time a perpetrator is actually arrested, it is likely that the behavior is well entrenched and much harder to break than at an earlier stage of intervention (something that rarely occurs).

More studies are needed concerning the effectiveness of counseling programs addressing male violence against women. Long-term follow-up is still largely unknown. In any case, counseling, whether voluntary or court-mandated, should not be regarded as a panacea[37] or as a means for men to avoid the consequences of their violent behavior. A combination of prevention education, law enforcement, and thoroughgoing systemic change addressing the root causes of abusive power is the only context in which lasting rehabilitation of violent individuals can succeed.

A Last Reminder to Referring Pastors: Not All Offenders Are Treatable

A final caution for pastors using an assess-and-refer approach to working with offenders: Not all offenders are treatable. Most good programs do *not* accept all referrals but instead conduct an in-depth evaluation to determine what type of offender the man is according to some fairly detailed and clinically proven assessment instrument,[38] as well as the length of time he has offended, the number of known victims, and so on. A prognosis is assigned depending on where he falls on the assessment scale. Men with very guarded or poor prognoses are not accepted for treatment. Stronger measures of containment and accountability are recommended in such cases for the protection of victims and their families. Pastors should understand that these limitations are appropriate and not press for treatment when it would only create a false hope (or evasion of responsibility) for the offender and a false sense of safety or justice for victims.

Reporting Offenders

One question pertaining to offenders that is still fraught with confusion, hesitancy, and fear is the ethical question of whether clergy need to report abuse disclosed to them in the course of pastoral counseling or confession. Traditionally, such disclosures have been assumed, usually by both parishioners and clergy, to be strictly protected, and the legal system has generally refrained from disturbing this assumption.

However, since the first mandatory child abuse reporting law in 1963, the realm of confidentiality for all counseling professionals has changed dramatically, based on the clinical recognition that child abuse could be observed and reported. By 1974, mandatory child abuse reporting laws were passed in all fifty states, the District of Columbia, and Puerto Rico.[39] Statutes concerning elder abuse generally followed about a decade later.[40] A more recent wave of reporting legislation has involved other dependent adults, for example, certain developmentally disabled persons age eighteen or older but legally under the care or conservatorship of another adult. Most recently, five states have passed laws mandating reports of spouse abuse.[41] The battered women's movement has been divided on this. Objections include concerns about preserving adult women's self-determination, women's fear of retaliation by the defendant, and the chilling effect on battered women seeking emergency medical care. Such laws also raise serious questions about what kind of agencies might be developed to investigate and handle such reports, the lack of training of existing law enforcement personnel to handle reports to police, and the possible consequences to battered women given the nonresponsiveness of the criminal justice system. In any case, taken together, such reporting laws represent a growing political view that the specific interests of certain individuals at risk for harm, and the interests of society, can override the general ethic of confidentiality in the helping professions.

The second area in which counselor confidentiality has been modified even more recently has to do with the "duty to warn." A landmark ruling in 1976, Tarasoff v. Regents of the University of California,[42] established that when a counselee has threatened harm against someone or is assessed to be dangerous, it is the duty of the counselor not only to notify police, but also to warn the potential victim. The court wrote, "In this risk-infested society, we can hardly tolerate the further exposure to danger that would result from a concealed knowledge of the therapist that his patient was lethal."[43]

Where clergy fit into this general picture established for counseling professions is problematic and varies from state to state. In many states, clergy are not named in reporting laws nor are they included in laws governing professional behavior—because of the power of church lobbying groups that insist that such regulation encroaches improperly on the separation of church and state established by the First Amendment to the Constitution. No attempt to establish a category for clergy malpractice has succeeded so far.[44]

The legal mandate to report is a gray area for clergy in many cases where it would be clear-cut for all other helping professionals. Statutory law—that is, the law actually written into code—often leaves clergy out of lists of those mandated to report, leaving the question open. In the case of child abuse reporting, only four states specifically name clergy as mandated reporters.[45] Four states specifically exempt *penitential* communication from child abuse reporting requirements,[46] while four states specifically state that clergy's duty to report overrides the clergy-penitent privilege.[47] Nearly half the states (twenty-two) impose a mandatory reporting duty on *all* persons, and this would clearly include clergy.[48]

Case law, on the other hand—that is, interpretations of the written law decided by specific court cases which then become precedent—amplifies what is in the written code. Case law could develop in criminal court—that is, if the state prosecutor were to bring a pastor to trial for failing to report. Historically, this scenario has been rare.[49] However, case law is also developing in civil court. A victim or family member of a victim of violent crime, under some circumstances, may be able to sue a pastor for failing to report and attempt to collect damages for the subsequent injury to the victim that might have been averted if the clergyperson had reported.[50]

While there may be liability for failure to report, there is none for reporting. Every state grants legal immunity to anyone who reports child abuse; in other words, a person who in good faith reports suspected or known child abuse cannot be sued for so doing.[51]

Misconceptions about Clergy Privilege

Most clergy and parishioners commonly assume a level of confidentiality that does not exist in either church canons or state law. The clergy privilege of confidentiality does not have a higher protection than that of therapists and medical professionals.[52] In fact, it is in many cases less protected. All fifty states (two quite recently) now have statutes establishing some clergy confidentiality. Private communications of a confessional or penitential nature are generally subsumed under "the pursuance of church discipline" and protected, whether or not in the form of sacramental confession, since many denominations do not have a confession rite.[53] However, many communications are *not* in all cases protected: general conversation, conversation during which a third party is present (possibly even in marital counseling), conversation in a group, or nonverbal communication (for example, handing over a gun).[54] Communications or information obtained while not specifically fulfilling the duties of a pastor are generally not held to be confidential. The privilege may also be challenged in cases where the clergyperson is not being asked actually to testify in court, but rather to give preliminary evidence in response to interrogatories,[55] or to report to an agency. Nonordained lay ministers are rarely granted any privilege.

Rule vs. Duty: Framing the Right Dilemma

In one sense, all these discussions of what is and is not permitted by law, and what constitutes liability for lawsuits, begs the question. Clergy can become caught up and panicked by discussions of liability and conflicting rulings. However, this presumes that the primary dilemma is one of competing loyalties to rules that are in conflict—the rule of silence of the church versus the (complicated and ever-changing) laws of the land. In general, arguments that follow this line of thought focus on the assertion of absolute clergy confidentiality and the objection to state interference. Even in cases of abuse, those who adhere first to the principle of clergy right to silence have argued that child protection laws should be resisted as an "abrogation of the clergy-penitent privilege."[56] The primary argument given beyond the separation of church and state is that persons would not be likely to seek out a clergyperson for help if they thought their communications would not be kept secret[57] or that reporting would be viewed as a betrayal by an offender and that this would irreparably damage the pastoral relationship.[58]

It is helpful to reframe the dilemma from one of competing rules to one of underlying ethical mandates or duties. Seen in this light, there is a duty to disclose as well as a duty to silence. Ethicist Sissela Bok has outlined three general premises for keeping professional secrets: the individual's autonomy over personal information (touching on the much-debated "right to privacy"), the mutual respect and trust assumed in a special relationship, and the premise that if we promise secrecy we are agreeing to a limit on our freedom. A promise of confidentiality constitutes a *prima facie* duty to honor that pledge.[59] A fourth premise enters in regard to professional confidentiality, that is, society's need for safe places for disclosure, a "professional refuge" where persons can go for help they might otherwise be too afraid to seek.[60] Bok, however, also states the following:

But of course there are reasons to override the force of all these premises, as when secrecy will allow violence to be done to innocent persons, or turn someone into an unwitting accomplice in a crime. At such times, autonomy and relationship no longer provide sufficient legitimacy. And the promise of silence should never be given, or if given, can be breached.[61]

Regarding professional privilege, she also cautions:

Such claims to individual and social utility touch on the raison d'être *of the professions themselves; but they are also potentially treacherous. For if it were found that a professional group or subspecialty not only did not help but actually hurt individuals, and increased the social burden of, say, illness or crime, then there would be a strong case for not allowing it to promise professional confidentiality. To question its special reason for being able to promise confidentiality of unusual strength is therefore seen as an attack on its special purposes, and on the power it acquires in being able to give assurances beyond those which non-professionals offer.*[62]

By this reasoning, to the degree that professional confidentiality actually causes harm, it cannot be justified on ethical philosophical grounds.

Marie Fortune has convincingly argued that the duty to disclose actual or potential abuse is primary and has biblical foundations in the Hebrew custom of hospitality and protection for the vulnerable and in the biblical principle of justice-making and the requirement of repentance and change.[63]

To Whom Is My Primary Commitment?

The dilemma of competing duties is perhaps solved by asking the question: To whom is my primary commitment? The purpose of confidentiality is to protect not the clergy[64] or, for that matter, the church, but the vulnerable and those served. Marie Fortune makes the helpful distinction between confidentiality and secrecy. While secrecy is absolute and therefore can collude with the secrecy of abuse, confidentiality is a trust:

Confidentiality means to hold information in trust and to share it with others only in the interest of the person involved, with their permission, in order to seek consultation with another professional. Information may also be shared without violating confidentiality in order to protect others from harm. Confidentiality is intended as a means to help an individual get help for a problem and prevent further harm to herself or others. Confidentiality is not intended to protect abusers from being held accountable for their actions or to keep them from getting the help they need. Shielding them from the consequence of their behavior will likely further endanger their victims and will deny them the repentance they need.[65]

Reporting Abuse

In actual practice, although some offenders do come forward and confess, a more typical situation is one in which the victim herself or another family member discloses the abuse.[66] Once pastors are ethically clear that they have a duty to disclose, two fears typically linger that have to do with the well-being of those served. Clergy often fear that by reporting they will make the violent situation worse or trigger retaliation on the part of the offender against the victim. Child protective services professionals say that in the case of child abuse this is largely unfounded, and that the knowledge of official scrutiny tends to make child abusers more cautious.[67] In a case of violence being perpetrated against an adult, the principle of self-determination of the victim should take precedence. Clergy should take the lead of the victim in reporting rape, battering, or other crimes against an adult woman.

Another fear is the fear of destroying the pastoral relationship and thereby withdrawing perhaps the only means of help and support from the perpetrator and the victim(s). While this is frightening, and initially there may be chaos and anger directed by victims and perpetrator alike at a pastor who reports, this can be mitigated by the way in which reporting is presented and accomplished. If it is framed in terms of needing additional help and support for the persons involved, rather than as a punitive action, reporting is as likely to enhance trust as to destroy it.

Respect for the person who is disclosing abuse, whether the perpetrator, victim, or other family member, is also conveyed in offering that person maximum involvement in the reporting process. Encouraging the person to make the report him- or herself is the strongest way to preserve a pastoral alliance with the person into the future. It is also important for the pastor to offer assurance that she or he will not abandon the person once the report is made. The pastor can offer to be present, for example, when the social worker comes out, to network with the social worker, therapists, and other referrals to see that help is found. Even if the person does not want to make the report him- or herself, the pastor should be open with the person about the facts of the report that is made. Anonymous reporting, while it relieves a pastor of having to deal in more depth with these awkward and sometimes frightening situations, is inadvisable because it removes the pastor from being able to help further,[68] and it creates a parallel process in which another layer of secrecy is overlaid on the secret of the abuse. Now the pastor is also keeping secrets from the parishioner or counselee.

Reporting also sends a message that the pastor takes abuse seriously and that safety is the first priority. This provides a secure container for the pastoral relationship. Keeping silence, while it may be on the surface more to the liking of the person who first told of the abuse, or may feel more comfortable to the pastor, sends a message of collusion with abuse and not a message of ultimate reliability and care. *Breaking silence* is the first tenet of interrupting and ending violence against women.

A Note about Sacramental Confession

Sometimes, in denominations that offer sacramental or formal confession (Roman Catholic, Eastern Orthodox, Episcopal, Lutheran), perpetrators will ask to make confession and surprise the priest or pastor with a disclosure that they have committed a violent crime or been abusive. The dilemma here is horrific. As discussed above, the seal of the confessional is the one context in which confidentiality can never be broken.[69] In the Roman Catholic Church, breaking the seal carries the highest penalty, that of excommunication.[70]

Priests are reluctant to violate the seal, not only feeling that they are bound *pro forma* by canonical or constitutional requirements, but that the absolute trust of the confessional situation would be ruptured for everyone if the confidentiality could be broken for any reason. And yet, pro forma confession and absolution in and of themselves are generally ineffective in bringing about any change, and may, in fact, simply play into patterns of repeated perpetration followed by temporary contrition. Some perpetrators, in fact, may deliberately seek out sacramental confession as a way of relieving the burden of their secrets, believing that nothing can be done about it and that they will not be forced to change.

While I am very uneasy with the obvious ramifications of this absolute secrecy on possible further violence, I recognize that priests who are committed to the absolute seal of the confessional also need guidance. Consensus wisdom about confessions of violent acts seems to be to maintain the sanctity of the seal but to (1) incorporate referrals and education into the counsel and admonitions to the penitent, (2) encourage the penitent to report himself while he is there with you, as you would in any counseling situation; and even if he cannot or will not take this step, (3) urge the seeking of appropriate professional help. Because in the Roman Catholic Church, canons forbid a priest to require a penitent to break the seal himself, this cannot be strictly *assigned* as penance. It is well within the limits of godly admonition and counsel. In any case—for example, the case of confessions of extreme or repeated acts of violence or repeated confessions and absolutions that clearly are having no effect on changing behavior—absolution can be withheld or suspended pending clear evidence of amendment of life. This is within the sole discretion given to the priest as arbiter. All of these measures can give a strong message, especially depending on how strongly the offender believes in the practice of confession and how highly he and his community esteem the clergy and the church.

A Perpetrator in the Congregation

What if the perpetrator is someone in your congregation? What if one parishioner has revealed abuse at the hands of another? What if you hear about it secondhand? This is a nightmare scenario, and every pastor or lay helper dreads being caught between conflicting loyalties to different parishioners, or feeling that if she or he says nothing it is collusion. Two general rules can be kept in mind to help in such a fragile situation: The safety and self-determination of the victim in any violent situation must come first; and taking steps to report or contain abuse, when it is safe and agreeable to the victim to do so, is actually helping the perpetrator, although he may not see it that way.
Some guidelines:

1. Do not unilaterally take the initiative to confront, challenge, counsel, or somehow try to heal an abuser. There are two considerations here: first and

foremost, the woman's safety and her self-determination. If you are tempted to confront a perpetrator, disclose this to the victim first, discuss the pros and cons with her, find out what would be most helpful to her, and *heed her response*. Actions taken apart from the victim's knowledge and consent serve further to disempower her, even though the intent is to be helpful to her. Such actions may be more an attempt to rescue the woman (see chap. 10) than a well thought-out strategy for providing appropriate support. And in cases where the victim has an ongoing relationship to the perpetrator, her sense of what is safe must be trusted. Your confrontation could endanger her.

Second, what a perpetrator of violence needs most is containment. Healing and counseling work, if done at all, must be preceded by the establishment—usually from outside himself, either by police, the courts, or sometimes fear of losing the woman—of strong limits aimed at stopping the violence he cannot stop by himself. Healing work also must be preceded by the man's acceptance of full responsibility for his violence—beyond quick apologies.

2. If the perpetrator comes to you: The assess-and-refer model has been discussed in detail. It is crucial to be prepared with referrals to agencies and practitioners with whom you have made personal contact and in whom you have confidence both philosophically and practically. Such a referral should be followed up with appropriate inquiries about progress and with support for continuing the work. The pastor should be on guard against inadvertently agreeing or colluding with denial, minimization, and blaming. In one study, incest perpetrators themselves stated that they were most helped by clergy who were knowledgeable, firm about the behavior being wrong, and who encouraged them to self-report and seek help.[71] Rather than taking either a minimizing, timid stance or a hostile, blaming, or rebuking one, it is most helpful to the offender to try to create an alliance in which your role is to support his desire to change, to provide him with educational information and referrals, and to be someone he can trust for honesty, safety, and containment (including reporting and legal recourse if needed).

3. Gender matters. Reflect on how your own experiences as a man or a woman may condition the way you feel and are likely to respond toward this congregant. It is important for men to consider their own gender socialization, their own relationship to issues of power and control, how they will handle the anger or fear that may be aroused by this man, or how they might be tempted to be a rescuer. It is important for women to be aware of possible experiences of intimidation or victimization in the past, their identification with the victim, their own feelings of anger or fear, and what they need to do to protect themselves while remaining assertive.[72]

4. Do not neglect your own safety. This may be especially true for women pastors and lay ministers, but it is also true for men. One male pastor at a domestic violence training shared the story of having been shot at by a batterer when he went to the house to try to intervene on the wife's behalf. Even if a woman asks you to accompany her to a meeting with her perpetrator or asks you

to come to her home (or his home, if different), you do not need to say yes to such requests in order still to be helpful to her. A few guidelines for safety:

a. Discourage home visits where you know violence is occurring. Respond to requests for meetings from either the victim or the perpetrator by suggesting that they come to your office and at times when other people are present and available to help. If a known perpetrator is coming for a meeting with you, ask someone in your office (with whom you can ethically share at least that you have some concern about things becoming volatile) to be available nearby to call police or provide assistance if needed.

b. If a woman asks you to go with her to meet or confront her perpetrator and you are willing to be a part of such a meeting, request that the meeting take place in a neutral, public location. In some instances it might be appropriate to suggest that several persons accompany her, not just yourself. This draws on the twelve-step model of an "intervention" and increases safety with numbers.

c. In situations where it is appropriate (for example, a battered woman wanting to go home for clothing or personal possessions), suggest that the police be called for a "civil standby," a procedure in which police meet the woman outside her home and accompany her inside long enough for her to gather her belongings or accomplish her business there.

d. Do not under any circumstance take a gun or other weapon that could escalate a situation or be used against you or her. However, have a plan in mind for what to do in case of a violent attack. If you are going into a situation that has potential for violence, be sure to notice where the exits and phones are, and try to think who in that setting could help in an emergency.

5. Set firm guidelines for the nature and extent of the offender's continued participation in the congregation.[73] In many cases, it is not necessary to ban the offender from public worship or from continuing to receive pastoral care. On the contrary, being willing to stand with the perpetrator as he begins on the journey of accepting responsibility, living with consequences, and undertaking true amendment of life requires that we remain in relationship with him. However, because safety for victims must be paramount, the safety of past or potential victims in the congregation must also be honestly and openly assessed. Because abuse thrives in a climate of secrecy, there can be no private deals between pastor and abuser. Depending on the type and severity of the abuse, the abuser's access to the church building (especially locations and times of the week when children or women gather) and to pertinent programs and activities (such as Sunday school) must be formally prohibited. Until such a time as appropriate rehabilitation is successfully completed, the offender should also be removed from any position of leadership or moral authority as a sign to the congregation and especially to victims that violence will not be ignored or even rewarded.[74]

Conclusion

There are no easy solutions or quick fixes to violence against women. Strong containment, a commitment to safety first, an understanding of the socialization of men to deny feelings and to enforce control to get their needs met, peer support for unlearning violence, and faithfulness to the theological precept that repentance requires amendment of life and that forgiveness requires justice—these are the foundations for appropriate pastoral response to men who use violence against women.

Empowering Women

[Jesus] unrolled the scroll and found the place where it was written:
"The Spirit of the Lord is upon me,
because he has anointed me to bring good news to the poor.
He has sent me to proclaim release to the captives
and recovery of sight to the blind,
to let the oppressed go free,
to proclaim the year of the Lord's favor."
And he rolled up the scroll, gave it back to the attendant, and sat down. The eyes
of all in the synagogue were fixed on him. Then he began to say to them, "Today
this scripture has been fulfilled in your hearing."

(Luke 4:17b-21)

It may be that she is in your parish and believes from something you said in a sermon or something you announced in the bulletin that you will be safe to tell. Or it may be that a colleague has referred this woman to you because you know something about the issue of violence against women. Or it may be simply that you are a woman. Or a sympathetic man who seems very different from her abuser(s), and who, she may hope, somehow will redeem men for her. Whatever it was that made you seem safe, now she is calling you, now she is here with you in your office. She is entrusting you with a story. It is a sacred story: one of betrayal, of shame and half-buried anger, and of terror. How will you receive her sacred story? How will you hold it in your hands, hold it out so that the two of you can look at it together in safety and in reverence?

Counseling or giving support to a person in a dangerous crisis past or present, a victim of violence, can be frightening and overwhelming. In any counseling or support session with anyone seeking help, there are things that one can do, skills to learn, and certain things to avoid. But skills alone, though powerful, will not support you, the caregiver, through fear, doubt, and struggle with the feelings it arouses in you. The importance of *self*-care has been emphasized in chapter 9. Self-care must precede and surround any of our work with victims, or we will surely sink into our own internal issues, into fatigue, and into burnout.

Perhaps the most important rubric of all is that it is *not necessary to have the answers to her problems.* In fact, we can't. She alone has them. When we lose sight of this, we can bear in mind the sacredness of her story. It is *her* story, from beginning to end. If we honor the "Thou" in her—even when she herself does not—by believing her, by reminding her of her courage, her power, her God-given right to abundant joy, and if, on a practical level, we keep her safety always as a first priority and are scrupulously clear about our boundaries, then we are not likely to make "mistakes." (We may make lapses in empathy and may fail in our insights because we are human, but this in itself can be healing rather than disruptive if we remain undefensive and committed to an honest process.) By simply offering presence, belief, and an unshakable confidence that she deserves a life free of violence—especially when she herself does not share that confidence—we are giving a gift of healing and empowerment.

So, taking a deep breath and giving *ourselves* the gift of confidence to be with this fragile, strong, frightened, brave woman, how do we begin?

Immediate Crisis Response: Sexual Assault/Acute Battering Incident

Confidence in caring for victims of violence is built on a foundation of emergency skills, which help us to be flexible and at least to a functional degree "ready for anything."

In perhaps the most frightening scenario, a woman calls in the middle of an acute battering incident. This was what I feared and dreaded most when I worked on hotlines, and it did happen, although only twice. In neither case was I able to save the woman from being beaten. Because the batterer was already coming in the door when each woman called and she didn't have time to go to a safer place, and because neither woman gave me a name (it could have been any woman in a large metropolitan area), I could not call the police. These were terrible moments, and I have never completely gotten over wondering what I could have done differently and better in the few seconds on the phone with each of these women. The tragic answer is probably nothing. Two women clients in another agency where I worked were murdered by their batterers, and the entire agency staff went into shock and grief each time. The hotline counselors, support group facilitator, and batterer's counselor were especially devastated by these horrible incidents because they felt so responsible. But they had done everything possible within their roles to protect and empower these women. One of the murdered clients was even a model of self-determination and strength for many other women in her support group. In the face of a determined and homicidal batterer, even legal measures and police intervention have limits to the safety they can guarantee. Even as committed and trained caregivers, we fail and our failures haunt us.

Acknowledging our limits, we marshall our skills and do the best we can. The most important skill base is knowing first steps in a crisis response:[1]

1. *Are you safe right now?* If the answer is no, then the first priority is for the woman to *hang up the phone and get to a safe place.* She may need you to suggest some options: Go to a neighbor's or to a lighted place where there are

people—a laundromat, twenty-four-hour convenience store, grocery, or pharmacy. If she is alone in a phone booth at night, also suggest that she go to one of these more populated and well-lighted places. Try to get her full name and present location. Encourage her or offer to call the police *immediately*. *Do not stay on the phone with her any longer than necessary to confirm that she is leaving and will call you as soon as she gets there and has called the police.*

2. If she believes she is safe now, explore this: Where is the person who hurt you? Is he coming back? Are you safe where you are? Is anyone there with you? If you do not believe she is safe, again, encourage her to go to a safer place.

3. Get her phone number in case you are disconnected. If her number is not local, call her back so that a long-distance call on the phone will not arouse the batterer's suspicion. Ask if and when it's safe to call her back and whether she would like you to call again to check in with her, and if so, when.

4. Ask about her medical situation: *Are you hurt? Do you need medical attention?* If she was just raped or beaten, encourage her or offer to call the police or 911. Take into account that she may be in shock and minimizing her injury. The police can assess this and get her an ambulance if necessary. Also, she may want the evidence later, although in the immediate aftermath of the crisis she is not likely to be thinking of legal steps.

These are the first, preliminary steps before the main body of the crisis counseling session can responsibly take place.

Crisis Response: Suicide

Perhaps the other most frightening scenario, equally a crisis, is a suicide call. Battered women, rape and incest victims, and other survivors of trauma do sometimes attempt or wish to attempt suicide. The main thing to know is that *it is not necessary to be an expert or a clinician successfully and quickly to make a preliminary suicide assessment and get the person appropriate help.* She called you. This means some part of her trusted you and reached out to you for help, even if there is a part of her that is trying or threatening to end her life. You can trust that there is a connection there and depend on that as well as your skills to keep *yourself* from panicking. In a suicide crisis, the following steps should be taken:[2]

1. If the person says that she has already taken steps to end her life, try immediately to find out the person's location and call police or paramedics. (Do not depend on having the phone call traced—it can take too long if the person has already made the suicide attempt.)

2. If the person has not actually harmed herself (which is most often the case) but she tells you or you suspect that she is suicidal, for *any* reason including your own intuition or just a sense that the person seems very depressed, reflect what you think you are hearing, and *ask*: "You sound really down/at the end of your rope/hopeless . . . are you thinking about killing yourself?" Asking the question will not "give the person ideas" or push the person further in the direction of suicide. On the contrary, naming the

thoughts may be enough to relieve some of the pressure and help the person not to act on them.

Do not ignore even vague clues and suggestions. Clues are present in approximately 80 percent of suicidal deaths.[3] It is a myth that people who talk about suicide don't commit it. Clues may include such indirect comments as "I can't stand it any more," "Everyone would be better off without me," "This is the last time I'll have to deal with this," or even queries about wills and funerals.[4]

3. Also be aware that depression is not the only mood or state in which suicide can occur.[5] If the person seems disoriented (as seen in connection with alcohol, drugs, or psychosis), in a state of defiant frustration (determined to seize control of one's fate, even if the only control left seems to be to kill oneself, the ultimate "I quit!"), or what one expert calls "dependent-dissatisfied" (feeling helpless and trapped by a state of dependency from which there appears to be no exit), or if your own sense continues to be strong in spite of denials, explore the level of risk. This is done in some very specific, concrete ways:

a. Have you thought about how you would do it? Do you have a plan? (If not, probe a little further: Have you ever fantasized about it? What did you do in your fantasy?) Other indications of a plan might be giving away valued possessions, saying goodbye to loved ones, writing a suicide note, sending the children to stay with a relative for the weekend, making out a will, or otherwise showing signs of wrapping up her affairs.

b. If any sort of plan or fantasy emerges, ask if she has the means to carry out the plan; for example, if she is thinking about taking pills, does she have them in her house?

c. Ask her directly how likely she thinks it is that she might actually do it. Most people are very honest about this and will ponder the question seriously with you.

d. Find out about her history: "Have you ever tried to hurt yourself or to commit suicide before?" If she has ever attempted suicide before, the risk is much higher. Eight or nine out of ten repeated attempters ultimately do kill themselves, so this is a very serious sign.[6] Family history is also a risk factor—you might ask if anyone else in her family ever attempted suicide.[7]

e. The risk is also much higher if, at the time of your intervention, she is intoxicated with drugs or alcohol, and/or if she is alone and the means are immediately available.

f. Drug and alcohol abuse, psychosis, severe depression, recent loss, recent physical trauma, a history of unsuccessful medical treatment, and the anniversary of a trauma are all risk factors as well. Consider what you already know about the person, and explore these areas to the extent that it seems possible without "grilling" her or interrogating her. And remember: A history of physical, emotional, or sexual abuse is *in and of itself* a risk factor.[8]

4. Try to reduce lethality:

a. Explore what other support systems she has—supportive family members she can talk to? a therapist? a friend? Try to help her reduce her isolation without taking this on as a twenty-four-hour burden for yourself alone.

b. If she has the means immediately available, try to reduce the lethality of the situation by asking her to get rid of them—for example, flush the pills down the toilet, unload the gun and throw away the ammunition, throw away the razor in a place she can't retrieve it or give it to someone.

5. Do not confuse expression of emotion with lethality.

Validate and do not try to contradict or argue her out of her feelings of pain, anger, or despair. Let her know that her feelings are important and understandable. If she is crying, let her take time to let it out. If she is screaming, yelling, or raging directly at you, try to help her regain self-control by making supportive, de-escalating statements such as: "OK, try to slow down now, I want to be able to help you, but it's hard for me to understand you. . . . Take a deep breath and count to ten with me. . . . I know you're angry and you have a right to be, but I want to hear you, and it's hard when you're directing it at me. . . . Take it easy now, and let me try to help you."

6. Offer realistic hope, support, and positive reframing. Without negating any of her pain, try to notice positive aspects in the situation and bring them to her attention—her courage in sharing her pain with you and in reaching out, good things in her life that she herself has mentioned (don't try to fabricate these or jolly her up), even her ability to feel so deeply as a sign of her sensitivity and worth.

7. Make a contract. This is the basic, standard way of working with someone who is suicidal. A contract should include two elements—an agreement not to kill herself before speaking with you or another professional and a time frame. The time frame for checking in is typically twenty-four hours, but if she is feeling very suicidal, it may be necessary for her to check in hourly or sooner. If the risk is not too great, the time frame may be longer.

She should say the agreement back to you herself. Be aware of evasiveness and press for a real commitment. If possible, try to get it in writing: "I will not kill myself without talking to you or my therapist first. I agree to call you back to check in within twenty-four hours."

Try also to build into the contract an agreement that if she is feeling suicidal, she will go to a safe place.

8. Follow up. A contract is a *temporary* measure and needs follow-up. Be aware that *most suicides actually occur within about three months following the beginning of "improvement,"* when the individual has the energy to carry out the suicide plan.[9]

As a pastor, the follow-up task is *not* to do the ongoing counseling needed, which is beyond the scope of general pastoral care, but to help her to make a good connection with a licensed therapist whose job it is to be available for emergencies on a twenty-four-hour basis, and who has the necessary training to treat suicidal conditions. You may make an agreement to follow up on therapist referrals a part of a follow-up contract with the suicidal person. At the same time, be alert to clues thrown in your direction during the follow-up phase. Missed appointments, odd telephone messages, anything that seems "off" should be followed up promptly.

The pastor's role in follow-up, while not a substitute for psychotherapy, legitimately involves exploring the meaning of the wish to kill herself, her motives and problems, and helping her to deal with the underlying problems and generating alternatives. Exploring options, past coping mechanisms, and continuing to build a wider support system—both within and beyond the church community—are all appropriately the province of pastoral care.

In more depth, the pastor has a *primary* follow-up role in exploring the spiritual meaning of the suicidal feelings and the theological dimensions of despair, rage, fear, and pain.

Exploring questions of meaning and God's purposes for the person as well as ethical questions and the person's moral values about suicide and life and death are all important areas for pastoral conversation.

9. If after several attempts you are *not* able to get a contract, and you believe the risk is imminent, you will need to *call the police or paramedics* and ask them to take the person into protective custody. In most states, in cases of suicide, this means psychiatric observation in a hospital. This is obviously a last resort and does run the risk of rupturing trust and rapport. It is a frightening thing to do and feels terribly coercive. However, in the long run, your concern for her safety as your first priority is a sign of your fidelity, and it is possible, over time, to rebuild the safety in your relationship on this foundation. No one is 100 percent suicidal.[10] Crisis expert Burl Gilliland writes: "People with the strongest death wishes are invariably ambivalent, confused and gasping for life. Their emotions and their perspectives are paralyzed. Their patterns are illogical and their sense of available options is frozen in an all-or-nothing, black-or-white mode. They may be able to see only two alternatives—misery and death. They are typically unable to project themselves ahead to happier, more successful times."[11] Even though strong action may seem to be against her will, to ignore or minimize the suicidal person's communication of her intentions[12] may, paradoxically, reinforce her sense of despair and isolation. It is important to remember, if you come to this difficult juncture, that there was a part of her that wanted to live, or she would not have reached out to you.

In addition to the above steps, a few "don'ts" have been identified by experts on suicide:[13]

1. Don't lecture, blame, or preach to the suicidal person.
2. Don't criticize the person or her choices or behaviors.
3. Don't debate the pros and cons.
4. Don't be misled by the person's telling you the crisis is past.
5. Don't deny her suicidal ideas.
6. Don't try to challenge for shock effects.

7. Don't leave her isolated, unobserved, and disconnected.

8. Don't diagnose and analyze behavior or confront her with interpretations, especially during the acute phase.

9. Don't be passive.

10. Don't overreact. Keep calm.

11. Don't keep her suicidal risk a secret (be trapped in the confidentiality issue). Her safety comes first.

12. Don't get sidetracked on extraneous or external issues or persons.

13. Don't glamorize, martyrize, glorify, or deify suicidal behavior in others, past or present.

14. Don't forget to follow up.

Suicide presents an important challenge to the pastoral perspective, because at its very core, suicide is a profound matter of hope and despair, a matter of transcendent meaning. It is the loss of hope that distinguishes suicidality from nonsuicidal anxiety and depression.[14] This is a theological matter! In anxiety and depression, one faces a traumatic state in the future (anxiety) or tries to deal with it in the present/past (depression). In a suicidal state, not only has the present become unmanageable and unbearable, the future has become unimaginable. It is the pastor's role to be a bearer of hope to the hopeless person until she can once again catch some glimpse of future possibility. The affirmation of God's abiding love and care can do much to lighten her sense of despair. Faith that she is going to make it can be contagious.[15]

This is emphatically *not* to say that the pastor should be in the business of trying to jolly up the suicidal person. To do so would be to give the message that her pain is trivial and that the valley of despair into which she has entered is too fearful for the pastor to journey with her. She is once again discounted and left alone, a reinforcement of her suicidal condition. To the extent that we can tolerate it ourselves, it is our priestly work to travel to the depths of despair with her—carrying the beacon of faithful hope and the promise of God's love as a lamp on the path at a time when perhaps her own light is too fragile to light the way on its own. Part of this is allowing for the free expression of painful emotions, and part is exploring the meaning of her longing for death—which may be very hard for us to hold.

Paul writes: "We know that the whole creation has been groaning in labor pains until now; and not only the creation, but we ourselves, who have the first fruits of the Spirit, groan inwardly while we wait for adoption, the redemption of our bodies. For in hope we were saved. Now hope that is seen is not hope. For who hopes for what is seen? But if we hope for what we do not see, we wait for it with patience" (Rom. 8:22-25). Jungian analyst James Hillman comments on this passage that a concrete hope, a hope for something one knows, is no real hope.[16] We cannot inspire someone with concrete promises or even imaginary pictures of a better future. Hope by definition is ineffable. What we can do is hold on to our *own* capacity for hope as we descend with the suicidal person, carrying it for her, as it were, while she comes to understanding the unique meaning and perspective of what has brought her to this impasse in her life.

Crisis Counseling beyond the Acute Emergency

Once you have ascertained the safety of the person at risk, and once there is no issue of suicidality, then it is possible to proceed with second-stage crisis intervention. This may be very soon in the aftermath of an acute crisis event, or it may be much longer, even years, after the actual trauma. Crisis aftermath begins in the moment in which the woman realizes that there was a crisis and seeks help for the first time.

"Crisis" may be defined as "a perception of an event or situation as an intolerable difficulty that exceeds the resources and coping mechanisms of the person."[17] Ordinary coping mechanisms and habitual choices no longer work. The person feels immobilized and out of control. Constriction occurs, in which the range of options that would occur to the person under other circumstances seems narrowed to a few terrible choices or none.

Crisis counseling is somewhat different from pastoral counseling in several respects. It is likely to be more structured for the sake of helping to restore clarity to one in crisis. It focuses on the immediate events or the trauma that precipitated her seeking help and usually ranges much less over questions of the person's history, upbringing, philosophy, theology, or the meaning of events. A crisis session has several essential components. There are a number of models for this, and all contain similar components.[18]

I use a model with five basic steps.[19] In this model, a cue for moving to the next step is when she starts to repeat.

1. *Instill calm; be reassuring.* This step is necessary when the person "breaks down" with crying, sobbing, screaming, or other dramatic emotional re-sponses. No matter what you may be feeling inside, it is of utmost importance to convey the message that you can hear and hold whatever she has to tell, and that you will not go into crisis too. Some specific techniques for helping her to move out of her own panic include: "Take a deep breath." "That's good . . . that's right." "It's OK now." "It's OK to cry; let it out." "I can hear you're upset, and I can really understand that." It is healing and validating for her to let out her feeling in the safety of that emotional "container" you provide by your presence (either in person or on the phone). This is very different from crying and shaking all alone.

Usually this intensity lessens naturally after a few minutes, but if you feel that she cannot wind down without assistance to a point where she can begin to talk, you can use some interventions to help her calm herself. For example, "OK, I hear you. Now for me to help you, I need for you to talk to me. Can you tell me what's happened?" "Take a deep breath and try to count to ten with me. . . . "

2. *Get the story clear. What happened?* What happened that made you decide to call now—if not the first time, as with battering? What's different about this time that made you decide to call?

In this *crisis* intervention session, as distinct from a regular pastoral counseling session, try to focus on the immediate event and less on previous events or longer history of assault or abuse. That part of her story can come later when she is not in acute crisis.

Help her to focus by using active listening skills, that is, feeding back to her what she has told you as accurately as possible without interpretation, judgment, or advice. For example: "I hear you saying. . . ." "Let me see if I'm understanding it right: this is what happened. . . ." "So you're thinking/feeling . . . ?" Summarizing and paraphrasing what she has told is a useful way not only for the counselor to get clear on the story, but for the woman in crisis to hear more clearly what she herself has just said and to make more sense of her experience in her own mind. This also gives her the message that you take what she is presenting very seriously, that you believe her, and you do not feel a need to change, question, or embroider on what she has told.

Direct questioning is probably less useful in any case than simply reflecting back and letting the story unfold in the sequence she wants to present. At times, however, you may want to ask a question for clarification. In general, it is better to use open-ended questions (one that is not answered simply by a yes or a no). For example: "What happened then?" "What injuries do you have?" "What made you decide to call now?"

One little warning about questions I have found particularly useful: "Why" questions are often heard by a counselee as judgmental or challenging, even when that is not the intent, and should be avoided. Of course, a question like "Why did you provoke him like that?" is blatantly inappropriate, but more subtle questions like "Why do you think so?" "Why do you feel . . . ?" "Why do you think he did . . . ?" are also undermining rather than clarifying. The "Why" question at best is a powerful and potentially defense-arousing tool, used mainly in cognitive-style confrontation or depth-therapeutic interpretation, and does not normally have any place in crisis counseling.

3. *Validate her feelings.* The pitfall here is cutting this step off too soon because it can be so hard and painful to listen to. The temptation is to cut to step 4, problem-solving. But that is something she may be more likely to be able to do for herself without you if her feelings are finally heard, validated, and not discounted. You may be the first person she has ever told, and your validation is essential in her having the courage to continue breaking silence and seeking help. Some examples: "I can understand your feeling that way/angry/sad/confused. . . ." "That sounds really hard for you." "That's certainly tough." "It's OK to have mixed feelings." "No, you don't deserve that, and I would be angry too."

4. *Problem-solving.* Make every attempt to have a good summary from step 2 and a fairly thorough exploration of step 3 *before* entering this step. A good

way to begin with problem-solving is to *explore her own past coping mechanisms*. Remember that crisis may have temporarily made it hard for her to think and plan clearly. This does not mean that she is without the resources to do this. Draw on past successes, however small. "What have you done before?" "What's worked, not worked?" *Explore her options; do not give advice*: savings, staying with friends or relatives where he wouldn't think of looking for her, can she take time off from work? and so on. This is the step in which you will *make relevant referrals*. Having an up-to-date and heavily annotated rolodex is critical. A very helpful focusing question in this step is: "What do you think you want to do now?" In concluding this step, try to *get an action plan*, even if it is simply to think it over and call back again in a week. Summarize the action plan back to her, including any referrals made.[20]

5. *Closing.* There are several elements to a good closing.

a. Express *appreciation and respect* directly: "I'm really *glad* you called."

b. *Validate her courage*: "It takes a lot of courage to take this step."

c. Assure *confidentiality* (and explain exceptions, if any).

d. Check and be sure that you have *not missed anything* important; let her know that you care about trying to meet *her expectations from you*: "Was there anything you were wanting from this call/meeting that you still need?" (Go back through the steps if necessary.)

e. Let her know clearly *when she can reach you again and of any limits on your availability or limits on what you can provide (making a referral for further help if you have not already done so).*

f. *Repeat her action plan and tell her you care.*

This is the scaffolding upon which a good crisis session can be built, and there are numerous similar variations. As many years as I have used this model, I still keep it in outline form on an index card, and I use it—especially if I am tired, sick, preoccupied with other matters, or taken by surprise (I think she is calling about the parish picnic and suddenly we are in the middle of a crisis call). When I was doing twenty-four-hour hotline on-call for a shelter, and a call would come over the beeper in the wee hours of the morning, I would pause a moment to make sure I was fully awake, and I would quickly scan the card to orient myself. I have found that it is always helpful, no matter how "experienced" or "trained" I think I am.

Crisis also elicits deeper-than-usual responses in us as we try to offer support and help. Our own buttons are pushed. Our own experiences of grief, terror, rage, betrayal, or entrapment are brought close to the surface. Especially those experiences and feelings which we have not fully processed ourselves will be activated in ways that may not be fully conscious and that may, indeed, trip us up, if not in the actual counseling, then in other parts of our lives. One pastor I know was brought up never to be afraid, because fear wasn't manly. When he counsels, it is hard for him simply to dwell in someone's fear without trying to soothe it or fix it. Another pastor admits that she becomes seriously depressed when angry herself and hides her anger from the world and from her own knowing. It is difficult for her to explore the anger being presented by those who come to her for help, even though she knows in theory that they need to "get in touch with" their anger. In my own pastoring, I sometimes feel impatient, because I may believe the abused person "should" feel more angry, or "should" feel more urgency about getting out of the dangerous situation. I find it difficult at times to "sit on" my own reactions to her situation and be present with her in her own feelings and the timing of her own process.

Nor will the person necessarily behave like a "good" victim—pleasant, cooperative, undemanding, reasonable, grateful for our attentions. Survivors will sometimes emotionally attack a caregiver, unconsciously doing to the pastor what was done to them. A friend who worked with deaf children first described this phenomenon to me: she was often attacked by children whom she taught for the first time to use sign language and communicate. She was puzzled and hurt because she felt that she was the most loving person in their young lives. It then occurred to her that, by being present to their pain and teaching them the language to name it, she also was the one who was near enough to receive the accumulated years of pent-up rage and anguish as soon as they could communicate. She stopped taking it personally and found that, if she could honor their feelings without taking on the blame for what had happened to them, a deep trust evolved over time. There are many parallels in working with survivors of abuse and trauma.

Because of the enormity of their pain, survivors will also sometimes pressure the pastor for more time than is conceivable, more energy than is available. Their own fractured boundaries and intense need may make it difficult for them to recognize that others can be truly committed to helping them and at the same time need to set limits on what can be given. Rage and despair can set in when limits are set, and yet without limits both partners in the pastoral relationship will spiral down into exhaustion and frustration. Pastors will experience some survivors in a state of deep dependency, regressing to the developmental stage of the earliest wound. We will be tempted to try to meet the expectation (hers colliding with ours) that we will be able to provide a spiritual-magical cure. What is needed is to maintain good boundaries and recognize our own human limitations, while staying firmly committed to the survivor and to the truth.

Pastors should also be alert to the phenomenon of survivors (unconsciously) seeking inappropriate "help" to avoid real help because facing the return of memories and the challenge of true change is terrifying. This can be a trap for all of us who want to help. The survivor is seeking us out, begging us for more of our time and wisdom, telling us that we are what she needs. Our own rescue fantasies are inflated by the praise and apparent need for what we have to give. But at all times we must ask ourselves whether a referral would actually be in her better interests. Sometimes seeking help from us is avoiding the help she really needs.

To walk with a survivor on her path of pain and recovery is a profound experience, but the pastor should be prepared to feel pain, horror, anger, and fear, as well as personal hurt and exhaustion along the way. Ruth Schmidt, a rape survivor, has written:

> I am an uncomfortable person. . . . Touch my anger. It is damp from tears. It is hot from smoldering. It is heavy and difficult to carry. Taste my anger, it is bitter. Smell my anger, it is rancid, it is filled with sweat from a heaving man forcing himself upon me and into me.
>
> Understand my anger, for you have brought it upon me. "Happy are those who are persecuted in the cause of right; theirs is the kingdom of heaven." I do not know this heaven.[21]

It is painful to be present to such pain and rage. But the capacity to hear and be big enough to contain it, without breaking down ourselves, without shrinking from the survivor or writing her off as demented or too angry, is the very gift that will help her to heal herself. As we can tolerate her depths of pain, so, too, she can accept them and begin to recover her life. Again, this cannot be done without healing our own wounds and being able to tell the difference between what is our own pain and what is hers.

Empowerment-Based Pastoral Counseling

Counseling with a view toward empowering the person counseled and respecting her process is the foundation of all good counseling—peer, pastoral, or psychotherapeutic. It is particularly crucial in counseling a victim of violent trauma. The experience that she brings for healing is a wound to her power. What she needs more than anything is the restoration of a sense that she can be powerful and fully alive once again. Beyond all specific skills and techniques, and beyond all the resources about which a counselor may be knowledgeable, the most healing thing of all will be the counselor's absolute conviction that she is the one in charge of her recovery from trauma, and that she has the inner strength and courage to overcome what happened to her. She has demonstrated that strength and courage in concrete ways: by coming to you, by telling her story, by surviving in whatever way she could. She is already whole. She needs to reclaim that wholeness.

It is the relationship that heals.[22] The basis of an empowering counseling relationship includes three components: (1) *empathy*—reflecting accurately and fully the counselee's feelings as she has expressed them, without adding, interpreting, or judging; (2) *respect*—communicating acceptance of the counselee as a person, what Carl Rogers described as "unconditional positive regard;" and (3) *warmth*—showing attentiveness and caring through nonverbal behaviors. Warmth does *not*, however, require any physical touching, while respect *precludes* it under most circumstances. More will be said about this below.

Facilitative responding includes the most attentive listening, active listening that is not rote repetition but mirroring back of the fullness of the material being received. Nonverbal signs of attentiveness such as eye contact and a relaxed but alert and interested body position are important. Such behaviors as eating one's lunch, picking up the phone, or leaning back too comfortably in one's chair may be acceptable during a casual conversation but destroy trust and rapport with a victim of violent trauma. They send a nonverbal message that her story is not very serious or important.

The power of simply mirroring responses should not be underestimated. Very little guidance or direction is necessary. George Gazda has described this as "facilitative responding:"[23]

> *Facilitative responses serve as a mirror of the helpee's psychic self, assisting the helpee to get a complete and accurate picture of his/her self. When helpees see their views more clearly, they may become able to test the validity of their perception, their memory, their judgment. They may discover contradictions within their statements or omissions in what they have said or believe. They may decide that some of their assumptions are unrealistic. This experience of self-exploration leads to better and more complete understanding of the situation and of self, both of which are necessary prerequisites to problem-solving and growth.*

At its deepest, pastoral counseling, like peer counseling, may need to explore discrepancies, inconsistencies, or irrational patterns of thinking that the counselee has presented and that are not helpful to her. This is the area of gentle confrontation. It is extremely important that the threatening nature of such confrontation be understood, and that no questioning or pointing out of inconsistencies be undertaken without a firmly established base of empathy, respect, warmth, and unconditional positive regard. Even then, such interventions must not be to impose the point of view of the counselor, but to propose alternatives that might be helpful to the counselee and are aimed toward her good and not the counselor's own needs. The counselee must feel free to refuse any such line of exploration and reject any observation that feels intrusive. If she is angry, this must be met with nondefensiveness and nonjudgment.

Ethical Judgments concerning Safety

Perhaps the most difficult situations involve the counselee's making decisions that the pastoral counselor believes are unwise, even dangerous. It is important, perhaps especially at this juncture, not to impose judgments or give advice. This is perceived, rightly, as taking power out of her hands. Is it ever justifiable to do this?

Because abuse or sexual assault is a violation of the woman's autonomy, her self-determination, her very bodily integrity,[24] any powerful unilateral intervention may be experienced as revictimization and a confirmation of her loss of control over her own life. In cases where a woman is making a decision that we feel is wrong or even dangerous, such as returning to her batterer, it is counterproductive to plead, argue, criticize, or try to forbid her. However, it is well within the bounds of mutual respect and a commitment to truthfulness to express our grave concern, using "I" statements such as: "I respect your decision. You know better than anyone else what is right for you now. I do want you to know, though, that I'm concerned about your safety." Depending on the level of trust already established, you may even want to venture, "I disagree with you," while making it clear that no matter what she chooses it is her choice and you will not abandon her for it.

We can also tell or remind her of information which, if this is done in a noncoercive way, empowers her with knowledge—whether she changes her mind or not. For example: "Remember the cycle of violence and the respite stage. Many men say they're sorry and mean it, but the abuse still escalates." Regardless of her decision, remind her that you will continue to be there for her and that she does not need to worry if she chooses to do something you don't feel good about—you will not abandon her or blame her, no matter what happens.

In the worst-case scenario, in more directly dangerous situations, such as suicide, child abuse, or threats of harm to others, it does become necessary to take a more active stance and call the police, paramedics, child protective services, or some other emergency agency. Even in such situations, however, it is possible to do so by giving the survivor as much choice as possible[25] and by explaining one's actions and choices so that her sense of having something done *to* her against her will is at least mitigated. Such explanations may take the form of de-escalating drama and responding with a method named "SET," an acronym for "support-empathy-truth."[26] Support here means a statement reaffirming your caring. Empathy means reflecting back how badly you perceive the survivor to be feeling, as accurately and warmly as you can. Truth is a statement of what you are feeling and thinking about what is happening, what you need to do about it, and why or how it would be unethical or wrong for you not to do so (for example, "Your safety is my first priority").

Finally, give the survivor as much choice and opportunity for self-determination as possible. Invite a person who is disclosing child abuse to make the child protective services report herself, with you standing by to support her. Ask a suicidal woman if she would prefer you to call the paramedics or if she would like to do it or arrange to check into a hospital herself. (Be sure to see that she does it.) Urge a battered woman to go to a neighbor's house or nearby convenience store and call the police herself. Even in the most dire of crisis situations, the old rubric "Never do anything for persons that they should do for themselves" still pertains and preserves your commitment to empowerment and restoring self-determination to the survivor as quickly and fully as possible, while holding her safety as your first priority.

Finally, when in doubt, *use consultation*. Without inappropriately divulging the survivor's confidences, consult with a colleague in ministry who may have experience with a similar situation. Consult with a therapist or social worker in the community. Consult with local police. How much could they actually do for her? Would they be able to provide a civil standby? Assign a patrol car to her house? There are often legal limits to what police are able to do in advance of any actual crime. Consult with the hospital. What happens when someone is held for observation? What will happen if paramedics are called? Familiarize yourself with the child abuse reporting agency that serves your community. What will they do when a report is made? All of this can be done in advance of any real crisis and can fund your own crisis response with a solid base of information to ground you and give you more calm and confidence when an actual emergency arises.

Limits and Boundaries of Pastoral Care and Counseling

Especially in the context of a growing awareness of clergy sexual abuse of parishioners, more attention is being paid to the appropriate boundaries of pastoral care in general and the limits of the counseling that can be provided by church counselors, clergy or lay, who do not possess clinical training beyond a basic seminary curriculum or lay ministry certification program.

Pastors, chaplains, spiritual directors, and pastoral counselors (whether clergy or lay) are *not* psychotherapists, unless they *also* possess clinical credentials (state licenses or professional certifications that ensure a minimum course of clinical/academic study and a minimum documentable number of hours of counseling experience under approved supervision in a specified variety of settings).[27] In most states, psychotherapists must be licensed under one of four categories requiring specified degrees: Psychiatrist (M.D.), Psychologist (Ph.D. in psychology), Clinical Social Worker (Master of Social Work), and Marriage, Family, Child or Licensed Professional Counselor (M.A. or M.S. in counseling psychology).[28] Psychoanalysts belong in one of these categories (usually at the M.D. or Ph.D. level), and in addition have received specialized training and certification from a Psychoanalytic or Jungian Institute.

Church insurance companies and denominational task forces on clergy professional ethics have increasingly adopted policies establishing appropriate boundaries for pastoral counseling. Many times, the result is to try to quantify these boundaries in an attempt to make trespasses measurable by an objective standard. However, pastoral counseling boundaries are not usually that simple.

Most often, such policies will limit unsupervised pastoral counseling to a certain number of sessions with a parishioner, usually six, as well as prohibiting fees for counseling (thereby resembling the model of a separate counseling practice).[29] While I agree strongly with the intent of such policies, I do not believe that this is a true safeguard against inappropriate, disempowering, or invasive pastoral counseling. Abuses can and do happen in the first session, while it can be argued that appropriate pastoral care may encompass many more than six sessions—for example, with a parishioner who is homebound or terminally ill.

I would propose that, in addition to such quantifiable boundaries, pastoral counseling be understood as belonging to a specialized subset of peer counseling or peer advocacy. The specialization, of course, refers to the spiritual dimension of pastoral care and the issues of meaning and faith often at issue in the content of counseling conversations. Especially in cases of pastoral counseling with victims of violent trauma, a peer advocacy model of problem-solving and relying on the person's own resources for change is the most effective because it is the most empowering. It scrupulously avoids fostering dependency, and it assumes that the answers reside with the person counseled.

Vincent D'Andrea and Peter Salovey have outlined "eight commandments of peer counseling." Originally designed for peer counselors in college dorms, residence hall advisors, hotline and grief counseling volunteers, and support group facilitators, their book *Peer Counseling* is extremely helpful in pastoral counseling as well.[30] The eight commandments are:

1. Be nonjudgmental.
2. Be empathetic (not a brick wall).
3. Don't give personal advice.
4. Don't ask questions that begin with "Why?"
5. Don't take responsibility for the other person's problem.
6. Don't interpret; do paraphrase (interpretation is reserved for psychotherapy).
7. Stick with the here and now.
8. Deal with feelings first.

The authors also present a useful graphic to mark out areas appropriate to peer counseling and areas that should be restricted to professional psychotherapy. Unlicensed pastoral counseling also should be limited, in my view, to these areas. The graphic is known as the "Johari Window"[31] (see Figure 11.1).

Information, thoughts, feelings, and memories known to the counselee and readily observable by others are the main arena for pastoral counseling. In addition, with the development of rapport and trust *over time*, gentle exploration of material that is observable but not entirely known in the consciousness of the counselee can be admitted. For example, if the woman tells a story of terrible pain and abuse, but is smiling, the discrepancy might be noted. In another example, a woman may say, "Everything is OK now," but look very sad and have tears in her eyes. Because this is readily observable, it is another discrepancy that may be useful to point out to her.

Peer and pastoral counseling stay out of the realm of a woman's secrets, unspoken fears, childhood history not readily presented, feelings, and fantasies. This is the realm known to self but not known to others. Probing for feelings that remain unexpressed or for private thoughts and fantasies is not the arena of pastoral counseling. This will be felt as intrusive and inappropriate. For example, to suspect that there is anger beneath expressed sadness, and to elicit this, a therapist might say, "I hear your sadness. I wonder if there isn't

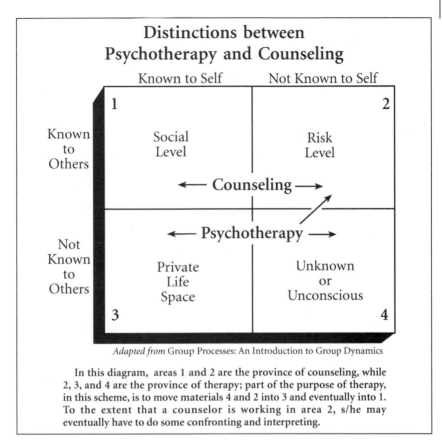

Distinctions between
Psychotherapy and Counseling

	Known to Self	Not Known to Self
Known to Others	1 — Social Level	Risk Level — 2
	← Counseling →	
	← Psychotherapy →	
Not Known to Others	Private Life Space — 3	Unknown or Unconscious — 4

Adapted from Group Processes: An Introduction to Group Dynamics

In this diagram, areas 1 and 2 are the province of counseling, while 2, 3, and 4 are the province of therapy; part of the purpose of therapy, in this scheme, is to move materials 4 and 2 into 3 and eventually into 1. To the extent that a counselor is working in area 2, s/he may eventually have to do some confronting and interpreting.

Figure 11.1   Johari Window

Reprinted from Vincent D'Andrea and Peter Salovey, *Peer Counseling: Skills and Perspectives* (Palo Alto, Calif.: Science and Behavior Books, 1983), p. 63.

also some anger?" or "If I were in your situation, I would probably feel pretty angry about that." The power of such an intervention, if not resisted and deflected by the counselee in the first place, will create a depth of intimacy and possibly dependency that cannot be followed up within the limits of time and training of the pastoral counselor. What if the anger is unleashed? Then what?

Finally, there is the arena of the unconscious, "not known to self or to others." This is the area of depth psychotherapy, usually long-term, and including such psychoanalytic techniques as interpretation of presumed hidden meanings behind certain behaviors, slips of the tongue, dreams, and verbal associations. This is emphatically *not* the arena of pastoral care and counseling. The intentional working with the transference inherent in such a therapeutic method is powerful and requires extensive training, supervised experience, and experience of such therapy for oneself. While certain aspects of pastoral counseling and spiritual direction may work with dreams, it is still essential that the counselee's own meanings are the focus and that interpretation is scrupulously avoided.

This view of the boundaries of pastoral counseling, while more complex, gets closer to the real intent of policies that limit pastoral counseling in order to minimize abuses. While less easily quantifiable, a pastor's counseling interventions, when questioned, can still be evaluated using a "standards of practice" model that clearly outlines appropriate and inappropriate areas for exploration and methods of intervention.

This also has implications for clergy training. The focus of pastoral counseling training at the seminary level shifts from trying to acquaint ministry students with the rudiments of clinical psychology for integration in their pastoral care work toward knowing the boundaries of appropriate pastoral care and learning techniques for being truly helpful and facilitative to parishioners within those boundaries of care.[32]

Supporting the Long-Term Recovery Process

Crisis intervention skills are essential in the acute stages of battering and sexual assault and at times in longer-term recovery when the survivor's anguish becomes acute. However, violence against women often results in post-traumatic stress-related disorders that are long-term, and sometimes involves symptoms and unhelpful modes of coping that are no longer connected in an obvious or immediately discernible way to the original traumatic cause. This kind of recovery requires a very different kind of support.

In general, as I have suggested above, the realm of deep past exploration and childhood history is the domain of professional, licensed psychotherapy. This is not to say, however, that the pastor does not have any role in this long-term healing process. On the contrary, the pastor's role, much as in suicide work, is one of hope-bearer and (re-)revealer of God's love and redemption.

It is also to be a prophetic voice of freedom. This is deeply meaningful in the context of traumatic reactions, because it is precisely freedom that trauma crushes. The difference in meaning between trauma and other negative experiences is not only in degree, but in the sense of being completely overwhelmed by a force greater than oneself and being placed in a situation of terror and helplessness that cannot be changed. Judith Herman writes, "Traumatic reactions occur when action is of no avail."[33] Trauma involves not only pain and fear, but a crushing defeat of volition and a ravaging of faith and meaning. Trauma involves the experience of captivity, and in situations of chronic abuse or long-term captivity the survivor may slowly become indoctrinated into the terrifying, ambiguous, special relationship of coercive control in which the perpetrator becomes the most powerful person in her life.[34] All her expectations of subsequent relationships are preconditioned and distorted by this experience of domination and loss of mutuality.

Faced with the often disturbed relating and anguished inner world of an abuse survivor, the pastor often feels overwhelmed and wishes for a quick fix or some theological palliative. She herself may feel her faith shaken by the story of the survivor. Her own personal vulnerability and fears may be heightened. The intensity of the survivor's most painful emotions, if allowed into the intimacy of the pastoral conversation, may feel overwhelming. A survivor is likely to feel not only fear but stark terror, not only anger but rage, not only sadness and grief but utter despair.

Conditioned as we are in the church to seek to do good and to eradicate evil, we are not so well equipped when it comes to acknowledging our own anger, and even more so, our own capacity for evil. We are prone to splitting off the evil as "out there" somewhere and disavowing it in ourselves. But to do so is not to admit the survivor's own feelings of guilt, shame, and (however unwilling) collaboration with evil into our pastoral conversation where they can be put into perspective, reflected upon, and healed. Unconscious reactions to the survivor's rage, if not reflected upon, can lead us to fearing her and even treating her as her perpetrator did.

We are also threatened by helplessness. We who have a strongly articulated theology of salvation sometimes find it unbearable not to be able to save another person in anguish, danger, or despair. We are possibly most likely to fall into the trap of rescuing or taking premature action on behalf of the survivor when we are feeling most at a loss. Paradoxically, we are most at risk for doing harm when we unconsciously fall into the rescuer's grandiose stance of specialness and omnipotence—which is always a defense against our own feeling of impotence. Boundary violations and fostering unhealthy dependency are often the result of such (fruitless) efforts to rescue the survivor. Pastors can learn from this warning sounded by psychoanalysts John Maltsberger and Dan Buie:

> The three most common narcissistic snares are the aspirations to heal all, know all, and love all. Since such gifts are no more accessible to the contemporary psychotherapist than they were to Faust, unless such trends are worked out . . . [the therapist] will be subjected to a sense of Faustian helplessness and discouragement, and tempted to solve his dilemma by resort[ing] to magical and destructive action.[35]

All of these traps are inherent in the work of supporting survivors of trauma and abuse. Rather than regarding them as aberrations or weaknesses on the part of an inexperienced helper, it is wiser to recognize that all of them will occur at some time during the work with *each* survivor if the relationship is at all deep. Rather than trying to eradicate such feelings and reactions as a helper, it is better to expect them, be able to reflect on them, and keep them conscious rather than acting them out. Prayer can be a powerful antidote to the overwhelming feelings of fear and helplessness of the pastoral helper.

Letting God carry what we cannot helps us more realistically to carry what we can.

Judith Herman has outlined three long-term tasks of recovery: (1) establishing of safety, boundaries, and trust; (2) exploration of the traumatic experience, integration of split-off traumatic memories into consciousness, and mourning losses;[36] (3) restructuring of the shattered elements of the self or building structure where none was allowed to develop—restoring healthy developmental progression from wherever it was interrupted and restoring connections to others by learning how to handle conflict and stress, how to take care of oneself, and learning what is "normal."[37] To these I would add a fourth phase: restoring meaning, purpose, faith, and hopefulness. While the pastor may have a strong role in stages one and three, and a more supportive role as an adjunct to professional therapy in stage two, it is in stage four that the pastoral relationship becomes paramount. Already implicit in stage three, *this is the theological task of healing.*

These four stages are not strictly sequential, but overlapping and cyclical. As new information is processed and new memories emerge, new capacities for relationship and for feeling are integrated and the stages cycle through again. The pastoral helper joins in this rhythmic dance, now being prominent and creative, now receding and supporting the delicate and heroic movements of others who are joined together with the survivor in the healing dance.[38]

Essential Messages of Hope

Finally, there are a few things that should be said clearly and directly to any victim of violent trauma, particularly upon first hearing her story, but also from time to time thereafter:

1. I believe you.[39]

2. This should never have happened to you. It is not God's will for you. (If the abuse occurred in the church, in your official capacity as clergy you may also add: "I'm sorry on behalf of the church I represent and love that this was allowed to happen to you.")

3. This is not your fault.

4. You do have choices now. You have a right to determine what happens to you and what you want to do now.

5. (For the sake of process and trust:) This is what I can provide you now (be very clear), and here are some other resources who can provide x, y, z. . . .

6. God cares about what happens to you and is with you. God's love is real.

The Role of a Spiritual Community in Healing

If the pastor meets with a survivor one-on-one, there is still a dimension of healing that is lacking. As important as the confidential pastoral relationship can be, it can in and of itself continue to model isolation and secrecy if the resources and love of the worshiping community are not offered. Not all survivors will want to share their stories with others, and no one should ever be coerced into doing so. However, a congregation that is educated and sensitized is a powerful witness to the larger themes that affect the survivor's life. Just having such a context, even if not one word of her individual story is ever told, can be tremendously healing.

It is not only the pastor's role, but the congregation's—in actions as well as words—to assure the victim-survivor of God's love and to provide her with an opportunity to build a spiritual support community for herself. Much of this work is in simply witnessing to the larger truths of violence against women and the objectification of oppressed groups. It is the work of making the parish a safe place where confidences are kept but destructive secrets are eradicated.

As the church, we are called to join in this movement to break silence and to restore justice. In the lectionary for the Baptism of Christ, we hear one of the great servant songs from the prophet Isaiah: "Here is my servant, whom I uphold, my chosen, in whom my soul delights; I have put my spirit upon him; he will bring forth justice to the nations. . . . A bruised reed he will not break, and a dimly burning wick he will not quench; he will faithfully bring forth justice" (Isa. 42:1ff.). This is a call, an anointing of each and every one of us.

First, we are called to see and hear the truth. There are a lot of reasons why we don't want to. But perhaps the most compelling is that, in addition to the forces of social inertia and unconscious collusion, if we were to acknowledge the truth of all this violence, its prevalence, and the pervasiveness of oppression of women, it would be too terrible. Who could bear it? If rape and battering were *not* as rare as the prevailing myths would have us believe, if they were *not* just the work of a small percentage of sociopathic criminals, then all women, and indeed, a great many men, are vulnerable. There is no "profile" that makes one woman more vulnerable to violence than another. We all are vulnerable. It is the (mostly subliminal) reality with which we live on a daily basis. But we will never change it until we allow ourselves to see it in all its tremendous proportions.

In very concrete ways, this means putting posters and flyers and tracts in the narthex of our churches, and preaching and teaching about violence against women until our congregations begin to trust and to know that this is a safe place to talk about what really happens in their lives. It means asking the right questions when we see bruises or frightened behavior. It means being alert to the statistical reality that, if one out of five women are adult survivors of childhood sexual abuse, one out of three women are raped, and as many as *one-half* of all women are battered, then proportionately as many women in our congregations are also victims—and they are waiting for a word of hope and healing from *us*.

Second, we must name the violence *as* violence. When we hear stories of individual women, we must remind ourselves to shift the focus *off* all the ways in which we are socialized to question her, doubt her, wonder what she did wrong or what in her psychological makeup made her vulnerable. We must hold the focus on the one who is responsible—the one who chose to cross the line, to violate her personhood, to harass, to terrorize, to stalk, to rape, to batter.

When we do this, we will start to get angry. Perhaps especially as Christians, this feels wrong to us. We are socialized—and women doubly so—to avoid anger, to smooth things over, to "forgive and forget," to "turn the other cheek." We push our anger underground, where it festers as depression, numbness, and distortion of the facts. We need to let our anger out again to breathe, and so to animate us—which literally means to "en-soul" us once again—to concern, solidarity, and action.

This is our third calling: We must mobilize our anger beyond helplessness and beyond sympathy to justice for victims/survivors. This means growing up and taking responsibility as a community to say to perpetrators that violence is unacceptable, that we will not resort to quick fixes and cheap, premature forgiveness without true repentance and change of life, and that we will stand for the righting of these wrongs—in our policies and in our relationships.

Finally, we are called to restore right relation, not just between individual men and women, and not in the sense of premature or cheap forgiveness, but in the sense of the whole community, the whole church, the whole society. This is the work of reconciliation to which we are called. (More will be said about this in the final chapter.) In concrete terms, this means that we can use language that does not exclude women and other oppressed groups or perpetuate stereotypes. We can ask ourselves as we prepare sermons, prayers, and religious education materials: How would this particular statement sound to the ears of someone who has been abused? For example, if we preach about sin, are we careful to do so in ways that will not seem to blame victims of violence for their victimization? If we preach about themes of sacrifice, endurance, or forgiveness, are we unwittingly exhorting abuse victims to denigrate their own feelings or even to stay in or return to violent situations?

A Word about Liturgies

Liturgies can be a powerful way for the church to acknowledge corporate complicity with evil and oppression, to lift up victims/survivors for healing and care, and to recommit as a community to justice and truthtelling.[40] Ritual, when used conscientiously and carefully, may even be a powerful instrument of healing in pastoral care and counseling.[41] A number of special liturgies for healing for survivors of abuse and violence are being developed,[42] and these have a place in the church because, by naming the violence and bringing it into particular focus, they interrupt the silence that has helped to perpetuate it. A beautiful *Litany for Healing* by Rev. Caroline Fairless is included as an appendix.

Some cautions about special liturgies, however, should be raised. First, special liturgies can have the unintended effect of taking abuse out of the mainstream of church life and worship. A one-time special liturgy (also true of workshops or forums, etc.) can inadvertently send the message that abuse is something unusual. And what is unusual is quickly forgotten. This is the second concern, that by creating a special liturgy and using it without a broader context of commitment, education, and incorporation into the regular ongoing life of the congregation, there is the tendency to say, "Oh, abuse? Yes, we did that."

Another concern is that special liturgies all too often are attempts to replace the long, hard process of grieving, raging, and recovery that survivors need to undergo. Premature forgiveness and premature assurances of healing often make pastors and congregations feel better but drive the survivor's less comfortable feelings underground.

A final concern I have is that we not inadvertently glorify victimhood by concentrating so much in our liturgies on healing. Authentic healing is not only a salve for pain and a mending of wounds, but a restoring of wholeness and right relation that justice requires. All too often, special liturgies of healing emphasize pain and convey a message that "we're all victims here," and do not challenge us to confront the church's corporate complicity and our individual responsibility to advocate for change.

When we anoint one another, we are not only applying a balm for pain, we are also touching one another with the living coal the seraph applied to Isaiah's lips (Isa. 6:6-7). This healing not only makes us feel better—it makes us prophets. Jesus, according to Luke, inaugurated his own ministry by reading the words of the prophet Isaiah (quoted at the beginning of this chapter). In his own house of worship, Jesus proclaimed the Good News of justice and liberation for all people.

The regular Sunday service of the Word, and the Eucharist itself, can be powerful liturgies of transformation and signs of promise and hope to survivors. It is here, I would propose, in the central worship of the life of a congregation, and not for the most part in special liturgies, that the most effective healing—in its *fullest* meaning, that of restoring wholeness—is accomplished:

When Sunday after Sunday we speak of the body broken, broken in order to embrace an ever-widening reality, we are speaking of hope and thanksgiving. The eucharistic hope and thanksgiving are born of surrender, but it is the surrender to the love of God, not to violence. Our eucharistic prayers echo with themes of creation and redemption, themes which connect at a deep spiritual level with those who, on the surface, have lost their hope, and despair of deliverance.[43]

These words and sacramental acts of promise—the Good News of justice spoken from the lectern and the pulpit, the prayers of solidarity and witness and commitment, and the eucharistic celebration of Communion and liberation—are the Passover feast of deliverance, the assurance of God's Realm of love and justice.

Conclusion:
The Call to Reconciliation

Cheap grace is the preaching of forgiveness without requiring repentance, baptism without church discipline, Communion without confession, absolution without personal confession. Cheap grace is grace without discipleship, grace without the cross, grace without Jesus Christ, living and incarnate. . . .

Costly grace is the gospel which must be sought again and again, the gift which must be asked for, the door at which a man [sic] must knock.

Such grace is costly because it calls us to follow, and it is grace because it calls us to follow Jesus Christ. . . . Costly grace is the incarnation of God.

—Dietrich Bonhoeffer, *The Cost of Discipleship*[1]

Beyond an Ethic of Instant Forgiveness

One of the most difficult issues, which comes up again and again in any discussion of violence against women, is the issue of forgiveness. One of the most common complaints of battered women and adult survivors of incest about their pastors is that they have been pressured into forgiving and "turning the other cheek" (Luke 6:29). As a whole church community, we consistently give signals to survivors of abuse that they should "forgive and forget," reminding them of Christ's forgiveness of his persecutors from the cross (Luke 23:34) or of the Lord's Prayer, "forgive us our trespasses as *we forgive* those who trespass against us" (Matt. 6:12ff.; cf. Luke 11).

All too often, survivors of violence are retraumatized by pastors and other well-meaning helpers who press forgiveness upon them as if it were something which, if they tried hard enough, they could simply will into happening. If the survivor tries to forgive, she can only fail, and her failure will reinforce all the self-blame and shame of her original abuse.

This message is not only said directly to victims. It is sometimes conveyed in ways that are manipulative and intrusive and that in the end only produce guilt and confusion. For example, I once attended an evening program on Christian meditation sponsored by a parish church. The facilitator, a Christian therapist, led us in a guided meditation. Without naming it as such, she induced a light trance state by asking us to become aware of our breathing and to relax our bodies bit by bit from head to toes and then asking us to picture ourselves floating in a warm cloud. Our clouds took us to a mountain. There we were to meet Jesus. When we could feel Jesus' arm around our shoulders, we were to notice someone coming up a path toward us. This was someone who had hurt us in our lives. Still feeling Jesus' arm lovingly around our shoulders, we were to say to the person, "I forgive you." We then were to get back on our cloud and slowly, when we were ready, come back to the room.

This was over ten years ago, and no one in the room raised any objections. But imagine the confusion, pain, and anger that might have been experienced by a survivor of rape, incest, or abuse. Totally unprepared, and in an extremely open and vulnerable trance state, she would have found even her spirituality invaded by an image or memory of the very person who once shattered her boundaries in the most violent way. Sadly, unsafe forms of guided imagery work are prevalent, both in Christian circles and among New Age practitioners. This type of spiritual exercise, even though done with the very best of intentions, is so coercive, intrusive, and manipulative that it is nothing short of spiritual rape.

Ellen Bass and Laura Davis write:

> It is insulting to suggest to any survivor that she should forgive the person who abused her. This advice minimizes and denies the validity of her feelings. Yet the issue of forgiveness is one that will be pressed on you again and again by people who are uncomfortable with your rage or want to have you back under their control. While you don't have to stay angry forever, you should not let anyone talk you into trading in your anger for the "higher good" of forgiveness.
>
> If you have strong religious ties, particularly Christian ones, you may feel it is your sacred duty to forgive. This just isn't true. If there is such a thing as divine forgiveness, it's God's job, not yours. . . .
>
> Trying to forgive is a futile short-circuit of the healing process. Trying to speed things along so you can "get to the forgiveness" is one of the fastest ways to undercut yourself. No one forgives by trying. If forgiveness of others is to be part of your healing (and it does not have to be), it will take place only when you've gone through all the stages of remembering, grief, anger, and moving on. It is not the grand prize. It is only a by-product. And it's not even a very important one.[2]

All too often, especially in the church, we see forgiveness as the final goal of any healing process. Whether this is motivated by genuine concern for victims, wishing them peacefulness and an ability to move on in their lives, or whether it is our *own* discomfort with their anger, grief, rage, or what seems to us like their "stuckness" that motivates us, we push women into trying to forgive "for their own good." We urge them to "get on with their lives"—ignoring the fact that their abuse and their healing are as much a part of their lives as any of the other parts that may be more comfortable for us.

We sometimes tell victims they should forgive because, after all, their perpetrator was probably abused as a child also.[3] This argument is confusing and only makes the victim feel more guilty for her own legitimate feelings of anger and pain. The fact that abusers frequently have histories of abuse may be useful in treating the abusers themselves, and points to their humanness. It does not, however, exonerate them from responsibility for the violent acts they committed. To imply this further minimizes the pain of the victim and retraumatizes her.

A survivor may also rush herself into premature forgiveness, partly because she believes it is expected of her, but also sometimes as an unconscious defense against feelings of rage and revenge that she cannot acknowledge. Forgiveness becomes a mask of niceness that keeps unacceptable feelings of hatred, loathing, and fantasies of revenge locked out of consciousness.[4] As un-Christian as she may feel her hatred and fantasies of revenge to be, these need to be worked through until they can be consciously tolerated and integrated—as righteous anger or righteous indignation.[5] These feelings are necessary for wholeness and recovery. Alice Miller writes, "Genuine forgiveness does not deny anger but faces it head-on. If I can feel outrage at the injustice I have suffered, can recognize my persecution as such, and can acknowledge and hate my persecutor for what he or she has done, only then will the way to forgiveness be open to me."[6] At the emergence of this stage of a survivor's process, it is more helpful to recall Jesus' fury at the money changers in the temple and the Hebrew prophets' many expressions of God's righteous wrath than to reinforce her sense of shame for her rage with saccharine images of Jesus "meek and gentle,"[7] "kind and good," as in the Christmas carol. If she is chided for her righteous anger, it will be driven back underground to fester as depression, shame, and self-injury.

Forgiveness Requires Remembering

Most often because we ourselves wish we could deny and forget about the violence that so pervades our lives, we urge victims to "forgive and forget":[8]

> Forgiveness is a word which has become more and more meaningless in our society. Some people mean that they want to simply forget what happened—just put it out of their mind. Others mean by forgiving that the offense or injury which occurred is okay, i.e., that somehow it becomes a non-offense. Neither of these meanings is adequate to the experience of rape or sexual abuse. A person can never forget these offenses. The memory of the event will always be in the victim's consciousness. It becomes a part of one's history as do one's positive experiences. And nothing can ever make the offense a non-offense. It will never be okay that a person was raped or molested. It is forever a wrong done to another human being.[9]

Forgiveness will always be premature, pseudo-, or at best partial forgiveness, unless and until the victim of violence has taken the long journey from victim to survivor, including uncovering enough of the factual story to know what really happened to her, solidly acknowledging it as real in its full magnitude, grieving what was taken from her, working through her pain and fear, claiming her anger and rage, and somehow integrating the experience to a place where she no longer feels powerless, but in touch with her own beauty, strength, and power.

Forgiveness Requires Justice

In addition to the internal process of healing that a survivor may undergo, there are many external factors as well—factors involving the perpetrator himself, and the response or lack of response of the church, the justice system, the victim's family and other support networks, and the whole community. Even if a survivor works through every stage necessary to her own healing, still, forgiveness requires justice.

The deepest form of justice involves the calling to account, subsequent repentance, and amendment of life of the perpetrator. Forgiveness is not a right.[10] One of the most liberating messages to battered women and other abuse victims concerning forgiveness has been articulated by Marie Fortune. In *Keeping the Faith*,[11] she examines the passage in the Gospel of Luke in which Jesus said about forgiveness, "Take heed to yourselves; if your brother sins, rebuke him, and if he repents, forgive him; and if he sins against you seven times in the day, and turns to you seven times and says, 'I repent,' you must forgive him" (Luke 17:1-4). She points out that first there is a rebuke—this may come from a helper, including the police. Then, the crucial phrase: *"if he repents . . . "*:

> This is a big if. Repentance here means more than remorse. Remorse is when he says, "I'm really sorry, honey, I didn't meant to hurt you; it will never happen again." Remorse usually gets expressed [in a battering relationship] during the honeymoon or "making up" period of the battering cycle. The remorse may even be very genuine, but it does not mean that he will not hit again.
>
> Repentance is more significant. To repent, in both the Old and New Testaments, means to turn away from, to change, never to repeat again. True repentance on the part of the abuser means that he never hits again and that he learns to relate to other people in ways that are not controlling, demanding, and dominating. True repentance is not easy; it takes hard work for him to change his abusive way of relating to you. But this is what is expected. Only when you have seen true repentance (and over a period of time) can you consider forgiveness.[12]

Nor is repentance a matter of bargaining:

> Sometimes a batterer will try to bargain with you: "If you forgive me, then I'll go get help for my problem." This is not the way it works. Repentance must come first; only then is true forgiveness possible. Do not give in to his request for your forgiveness. Premature forgiveness does not help him or you.[13]

This applies equally well to the battered woman anguishing over the pleas for forgiveness from her batterer, to the pastor wondering about granting absolution to a sex offender, to the bishop agonizing over the request for another chance from a pastor found guilty of sexual misconduct. Premature forgiveness may seem to smooth things over temporarily, and it appeals to most of us who were brought up to believe that being nice was a primary Christian virtue. But it has the effect of driving anger and pain underground where they then fester like a poisonous stream, under our houses and our churches and our communities. And it has the effect of relieving the abuser of any true responsibility to examine his behavior and to change. Because premature forgiveness bypasses consequences and rehabilitation for the offender, it is, in fact, tacit permission—perhaps even an invitation—to continue the violence.

And so, it is unreasonable and even inhumane to insist that the victim of violence strive to forgive her attacker, as if it were her job to do. The first step toward forgiveness is not in her hands at all. It depends upon the willingness and the ability of the attacker to examine himself, to confess (to someone who can exercise appropriate authority to help and insist upon his changing his behavior), and, most significantly, to turn his life around and stop the violence. She should not be pressured into forgiving anyone who has shown no genuine efforts toward amendment of life.

Note, too, that the perpetrator's confession is not the same as an apology to the victim. While certain popular books, including twelve-step literature, encourage a direct apology to persons harmed, many women do not need or want to hear directly from their abuser. This type of direct apology, even if genuine, can further traumatize the victim. It is motivated by his timetable, his need to heal, not hers. In this sense, it is still abuse—ignoring her needs to take care of his own. The most useful type of self-disclosure by a perpetrator is one in which he (a) takes full responsibility for his violence, without blame or qualification, and (b) tells someone who will not simply make him feel better or relieve his guilt, but someone who has true authority to hold him accountable for changing his behavior and—without bargaining—keeping his promises to reform his life.

This is the meaning of the quote from Dietrich Bonhoeffer above. "Cheap grace" is no solution. Bonhoeffer points to the "cost of discipleship," in which grace comes at no less a cost than following Christ. While it may not be realistic to demand that every perpetrator become a perfect imitator of Christ, we are always pointing toward discipleship, and this requires repentance and amendment of life.

If justice were possible only in the case of an offender's true repentance, forgiveness would seldom be possible at all. Sadly, few batterers and sex offenders ever achieve this. Few move beyond the minimization and denial so characteristic of the perpetrator profile. The prognosis for complete recovery from violent behavior is poor for most perpetrators, as noted in chapter 10. In more realistic terms, however, justice may also be expressed by actions of the legal system, or the belief and protection of a single other human being. Sometimes simply being really heard and understood by someone in a position of authority is enough. Restitution by the offender in some form, whether he has repented or not, may also be an element in making justice for some victims—for example, paying for her counseling, medical, or legal expenses (whether voluntarily or imposed by some authority)—although other victims will say they want nothing to do with his "guilt money." Marie Fortune writes, "One person standing up for her/him may be sufficient for the victim to experience justice. Whatever form it takes, justice is a prerequisite for a victim to move towards forgiveness. . . . If justice is the right relation between persons, then reconciliation is the making of justice where there was injustice."[14]

The Question of Self-Forgiveness

Ellen Bass and Laura Davis write:

The only forgiveness that is essential is for yourself. You must forgive yourself for having needed, for having been small. You must forgive yourself for coping the best you could. As one woman said, "I've had to forgive my genitals for responding. I've had to forgive myself for not being able to second-guess my father and avoid the abuse."

You must forgive yourself for the limitations you've lived with as an adult. You must forgive yourself for repeating your victimization, for not knowing how to pro- tect your own children, or for abusing others. You must forgive yourself for needing time to heal now, and you must give yourself, as generously as you can, all your compassion and understanding, so you can direct your attention and energy toward your own healing. This forgiveness is what's essential.[15]

Most, if not all, survivors blame themselves, at least in part, for what hap- pened to them. This is often reinforced by the perpetrator's direct or indirect messages that impute responsibility and culpability to the victim herself. In this sense, self-forgiveness can be seen as a necessary step, as a releasing from self-blame and condemnation.

There is still a trap, however, in any form of self-forgiveness—particularly if the suggestion is made not by the survivor herself but by someone in a help- ing role. Any suggestion that she needs to forgive herself may still be heard as taking culpability on herself. Otherwise, what would there be to forgive? When survivors have come to me for pastoral care or for confession, I have given an assurance of pardon if it is truly on their own initiative and needed to relieve a burden of pain. But I have always accompanied it with equal as- surances that the abuse was not their fault, and they need not blame them- selves for violence committed against them.

If the survivor is bent on taking responsibility, it may be helpful to redirect this from a burden of guilt for what was done to her toward taking responsi- bility and authority for her recovery. Judith Herman writes, "Paradoxically, acceptance of this apparent injustice is the beginning of empowerment. The only way that the survivor can take full control of her recovery is to take re- sponsibility for it. The only way she can discover her undestroyed strengths is to use them to their fullest."[16] In some cases recovery will include recognizing and stopping re-abuse of others. If the survivor has recapitulated (usually un- consciously) the abuse she herself experienced on a child of her own or some- one else's, the road to self-forgiveness will be difficult but must follow without any short-cuts the path of taking responsibility and amending her life.

There is one other tragic occasion on which self-forgiveness becomes es- sential. At times, survivors have also been forced to be perpetrators by their own abuser. Battered women sometimes cannot protect their children from their abuser, and sexual abuse survivors sometimes report being forced to abuse other children. In extreme cases, ritual abuse survivors even report having been forced to participate in ritual maiming and murder. Although forced or trapped into circumstances that made moral choice impossible, survivors bear intense shame and guilt for wrongs of omission or commission, however motivated by fear or coercion. Herman writes, "The survivor needs to mourn for the loss of her moral integrity and to find her own way to atone for what cannot be undone. This restitution in no way exonerates the perpetrator of his crimes; rather, it reaffirms the survivor's claim to moral choice in the present."[17] In such a case, the pastor's understanding and supportive presence and, when the time is right, depending on the traditions and expectations of the survivor, authoritative pardon/sacramental absolution, can be deeply healing.

Forgiveness as Letting Go

Forgiveness, if and when it does finally occur in the life of an individual survivor of violence, happens some time fairly far along in the process of healing—although it is not the goal, and not even necessarily the end-point in the healing process. It has as its prerequisite some manifestation of justice, and it cannot come fully before the victim has worked through the horror of what happened to her and all the feelings surrounding her experience. Forgiveness is not forgetting, or erasing the experience of the violence, or excusing the violence. Forgiveness is not required of a victim.[18] If she dies before she experiences forgiveness, she will not be consigned to hell.

The word most often used in the gospel accounts of Jesus' teachings on forgiveness[19] is *aphiemi*,[20] which means to send or let off or away.[21] Nearly all the words for forgiveness in both the Old and New Testaments carry a similar meaning.[22] When we "forgive our debtors" (Luke 11:4), we are releasing them from any obligation to us. The major exception in Hebrew is *kaphar*, which means to cover. Only God ever forgives, blots out, or "covers" sins in this sense; it is not required of human persons.[23]

At certain times, for some survivors, this releasing or letting go becomes possible once the anger, grief, and other feelings are truly worked through. Viewed in this way, as letting go, forgiveness is not done out of sentimentality toward the offender, but as a step toward wholeness for the survivor herself. It is a releasing of all the heavy burden of rage and hatred and moving forward in life with a new lightness of breath and of step.

Nor does this letting go mean that the survivor will never feel anger, grief, fear, or horror again. It simply means that the perpetrator no longer has such a hold on her life, even in memory. The experience of trauma will always be a part of her life, but is no longer her whole life, her identity—no longer a defining and all-consuming preoccupation.

In a letter written to her father, who had molested her as a child, one survivor wrote eloquently about the meaning of forgiveness as letting go:[24]

> Dad,
>
> I believe God wants me to forgive. Why? You don't deserve it—God knows that. All the demons in hell know it. You don't even want it. So why would I forgive you?

For me! As I forgive you I let go of you—the sorrow, the rage, the memories, and gain peace—imperceptibly, minute bits at a time. I do not forgive because you deserve it, but because I deserve it and God asks it of me. I cannot live with my bitterness any longer, for it has nearly destroyed me.

I forgive you. I ask God to forgive you. I release you.

Forgiveness Is a Gift of Grace

Finally, even if all the conditions are "right," forgiveness is not something that the victim owes anybody or should feel obligated to do. In the final analysis, it is not something she does, no matter how hard she tries, and no matter how much she wants to do it.

In nearly all passages of the Old Testament, and most in the Epistles, it is God who forgives sins, not human beings. Joseph rebuked his brothers for trying to trick him into forgiving them, saying, "Fear not, for am I in the place of God?" (Gen. 50:19).

This is echoed in much of Paul's theology, in which the whole matter of forgiveness is not between people, but between God and humanity (Rom. 4:6-8). This forgiveness, which Paul uses interchangeably with the word for redemption, is accomplished in his view by God through the mediation of Christ (for example, Acts 26:18; Eph. 1:7-8; Col. 1:14; 2:13).

New Testament scholar Krister Stendahl has asserted that the modern church's emphasis on sin and forgiveness is not a correct interpretation of Paul, and that it says more about our own psychological preoccupation with guilt than about Paul or, for that matter, God.[25]

Ultimately, then, forgiveness is something we can let go of and give up to God. We can turn this over to the "wideness in God's mercy"[26] and be released from the pressure and the burden of making it happen ourselves. This in itself is a crucial part of the letting go, *aphesis*, of forgiveness.

The one remaining word for forgiveness that frequently appears in the Epistles (2 Cor. 2:7, 10; 12:13; Eph. 4:31-32; Col. 2:13; 3:13), and once in the Gospel of Luke (Luke 7:42-43), is *charizomai*, which means to be gracious. Paul often exhorts the members of his churches to show forbearance, compassion, and kindness toward one another, and to "forgive each other as the Lord has forgiven you" (Col. 3:13; cf. Eph. 4:31-32).

But this *charizomai* is too often misunderstood, again, as something effortful on the part of the forgiver. To be gracious is to *be graced*. It is a *charisma*, a gift of the Holy Spirit. At a certain time, for some people, when pain has been worked through and justice has in some sense been achieved, it simply descends. Much of the inner conflict, doubt, fear, and hatred are lifted away. The memory of the experience is not erased or covered over, and anger and even fear are still present in very appropriate ways. But the experience no longer has power over the person in the same way.

There is no word in the English language that adequately describes the experience of this spiritual gift. Rather than the transitive verb "to forgive him," which implies an active effort, we need a word like "to be forgiven of him," which conveys the sense of receiving this forgiveness of the other.

At times, this may come as a sense of realization or discovery after the fact.[27] There is a new lightness, a new ability to move on, a sense of peace.

Perhaps the best pastoral counsel to give someone who without any external pressure or coercion truly wants to forgive her offender, is this: Do not blame yourself if you cannot forgive yet. Forgiveness is a gift of grace, and if it is right for it to happen, it will be given to you by God in God's own good time. In the meantime, don't worry, and let it go.

From Forgiveness to Reconciliation: The Restoring of the Community

Finally, recalling the discussion of power that laid the framework for the exploration of violence against women in this book, there is a context of accountability *in community*, which is the test of all authentic power. It is, finally, in community that we are all called to account. Power-in-community, whether it is a nurturing, caretaking power-for, an interpersonal power-with, or a charismatic power-within, is power authorized by the whole people. Violence against women is not only an abuse of an individual person, but a violation of trust and a rupturing of right relation with the entire community.

When viewed in this light, insisting upon the forgiveness of an individual perpetrator by an individual victim misses the point. Even if such forgiveness were accomplished, if it takes place in private, or relatively so, the wound to the community is not healed. Deep change must put down roots, and when those roots go deep into the earth, the whole earth is rearranged by their movement. This is the thorough change, not of individual forgiveness, but of *reconciliation*.[28]

Reconciliation is often misunderstood in the church to mean an atmosphere of niceness and the suppression of conflict. Reconciliation has often meant the disenfranchised being reconciled to the dominant reality.[29] But this is contrary to the biblical sense of reconciliation. The three Greek words in the New Testament most often translated into English as "reconciliation" or "to reconcile" are *apokatallatto*, or *katallasso/katallage*, and *diallattomai*, all of which mean a *thorough change*.[30] To be reconciled is to be changed through and through. This is the precise meaning of the passage in Paul's second letter to the church in Corinth:

> *All this is from God, who through Christ reconciled us to himself and gave us the ministry of reconciliation; that is, in Christ, God was reconciling the world to himself, not counting their trespasses against them, and entrusting the message of reconciliation to us. So we are ambassadors for Christ, since God is making his appeal through us; we entreat you on behalf of Christ, be reconciled to God. (2 Cor. 5:18-19)*

It is in this sense of thoroughgoing change that Paul promises unity and peace between Jew and Greek (Eph. 2:14-16), humanity and God (Rom. 5:10, Col. 1:19-23).

We are called by the gospel to restore right relation, not just between individual men and women, and not in the sense of premature or cheap forgiveness, but in the sense of the whole community, the whole church, the whole society[31]—even, as Paul says, the world (*kosmos*). We are called by baptism to be *re-concilers*, that is, restorers of the *concilium*—the *whole* community of God, called and blessed as God's children, and equally precious in God's sight. We are called to make the connections between violence against women and all forms of violence—racism, heterosexism, classism, and all forms of oppression, all of which serve to maintain structures of power and privilege at the expense of the majority of the planet's people and creatures.

To recall once again the words of Martin Buber, "Inscrutably involved, we live in the currents of universal reciprocity."[32] This "I-Thou" relationship refuses to brand any person as an It, and replaces aggression and domination with relationality, truth-telling, and care. Objectification, the "I-It" relationship, is the root of all violence. Reconciliation means rooting out "I-It" exploitation of people and replanting the garden once again with relationships of "I-Thou-We."

This is, at heart, an eschatological perspective. Jesus' prophetic ministry was radical precisely because he lived and taught in *kairos* time: eternity in this moment, now! Salvation, liberation, the Realm of God is here! We are all, as a community, called to repent, that is, to turn around, because in Jesus' words, the Kingdom of God is already here. And we must turn to see it—and then to do it and be it. We are finally called to do justice, not to make God's Realm happen, but to live in the Realm that is already in God's *kairos* time around us, in us, and through us. Wars should cease; people should be fed and clothed and have meaningful work; races should live in harmony and dignity; women should be ordained in every church—not only because that is how we wish things to be in the future, but because that is how it already is in the Realm of God, and we have to live it.

As pastors, it is our calling to be ambassadors for Christ in the ministry of reconciliation, as St. Paul has written. In carrying out this ministry, our prophetic as well as our pastoral abilities are required, because this ministry is one of heralding thoroughgoing change—not just for individuals, but for the church and for society. We must shift our primary focus away from our long-accustomed insistence upon individual forgiveness, and point—however haltingly and imperfectly, hindered by our own human limitations—toward the reconciliation that is true transformation, the reestablishment of right relation that is the Realm of God. This reconciliation lifts us beyond the restoring of harmony between individuals to the restoring of compassion to the whole world.

NOTES

PREFACE

1. A few books come close and have been important resources for my classes and for this project: Marie Fortune, *Sexual Violence* (New York: Pilgrim Press, 1983); and two anthologies: Joanne Carlson Brown and Carole R. Bohn, eds., *Christianity, Patriarchy, and Abuse* (New York: Pilgrim Press, 1989); and Mary Pellauer, Barbara Chester, and Jane Boyajian, *Sexual Assault and Abuse: A Handbook for Clergy and Religious Professionals* (San Francisco: HarperSanFrancisco, 1987).

2. Judith Herman, *Trauma and Recovery* (New York: Basic Books, 1992), 8–9.

3. Elie Wiesel, *A Jew Today*, trans. Marion Wiesel (New York: Vintage/Random House, 1978), 236.

INTRODUCTION: THE RAPE OF TAMAR

1. *In Memory of Her: A Feminist Theological Reconstruction of Christian Origins* (New York: Crossroad, 1983), 31.

2. For example, it is only assigned in the Daily Office of the Episcopal Church, year 1 of two, on the Sunday and Monday of Proper 14 in Pentecost (*Book of Common Prayer* [New York: Church Hymnal Corporation 1979/Seabury Press, 1979], 978), and the Daily Lectionary of the Lutheran Church for Sunday and Monday in the week of Pentecost 13 (*Lutheran Book of Worship* [Minneapolis: Augsburg, 1978], 183). It only appears once every other year in the complete successive reading of 2 Samuel in the Daily Office, on a Sunday when it would almost certainly be eclipsed by the regular Sunday lectionary in any public service of worship—year 1, Proper 10, Season after Pentecost (*Book of Common Prayer*, 974).

3. Walter Brueggemann has emphasized the importance of our considering all the biblical text; e.g., speech presented at Trinity Institute West, Grace Cathedral, San Francisco, January 1992; and on this text in particular, see *First and Second Samuel*, Interpretation: a Bible Commentary for Teaching and Preaching, ed. J. L. Mays, P. D. Miller, Jr., and P. J. Achtemeier (Louisville: John Knox Press, 1990), 6.

4. This realization concerning the impossibility of objectivity in historical narration is a fairly recent phenomenon in the history of knowledge and is a domain of Postmodernism, especially beginning with Spinoza. For a discussion of the (patriarchal) bias of narrators in the Old Testament, with particular attention to literary criticism, see Mieke Bal, *Death and Dissymetry: The Politics of Coherence in the Book of Judges* (Chicago: University of Chicago Press, 1988); and Mieke Bal, ed., *Anti-Covenant: Counter-Reading Women's Lives in the Hebrew Bible* (Sheffield, England: Almond Press/Sheffield Academic Press), 1989.

5. Contra Barbara Green, Dominican School of Theology and Philosophy, Berkeley, who contends that a case can be made on the basis of rhetoric that Amnon is portrayed as a villain (personal communication, March 1993). Cf. Charles Conroy (*Absalom Absalom!* Analecta Biblica 81 [Rome: Biblical Institute Press, 1978]), who does identify the narrator as aligning mostly with Amnon's internal state, but also sees Amnon as being progressively portrayed in a bad light (22ff.

and 111). David Biale points out that the perpetrator is condemned, but the victim does not receive sympathy. These are two separate matters. The story of David and Bathsheba is also told from David's point of view and is at the same time critical of him. In neither story, however, does the narrator ever take the part of the woman (personal communication, October 1993).

6. Biale points out that an interesting *midrash* utilizes this text as making the distinction between "love which is temporary and love which is permanent." The passage goes on to say that the only love that is permanent as described in the Bible is the love between David and Jonathan. It acknowledges that one does not truly "love" as Amnon "loved" Tamar, but counterposes only the love of a man for a man as permanent, raising the questions: Is this example assumed to be nonerotic? In the view of the rabbi author, can love for a woman ever be other than temporary love, infatuation, or lust (personal communication, October 1993)?

7. P. Kyle McCarter, Jr., *2 Samuel: A New Translation with Introduction, Notes and Commentary*, The Anchor Bible Series (Garden City, N.Y.: Doubleday, 1984), 321.

8. Sanhedrin 21a, cited in McCarter, *2 Samuel*, 321.

9. Cf. Judges 14:20. McCarter, *2 Samuel*, 321.

10. Brueggemann, *1 and 2 Samuel*, 287.

11. Phyllis Trible, *Texts of Terror: Literary-Feminist Readings of Biblical Narratives* (Philadelphia: Fortress Press, 1984), 46. Brueggemann (*1 and 2 Samuel*) also comments on this word as conveying a meaning of "unprincipled self-indulgence" (287).

12. Ilona Rashkow, *The Phallacy of Genesis: A Feminist Psychoanalytic Approach*, in Literary Currents in Biblical Interpretation, ed. D. N. Fewell and D. Gunn (Louisville: Westminster/John Knox Press, 1993), 86. She also cites Ezekiel 32:21–29 and Psalm 88:6.

13. Brueggemann, *1 and 2 Samuel*, 287.

14. Cf. Conroy, *Absalom*, 24, 33.

15. Cf. Brueggemann, *1 and 2 Samuel*, 2–3 on "a long-established practice of an 'innocent' or 'pious' reading of the Samuel narrative," which ignores the realism and brutality represented in the text. See also Meir Sternberg, *The Poetics of Biblical Narrative: Ideological Literature and the Drama of Reading* (Bloomington, Ind.: Indiana University Press, 1985), 422, on the telescoping and elision in 2 Samuel 13:14–20 as "tactful mention of awkward subjects."

16. Compare this story with another narrator's terse account of a rape—or is it minimization?—in the story of the rape of the Levite's concubine in Judges 19:25. All that is written of a night-long gang rape is ". . . and they knew (*yd`*) her, and abused (`*ll*) her all night until morning." For more details, see Trible, *Texts of Terror*, 76–77. Some literary scholars of the Bible have argued more generally that brevity and gaps are purposeful, artistic choices. Erich Auerbach, *Mimesis*, trans. W. Trask (Princeton, N.J.: Princeton University Press, 1953); Robert Alter, *The Art of Biblical Narrative* (New York: Basic Books, 1981). For an example close to Tamar, see Alter's discussion of David's wife Michal and the possible meaning of gaps, p. 125. On reading gaps in Tamar's story, see Sternberg, *Poetics*, 251–52, 313.

17. Contrast this reversal of sentiment with the story of the rape of Dinah (Gen. 34), in which another rapist-prince, Shechem, rapes first and "loves" second.

18. David Biale (*Eros and the Jews: From Biblical Israel to Contemporary America* [New York: Basic Books/HarperCollins, 1992], 20) proposes that, in fact, it is David's adultery with Bathsheba that initiates a long intergenerational chain of sexual violations, which has implications for our contemporary understandings of intergenerational repetition of sexual abuse in families.

19. Trible, *Texts of Terror*, 45–46.

20. Reflected in Exodus 22:16–17, Deuteronomy 22:28, and the forcible appropriation of women during war in Deuteronomy 21:10.

21. Some controversy exists over the interpretation of incest laws of Leviticus 18:9,11, and whether these were in effect at the time of David. It is reasonable to assume, however, that given David's own bending of the laws, he would have permitted the marriage. See, for example, McCarter, *Absalom*, 324.

22. Compare this to Genesis 38, in which (a different) Tamar manages to claim her right to bear a child by deceiving her father-in-law, Judah, who had wronged her by depriving her of that right.

23. For example, consider how the brothers of Dinah and her father Jacob view her rape by Shechem as a defilement (Gen. 34:5, 13). Shechem and his father, Hamor, seem to be following the custom of equating rape with a form of betrothal. Much of what ensues (13–25), although deceitful, is a complicated negotiation over property and commerce. The final revenge is wrought by murder, but also by plunder and capture of wives and "little ones"—in their view, committing property theft to avenge property theft (25–31).

24. There is little mention of this in standard texts—for example, Roland DeVaux, *Ancient Israel*, 2 vols. (New York: McGraw-Hill, 1961)—and an absence of concrete evidence. However, many scholars concur that this is likely (David Biale, personal communication, October 1993).

25. Phyllis Trible suggests that this is not minimizing, but rather that the terseness of her brother's response is ironic and pained (personal communication, June 1992). In *Texts of Terror*, she writes, "rather than minimizing the crime, euphemisms such as 'with you' or 'this deed' underscore its horror. They cover the unspeakable, even as Jonadab's innocent vocabulary promoted rape" (51). But is this really the effect? Does not the keeping of silence, as with any family's keeping of an incest secret, always serve to collude with the crime and to disempower the victim?

26. Trible (*Texts of Terror*) asserts that the use of the word "now" (*attah*) means "for the time being" (51). It is true that Absalom appears to be biding his time. But in point of fact, Tamar herself never speaks again in the historical record.

27. Hans Wilhelm Hertzberg, *1 and 2 Samuel: A Commentary*, trans. J. S. Bowden (Philadelphia: Westminster Press, 1964), 324; and McCarter, *Absalom*, 326.

28. Cf. the use of the same word in Isaiah 54:1: "the children of a desolate woman will be more numerous than the children of a married woman." Cited in McCarter, *Absalom*, 326.

29. It is not clear how much time had elapsed from the time of the rape to this birth, but it is likely that Tamar died sometime probably fairly early in a period of seven years, counting the two years before Absalom carried out his plot against Amnon (13:23), three more years living in virtual exile in Geshur (13:38), and two more full years in Jerusalem before going before the king (14:28). The chronology of baby Tamar's birth is apparently placed by the narrator after Absalom's return to Jerusalem but before his approach to the king. The elder Tamar might have died at any time prior to the baby Tamar's birth.

30. Hertzberg, *1 and 2 Samuel*, 322.

31. First identified by Leonhart Rost, *Die Überlieferung von der Thronnachfolge Davids* (Stuttgart: Kohlhammer, 1926), cited in McCarter, *2 Samuel*, and in Judith Todd, "Can Their Voices Be Heard?: Narratives about Women in 1 Samuel 16 through 1 Kings 2" (Ph.D. diss., Graduate Theological Union, Berkeley, Calif., April 1990). See also Conroy, *Absalom*.

32. For a thorough review of the major theories of both narrative (original) and later redactive sources, see McCarter, *2 Samuel*, 3–19, and Todd, "Can Their Voices?" 152–202. See also questions of methodology, text-critical problems, and a review of literature in Conroy, *Absalom*, 1–13.

33. Chapter 13 is not identified as part of the Deuteronomistic redaction layers that comprise the major editorial voice(s) named in the major scholarship on this topic; e.g., Frank Moore Cross, *Canaanite Myth and Hebrew Epic* (Cambridge, Mass.: Harvard Univ. Press, 1973), or T. Veijola, *Die ewige Dynastie. David und die Entstehung seiner Dynastie nach der deuteronomistischen Darstellung*, Annales Academiae Scientiarum Fennicae B 193 (Helsinki: Suomalainen Tiedeakatemia, 1975), cited in McCarter, *2 Samuel*, 7–8.

34. Rost, *Die Überlieferung*; Martin Noth, *The Deuteronomistic History*, trans. J. Doull et al., JSOT Supplement Series 15 (Sheffield, England: JSOT Press, 1981); Gerhard von Rad, *Old Testament Theology*, 2 vols., trans. D. Stalker (New York: Harper & Row, 1962), 1:339; James Flanagan, "Court History or Succession Document? A Study of 2 Samuel 9–20 and 1 Kings 1–2," *Journal of Biblical Literature* 91 (1972), 172–81, and others, cited in McCarter, *2 Samuel*, 4–15.

35. McCarter, *2 Samuel*, 15.

36. Aspects of E. Wurthwein, *Die Erzählung von der Thronfolge Davids—theologische oder politische Geschichtsschreibung?* Theologische Studien 115 (Zurich: Theologischer Verlag, 1974); Veijola, *Die ewige Dynastie*; F. Langlamet, "Pour ou contre Solomon? La redaction prosalomoni-enne de 1 Rois, 1–2," *Revue Biblique* 83: 321–79, 481–529; and others, cited in McCarter, *2 Samuel*, 15.

37. See especially von Rad, *Old Testament Theology*.

38. First identified by Noth, *Deuteronomistic History*, cited in Todd, "Can Their Voices?" 152, and McCarter, *2 Samuel*, 5.

39. The dating of these redactive layers is also disputed. Particularly at issue is whether the editing was during exilic or pre-exilic times. Major scholars involved in this debate include Cross, *Canaanite Myth*; Veijola, *Die ewige Dynastie*; and others, cited in McCarter, *2 Samuel*, 4–8.

40. Schüssler Fiorenza, *In Memory of Her*, 43, cited in Todd, "Can Their Voices?" 152–53.

41. William F. Stinespring, Preface, *New Oxford Annotated Bible* (New York: Oxford University Press, 1962), and *New Oxford Annotated Bible with the Apocrypha, Expanded Edition* (New York: Oxford University Press, 1977).

42. Stinespring, *New Oxford Annotated Bible*, 330, 374.

43. McCarter, *2 Samuel*, 327–28.

44. David Gunn, *The Story of King David: Genre and Interpretation*, JSOT Supplement Series 6 (Sheffield, England: JSOT Press, 1978), 100, cited in McCarter, *2 Samuel*, 328. Conroy (*Absalom*, 18–19) also examines the words "love" and "in love" and frames the story as opening with love and ending with hate, based on his literary analysis of the text. Conroy is sympathetic to Tamar (e.g., 23, 25), but could perhaps go further in questioning Amnon's "love." Barbara Green, in an interesting reading, finds the use of the word for "love" to be one more example of Amnon's being portrayed literarily in a negative light—in this case, as a liar (personal communication, March 1993).

45. McCarter, *2 Samuel*, 328.

46. Hertzberg, *1 and 2 Samuel*, 324; also Siegfried Herrmann, *A History of Israel in Old Testament Times*, rev. ed., trans. J. Bowden (Philadelphia: Fortress Press, 1981), 164, cited in Todd, "Can Their Voices?" 153.

47. David Biale, personal communication, October 1993.

48. For feminist examination of biblical stories of women blending literary and psychoanalytic approaches, see J. Cheryl Exum, *Fragmented Women: Feminist (Sub)Versions of Biblical Narratives* (Valley Forge, Pa.: Trinity Press International, 1993). Her analysis of texts concerning David's wife Michal in 1 and 2 Samuel are of particular relevance to the story of Tamar in 2 Samuel 13.

49. Trible, *Texts of Terror*.

50. The themes of justice and counsel in the reign of David are the focus of Keith Whitelam, *The Just King: Monarchical and Judicial Authority in Ancient Israel* (Sheffield, England: JSOT Press, 1979), cited in Todd, "Can Their Voices?" 196.

51. Citing Whitelam, *Just King*, 33.

52. Todd, "Can Their Voices?", 196.

53. Todd similarly highlights other overlooked wise women, including the wise woman of Tekoa and Bathsheba ("Can Their Voices?" 182ff.). See also Claudia Camp, "The Wise Women of 2 Samuel: A Role Model for Women in Early Israel." *Catholic Biblical Quarterly* 43 (1981), 14–29; and Jo Ann Hackett, "In the Days of Jael: Reclaiming the History of Women in Ancient Israel," in *Immaculate and Powerful: The Female in Sacred Image and Social Reality*, ed. C. Atkinson, C. Buchanan and M. Miles, Harvard Women's Studies in Religion Series (Boston: Beacon, 1985), 15–38.

54. Tamar fares much better in Walter Brueggemann's recent commentary (*1 and 2 Samuel*, 286–91). He acknowledges her response to Amnon as "shrewd and discerning," following Trible, and suggests that the accumulated arguments function literarily as a "massive indictment of Amnon, and implicitly David's earlier act of lust as well" (287). Brueggemann acknowledges the humiliation and oppression of the rape act (287). He also reads Tamar's act of public lamentation

as an act of noncompliance with a cover-up by Amnon (288). He acknowledges Absalom's re-marks to Tamar as possibly sounding dismissive. He misses, however, that in taking matters into his own hands, Absalom has reappropriated the matter as men's business. Brueggemann asserts that Tamar is avenged, without questioning the paternalism of Amnon's response, even if seen in the best light. Nor does he mention Tamar's absence in the account of the king's mourning at the end of 2 Samuel 13.

55. Rashkow, *Phallacy of Genesis*, esp. 21ff. This is her central premise.

56. Schüssler Fiorenza, *In Memory of Her*, 31.

57. See Brueggemann, *1 and 2 Samuel*, 1–7.

58. Article VI of the "Articles of Religion" (1801) of the Episcopal Church (BCP, 868). This article was part of the original Ten Articles of Religion of the Church of England, 1536.

CHAPTER 1: POWER AND VIOLENCE AGAINST WOMEN

1. Martin Buber, *I and Thou*, trans. W. Kaufman (New York: Charles Scribner's Sons, 1970), 67.

2. Mary Daly coined the term *re-membering* in her book *Gyn/Ecology: The Metaethics of Radical Feminism* (Boston: Beacon Press, 1978). *Re-membering* is defined as "1) Re-calling the Original intuition of integrity; healing the dismembered Self—the Goddess within women; Re-calling the Primordial connections/conversations among women, animals, and other Elemental beings. 2) Realizing the power to See and to Spell Out connections among apparently disparate phenomena: Spinning and Creating," also related to "*Re-calling*": "1) persistent/insistent Calling of the Wild; recurring invitation to Realms of Deep Memory. 2) Active unforgetting of partici-pation in Be-ing; Re-membering and giving voice to Original powers, intuitions, memories" (Daly, with Jane Caputi, *Webster's First New Intergalactic Wickedary of the English Language* [Boston: Beacon Press, 1987], 92–93).

3. Buber, *I and Thou*, 78.

4. Ibid., esp. 59, 63–64. Buber considered this inevitable: "This, however, is the sublime melancholy of our lot that every You must become an It in our world. . . . Genuine contemplation never lasts long; the natural being that only now revealed itself to me in the mystery of reciprocity has again become describable, analyzable, classifiable . . ." (68). Genuine, deep, unmediated en-counters with You are fleeting. "One cannot live in the pure present: it would consume us if care were not taken that it is overcome quickly and thoroughly. But in pure past one can live; in fact, only there can a life be arranged. One only has to fill every moment with experiencing and using, and it ceases to burn. And in all the seriousness of truth, listen: without It a human being cannot live. But whoever lives only with that is not human" (85). "Each such encounter is, as well, a glimpse of the eternal You, the divine" (123).

5. Ibid., 62.

6. Ibid., 69.

7. Following are some of the major analyses of power. Political-philosophical analyses: Hannah Arendt, *The Human Condition* (Chicago: Univ. of Chicago Press, 1958), esp. 199–207; Dorothy Emmet, "The Concept of Power," *Proceedings of the Aristotelian Society* (London) n.s. 54 (1953–54); Michel Foucault, *Power/Knowledge: Selected Interviews and Other Writings 1972–1977*, ed. Colin Gordon (New York: Pantheon, 1980); Steven Lukes, *Power: A Radical Analysis* (London: Macmillan, 1974); Steven Lukes, ed., *Power* (Oxford: Basil Blackwell, 1986); and Mariana Val-verde, *Sex, Power and Pleasure* (Philadelphia: New Society Pub., 1987). Theological examinations of power include: Paul Tillich, *Love, Power and Justice: Ontological Analyses and Ethical Applica-tions* (New York: Oxford University Press, 1954); Bernard Loomer, "Two Conceptions of Power," *Process Studies* 6/1 (Spring 1976), 5–32; Rita Nakashima Brock, *Journeys by Heart: a Christology of Erotic Power* (New York: Crossroad, 1988); Rebecca Chopp, *The Power to Speak: Feminism, Lan-guage, God* (New York: Crossroad, 1989); Carter Heyward, *The Redemption of God: A Theology of Mutual Relation* (Lanham, Md.: University Press of America, 1982), and *Touching Our Strength: The Erotic as Power and the Love of God* (San Francisco: Harper & Row, 1989); and Walter Wink,

Naming the Powers (Philadelphia: Fortress Press, 1984), *Unmasking the Powers: The Invisible Forces That Determine Human Existence* (Philadelphia: Fortress Press, 1986), and esp. *Engaging the Powers: Discernment and Resistance in a World of Domination* (Minneapolis: Fortress Press, 1992); James Newton Poling, *The Abuse of Power: A Theological Problem* (Nashville: Abingdom, 1991). Psychological examinations of power include Rollo May, *Power and Innocence: A Search for the Sources of Violence* (New York: Norton, 1972). Ethical examinations of power include: Karen Lebacqz, *Professional Ethics: Power and Paradox* (Nashville: Abingdon, 1985); Adolf Guggenbuhl-Craig, *Power in the Helping Professions* (Dallas: Spring, 1971); Peter Rutter, *Sex in the Forbidden Zone: When Men in Power Betray Women's Trust* (Los Angeles: Jeremy Tarcher, 1989); and Martha Ellen Stortz, *Pastor Power* (Nashville: Abingdon, 1993). Further feminist examinations of power include: Riane Eisler, *The Chalice and the Blade: Our History, Our Future* (San Francisco: Harper & Row, 1987), and Eisler with David Loye, *The Partnership Way* (San Francisco: HarperSanFrancisco, 1990); Starhawk, *Truth or Dare: Encounters with Power, Authority, and Mystery* (San Francisco: Harper & Row, 1987); Nancy Hartsock, *Money, Sex and Power: Toward a Feminist Historical Materialism* (Boston: Northeastern University Press, 1983; and Haunani-Kay Trask, *Eros and Power: The Promise of Feminist Theory* (Philadelphia: Univ. of Pennsylvania Press, 1986).

8. The pronoun *his* is used here because statistics show that 95 to 98 percent of battering is done by men against women. Richard Gelles, "The Myth of Battered Husbands," *Ms.* (October 1979): 65–73.

9. Study by the American Psychological Association, 1992: "Big World, Small Screen," summarized in *Congressional Quarterly Researcher*, March 26, 1993, cited by Media Scope, a parents' television advocacy organization in Los Angeles, California. See also "Violence on TV," *TV Guide*, August 22, 1992, 12–23.

10. Neil Hickey, "How Much Violence?" *TV Guide*, August 22, 1992, 10.

11. Ibid.

12. National Commission on the Causes and Prevention of Violence (1968), Surgeon General's Report (1972), National Institute of Mental Health (1982), and the U.S. Attorney General's Task Force on Family Violence (1984), cited in Hickey, "How Much Violence?" 11.

13. Editorial, "Violence in Video Games," *Oakland Tribune*, October 14, 1993, A-8.

14. "Violence in Video Games," A-8; and Melissa Reed, "From the Director," *Lifeline*, Mid-Peninsula Support Network for Battered Women, 14/3 (Summer 1993): 2.

15. Reed, "Director," 2. The British Board of Film Classification has banned sales of this game to minors under age fifteen.

16. Sigmund Freud, *The Ego and the Id*, trans. James Strachey, vol. 19 of *The Standard Edition* (London: Hogarth Press, 1961). Walter Kaufman first made this point in the introduction to Buber, *I and Thou*, 15.

17. Late in his life, Freud also postulated a separate "aggression instinct." See *Civilization and Its Discontents*, trans. James Strachey (New York: W. W. Norton, 1961).

18. On the archtype of the Self, see C. G. Jung, "The Self," 1–6, and "Christ, a Symbol of the Self," 36–71, in *Aion: Researches into the Phenomenology of the Self*, Bollingen Series 20, vol. 9/2 of *The Collected Works of C. G. Jung* (Princeton, N.J.: Princeton University Press, 1959). On the collective unconscious, see his "Archetypes of the Collective Unconscious" and "The Concept of the Collective Unconscious," in *The Archetypes and the Collective Unconscious*, Bollingen Series 20, vol. 9/1 of *The Collected Works of C. G. Jung* (Princeton, N.J.: Princeton University Press,), 3–41, 42–53.

19. Jung writes of an "ocean of divinity" in *Two Essays on Analytical Psychology*, Bollingen Series 20, vol. 7 of *The Collected Works of C. G. Jung* (Princeton: Princeton University Press, 1966), 476. Concerns with religion and the divine permeate the work of Jung, himself a pastor's son, and are particularly represented in his considerations of the archetypes of wholeness, mandala imagery, and the archetype of the Self. This was a profound rupture with Freud's almost entirely atheistic framework. Freud wrote a scathing dismissal of an "oceanic" or religious feeling as neurotic in origin, in *Civilization and Its Discontents*, 11ff. But Freud himself was drawn to intense consideration of the question of religion late in his life, particularly within the context of

the rise of Hitler. His *Moses and Monotheism* (trans. Katherine Jones [New York: Vintage/Random House, 1967]) appeared in 1939, the year World War II began and the year of his death. For a consideration of Freud's religious issues, see Hans Küng, *Freud and the Problem of God* (New Haven: Yale University Press, 1979).

20. The term *Third World* has been strongly challenged by people who live in the regions commonly associated with the term as condescending and making their cultures stand in reference to the *First World*. Instead, they offer the term *Two-thirds world*, to indicate that the majority of the world's populations reside in their countries. See Vinay Samuel and Christopher Sugden, *Lambeth: A View from the Two Thirds World* (Harrisburg, Pa.: Morehouse Publishers, 1989), 1.

21. Robert Alter (*The World of Biblical Literature* [New York: Basic Books, 1992], 114) has shown how this story of the violation of the fraternal bond makes literary allusion to the Joseph story of fraternal reconciliation in Genesis 45. Robert Alter, Alter draws out further allusions to the Joseph story and Potiphar's wife (Genesis 39), contrasting Joseph's ability as a man to escape, with Tamar's inability to escape as a woman overpowered physically by a man.

22. See Alter's reading (*Biblical Literature*, 115) as "this one" and "this creature."

23. The "power shuffle" exercise was first developed by Ricky Sherover-Marcuse, Harrison Simms, and Hugh Vasquez, and later published in Alan Creighton and Paul Kivel, *Helping Teens Stop Violence* (Alameda, Calif.: Hunter House, 1992). For an introduction to the broader "co-counseling movement from which it was derived, see Harvey Jackins, *The Human Side of Human Beings: The Theory of Re-Evaluation Counseling* (Seattle: Rational Island Pub., 1978).

24. For an analysis of how one -ism serves and maintains another, see Suzanne Pharr, *Homophobia: A Weapon of Sexism* (Little Rock, Ark./Inverness, Calif.: Women's Project/Chardon Press, 1988).

25. bell hooks, "Sisterhood: Political Solidarity," in *Feminist Theory: From Margin to Center* (Boston: South End Press, 1984), 43–66.

26. This may be a natural outgrowth of the roots of the program in the cocounseling movement, in which catharsis of blocked personal emotions is considered a key to healing.

27. This departs from Buber, who states in his opening sentence in *I and Thou*, "The world is twofold for man in accordance with his twofold attitude" (53; cf. 125). Concerning God, Buber writes, "God and man, being consubstantial, are actually and forever Two, the two partners of the primal relationship that, from God to man, is called mission and commandment . . . " (133). I envision an understanding in which God not only flows in and through the binary pair of two human subjects but also is the energy of love between them and beyond them to hold and contain them.

28. Here I borrow from the British object relations theorist D. W. Winnicott, who coined the phrases *holding environment* and *facilitating environment* to describe the earliest essential function of the primary parent (in Winnicott's view, the mother) to hold the infant, knitting the infant together with physical touch and emotional constancy until the infant can begin to hold himself or herself. The holding environment classically is an environment in which the whole person is allowed to be, without splitting off or disavowing any of his or her component thoughts, feelings, or impulses. See, for example, D. W. Winnicott, *Maturational Processes and the Facilitating Environment*, vol. 64 of *The International Psycho-Analytical Library* (London: The Hogarth Press and the Institute of Psycho-Analysis, 1965).

29. Buber, *I and Thou*, 155–56.

30. The understanding of God as "ground of being" (cf. Acts 17:28) is a central theme of existential theology, which also makes reference to Eastern religions, particularly Hinduism, as described by Paul Tillich, *Systematic Theology* (Chicago: Chicago University Press, 1967), 1:155–57; and *The Courage to Be* (New Haven: Yale University Press, 1952), esp. 157–58.

31. Rollo May, *Power and Innocence: A Search for the Sources of Violence* (New York: W. W. Norton, 1972).

32. Ibid., 40–45.

33. Ibid., 45.

34. For an interesting discussion of this distinction, see Carter Heyward, *Touching Our Strength: The Erotic as Power and the Love of God* (San Francisco: Harper & Row, 1989), 34.

35. Philosopher Dorothy Emmet has named a number of meanings and nuances for power in *Function, Purpose, and Powers: Some Concepts in the Study of Individuals and Societies*, 2d ed. (Philadelphia: Temple University Press, 1972), esp. 222–28. See also an inventory of nine different "powers of the allegedly powerless" articulated by Berenice Carroll, "Peace Research: The Cult of Power," in *Journal of Conflict Resolution* 4 (1972): 96, cited in Hartsock, *Money, Sex and Power*, 225.

36. Starhawk, *Truth or Dare*. Very similar to Starhawk's typology are Riane Eisler, *The Chalice and the Blade: Our History, Our Future*, and Eisler with David Loye, *The Partnership Way* (San Francisco: HarperSanFrancisco, 1990), in which she describes power over others as *dominator power* and proposes as an alternative a *partnership way* that closely resembles Starhawk's *power-with*. An excellent review of literature on power with particular attention to feminist theology and ethics is Rosalie Walker's "Feminist Discourse on Power: Toward a Vision of Erotic Power as Women's Spirituality," M.A. thesis, Pacific School of Religion, Berkeley, Calif., 1991.

Less popularly known feminist theories of power that also argue against power as dominance are Carroll, "Peace Research"; Hanna Pitkin, *Wittgenstein and Justice* (Berkeley, Calif.: University of California, 1972), and Elizabeth Janeway, *Powers of the Weak* (New York: 1980), all cited in Hartsock, *Money, Sex and Power*, 224–25.

Other authors have also begun describing power in ways that challenge the usual definition of power as power-over, expanding in both the direction of power between people that is shared more reciprocally and power within oneself that is derived from a stronger sense of internal authority and wisdom. Rollo May's categories of *nutrient power* (power used for the other in nurturing, parenting, or teaching ways) and *integrative power* are examples of attempts to expand power beyond dominance. So is Dorothy Emmet's category of coactive power, as opposed to power that she terms coercive.

Theologian Bernard Loomer has written on power as *relational power*, which has as its goal to strengthen relationships between people, rather than individual conquest. This is power to be influenced rather than to influence, which Loomer asserts is greater in size, exemplified by the suffering, relational power of Jesus. Bernard Loomer, "Two Conceptions of Power," *Process Studies* 6 (1976), 5–32. Of relevance also is the work of Jean Baker Miller and other psychologists at the Stone Center in Wellesley, Massachusetts, and of theologian Carter Heyward, on the importance of mutuality as a proper relational stance and the concept of the self-in-relation as the proper framework for identity rather than an individualistic concept of the self. See Jean Baker Miller, "Connections, Disconnections, and Violations," *Stone Center Work in Progress*, no. 33 1988, and *Toward a New Psychology of Women*, 2d ed. (Boston: Beacon Press, 1987).

Some theorists and theologians have also argued that the redemption of the concept of *eros* is concerned with the revisioning of power. *Eros*, expanded beyond its narrow definition as sexual love toward a definition as a passionate power directed toward both self and others, is necessary to the energetic and life-loving movement toward mutuality and shared power. In the words of Rita Nakashima Brock, "Erotic power is the power of our primal interrelatedness. Erotic power, as it creates and connects hearts, involves the whole person in relationships of self-awareness, vulnerability, openness, and caring." See esp. Rita Nakashima Brock, *Journey by Heart: A Christology of Erotic Power* (New York: Crossroad, 1988), 26; see also Catherine Keller, *From a Broken Web: Separation, Sexism, and Self* (Boston: Beacon, 1986); and Heyward, *Touching Our Strength*.

Power and its relation to sex, relationships, and economics is explored from a feminist framework by Hartsock, *Money, Sex and Power*; Valverde, *Sex, Power, and Pleasure*; Phyllis Chesler and Emily Jane Goodman, *Women, Money and Power* (New York: William Morrow and Co., 1976); and hooks, *Feminist Theory*.

37. Winnicott, *Maturational Processes*, esp. 140–52.

38. Cf. writings on community as a basis for revisioning a new or good society: Robert Bellah et al., *Habits of the Heart: Individualism and Commitment in American Life* (Berkeley, Calif.:

University of California Press, 1985), and *The Good Society* (New York: Knopf, 1991); M. Scott Peck, *The Different Drum: Community Making and Peace* (New York: Simon and Schuster, 1987).

39. Some authors have gone so far as to propose a prepatriarchal golden age in which goddesses were worshiped and peaceful, matriarchal social structures prevailed. See Eisler, *The Chalice and the Blade*; and Marija Gimbutas, *The Goddesses and Gods of Old Europe: Myth and Cult Images* (Berkeley: University of California Press, 1972); *The Language of the Goddess* (San Francisco: Harper & Row, 1989); and *The Civilization of the Goddess* (San Francisco: Harper & Row, 1991). Verification of these claims poses difficulties. The authors have necessarily based their theories of prepatriarchal history on archaeological evidence from preliterate cultures; unfortunately no texts are available to collaborate the interpretation of archaeological remains. Nevertheless, these interpretations have served as the inspiration or justification for a strong contemporary goddess-worshiping religious movement, as well as for numerous works of literature in which the longing for this kind of cooperative society and the sense of anger and despair at its supposed destruction is poured out in a lyrical and romantic form. Two immensely popular examples are Marion Zimmer Bradley, *The Mists of Avalon* (New York: Knopf, 1982), and Jean Auel, *The Clan of the Cave Bear* (New York: Crown Publishers, 1980).

40. See, for example, Philip L. Culbertson, *Counseling Men* (Minneapolis: Fortress Press, 1994), esp. 11–16.

41. This term is from Matthew Fox, *Original Blessing* (Santa Fe, N.M.: Bear and Co., 1983); for a well reasoned discussion of sin, goodness, and grace, see also John Macquarrie, *The Faith of the People of God: A Lay Theology* (New York: Charles Scribner's Sons, 1972). Macquarrie writes: "While I have stressed the universality of sin, as any realistic account of man must do, I do not think that one can accept the doctrine that man is totally immersed in sin, the doctrine of 'total depravity.' For if man were totally depraved, he would not even be conscious of his sinful state or made uneasy by it. Only because there persists in the human race something of an original righteousness, more original than original sin, can there be awareness of sin and any desire to overcome it. In more theological language, this original righteousness can be expressed by saying that man was made in the image of God; and although that image has been marred by sin, it has not been totally effaced" (63–64).

42. This departs somewhat from Starhawk's (*Truth or Dare: Encounters with Power, Authority, and Mystery* [San Francisco: Harper & Row, 1987]) original definition of power-with as "the power of a strong individual in a group of equals, the power not to command, but to suggest and be listened to, to begin something and see it happen" (10). Tamar's exercise of power-with fails if judged by the response of the men around her, if power-with is defined only as the power to be listened to and have influence. Tamar was not received, and yet her approach was one of mutuality. I believe that the exercise of power-with is an intention and commitment to mutuality, which is not wholly contingent upon the response or lack of response of the other.

43. The term *deconstruction* is used literally to mean the critique and dismantling of existing structures and not to be confused with the sense used by postmodernist French feminist philosophers, who focus on textual criticism, drawing on the work of Jacques Derrida.

44. For example, Hanna Pitkin, *Wittgenstein and Justice*, and Carroll, "Peace Research"; both cited in Hartsock, *Money, Sex, and Power*, 224–25.

45. Hartsock, *Money, Sex, and Power*.

46. For some detailed proposals for feminist collective leadership, see especially Starhawk, *Dreaming the Dark*; Mudflower Collective, *God's Fierce Whimsy: Christian Feminism and Theological Education* (New York: Pilgrim Press, 1985); Eisler and Loye, *Partnership Way*; and Lynn Rhodes, *Co-Creating: A Feminist Vision of Ministry* (Philadelphia: Westminster, 1987). Rhodes discusses authority as empowerment, a mutual exchange rooted in an honest examination of our own experience of life and sacred meaning, and she proposes ministry as a vision of friendship and solidarity.

47. Attrib. Sigmund Freud.

48. A classic analysis of charismatic power and its dangers is Max Weber, "The Meaning of Discipline," in H. H. Gerth and C. Wright Mills, eds., *From Max Weber: Essays in Sociology* (New York:

Oxford University Press, 1958), 262, summarized in Martha Ellen Stortz, *PastorPower*, 81, 139 fn. 4. Stortz, in her own critique of Starhawk's typology, emphasizes the dangers of charismatic leadership as power-within in " 'Clothed with Power from On High': Reflections on Power and Service in Ministry," *Word and World* 9/4 (Fall 1989), 328–36; and in *PastorPower*, 69–97. Dorothy Emmet distinguishes between the charismatist who uses hypnotic power to dominate and subordinate others and the more benevolent charismatic leader whose ultimate aim is to strengthen the will of those influenced and eventually let them go their own way, using the image of coach as a positive paradigm of charismatic power, in "Function, Purpose, and Powers," 233–34.

49. Verneice Thompson, consultation report to the Mid-Peninsula Support Network for Battered Women, Mountain View, Calif., Spring 1988.

50. A few authors have begun to address the pain of this phenomenon: Janice Raymond, *A Passion for Friends: Toward a Philosophy of Female Affection* (Boston: Beacon Press, 1986); Hartsock, *Money, Sex, and Power*; Luise Eichenbaum and Susie Orbach, *Between Women: Love, Envy, and Competition in Women's Friendship* (New York: Viking/Penguin, 1988); Marilyn Steele, "Redefining Authority: The Heroic Feminine," presented at Redefining the Givens: The Evolution of the Female Self, seminar series sponsored by Saturday Seminars, Berkeley, Calif., April 9, 1992.

51. Similar observations have been made by Stortz, *PastorPower*, and Edwin Friedman, *Generation to Generation: Family Process in Church and Synagogue* (New York: Guilford Press, 1985).

52. Cf. Hugh F. Halverstadt, *Managing Church Conflict* (Louisville: Westminster/John Knox Press, 1991).

53. Stortz, *PastorPower*; Karen Lebacqz, *Professional Ethics*, 109ff.; Rollo May, *Power*.

54. For example, see Nel Noddings, *Caring: A Feminine Approach to Ethics and Moral Education* (Berkeley, Calif.: University of Berkeley Press, 1984); and Sara Ruddick, *Maternal Thinking: Toward a Politics of Peace* (New York: Ballantine, 1990).

55. Contrary to some Marxist and feminist theories of education, I do not reject out of hand all pedagogies that, to use terminology from Paolo Freire, involve a "transfer of knowledge." Marxist, feminist, and liberation pedagogies that insist in all instances upon leaderless learning and the elimination of any expert, in my experience, severely limit the range of learning possible. Just as leadership is not in and of itself a negative construct, neither is legitimate expertise. For elaborations of alternative pedagogies, see Paolo Freire, *The Pedagogy of the Oppressed*, rev. ed., trans. Myrna Berman Ramos (New York: Continuum, 1992); and Mudflower Collective, *God's Fierce Whimsy*.

56. Rita Nakashima Brock, Panel "Contextualizing Dominant Christologies in North America," national meeting of the American Academy of Religion, Anaheim, Calif., November 1989.

57. Hartsock, *Money, Sex, and Power*, 3–4, 31; Stortz, *PastorPower*, 95. Stortz points out that the reverse could also be true—that every theory of community implies a theory of power (140 fn. 18).

58. Edwin H. Friedman (*Generation to Generation*, 229) discusses the body as an apt analogy for the differentiation of leadership in an organization. Martin Buber (*Meetings*, ed. Maurice Friedman [LaSalle, Ill.: Open Court, 1973], 38–39) wrote on the importance of "the living double kernels of humanity: genuine community and genuine leadership"—after visiting a Hasidic community as a small child in Sadagora: "the palace of the rebbe, its showy splendor, repelled me. The Prayer House of the Hasidim with its enraptured worshipers seemed strange to me. But when I saw the rebbe striding through the rows of the waiting, I felt 'leader,' and when I saw the Hasidim dance with the Torah, I felt 'community.' At that time there rose in me a presentiment of the fact that common reverence and common joy of soul are the foundations of genuine human community."

59. Michael Lerner writes of "communities of compassion" and the need for the "forging of a new 'We' " in *Surplus Powerlessness: The Psychodynamics of Everyday Life . . . and the Psychology of Individual and Social Transformation* (Atlantic Highlands, N.J.: Humanities Press International, 1991), esp. 339–50, 388–91.

60. Borrowing from Alice Miller, *For Your Own Good: Hidden Cruelty in Child-Rearing and the Roots of Violence*, trans. Hildegarde and Hunter Hannum (New York: Farrar, Straus, Giroux, 1983).

61. Hannah Arendt, *The Human Condition* (Chicago: Univ. of Chicago Press, 1958), 201.

62. Ibid., 202.

63. Starhawk (*Truth or Dare*, 1–27) uses the term pejoratively. Richard Sennett (*Authority* [New York: W. W. Norton, 1980]) examines traditional forms of authority (father-in-family, lord-in-society), why we tend to fear authority (because we fear being deceived), the bonds that rebellion paradoxically establishes, and ways to reinfuse authority with ideals. He concludes: "Belief in visible, legible authority is not a *practical* reflection of the public world; it is an *imaginative* demand. To ask that power be nurturing and restrained is unreal—or that, at least, is the version of reality our masters have inculcated in us. Authority, however, is itself inherently an act of imagination. It is not a thing; it is a search for solidity and security in the strength of others which will seem like a thing. To believe the search can be consummated is truly an illusion, and a dangerous one. Only tyrants fit the bill. But to believe the search should not be conducted at all is also dangerous. Then whatever is, is absolute" (197).

64. Anthony Giddens (*The Transformation of Intimacy: Sexuality, Love and Eroticism in Modern Societies* [Stanford, Calif.: Stanford University Press, 1992], esp. 184–92) proposes a democratization of private life, in which the principle of "no rights without obligations" and accountability based on trust would pertain as much in intimate, personal, and domestic life as well as in public life. In his conclusion, he suggests that such a "life politics" points toward a renewal of spirituality (203).

65. Kaufman, Introduction, *I and Thou.*

66. The work of the 1970s was largely in raising a critique of patriarchal language. Mary Daly's trenchant critique of male God-language (*Beyond God the Father: Toward a Philosophy of Women's Liberation* (Boston: Beacon Press, 1973) is still relevant. See also Mary Daly, *Gyn/Ecology*; and Naomi Goldenberg, *The Changing of the Gods: Feminism and the End of Traditional Religions* (Boston: Beacon Press, 1979). Efforts at new construction of God-language are growing. Two of the best known are Letty Russell, "Changing Language and the Church," in *The Liberating Word: A Guide to Nonsexist Interpretation of the Bible*, ed. Letty Russell (Philadelphia: Westminster, 1976), 82–98; and Sally McFague, *Models of God: Theology for an Ecological, Nuclear Age* (Philadelphia: Fortress Press, 1987).

67. Jon Sobrino and Juan Hernandez Pico, *Theology of Christian Solidarity*, trans. P. Berryman (Maryknoll, N.Y.: Orbis, 1985); Gustavo Gutierrez, *We Drink from Our Own Wells: The Spiritual Journey of a People*, trans. Matthew J. O'Connell (Maryknoll, N.Y.: Orbis, 1984); Desmond Mpilo Tutu, *Hope and Suffering: Sermons and Speeches* (Grand Rapids, Mich.: Wm. B. Eerdmans, 1983).

68. John B. Cobb, *Christ in a Pluralistic Age* (Philadelphia: Westminster, 1975), and with David Ray Griffin, *Process Theology: An Introductory Exposition* (Philadelphia: Westminster, 1976); Bernard Loomer, *The Size of God: the Theology of Bernard Loomer in Context*, ed. William Dean and Larry Axel (Macon, Ga.: Mercer University Press, 1987); *Process Theology: Basic Writings*, ed. Ewert H. Cousins (New York: Newman Press, 1971).

69. Paul Tillich, *Systematic Theology*. Langdon Gilkey (*Naming the Whirlwind: the Renewal of God-Language* [Indianapolis: Bobbs-Merrill Educational Pub., 1969]), among others, also draws from Eastern and particularly Buddhist thought to describe the infinity and transcendence of God in language of Nothingness and mystery. Such radical otherness, however, creates other problems for women, who are more traditionally identified with body, earth, and embodiment.

70. See esp. Virginia Ramey Molleukott, *The Biblical Images of God as Female* (New York: Crossroad, 1983).

71. See, for example, artistic representations by Meinrad Craighead, *The Mother's Songs: Images of God the Mother* (New York: Paulist Press, 1986).

72. Three of the best resources for inclusive language are Gail Ramshaw, *God beyond Gender: Feminist-Christian God-Language* (Minneapolis: Fortress Press, 1994); "Guidelines for Inclusive Use of the English Language" (Evangelical Lutheran Church in America, 1989); and *Language, Thought, and Social Justice: In a Manner of Speaking* (National Council of the Churches of Christ in the U.S.A., 1986).

73. Heyward, *Redemption of God*; McFague, *Models of God*.

74. Sallie McFague, *Metaphorical Theology: Models of God in Religious Language* (Philadelphia: Fortress Press, 1982), 43.

75. Tillich, *The Courage to Be*; and *Systematic Theology*.

76. One good discussion of this is Harold Kushner, *When Bad Things Happen to Good People* (New York: Schocken, 1981), reprinted in paperback (New York: Avon, 1983). The understanding of God as a fellow sufferer is also found as a central premise of many process theologians, stemming from Alfred North Whitehead and further developed by John Cobb. See, for example, John Cobb, *A Christian Natural Theology: Based on the Thought of Alfred North Whitehead* (Philadelphia: Westminster, 1965); Loomer, *Size of God*. Powerful expressions of divine cosuffering also exist in other religions, for example, the tradition of the Boddhisattva in Buddhism and the compassionate goddess Kuan Yin.

77. This was the conclusion of Elie Wiesel in wrestling with the unspeakable horror of the Nazi Holocaust. Either God was omnipotent and allowed the ghastly deaths of the children in the concentration camps, or God was not omnipotent in the sense of being able to prevent such suffering. Wiesel chose to believe in a God who suffers with humanity and to relinquish the concept of God's omnipotence. Other Jewish theologians took another path: No personal God could possibly exist who could permit such atrocity; therefore, the death of God is the starting point for a post-Holocaust theology. See Richard L. Rubenstein, *After Auschwitz: Radical Theology and Contemporary Judaism* (Indianapolis: Bobbs-Merrill Educational Publishing, 1966), esp. 227–64. Contra Wiesel, "Against Despair," in *A Jew Today*, trans. M. Wiesel (New York: Vintage/Random House, 1978), 183–97. See also Heyward, *Redemption of God*.

78. For example John Cobb, *Christian Natural Theology*.

79. Buber, *I and Thou*, 155.

80. Cf. McFague, *Metaphorical Theology* and *Models of God*.

81. Heyward (*Redemption of God*) has even proposed that in our mutual engagement with God humanity may be the source of God's own redemption.

CHAPTER 2: PORNOGRAPHY AND THE CONNECTION TO VIOLENCE

1. H. Rider Haggard, *She* (1887), ed. D. Karlin (Oxford: Oxford Univ. Press, 1991), 189.

2. Pauline Reage (pseudonym), *The Story of O* (1954), trans. Sabine d'Estree (New York: Ballantine, 1973), 95–96.

3. Vicky Noble, *Shakti Woman* (San Francisco: HarperSanFrancisco, 1991), 11–36.

4. Marija Gimbutas, *The Goddesses and Gods of Old Europe: Myth and Cult Images* (Berkeley: Univ. of California Press, 1972), *The Civilization of the Goddess* (San Francisco: HarperSanFrancisco, 1991) and *The Language of the Goddess* (San Francisco: Harper & Row, 1989); Merlin Stone, *When God Was a Woman* (New York: Harcourt Brace Jovanovich, 1978); Monica Sjoo and Barbara Mor, *The Ancient Religion of the Great Cosmic Mother of All* (Trondheim, Norway: Rainbow Press, 1981); Riane Eisler, *The Chalice and the Blade: Our History, Our Future* (San Francisco: Harper & Row, 1987). Whether or not a peaceful, goddess-oriented, prepatriarchal culture ever existed, as these authors suggest, I leave to the archaeologists and anthropologists to decide. It seems clear that more warlike cultures with male gods did, at certain times and places, overthrow more peaceful goddess cultures, for example, at Knossos (cited in Eisler, *The Chalice and the Blade*). In other settings, it is likely that both coexisted to some degree, worshiping both male and female deities with a variety of attributes, as in ancient Greece. Female priestesses figured more prominently in some ancient Near Eastern religions, for example, at Sumer. See Savina J. Teubal, *Sarah the Priestess: The First Matriarch of Genesis* (Athens, Ohio: Swallow Press, 1984). See also Walter Wink, *Engaging the Powers: Discernment and Resistance in a World of Domination* (Philadelphia: Fortress Press, 1992), 39–43.

5. Carol J. Adams, ed., *Ecofeminism and the Sacred* (New York: Continuum, 1993); Rosemary Radford Ruether, *Gaia and God: An Ecofeminist Theology of Earth Healing* (San Francisco: HarperSanFrancisco, 1992); Vandana Shiva, *Staying Alive: Women, Ecology, and Development*

(London: Zed Books, 1989). On the link between ecological damage and economic justice, see Carol S. Robb and Carl J. Casebolt, eds., *Covenant for a New Creation: Ethics, Religion and Public Policy* (Maryknoll, N.Y.: Orbis, and Berkeley, Calif.: Graduate Theological Union, 1991).

6. Some of the feminist spirituality literature and other feminist literature exalts these stereotypical aspects of the feminine in an effort to reclaim their value in a society that denigrates and devalues so-called "feminine" qualities. However, this movement can fall into the essentialist trap of perpetuating stereotypes, rather than actually reclaiming power for women as it purports to do by revaluing the feminine archetype.

7. Timothy Beneke, *Men on Rape* (New York: St. Martin's Press, 1982), 25–29.

8. Ernest Becker, *The Denial of Death* (New York: Basic Books, 1973). Becker contends in this classic psychosocial study that it is the denial of death, and not the sublimation of sexuality as Freud thought, that is the primary motivator and shaper of all civilization. See also Norman O. Brown, *Life against Death: The Psychoanalytical Meaning of History* (New York: Viking Books, 1959), one of the central sources for Becker's thesis.

9. Carolyn Merchant, *The Death of Nature: Women, Ecology and the Scientific Revolution* (San Francisco: HarperSanFrancisco, 1980); Susan Griffin, *Pornography and Silence: Culture's Revenge Against Nature* (New York: Harper & Row, 1981), and *Women and Nature: The Roaring Inside Her* (New York: Harper & Row, 1978); Dorothy Dinnerstein, *The Mermaid and the Minotaur* (New York: Harper & Row, 1976); Sherry Ortner, "Is Female to Male as Nature Is to Culture?" in *Woman, Culture, and Society*, ed. Michelle Zimbalist Rosaldo and Louise Lamphere (Stanford, Calif.: Stanford University Press, 1974).

10. H. Rider Haggard, *She*. Haggard's character Ayesha, "She-Who-Must-Be-Obeyed," is at first portrayed as an all-powerful, supernaturally beautiful, and commanding woman—not, incidentally, an "exotic" woman of color discovered by colonialist adventurers—who has mastered the secret of eternal life. Predictably, in the end, her secret is unmasked and the climax of the book is achieved with her withering and dying. Interestingly, C. G. Jung considered *She* to be representative of the *anima* (the archetype of man's feminine soul). C. G. Jung, "Marriage as a Psychological Relationship," in *The Development of Personality* (1954), Bollingen Series 20, Collected Works of C. G. Jung, vol. 17, 3d ed. (Princeton, N.J.: Princeton University Press, 1970), 200.

11. Sherry Ortner, "Is Female to Male as Nature Is to Culture?" See also Susan Griffin, *Pornography and Silence* and *Women and Nature*.

12. Melanie Klein, *Envy and Gratitude* (1957), cited in Dinnerstein, *The Mermaid and the Minotaur*; Nancy Chodorow, *The Reproduction of Mothering: Psychoanalysis and the Sociology of Gender* (Berkeley, Calif.: Univ. of California Press, 1978); Carolyn Merchant, *The Death of Nature*. For a complementary Jungian View, see Erich Neuman, *The Fear of the Feminine*, Bollingen Series 61/4 (Princeton, N.J.: Princeton University Press, 1994).

13. Marta Weigle, *Creation and Procreation: Feminist Reflections on Mythologies of Cosmogony and Parturition* (Philadelphia: Univ. of Pennsylvania Press, 1989). See also P. Cooper-White, review of Weigle in *Bulletin of the Center for Theology and Natural Sciences*, Berkeley, Calif., 11/4 (Autumn 1991), 24–25.

14. For an elaboration of this theme, and a scathing critique of the traditional treatment of women by the mental health profession, see Phyllis Chesler, *Women and Madness* (1972), reprinted with new introduction (San Diego: Harvest/Harcourt Brace Jovanovich, 1989).

15. Linda Schierse Leonard, *Meeting the Madwoman: An Inner Challenge for the Feminine Spirit* (New York: Bantam, 1993).

16. Helen B. Lewis, "Madness in Women," in *Women and Mental Health*, ed. Elizabeth Howell and Marjorie Bayes (New York: Basic Books, 1981), 219.

17. G. J. Barker-Benfield, *The Horrors of the Half-Known Life: Male Attitudes toward Women and Sexuality in the Nineteenth Century* (New York: Harper & Row, 1976), cited in Mary Daly, *Gyn/Ecology: the Metaethics of Radical Feminism* (Boston: Beacon Press, 1978), 241.

18. Ibid., cited in Daly, *Gyn/Ecology*, 241, and esp. fn. 30.

19. See "sex ratio" information given for each disorder in American Psychiatric Association, *Diagnostic and Statistical Manual of Mental Disorders*, 4th ed. (DSM-IV) (Washington, D.C.: APA, 1994). It can also be argued that a number of disorders disproportionately affecting men also reflect exaggerations of stereotypical masculinity—for example, antisocial personality disorder (647) (characterized in childhood by lying, stealing, truancy, vandalism, initiating fights, and physical cruelty, and in adulthood by deceitfulness, failure to honor financial obligations, to function as a responsible parent or plan ahead, an inability to sustain consistent work, and criminal acts including destruction of property, harassment, stealing, driving under the influence, and repeated violence).

20. This theory is elaborated in Robert Seidenberg and Karen DeCrow, *Women Who Marry Houses: Panic and Protest in Agoraphobia* (New York: McGraw-Hill, 1983).

21. Kim Chernin, *The Hungry Self: Women, Eating and Identity* (New York: Harper & Row, 1985); Naomi Wolf, *The Beauty Myth* (New York: Anchor/Doubleday, 1992, 179–219; Susie Orbach, *Hunger Strike: The Anorectic's Struggle as a Metaphor for Our Age* (New York: W. W. Norton, 1986).

22. Margot Kaessmann, "Bible Study: Spirit of Freedom, Not of Slavery," in World Council of Churches, *Women in a Changing World* 30 (June 1991), 16.

23. Caroline Fairless, "What Does Love Require? A Family Violence Manual for the Church Community," unpublished M.Div. honors thesis, Church Divinity School of the Pacific, Berkeley, Calif., May 1989, 17.

24. Kaessmann, "Bible Study," 15.

25. Thomas Aquinas, *Summa Theologiae* II-II, 26, 10c, cited in Mary Daly, *The Church and the Second Sex* (New York: Harper Colophon, 1975), 91.

26. Ibid., I, 93, 4, ad 1. cited in Daly, *The Church and the Second Sex*, 93.

27. Kaessmann, "Bible Study," 16.

28. Preserved Smith, *The Life and Letters of Martin Luther* (Boston: Houghton Mifflin, 1911), 180, cited in Fairless, "What Does Love Require?" 20.

29. Kaessmann, "Bible Study," 15.

30. Cited in Joy Bussert, *Battered Women* (Minneapolis: Augsburg Fortress, 1986), 11–12.

31. Cited in Kaessmann, "Bible Study," 16.

32. Karl Barth, *Church Dogmatics: the Doctrine of Creation*, ed. Bromily and Torrance, trans. A. T. Mackay et al. (Edinburgh: T. and T. Clark, 1961), 3/4: 169; cited in Fairless, "What Does Love Require?" 19.

33. Ibid., 170; cited in Fairless, "What Does Love Require?" 19.

34. "The Apparel of Women," in *Tertullian: Disciplinary, Moral and Ascetical Works*, trans. Rudolph Arbesmann et al., ed. Roy Deferrari et al. The Fathers of the Church Series (New York: Fathers of the Church, Inc., 1959), 118. Cited variously in Fairless, "What Does Love Require?" 17; and Kaessmann, "Bible Study," 15.

35. Cited in Kaessmann, "Bible Study," 15

36. Excerpt from poem "The Anatomy of the World," cited in Merchant, "Death of Nature," 133.

37. For an elaboration of this theme, see Mary Daly, *Beyond God the Father: Toward a Philosophy of Women's Liberation* (Boston: Beacon Press, 1973), esp. chap. 2; and Nel Noddings, *Women and Evil* (Berkeley, Calif.: University of California Press, 1989), esp. chap. 2 "The Devil's Gateway," 35–58.

38. Heinrich Kramer and James Sprenger, *Malleus Maleficarum*, trans. M. Summers (London: Arrow Books, 1971), cited in Andrea Dworkin, *Woman Hating* (New York: Penguin-Plume, 1974), 130–31.

39. Phyllis Trible, *God and the Rhetoric of Sexuality* (Philadelphia: Fortress Press, 1978), 113–14.

40. Kramer and Sprenger, *Malleus Maleficarum*, cited in Dworkin, *Woman Hating*, 131.

41. Ibid., cited in Dworkin, *Woman Hating*, 132.

42. Ibid., cited in Dworkin, *Woman Hating*, 130.

43. For more details on the witch craze as persecution of women, see Marianne Hester, "The Witch-Craze in Sixteenth- and Seventeenth-Century England as Social Control of Women," in J. Radford and D. E. H. Russell, *Femicide*, 27–39; Dworkin, "Women Hating," 118–54; Barbara Ehrenreich and Deirdre English, *Witches, Midwives, and Nurses: a History of Women Healers*, 2d ed. (Old Westbury, N.Y.: Feminist Press, 1973); and Mary Daly, "European Witchburnings: Purifying the Body of Christ," in *Gyn/Ecology* 178–222; and Starhawk, "The Burning Times: Notes on a Crucial Period of History," in *Dreaming the Dark: Magic, Sex and Politics* (Boston: Beacon Press, 1982), 183–219.

44. Ibid. The term "witch-craze" is from Hugh Trevor-Roper, *The European Witch-craze of the Sixteenth and Seventeenth Centuries* (Harmondsworth: Penguin, 1969).

45. Articulated by a Synod in 785; cited in Dworkin, *Woman Hating*, 126.

46. See Dworkin, *Woman Hating*, 128–29.

47. See Hester, "The Witch-Craze."

48. Jane Caputi and Diana Russell, "Femicide: Sexist Terrorism Against Women," in Radford and Russell, *Femicide*, 13, 15.

49. Laura Lederer, ed., *Take Back the Night: Women on Pornography* (New York: William Morrow and Co., 1980).

50. Irene Diamond, "Pornography and Repression: A Reconsideration of 'Who' and 'What' "; Pauline B. Bart and Margaret Jozsa, "Dirty Books, Dirty Films, and Dirty Data"; Diana E. H. Russell, "Pornography and Violence: What Does the New Research Say?" in *Take Back the Night*, ed. Laura Lederer, 187–238; Diana Russell, *Against Pornography: The Evidence of Harm* (Berkeley, Calif.: Russell Publications, 1993). See esp. a summary of research and arguments on causation in "A Theory about the Causative Role of Pornography," 118–48.

51. Jane Caputi, citing studies by Kathleen Barry, Susan Brownmiller, Andrea Dworkin, Susan Griffin, Laura Lederer, and Diana Russell, in "Advertising Femicide: Lethal Violence Against Women in Pornography and Gorenography," in Radford and Russell, *Femicide*, 203–4.

52. Caputi, "Advertising Femicide," 204.

53. R. K. Ressler, A. W. Burgess and J. E. Douglas, *Sexual Homicide: Patterns and Motives* (Lexington, Mass.: Lexington Books/D.C. Health and Co., 1988), cited in Caputi, "Advertising Femicide," 204.

54. Deborah Cameron, " 'That's Entertainment'?: Jack the Ripper and the Selling of Sexual Violence," in Radford and Russell, *Femicide*, 184–88.

55. Caputi, "Advertising Femicide," 212.

56. Ibid.

57. U.S. Attorney General's Commission on Pornography, *Final Report* (Nashville, Tenn.: Rutledge Hill Press, 1986), 39.

58. Caputi, "Advertising Femicide," 217.

59. Neil Malamuth and Edward Donnerstein, "The Effects of Aggressive-Pornographic Mass Media Stimuli," *Advances in Experimental Social Psychology* 15, ed. L. Berkowitz (New York: Academic Press, 1982); Park Dietz and B. Evans, "Pornographic Images, and Prevalence of Paraphilia," *American Journal of Psychiatry* 139 (1982), 1493–95.

60. U.S. Attorney General's Commission on Pornography, *Final Report*, 40.

61. Reproduced in Russell, *Against Pornography*, i.

62. Ibid., 13.

63. March 1983, reprinted in Russell, *Against Pornography*, 41.

64. Ibid., 56.

65. August 1975, reprinted in Russell, *Against Pornography*, 73.

66. National Research Bureau, 1992, cited in Russell, *Against Pornography*, 11.

67. Ibid., 12.

68. Women against Pornography, n.d., "Did You Know That . . . ?"

69. "A Newsweek Poll: Mixed Feelings about Pornography," *Newsweek*, March 18, 1985.

70. Daniel S. Campagna and Donald L. Poffenberger, *The Sexual Trafficking in Children: An Investigation of the Child Sex Trade* (Dover, Mass.: Auburn House, 1988).

71. Ibid. See also Russell, *Against Pornography*.

72. Laura Lederer, "Then and Now: An Interview with a Former Pornography Model," in *Take Back the Night*, ed. Laura Lederer, 57–70; Kathleen Barry, *Female Sexual Slavery* (Englewood Cliffs, N.J.: Prentice-Hall, 1979); Diana E. H. Russell and Nicole Van de Ven, eds., *Crimes Against Women: Proceedings of the International Tribunal* (Millbrae, Calif.: Les Femmes, 1976).

73. Gloria Steinem, "Linda Lovelace's 'Ordeal,' " *Ms.*, May 1980, also cited in Susan Griffin, *Pornography and Silence*, 113.

74. Reprinted in Russell, *Against Pornography*, 102.

75. Melissa Farley, "The Rampage Against *Penthouse*," in Radford and Russell, *Femicide*, 339.

76. Ibid., 340–41.

77. In an introduction to *The Story of O* entitled "Happiness in Slavery," Jean Paulhan of l'Academie Francaise writes concerning the mystery of the supposedly unknown identity of "Pauline Reage": "That you are a woman I have little doubt. . . . And yet, in her own way O expresses a virile ideal. Virile, or at least masculine. At last a woman who admits it! Admits what? Something that women have always refused till now to admit (and today more than ever before). Something that men have always reproached them with: that they never cease obeying their nature, the call of their blood, that everything in them, even their minds, is sex. That they have constantly to be nourished, constantly washed and made up, constantly beaten. That all they need is a good master, one who is not too lax or too kind. . . . In short, that we must, when we go to see them, take a whip along" (xxiv-xxv). The further linkage between this attitude about the sexual bondage of women and racism is made explicit as this writer begins his introduction with a story of "two hundred Negroes" in Barbados, who, supposedly, after their emancipation in 1838 came to beg their master to take them back into bondage (xxi).

In a recent article in *The New Yorker* (John De St. Jorre, "The Unmasking of O," August 1, 1994, pp. 42ff.), Pauline Reage was identified as Dominique Aury, a prominent French woman of letters and winner of the Legion d'Honneur. Aury wrote *The Story of O* for Jean Paulhan himself in a desperate attempt to keep him as her lover. *The Story of O* is still described in this contemporary article as "a rather beautiful book" and a "sexual landmark" (42).

78. Dworkin, *Woman Hating*, 58–59, also citing Pauline Reage, *Story of O*.

79. U.S. Attorney General's Commission on Pornography, *Final Report*, 40–41.

80. Marie Fortune makes this distinction in the context of her ethical analysis of sexual violence, in *Sexual Violence: the Unmentionable Sin* (New York: Pilgrim Press, 1983), esp. 231–36, and in "Violence against Women: The Way Things Are Is Not the Way Things Have to Be" (Seattle, Wash.: Center for the Prevention of Sexual and Domestic Violence). For a discussion on pornography vs. erotica, issues of "obscenity" and censorship vs. freedom of the press, and whether or not pornography causes or influences violence, see Susanne Kappeler, *The Pornography of Representation* (Minneapolis: Univ. of Minnesota Press, 1986).

81. Audre Lorde, "Uses of the Erotic: The Erotic as Power," in *Take Back the Night*, ed. Laura Lederer, 295–300; Susan Griffin, *Pornography and Silence*; Carter Heyward, "The Erotic as the Power of God," in *Touching Our Strength*; Rita Nakashima Brock, *Journey by Heart: a Christology of Erotic Power* (New York: Crossroad, 1988).

82. Lorde, "Uses of the Erotic," 296.

83. Ibid.

84. Anthony Giddens, *The Transformation of Intimacy: Sexuality, Love and Eroticism in Modern Societies* (Stanford, Calif.: Stanford University Press, 1992), 119–20.

85. Gloria Steinem, "Erotica and Pornography: A Clear and Present Difference," in *Take Back the Night*, ed. Laura Lederer, 37.

86. Susan Griffin, *Pornography and Silence*.

87. *Pornography and Civil Rights: A New Day for Women's Equality* (Minneapolis: Organizing against Pornography, 1988), cited in Caputi, "Advertising Femicide," 206–7. See also Catherine MacKinnon, *Only Words* (Cambridge, Mass.: Harvard University Press, 1993).

88. Griffin, *Pornography and Silence*, 36.

89. See, e.g., C. G. Jung, *Two Essays on Analytical Psychology* (1917/1926/1943 and 1928), Bollingen Series 20, The Collected Works of C. G. Jung (Princeton: Princeton University Press, 1966), 7:90ff; "The Shadow" in *Aion: Researches into the Phenomenology of the Self* (1951), Bollingen Series 20, 9/2.

CHAPTER 3: SEXUAL HARASSMENT

1. Maureen Longworth, M.D., told this story at a conference sponsored by the National Women's Political Caucus, "A Sexual Harassment Speak-Out," Laney College, Oakland, March 7, 1992, where she also spoke of a film she produced in 1984 to educate doctors about sexism in medicine. She says that she still receives hostile sexual remarks from male physicians when she shows the films at even the most highly respected hospitals. For an account of the conference, see Candy J. Cooper, "Women Speak Out on Abuse," *San Francisco Examiner*, Sunday, March 8, 1992, B-1, B-4.

2. Doe Fiedler et al. v. Dana Properties, Inc., and Fairfield North et al., U.S. District Court, Sacramento, California. Summarized in Barbara Deane, "At His Mercy," *Redbook*, May 1992, 98–127; Robin Abcarian, "Harassed at Home," *Los Angeles Times*, Sunday, November 24, 1992, E1, E8; personal communication, November 1993, Leslie Levy, attorney for the plaintiffs.

3. WRATH, 607 Elmira Road, Suite #299, Vacaville, CA 95687.

4. Katherine Lanpher, "Reading, 'Riting, and 'Rassment," *Ms.* (May/June 1992), 90–91; [n.a.], "Sticking Up for Teenage Girls," *Glamour*, August 1992, 114.

5. Lanpher, "Reading, 'Riting, and 'Rassment," 91.

6. The names and exact details of this story have been altered to protect the anonymity of the victim. Reprinted by permission.

7. Glenna Matthews, author of *Just a Housewife: The Rise and Fall of Domesticity in America* (New York: Oxford University Press, 1987). Dr. Matthews told her story at National Women's Political Caucus, "A Sexual Harassment Speak-Out," Laney College, Oakland, Calif., March 7, 1992.

8. Interview by Candy J. Cooper, "Women Speak Out on Abuse," *San Francisco Examiner*, Sunday, March 8, 1992, B-4.

9. For a practical interpretation of this section, see Susan L. Webb, *Step Forward: Sexual Harassment in the Workplace: What You Need to Know!* (New York: Mastermedia, 1991), 41.

10. This distinction between "quid pro quo" and "condition of work" harassment is detailed in Catharine MacKinnon, *Sexual Harassment of Working Women: A Case of Sex Discrimination* (New Haven: Yale University Press, 1979), 32–47.

11. Carol Robb, "Sexual Harassment: The Sexual Significance of Work," work in progress, presented at San Francisco Theological Seminary, Spring 1990.

12. Katherine A. Benson, "Comment on Crocker's 'An Analysis of University Definitions of Sexual Harassment,' *Signs: Journal of Women in Culture and Society* 9/3 (1984), 516, cited in Robb, 27.

13. Peter Rutter, *Sex in the Forbidden Zone* (Los Angeles: Jeremy Tarcher, 1989), 68.

14. For more detailed discussion of the consequences for victims, see Barbara Chester, "Sexual Harassment: Victim Responses," in *Sexual Assault and Abuse: A Handbook for Clergy and Religious Professionals*, ed. Mary D. Pellauer, Barbara Chester, and Jane Boyajian (San Francisco: HarperSanFrancisco, 1987), 161–71.

15. MacKinnon, *Sexual Harassment*, 30.

16. Stingley v. State of Arizona et al., U.S. District Court, D. Arizona, No. Civ 91–122 TUC JMR, July 27, 1992. Yolanda Stingley, who had been harassed at work both racially and sexually, brought a case against her employer, the Dept. of Corrections of the State of Arizona. The U.S. District Court of Arizona ruled that "the proper perspective from which to evaluate the hostility of the environment is the 'reasonable person of the same gender and race or color' standard," citing Ellison v. Brady's "reasonable woman" standard as precedent. Ellison, which established the "reasonable woman" standard, will be described in detail later in the chapter. The "reasonable black person" standard as applied to racial harassment cases was established in another case

around the same time, Harris v. International Paper, U.S. District Court, D. Maine, 765 F.Supp. 1509 (D.Me. 1991), March 28, 1991.

17. May D. Faucher and Kenneth J. McCulloch, "Sexual Harassment in the Workplace," in Gail Ann Neugarten and Jay M. Shafritz, eds., *Sexuality in Organizations: Romantic and Coercive Behaviors at Work* (Oak Park, Ill.: Moore Press, 1980), 88; cited in Robb, 15–16.

18. Cynthia Grant Bowman, "Street Harassment and the Informal Ghettoization of Women," *Harvard Law Review* 106/3 (Jan. 1993), 517.

19. MacKinnon, *Sexual Harassment*, 49.

20. American Psychiatric Association, *Diagnostic and Statistical Manual*, 4th ed. rev. (DSM-IV), (Washington, D.C.: American Psychiatric Association, 1994), 522, 527, 532.

21. Steven White, M.D., and Chris Hatcher, M.D., "Violence and Trauma Response," *Occupational Medicine: State-of-the-Art Reviews*, vol. 3, no. 4 (Oct.–Dec. 1988), 677–94, cited in "Terror and Violence in the Workplace," *The 1993 National Employer*, 10th ed. (San Francisco: Littler, Mendelson, Fastiff, Tichy & Mathiason, 1993). Other warning signs, the presence of which compounds the probability of violence, include ominous generalized threats, menacing gestures or flashing of concealed weapons, bizarre thoughts, obsessive grudges, an obsession with weapons and gun magazines, lack of interests outside the job, being a loner, being paranoid, and environmental factors of extreme stress, exposure to violence on the job from nonemployees, labor disputes, layoffs, or personal problems. See *The 1993 National Employer*, 160 and 170–71.

22. For a clinical discussion of erotomania, the delusional disorder underlying this form of stalking, see Jonathan H. Segal, "Erotomania Revisited: From Kraepelin to DSM-III-R," *American Journal of Psychiatry* 146/10 (Oct. 1989), 1261–66.

23. Calif. P.C. 6469.

24. Kerry Ellison, Plaintiff-Appellant v. Nicholas F. Brady, Secretary of the Treasury, Defendant-Appelle, United States Court of Appeals, 9th Circuit, No. 89–15248, 1991, 878ff.; also citing Kathryn Abrams, "Gender Discrimination and the Transformation of Workplace Norms," 42 Vand.L.Rev. 1183, 1205 (1989). That there might be two different perspectives on the questions of unwelcomeness and pervasiveness or severity was already established in Lipsett v. University of Puerto Rico, First Circuit Court of Appeals 864 F.2d 881, 1988. Similar rulings were being made in the same time period concerning racial harassment. (See this chapter, above.)

25. MacKinnon, *Sexual Harassment*, 54.

26. Ibid., 54–55.

27. Karen Lebacqz, "Reflections on the Thomas Hearings," *Center for Women and Religion Newsletter* (Berkeley, Calif.: Graduate Theological Union), November 1991, 1–2.

28. Lynn Wehrli, "Sexual Harassment at the Workplace: A Feminist Analysis and Strategy for Social Change," M.A. thesis, Massachusetts Institute of Technology, December 1976, cited in MacKinnon, *Sexual Harassment*, 48.

29. MacKinnon, *Sexual Harassment*, 48.

30. Dierdre Silverman, "Sexual Harassment: Working Women's Dilemma," *Quest: A Feminist Quarterly* 3/3 (1976–77), 19; cited in MacKinnon, *Sexual Harassment*, 48.

31. For a more detailed list, see Webb, *Step Forward*, 97–101; for a more aggressive approach to direct confrontation, see Martha J. Langelan, *Back Off! How to Confront and Stop Sexual Harassment and Harassers* (New York: Fireside/Simon & Schuster, 1993); see also Mary P. Rowe, "Dealing with Sexual Harassment," *Harvard Business Review* 59/3 (May–June 1981), 42–46, also cited in Robb, 23.

32. Webb, *Step Forward*, 99.

33. If you have a sense that these early steps won't work, consider getting an initial consultation with an attorney. An attorney can be one factor that levels the imbalance of power between the harasser and the victim. Even talking to an attorney and coming up with a game plan can be empowering. An attorney can advise on how to keep a log, how to document, what to know about the law, and how the courts have been ruling. Economics can be a deterrent to many women at this stage. However, there are *pro bono* and community legal services. Contact the Bar Association in your area for listings.

34. See Webb, *Step Forward*, 98–99; and Langelan, *Back Off!* 115–26.

35. For this reason, even though it is an improvement over the "reasonable man" standard, shifting to a "reasonable woman" standard of what constitutes sexual harassment does not go far enough. Even this standard means that the definition of harassment remains murky, dependent upon the woman's perceptions, and hence opening her to attack on her credibility.

36. Drawn partly from Webb, *Step Forward*, 41–44, and from my own work on church and seminary policies.

37. For a good example of the use of an ombuds team, see *Naming the Unnamed: Sexual Harassment in the Church* (1982), Council on Women and the Church (United Presbyterian Church in the USA, 475 Riverside Drive, Room 1151, New York, NY 10115), 16–17.

38. David Owen-Ball, Esq., personal communication, November 1993.

39. Leslie Levy, Esq., personal communication, November 1993.

40. For example, a program called "Todos: Sherover Simms Alliance Building Institute" (formerly "New Bridges"), founded by the originators of the antioppression materials cited in this chapter, located at 678 13th Street, Suite 103, Oakland, CA 94612.

41. See flyer entitled "Five Ways Your Parish Can Work to Become a Safe Place," Evangelical Lutheran Church in America, Commission for Women, 8765 W. Higgins Road, Chicago, IL 60631.

42. "Sexual Harassment and Abuse," handout created by the ELCA Commission for Women with highlights of the 1989 Churchwide Assembly resolution on sexual harassment and abuse, printed on reverse side of "Five Ways. . . . " Available from 8765 W. Higgins Road, Chicago, IL 60631.

43. BCP, 305.

44. The Book of Confessions, 7:071.

45. *Naming the Unnamed*, 4.

CHAPTER 4: RAPE

1. Some resources for statistics include: Federal Bureau of Investigation, *Uniform Crime Reports* (Washington, D.C.: Federal Bureau of Investigation, 1990, 1991, et al.); Caroline Wolf Harlow, *Female Victims of Violent Crime* (Washington, D.C.: U.S. Department of Justice/Bureau of Justice Statistics, 1991); Mary P. Koss and Mary R. Harvey, *The Rape Victim: Clinical and Community Interventions* (Beverly Hills: Sage, 1991); National Victim Center/National Women's Study, "Rape in America: A Report to the Nation," April 23, 1992 (2111 Wilson Blvd., Suite 300, Arlington, VA 22201); Diana Russell, *The Politics of Rape: The Victim's Perspective* (New York: Stein and Day, 1975); Diana Russell, *Sexual Exploitation: Rape, Child Sexual Abuse and Sexual Harassment* (Beverly Hills: Sage, 1984); U.S. Department of Justice, Bureau of Justice Statistics, *Sourcebook of Criminal Justice Statistics*, 1991. FBI Uniform Crime Reports 1990, 1991, et al.

2. National Victim Center report, 1992, p. 5, says only 16 percent of rapes are reported; rape crisis centers generally agree on a 10 percent rape report rate; the Bureau of Justice Statistics, based on the National Crime Survey, states that about half of rapes or attempted rapes are reported. *BJS Data Reports*, 1986, 15.

3. Statistics are drawn from studies conducted in Seattle, Wash., Kansas City, Mo., and Boston City Hospital, cited in A. Nicholas Groth, with H. Jean Birnbaum, *Men Who Rape: The Psychology of the Offender* (New York: Plenum, 1979), 222.

4. For a study on women's fear of rape, see Stephanie Riger and Margaret Gordon, *The Female Fear* (New York: Free Press, 1989).

5. Diana Russell, *Rape in Marriage* (New York: Macmillan, 1982); David Finkelhor and Kersti Yllo, *License to Rape: Sexual Abuse of Wives* (New York: Holt, Rinehart and Winston, 1985).

6. Ruth Schmidt, "After the Fact: To Speak of Rape," *Christian Century*, Jan. 6–13, 1993, 14.

7. National Women's Study, National Victim Center, "Rape in America: A Report to the Nation," April 23, 1992 (2111 Wilson Blvd., Suite 300, Arlington, VA 22201), 7–8. Similar conclusions appear in Dean Kirkpatrick et al., "Mental Health Correlates of Criminal Victimization," *Journal of Consulting and Clinical Psychology* 53/6 (1985), 866–73.

8. Henry Campbell Black, *Black's Law Dictionary*, 6th rev. ed. (St. Paul, Minn.: West Publishing Company, 1990), 1260. The complete definition reads: "Unlawful sexual intercourse with a female without her consent. The unlawful carnal knowledge of a woman by a man forcibly and against her will. The act of sexual intercourse committed by a man with a woman not his wife and without her consent, committed when the woman's resistance is overcome by force or fear, or under other prohibitive conditions. (State v. Lora, 213 Kan. 184, 515 P.2d 1086, 1093). A male who has sexual intercourse with a female not his wife is guilty of rape if: (a) he compels her to submit by force or by threat of imminent death, serious bodily injury, extreme pain or kidnapping, to be inflicted on anyone; or (b) he has substantially impaired her power to appraise or control her conduct by administering or employing without her knowledge drugs, intoxicants or other means for the purpose of preventing resistance; or (c) the female is unconscious; or (d) the female is less than 10 years old. (Model Penal Code -213.1) Under some statutes, crime embraces unnatural as well as natural sexual intercourse, e.g. M.G.L.A. (Mass.) C.277 -39; and, may include intercourse between two males." Many states still conform to this quite narrow definition, for example, California, in which rape is defined as sexual intercourse by a man without the consent of a woman, and in which there must be some penetration of the vagina by the penis.

9. See Martha R. Burt, "Cultural Myth, Violence against Women, and the Law," *The Drew Gateway* 58 (1988), 25–27.

10. Groth and Birnbaum, *Men Who Rape*, 3.

11. Sam Green, "Lecturer [Nancy Lemon] Takes On Marital Rape Law," *Oakland Tribune*, July 13, 1992. For longer studies of marital rape, see Diana Russell, *Rape in Marriage*;. Finkelhor and Yllo, *License to Rape*.

12. Susan Griffin, "Rape—the All-American Crime," *Ramparts*, September 1971, 35, cited in Susan Schechter, *Women and Male Violence: The Visions and Struggles of the Battered Women's Movement* (Boston: South End Press, 1982).

13. Andra Medea and Kathleen Thompson, *Against Rape* (New York: Noonday Press, 1974), 11.

14. For a comprehensive discussion of rape in history, see Susan Brownmiller, "In the Beginning Was the Law," in *Against Our Will: Men, Women and Rape* (New York: Fawcett Columbine, 1993), 16–30.

15. Summarized from "The History of Rape," *YWCA Rape Crisis Manual*, Mid-Peninsula Rape Crisis Center, Palo Alto, Calif. (September 1989), 6–7.

16. Toinette Eugene, "Swing Low, Sweet Chariot: A Womanist Response to Sexual Violence," *Daughters of Sarah* (Summer 1994), 11–14; Gail E. Wyatt, "The Sociocultural Context of African American and White American Women's Rape," *Journal of Social Issues* 48 (Spring 1992), 77–91; Darlene Clark Hine, "Rape and the Inner Lives of Black Women in the Middle West: Preliminary Thoughts on the Culture of Dissemblance," *Signs* 14/4 (1989), 912–20; Susan Brownmiller, "A Question of Race," in *Against Our Will: Men, Women and Rape*, 210–55.

17. Toinette Eugene, "Swing Low, Sweet Chariot." See also Mary Helen Washington, *Invented Lives: Narratives of Black Women, 1860–1960* (New York: Anchor, 1987), and Jacquelyn Grant, "Womanist Theology: Black Women's Experience as a Source for Doing Thelogy," in *African-American Religious Studies*, ed. Gayraud S. Wilmore (Duke University Press, 1989), 208–27.

18. Angela Davis, *Women, Race and Class* (New York: Random House, 1981), 7; cited in Schechter, *Women and Male Violence*, 41.

19. Darlene Clark Hine, "Rape and the Inner Lives of Black Women in the Middle West," *Signs: Journal of Women in Culture and Society* 14/4 (1989), 912–20.

20. Socialist Women's Caucus of Louisville, cited in Schechter, *Women and Male Violence*, 40.

21. Charlotte Bunch, "Women's Rights as Human Rights," in *Gender Violence: A Development and Human Rights Issue* (New Brunswick, N.J.: Center for Women's Global Leadership, 1991); Noreen Burrows, International Law and Human Rights: The Case of Women's Rights," in *Human Rights from Rhetoric to Reality*, ed. Tom Campbell (New York: Blackwell, 1986); Renny Golden, "Crimes against Humanity: Violence against Women," *Probe: National Assembly of*

Religious Women 11/2 (May–June 1993), 1ff.; Gayle Kirshenbaum, "Why Aren't Human Rights Women's Rights?" *Ms.* (July–August 1991), 90.

22. Colectivo de Mujeres de Medellin, "La violacion como ejercicio del poder autoritario," in *Micaela*, no. 84 (n.d.), 16–17, cited in *Women's World Isis* 26 (1991/2), 28.

23. "I Was Gang-Raped," in *South Tribune*, September 22, 1991; and H. Robertson, "At Last a Reaction to Rape?" *South*, September 11, 1991, cited in *Women's World Isis* 26 (1991/2), 31, 34.

24. Menachim Amir, *Patterns in Forcible Rape* (Chicago: Univ. of Chicago Press, 1971), cited in Schechter, *Women and Male Violence*, 35.

25. Neil Malamuth, "Rape Proclivity among Males," *Journal of Social Issues* 37 (1981), 138–57.

26. G. Terrence Wilson and David M. Lawson, "Expectancies, Alcohol, and Sexual Arousal in Male Social Drinkers," *Journal of Abnormal Psychology* 85 (1976), 587–94.

27. Children's Hospital, Washington D.C., as reported in Joyce Hollyday, "An Epidemic of Violence: Manifestations of Violence Against Women," *Sojourners* 13 (1984), 10–12.

28. Groth and Birnbaum, *Men Who Rape*, 5.

29. David Gelman et al., "The Mind of the Rapist," *Newsweek*, July 23, 1990, 47.

30. Groth and Birnbaum, *Men Who Rape*, 8–13.

31. Ibid., 13.

32. Bureau of Justice Statistics, cited in Gelman, "The Mind of the Rapist," 48.

33. YWCA, "The History of Rape," 6.

34. Martha Blackstock, Bay Area Women against Rape, Oakland, Calif. (personal communication, April 1994).

35. For an account of the New Bedford gang rape, see Mark Starr et al., "The Tavern Rape: Cheers and No Help," *Newsweek* 101 (March 21, 1983), 25; Mary Kay Blakely, "Who Were the Men?" *Ms.*, July 1983, 50ff. For an analysis of the media's role in blaming the victim in this case, see Helen Benedict, *Virgin or Vamp: How the Press Covers Sex Crimes* (New York: Oxford University Press, 1992), 89–146.

36. Brownmiller, cited in YWCA, "The History of Rape," 9.

37. Pauline Bart and Patricia O'Brien, *Stopping Rape: Successful Survival Strategies* (New York: Pergamon Press, 1985).

38. Ibid., 40.

39. This summary from Pauline Bart and Patricia O'Brien, 1984 study at the University of Chicago; and Sarah E. Ullman, at Brandeis University and Massachusetts Treatment Center; cited in *Voices: Newsletter of the Rape Crisis Center*, West and Central Contra Costa and Marin Counties, Spring 1992, 1–2.

40. Py Bateman, "Coming Out Alive," in *Her Wits about Her: Self-Defense Stories by Women*, ed. Denise Caignon and Gail Groves, 164.

41. Diana Russell, *The Politics of Rape*, 285.

42. Stephanie Townsend compares the tone of blame after the fact with the question posed to battered women: "Why don't you just leave?"

43. YWCA, "The History of Rape," 10.

44. BJS Data Reports, National Women's Survey, rape crisis centers.

45. James Denman, Men's Counselor, Battered Women's Alternatives, Concord, Calif., Panel "Living in a Violent Society: Healing Violent Relationships," 87. St. Cuthbert's Episcopal Church, Oakland, Calif., January 1991.

46. Bureau of Justice Statistics, *BJS Data Report* (Rockville, Md.: National Criminal Justice Reference Service/BJS Clearinghouse, 1986), 12; National Crime Survey, *Female Victims of Violent Crime*, 10.

47. *BJS Data Report* (1986), 12.

48. University of California–San Francisco, Rape Prevention Program, "Resources against Sexual Assault," rev. ed., 1992, 7.

49. *BJS Data Report* (1986), 15; Bart and O'Brien, *Stopping Rape*, 86–88.

50. Bart and O'Brien, *Stopping Rape*, 86–88.

51. *BJS Data Reports* (1986), 15.

52. *BJS Data Reports* (1986), 12; and National Women's Study, 4.

53. FBI, *Uniform Crime Report* (1991), 23.

54. Diana Russell, *Sexual Exploitation* (Phoenix: Sage, 1984).

55. "Resources against Sexual Assault," 7.

56. The broader definition of rape also admits sexual assault against men by women. While this is considered rare, it must be considered. Research on women offenders to date has focused mainly on child sexual assault. See David Finkelhor and Diana Russell, "Women as Perpetrators," in Finkelhor, *Child Sexual Abuse: New Theory and Research*, 171–85; and Groth with Birnbaum, *Men Who Rape*, 192.

57. John Donne, Holy Sonnets #10, in *Selections from Divine Poems, Sermons, Devotions and Prayers*, ed. John Booty (New York: Paulist Press, 1990).

58. *The Collected Works of St. Teresa of Avila, Vol. I: The Book of Her Life*, trans. K. Kavanaugh and O. Rodriguez (Washington, D.C.: Institute of Carmelite Studies/ICS Pub., 1976), 193–94.

59. Kenneth Clark, *Civilisation* (New York: Harper & Row, 1969), 191.

60. Gustav Klimt, *Danae*, reproduced in Alessandra Comini, *Gustav Klimt* (New York: George Braziller, 1975), Pl. 27.

61. Homer, *Hymn to Demeter*, trans. C. Boer (Dallas: Spring Publications, 1970), 92–93, cited in Naomi Ruth Lowinsky, *Stories from the Motherline: Reclaiming the Mother-Daughter Bond, Finding Our Feminine Souls* (Los Angeles: Jeremy Tarcher, 1992), 7–8.

62. Lowinsky, *Stories from the Motherline*, 7–8. For another feminist use of the Demeter-Persephone myth, see Phyllis Chesler, "Demeter Revisited," in *Women and Madness* (San Diego: Harcourt Brace Jovanovich, 1989), xxviii–xxxvii.

63. Lowinsky, *Stories from the Motherline*, 8.

64. Jean Shinoda Bolen, M.D., *Goddesses in Everywoman* (New York: Harper Colophon, 1984), 169–70, 173–74.

65. Thomas Moore, *Care of the Soul: a Guide for Cultivating Depth and Sacredness in Everyday Life* (New York: Harper Collins, 1992), 43–44.

66. Ibid., 47.

67. Mary Tennes, Ph.D., "Beyond Submission and towards Surrender: The Evolving Female Self," unpublished manuscript, presented at Redefining the Givens Seminar Series, Berkeley, Calif., February 1993. Reprinted by permission.

68. Joanne Carlson Brown and Rebecca Parker, "For God So Loved the World?" in *Christianity, Patriarchy and Abuse*, ed. Joanne Carlson Brown and Carole R. Bohn (New York: Pilgrim Press, 1989), 26; and Rebecca Parker, "Critique of Atonement," presentation for Center for Women and Religion luncheon at Earl Lectures, January 1991 (tape available through CWR, 2400 Ridge Road, Berkeley, CA 94709).

69. Ibid., 23; See also Rita Nakashima Brock, "And a Little Child Will Lead Us: Christology and Child Abuse," in *Christianity, Patriarchy and Abuse*, 42–61.

70. Brown and Parker, *Christianity, Patriarchy and Abuse*, 27; See Carter Heyward, *Redemption of God*, 54–57, 58, 167–69, and *Touching Our Strength*, 115ff., on the Christa sculpture.

71. Brown and Parker, *Christianity, Patriarchy and Abuse*, 27.

72. For example, see Jon Sobrino, *Christology at the Crossroads* (Maryknoll, N.Y.: Orbis Books, 1978). See the critique in Brown and Parker, *Christianity, Patriarchy, and Abuse*, 23. See also Sobrino and Juan Hernandez Pico, *Theology of Christian Solidarity*, trans. P. Berryman (Maryknoll, N.Y.: Orbis Books, 1985), which begins with a "proem" expressing God's solidarity on the cross with the people in their pain, misfortune, oppression, and death (vii–viii).

73. At the same time as I was formulating this section, Sally B. Purvis was coming to similar conclusions in *The Power of the Cross: Foundations for a Christian Feminist Ethic of Community* (Nashville: Abingdon Press, 1993): "The power of God in the cross is not the power to die but the power to live. It is power that does not try to control events to affect one's will but rather power

that brings forth life even from the desolation of defeat and death. The power of the cross is not the crucifixion but the resurrection—surprising, astonishing, utterly unpredictable" (74–75; see also 77 and 83–92).

74. Anonymous, "Speak Out," in *Voices* (Spring 1992), 3.

75. Named by Ann Wolbert Burgess, D.N.Sc., and Lynda Lytle Holmstrom, Ph.D., in "Rape Trauma Syndrome," *American Journal of Psychiatry* 131/9 (September 1974), 981–86. This was further elaborated by Burgess and Holmstrom in "The Rape Victim in the Emergency Ward," *American Journal of Nursing* 73/10 (1973), 1740–45; and Burgess and Holmstrom, *Rape: Victims in Crisis* (Bowie, Md.: Robert J. Brady Co., 1979). For another view of the healing process, see Judith H. Katz, *No Fairy Godmothers, No Magic Wands: The Healing Process After Rape* (Saratoga, Calif.: R & E Press, 1984, 1993).

76. See Burgess and Holmstrom, "Rape Trauma Syndrome," 982.

77. Burgess and Holmstrom, *Rape: Victims in Crisis*.

78. YWCA, "Counseling Techniques," *YWCA Rape Crisis Manual*, 8.

79. Burgess and Holmstrom, "Rape Trauma Syndrome," 983.

80. Ibid., 985.

81. This intervention material is drawn primarily from "Crisis Intervention with Rape Survivors," *YWCA Rape Crisis Manual*, 5.

82. Ruth Schmidt, "After the Fact," 16–17.

83. Drawn from Marsha and Dwight Blackstock, "The Bible and Healing from Sexual Assault," unpublished manuscript presented at a conference in July 1990 sponsored by Bay Area Women Against Rape, 357 MacArthur Blvd., Oakland, CA 94610; and Caroline Fairless, "What Does Love Require?" unpublished M.Div. honors thesis, Church Divinity School of the Pacific (Berkeley, Calif., May 1989), 99.

CHAPTER 5: BATTERING

1. "Eleanor" and "Alice" are not their real names. Details of this story have been altered to maintain confidentiality.

2. Ann Jones describes a very different outcome to a similar story. In the case of Connie Mullis, who was convicted of murder in a jury trial, one juror later said, "We couldn't let her go. It would have been open season on husbands in Atkinson County." Ann Jones, *Women Who Kill* (New York: Fawcett Crest, 1980), 344.

3. Statistics compiled by the National Clearinghouse for the Defense of Battered Women, 125 S. 9th St., Suite 302, Philadelphia, PA 19107; Jane O'Reilly, "Wife Beating: The Silent Crime," *Time*, September 5, 1983, 23; Karen Stout, "Intimate Femicide: A National Demographic Overview," *Violence Update* 1/6 (February 1991), 3. See also *Double-Time*, newsletter of the National Clearinghouse, for updated statistics.

4. *FBI Uniform Crime Reports*, 1990, 1991.

5. Statistics compiled in 1992 by the National Clearinghouse for the Defense of Battered Women; Angela Browne, *When Battered Women Kill* (New York: Free Press, 1987); Claudia McCormick, *Battered Women* (Chicago: Cook County Dept. of Corrections, 1977); Allison Bass, "Women Far Less Likely to Kill Than Men," *Boston Globe*, February 24, 1992, 27; Lenore E. Walker, *Terrifying Love: Why Battered Women Kill and How Society Responds* (New York: Harper & Row, 1989); Margo I. Wilson and Martin Daly, "Who Kills Whom in Spouse Killings?" *Criminology* 30/2 (May 1992), 189; Ann Jones, *Women Who Kill*, esp. 299–354.

6. Claiming self-defense in this type of situation has sometimes been called "the burning bed defense," after the story of Francine Hughes, who burned her husband in his bed while he slept—in self-defense against an escalating pattern of violence which she believed had turned deadly. Hughes's story is described in Ann Jones, *Women Who Kill*, 299–354. Temporary insanity is also sometimes used, but this raises serious questions about the perpetuation of labeling and pathologizing of women, and discounting the genuineness of her fear for her own life. Nor is psychiatric institutionalization a desirable option. For more detailed discussion of the issues and

problems relating to battered women's self-defense, see Lenore Walker, "Feminist Forensic Psychology," in *Feminist Theory: A Coming of Age*, Selected Proceedings of the Advanced Feminist Therapy Institute, Vail, Colo., April 1982, 274–83; Lenore Walker, Roberta Thyfault, and Angela Browne, "Beyond the Jurors' Ken: Battered Women," in *Vermont Law Review*, Fall 1981; Lenore Walker, "Battered Women Syndrome and Self-Defense (Symposium on Women and the Law)," *Notre Dame Journal of Law, Ethics and Public Policy* 6 (Summer 1992), 321–34; Elizabeth Schneider, "Describing and Changing: Women's Self-Defense Work and the Problem of Expert Testimony on Battering," *Women's Rights Law Reporter* 9/3–4 (Fall 1986), 195–225; Roberta Thyfault, "Self-Defense: Battered Woman Syndrome on Trial," *California Western Law Review* 20/3 (1984), 485–510; and Cynthia Gillespie, *Justifiable Homicide: Battered Women, Self-Defense and the Law* (Columbus, Ohio: Ohio State University Press, 1989). See also Angela Browne, *When Battered Women Kill*; and Lenore Walker, *Terrifying Love*.

7. Jones, *Women Who Kill*, 9.

8. Nancy Gibbs, " 'Til Death Do Us Part," *Time*, January 18, 1993, 38–95; National Clearinghouse for the Defense of Battered Women.

9. Rebecca Emerson Dobash and Russell P. Dobash, *Violence against Wives: A Case against the Patriarchy* (New York: Free Press, 1979); Domestic Abuse Intervention Project, 206 W. 4th Street, Duluth, MN 55806.

10. Domestic Abuse Intervention Project.

11. Marin Abused Women's Services, San Rafael, California.

12. Lenore Walker, *The Battered Woman* (New York: Harper Colophon, 1979), esp. 55–70.

13. See Rebecca Emerson Dobash and Russell P. Dobash, *Women, Violence and Social Change* (New York: Routledge, 1992), 229.

14. Lenore Walker, *The Battered Woman Syndrome* (New York: Springer, 1984), 97–99.

15. Walker, *The Battered Woman*, 58.

16. Marie Fortune, *Keeping the Faith: Questions and Answers for the Abused Woman* (San Francisco: Harper & Row, 1987), 24–26, 46–51.

17. C. Joan Parkes, Barbara Hart, and Jane Stuehling, *Seeing Justice: Legal Advocacy Principles and Practice*, vol. 1 (Harrisburg, Pa.: Pennsylvania Coalition against Domestic Violence, 1992), 7; Caroline Wolf Harlow, Bureau of Justice Statistics, *Female Victims of Crime*, 1991.

18. See example in Nancy Gibbs, " 'Til Death Do Us Part," 42.

19. Lenore Walker, *The Battered Woman*, ix; Murray Straus, Suzanne Steinmetz, and Richard Gelles, *Behind Closed Doors: Violence in the Family* (New York: Anchor/Doubleday, 1980).

20. A few researchers have also suggested that mutual battering is more prevalent than has been previously supposed, and that violence is equally or even more likely to be perpetrated by women partners as by men. However, such research claims can be called into question due to methods of gathering data (for example, not considering whether violence was committed in self-defense, not inquiring about varying degrees of resulting injury and relative dangerousness of each partner, and not taking safety of victims adequately into consideration in the interviewing process itself). A brief synopsis of this controversy is given in Pamela Cooper-White, "Peer vs. Clinical Counseling: Is There Room for Both in the Battered Women's Movement?" *Response to the Victimization of Women and Children* 13/3 (1990), 4; for more details, see Richard McNeely and G. Robinson-Simpson, "The Truth about Domestic Violence: A Falsely Framed Issue," *Social Work* 32/6 (1987), 485–90; Daniel Saunders et al., "Other 'Truths' About Domestic Violence: A Reply to McNeely and Robinson-Simpson," *Social Work* 33/2 (March/April 1988), 179–83; Dobash and Dobash, *Women, Violence and Social Change*. The Dobashes make the distinction between "family violence research," which adheres to a "value-free positivist stance," vs. "violence-against-women research," which takes as its starting point an advocacy stance (see esp. ch. 8, "Knowledge and Social Change," 251–82).

21. While the vast majority of battering occurs in heterosexual relationships, battering does also occur in both gay male and lesbian relationships. Although the gender configuration is different, the power dynamics are essentially the same. Societal and institutional oppression of gay and lesbian

persons, internalized homophobia, and lack of trust in the responsiveness of existing agencies and services make reporting and/or leaving even more difficult for the victim. For an in-depth discussion of lesbian battering, see Kerry Lobel, ed., for the National Coalition Against Domestic Violence, *Naming the Violence: Speaking Out about Lesbian Battering* (Seattle: Seal Press, 1986).

22. See, for example, Terry Davidson, "My Own Story: The Skeleton in the Parsonage," in *Conjugal Crime: Understanding and Changing the Wifebeating Pattern* (New York: Hawthorn, 1978), 131–54.

23. A more detailed discussion of the debate between peer advocates and clinical/professionally licensed psychotherapists in the intervention or treatment of battered women is given in Pamela Cooper-White, "Peer vs. Clinical Counseling—Is There a Place for Both in the Battered Women's Movement?" *Response to the Victimization of Women and Children*, 13/3 (1990), 2–6.

24. For an example of victim-blaming in the guise of feminist popular psychology, see Natalie Shainess, *Sweet Suffering: Woman as Victim* (Indianapolis: Bobbs-Merrill, 1984). For a critique of Shainess, see Dobash and Dobash, *Women, Violence and Social Change*, 222.

25. Lynn Bravo Rosewater, "Schizophrenia, Borderline or Battered?" in *Handbook of Feminist Therapy*, ed. L. B. Rosewater and L. E. A. Walker (New York: Springer, 1985), 215–25.

26. Listed under "Proposed Diagnostic Categories Needing Further Study," in American Psychiatric Association, *Diagnostic and Statistical Manual of Mental Disorders*, 3rd rev. ed. (DSM-III-R) (Washington, DC: APA, 1987), 373–4. This so-called "disorder," intended as a description of a masochistic character disorder, was likely to have been applied to battered women. It has been eliminated from DSM IV (Washington, DC: APA, 1994). For an account of the debate among clinicians on masochism, see John Leo, "Battling over Masochism: Psychiatrists and Feminists Debate 'Self-Defeating' Behavior," *Time*, December 2, 1985, 76.

27. Lenore Walker, *The Battered Woman Syndrome*.

28. Even so, because the symptomatology of PTSD is based on a male model of wartime experience and reaction to stress and terror, it may not be entirely appropriate in its details. For further discussion on the history of PTSD and the correlation between veterans and other trauma victims, see Judith Herman, *Trauma and Recovery* (New York: Basic Books, 1992).

29. Pioneered in the 1970s by practitioners including Murray Bowen (*Family Therapy in Clinical Practice* [New York: Jason Aronson, 1978]); Salvador Minuchin (*Families and Family Therapy* [Cambridge, Mass.: Harvard University Press, 1974]); Virginia Satir (*Conjoint Family Therapy*, 3d ed. [Palo Alto, Calif.: Science-Behavior Books, 1988]). For further critique, see Cooper-White, "Peer vs. Clinical Counseling"; and Dobash and Dobash, *Women, Violence and Social Change*, esp. 238–39.

30. Term created by Murray Bowen, *Family Therapy*.

31. Melody Beattie, *Codependent No More: How to Stop Controlling Others and Start Caring for Yourself* (New York:Harper/Hazelden, 1987).

32. Robin Norwood, *Women Who Love Too Much* (New York: Pocket Books, 1986).

33. Rose Moore, "Co-Dependency vs. Battered Woman Syndrome," *The Voice* (special edition, 1988), National Coalition Against Domestic Violence, reprints: P.O. Box 18749, Denver, CO 80218-0749); Patti Ford-McComb and Tania Stute Hubacher, "Co-Dependent or Abused?" Family Crisis Shelter, Portland, Maine; Laura Brown, "What's Love Got to Do with It: A Feminist Takes a Critical Look at the Women Who Love Too Much Movement," *Working Together* 7/2 (December 1986), Center for the Prevention of Sexual and Domestic Violence, Seattle, Wash.; Phyllis B. Frank and Gail Kadison Golden, "Blaming by Naming: Battered Women and the Epidemic of Codependence," *Social Work* 37/1 (January 1992); Evelina Giobbe, "Codependency and 12 Step Programs: Implications for Women" (Minneapolis, Minn.: WHISPER: Women Hurt in Systems of Prostitution Engaged in Revolt, n.d.); Kay Hagan, "Codependency and the Myth of Recovery: A Feminist Scrutiny," *Fugitive Information* (Escapadia Press, 1989); Wendy Kaminer, *I'm Dysfunctional, You're Dysfunctional* (Reading, Mass.: Addison-Wesley, 1992). A more extended

bibliography is printed in *Double-Time*, National Clearinghouse for the Defense of Battered Women, 1/3–4 (November 1992), 5–6.

34. Norwood, *Women Who Love Too Much*, 13, 22, 61–63, 204–208, also cited in Dobash and Dobash, *Women, Violence and Social Change*, 223.

35. Norwood, *Letters from Women Who Love Too Much*, (New York: Pocket Books, 1988), 98.

36. Ibid., 92; see also Norwood, *Women Who Love Too Much*, 203–4.

37. Norwood, *Letters*, 267.

38. Family Violence Project (now renamed the Family Violence Prevention Fund), "Domestic Violence, Drugs and Alcohol," Proceedings of the Conference of the Family Violence Project, October 1985, San Francisco, Calif. See also Walker, *The Battered Woman*, 25–26.

39. John Leo, "Battling Over Masochism"; Lenore Walker, "Inadequacies of the Masochistic Personality Diagnosis for Women," *Journal of Personality Disorders* 1/2 (Summer 1987), 183–89. Also see Paula J. Caplan, *The Myth of Women's Masochism* (Toronto: University of Toronto Press, 1985).

40. DSM-IV, 529.

41. DSM-IV, 530.

42. Some of the themes concerning sado-masochistic sexual practices that are being debated in a number of circles (including feminists, incest survivors, and S & M practitioners both heterosexual and lesbian/gay/bisexual) are summarized and addressed from a theological-ethical perspective in Carter Heyward, *Touching Our Strength* (San Francisco: Harper & Row, 1989), see esp. 105–10. Although I do not differ with Heyward's assessment that we live in a "praxis of alienation" and her suggestion that "sadomasochism is a social structure of alienated power" (105), I find her lack of differentiation between the impact of sado-masochistic fantasies and "activities with consenting adults"(109) very disturbing. Given the pervasiveness of violence and alienation that Heyward herself addresses, how can consent to violence ever be mutual or authentic? While I agree that more consciousness of our indoctrination into sadism is called for, I do not believe that consciousness requires enactment in order to "move through sadomasochism" (106). I am also troubled by her implication that boundaries are "walls that divide us" (110 and fn. 36); rather, I view boundaries as essential for individual and relational health and safety. The question of professional boundaries, particularly in psychotherapy, is raised more personally and provocatively in Heyward's most recent book, *When Boundaries Betray Us: Beyond Illusions of What Is Ethical in Therapy and Life* (San Francisco: HarperSanFrancisco, 1993). For review of this book, see Pamela Cooper-White, Marilyn Coffy, Jan Baltz, Jan Sollom-Brotherton, Marilyn Steele, Ida Thornton, and Nancy Ulmer, "Desperately Seeking Sophia's Shadow," *Journal of Pastoral Care*, 48/3 (Fall 1994), 287–92.

43. This insight comes from my own direct work with battered women and very helpful and thought-provoking conversations with Marilyn Steele, and Melissa Reed of the Mid-Peninsula Support Network.

44. Identified by Dobash and Dobash, in *Violence against Wives*, and more recently elaborated in *Women, Violence and Social Change*, 230–35.

45. Dobash and Dobash, *Women, Violence and Social Change*, 230–35.

46. For a biblically based answer to this, see Marie Fortune, *Keeping the Faith*, 28–30.

47. Lenore Walker, in *The Battered Woman*, describes the psychosocial theory of learned helplessness in great detail (42–54). Psychologist Martin Seligman's experiment with dogs is the classic example of learned helplessness. "Seligman and his researchers placed dogs in cages and administered electrical shocks at random and varied intervals. These dogs quickly learned that no matter what response they made, they could not control the shock. At first, the dogs attempted to escape through various voluntary movements. When nothing they did stopped the shocks, the dogs ceased any further voluntary activity and became compliant, passive, and submissive. When the researchers attempted to change this procedure and teach the dogs that they could escape by crossing to the other side of the cage, the dogs still would not respond. In fact, even when the door was left open and the dogs were shown the way out, they remained passive, refused to leave, and did not avoid the shock. It took repeated dragging of the dogs to the exit to teach them how to

respond voluntarily again. The earlier in life that the dogs received such treatment, the longer it took to overcome the effects of this so-called learned helplessness. However, once they did learn that they could make the voluntary response, their helplessness disappeared" (46).

48. Dobash and Dobash *Women, Violence and Social Change*, 223–30.

49. Ibid., 231.

50. Study at Michigan State University, cited in Terry Davidson, *Conjugal Crime: Understanding and Changing the Wifebeating Pattern* (New York: Hawthorn, 1978), 80. See also N. Zoe Hilton, "When Is an Assault Not an Assault? The Canadian Public's Attitudes towards Wife and Stranger Assault," *Journal of Family Violence* 4/4 (December 1989), 323–37; and a related study by R. Lance Shotland and Margaret Straw, "Bystander Response to an Assault: When a Man Attacks a Woman," *Journal of Personality and Social Psychology* 34/5 (November 1976), 990–99.

51. Donna Garske, Marin Abused Women's Services, San Rafael, Calif. (personal communication, October 1993).

52. See Garland F. White, Janet Katz, and Kathryn E. Scarborough, "The Impact of Professional Football Games upon Violent Assaults on Women," *Violence and Victims* 7/2 (1992). Authors found in a study of the relationships between the timing and outcomes of the Washington Redskins' football games and frequency of admissions to hospital emergency rooms in northern Virginia that the frequency of admissions of women victims of gunshots, stabbings, assaults, falls, lacerations, and being struck by objects increases when the team wins. They hypothesize that having a favorite team win may act as a trigger for assault in some males, and that viewing the successful use of violent acts may give the identifying fan a sense of license to dominate his surroundings.

53. Mildred D. Pagelow, *Woman-Battering: Victims and Their Experience* (Beverly Hills: Sage, 1981).

54. Ibid.; Jim M. Alsdurf, "Wife Abuse and the Church: The Response of Pastors," *Response* (Winter 1985), 9–11.

55. Lee H. Bowker, "Battered Women and the Clergy: An Evaluation," *Journal of Pastoral Care* 46/4 (1982), 226–34.

56. Details on how to assess danger are summarized in Carol Adams, *Woman-Battering*, Creative Pastoral Care and Counseling Series (Minneapolis: Fortress Press, 1994), 63–67.

57. J. N. Honeywell, "Counseling the Battered Wife," *Your Church*, January/February 1982, 38–39, 49–50, cited in Joy Bussert, *Battered Women: From a Theology of Suffering to an Ethic of Empowerment* (Minneapolis: Augsburg Fortress/Division for Ministry in North America, Lutheran Church in America, 1986), 63.

58. For further discussion on this point, see Susan Schechter, *Guide for Mental Health Professionals*, National Coalition against Domestic Violence, (P.O. Box 15127, Washington, D.C. 20003-0127), 1987. Specific to pastoral care, see Carol Adams, *Woman-Battering*, 47–49.

59. Mitzi Eilts, "Saving the Family: When Is the Covenant Broken?" in *Abuse and Religion: When Praying Isn't Enough*, ed. Anne L. Horton and Judith A. Williamson (Lexington, Mass.: Lexington Books, 1988), 207–14.

60. For example, Bishops' Committee on Marriage and Family Life, Bishops' Committee on Women in Society and in the Church, and the National Conference of Catholic Bishops, "When I Call for Help: A Pastoral Response to Domestic Violence against Women," September 30, 1992; Ann D. Weatherholt, "Are You Battered?" (1991, Forward Movement Publications, 412 Sycamore, Cincinnati, OH 45202); "About Anger," "About Wife Abuse," "Family Violence," and "About Child Abuse," from Scriptographic Booklets (Channing L. Bete Co., 200 State Road, So. Deerfield, MA 01373; 1-800-628-7733); Mary Pellauer, "If There Is Abuse in Your Home . . . " and "Ministry to Abusive Families," and a poster "Help for Victims of Violence in the Home," Family Resources, Division for Parish Services, Lutheran Church in America (now Division for Congregational Ministries, Evangelical Lutheran Church in America, 8765 W. Higgins Rd., Chicago, IL 60631). New congregational study guides are being developed also by the ELCA Division for Congregational Ministries and the Commission for Women.

61. For some carefully reasoned theological approaches, see Caroline Fairless, "What Does Love Require? A Family Violence Manual for the Church Community," unpublished M.Div. honors thesis, Church Divinity School of the Pacific, Berkeley, Calif., May 1989; Joy Bussert, *Battered Women*; Carol Adams, *Woman Battering*; Marie Fortune, *Keeping the Faith*.

CHAPTER 6: CLERGY SEXUAL ABUSE

1. "Katya" and "Peg" are not their real names. Details of their stories have been altered to maintain confidentiality. Both stories are reprinted by permission.

2. Marie Fortune, *Is Nothing Sacred? When Sex Invades the Pastor-Parishioner Relationship* (San Francisco: Harper & Row, 1989).

3. Peter Rutter, M.D., *Sex in the Forbidden Zone: When Men in Power Abuse Women's Trust* (Los Angeles: Jeremy Tarcher, 1989).

4. For an excellent review of related literature on therapist-client sexual contact, see Gary R. Schoener, "A Look at the Literature," in *Psychotherapists' Sexual Involvement with Clients: Intervention and Prevention* (Minneapolis: Walk-In Counseling Center, 1989), 11–50. Key prevalence studies include:

S. H. Kardener, M. Fuller, and I. Mensh, "A Survey of Physicians' Attitudes and Practices regarding Erotic and Nonerotic Contact with Clients," *American Journal of Psychiatry* 130 (1973), 1077–81; J. C. Holroyd and A. M. Brodsky, "Psychologists' Attitudes and Practices regarding Erotic and Nonerotic Physical Contact with Patients," *American Psychologist* 32 (1977), 843–49; Kenneth S. Pope, H. Levinson, and L. Schover, "Sexual Intimacy in Psychology Training: Results and Implications of a National Survey," *American Psychologist* 34 (1979), 682–89; J. Bouhoutsos, J. Holroyd, H. Herman, B. Forer, and M. Greenberg, "Sexual Intimacy between Psychotherapists and Patients," *Professional Psychology: Research and Practice* 14 (1983), 185–96; J. Hamilton and H. DeRosis, *Report of the Women's Committee to the Washington, D.C., Psychiatric Society* (Washington, D.C.: Washington Psychiatric Society, 1985); Kenneth S. Pope, P. Keith-Spiegel, and B. G. Tabachnick, "Sexual Attraction to Clients: The Human Therapist and the (Sometimes) Inhuman Training System," *American Psychologist* 41 (1986), 147–58; N. Gartrell, J. Herman, S. Olarte, M. Feldstein, and R. Localio, "Psychiatrist-Patient Sexual Contact: Results of a National Survey, I: Prevalence," *American Journal of Psychiatry* 143 (1986), 1126–31; N. Gartrell et al. "Reporting Practices of Psychiatrists Who Knew of Sexual Misconduct by Colleagues," *American Journal of Ortho-Psychiatry* 57 (1987), 287–95; Kenneth S. Pope, B. G. Tabachnick, and P. Keith-Spiegel, "Ethics of Practice: The Beliefs and Behaviors of Psychologists as Therapists," *American Psychologist* 42 (1987), 993–1006.

5. A range of 12 to 20.7 percent can be extrapolated from a *Christianity Today* survey, reported in "How Common Is Pastoral Indiscretion?" *Leadership* (Winter 1988), 1. A doctoral study at Fuller Seminary shows fully 38.6 percent of respondents having had sexual contact with a parishioner. See Richard Allen Blackmon, "The Hazards of the Ministry" (unpublished Ph.D. dissertation, Fuller Seminary, 1984).

6. *Leadership*, 12.

7. Ibid., 13.

8. Blackmon, "The Hazards of the Ministry." Anthony Kuchan reports that 11.2 percent of all sexual contact reported to helping professionals were clergy, in "Survey of Incidence of Psychotherapists' Sexual Contact with Clients in Wisconsin," in Schoener et al., ed., *Psychotherapists' Sexual Involvement*, 60.

9. For an alternative, less absolute point of view, see Karen Lebacqz and Ronald G. Barton in "Sex, Power and Ministry: The Case of the Normal Neurotic," *Quarterly Review* 10/1 (1990); and *Sex in the Parish*, Westminster Press, 1991.

10. Pamela Cooper-White, "Soul-Stealing: Power Relations in Pastoral Sexual Abuse," *Christian Century*, February 20, 1991, 196–99.

11. Bouhoutsos et al. ("Sexual Intimacy," 185–96), report that 92.4 percent of sexual contact was between male therapists and female clients.

12. See further explorations of this theme by Mary Pellauer, "Sex, Power and the Family of God," *Christianity and Crisis*, February 16, 1987.

13. It is largely to this complex reality that Karen Lebacqz and Ronald G. Barton speak in "Sex, Power and Ministry" and *Sex in the Parish*. They argue that it may be legitimate for single pastors to fall in love with single parishioners. Even in this less stringent treatment of the theme of pastor-parishioner dating, they also caution that a complex power dynamic must be taken into consideration. In *Sex in the Parish*, they further caution that certain public safeguards against secrecy and exploitation must be set up.

14. This discussion was first presented at a book panel at Pacific School of Religion, February 1992. See also Marie Fortune, "Violating the Pastoral Relation" (review of Lebacqz and Barton), *Christianity and Crisis* 51/16–17, November 18, 1991, 367–68; Pamela Cooper-White, "Sex in the Parish" (review of Lebacqz and Barton), *Christian Century*, April 1, 1992, 344–45.

15. Lebacqz and Barton, *Sex in the Parish*; Karen Lebacqz, "Pastor-Parishioner Sexuality: An Ethical Analysis," *Explor* (Winter 1988); Lebacqz and Barton, "Sex, Power and Ministry," 36–48.

16. 90 percent of victims reported harm in one study of therapist-patient sex (Bouhoutsos et al., "Sexual Intimacy," 185–96).

17. Rutter, *Sex In the Forbidden Zone*, 182–84.

18. See Lebacqz and Barton's helpful chapter on "the Bishop's dilemma" in *Sex in the Parish*.

19. Marie Fortune, *Clergy Misconduct: Sexual Abuse in the Ministerial Relationship Workshop Manual* (Seattle, Wash.: Center for the Prevention of Sexual and Domestic Violence, 1992), 20–21.

20. Schoener, *Psychotherapists' Involvement with Clients*, 402–4.

21. For this reason, clinical typologies are not designed to be used diagnostically, but for educational purposes. Clinical assessment is based on the prognosis for rehabilitation, by what means, and how it can be measurable and made accountable to future congregations.

22. Gary Schoener, personal communication; G. Lloyd Rediger, *Ministry and Sexuality: Cases, Counseling, and Care* (Minneapolis: Fortress Press, 1992), 24. One study showed 80 percent of offenders with more than one client (median=2, mean=2.6 clients). J. C. Holroyd and A. M. Brodsky, "Psychologists' attitudes and practices," 843–49. From a purely statistical point of view, if even half of offenders abuse at least two victims, then at least two-thirds of all victims will have been abused by a repeat offender. This has important implications for the importance of doing public investigations of single allegations, in order to allow other victims to come forward.

23. Similar theoretical models of multiple causation have been applied to child sexual abuse by David Finkelhor, in *Child Sexual Abuse: New Theory and Research* (New York: Free Press, 1984), 33–68; to sexual assault and battery of women by Diana Russell, *Sexual Exploitation: Rape, Child Sexual Abuse, and Sexual Harassment* (Beverly Hills: Sage, 1984); and to the causative role of pornography in rape by Diana Russell, *Against Pornography* (Berkeley, Calif.: Russell Publications, 1993), 118ff.

24. One recent exception is G. Lloyd Rediger, *Ministry and Sexuality*. Although Rediger's focus is on sexuality and not power and professional ethics per se, he does name abuse clearly and frames clergy sexual ethics in terms of professional responsibility.

25. E.g., Don Basham, *Lead Us Not into Temptation: Confronting Immorality in Ministry* (Old Tappan, N.J.: Chosen Books, 1986); [n.a.], "The War Within Continues: An Update on a Christian Leader's Struggle with Lust," *Leadership* (Winter 1988), 24–33; Randy Alcorn, "Strategies to Keep from Falling," *Leadership* (Winter 1988), 42–47; Andre Bustanoby, "Counseling the Seductive Female: Can We Offer Help and Yet Remain Safe?" *Leadership* (Winter 1988), 48–54. The best of this genre is Charles Rassieur, *The Problem Clergymen Don't Talk About* (Philadelphia: Westminster, 1976). While the emphasis of the book is still on resisting seduction by women parishioners, Rassieur does appeal to professionalism and a standard of care. Power dynamics remain largely unexplored.

26. E.g., Martin Shepard's widely read *The Love Treatment: Sexual Intimacy between Patients and Psychotherapists* (New York: Peter H. Wyden, 1971). For a review of these debates see Schoener, "A Look at the Literature," 13–24.

27. Gary Schoener and Jeanette H. Milgrom, "Sexual Exploitation by Clergy and Pastoral Counselors," in Schoener et al., *Psychotherapists' Sexual Involvement*, 230–32; Gary L. Harbaugh and E. Rogers, "Pastoral Burnout: A View from the Seminary," *Journal of Pastoral Care* 38/2 (1984), 99–106; Mary Pellauer, "Sex, Power and the Family of God," *Christianity and Crisis*, February 16, 1987, 49.

28. H. N. Malony, "Clergy Stress: Not So Bad After All?" *Ministry* (May 1989), 8–9.

29. Cf. Florence Rush, *The Best Kept Secret* (New York: Prentice-Hall, 1980).

30. Conrad Weiser gives a table summarizing studies of mental health of clergy and seminarians in *Healers—Harmed and Harmful* (Minneapolis: Fortress Press, 1994), 5. Some have suggested that the ministry attracts a certain type of narcissistic and competitive male personality—Andre Bustanoby, "The Pastor and the Other Woman," *Christianity Today*, August 30, 1974, 7–10; J. Reid Meloy, "Narcissistic Psychopathology and the Clergy," *Pastoral Psychology* 35/1 (1986), 50–55.

31. Cf. Samuel L. Bradshaw, "Ministers in Trouble: A Study of 140 Cases Evaluated at the Menninger Foundation," *Journal of Pastoral Care* 31/4 (December 1977), 236.

32. For an excellent understanding of narcissistic wounding, see Alice Miller, *The Drama of the Gifted Child: The Search for the True Self* (New York: Basic Books, 1981); specific to clergy, see J. Reid Meloy, "Narcissistic Psychopathology and the Clergy"; Conrad Weiser, *Healers—Harmed and Harmful*, esp. 67–81.

33. Pellauer, "Sex, Power and the Family of God," 49.

34. See, e.g., Robert J. Stout, "Clergy Divorce Spills into the Aisle," *Christianity Today*, February 5, 1982; and the emphasis on the theme of temptation in several articles in *Leadership*, Winter 1988.

35. See Ann-Janine Morey, "Blaming the Woman for the Abusive Male Pastor," *The Christian Century*, October 5, 1988, 866–69.

36. Gary Schoener and Jeanette H. Milgrom, "False or Misleading Complaints," in Schoener et al., *Psychotherapists' Sexual Involvement*, 147–56.

37. Cf. T. Gutheil, "Borderline Personality Disorder, Boundary Violations, and Patient-Therapist Sex: Medicolegal Pitfalls," *American Journal of Psychiatry* 146 (1989), 597–602.

38. For more detailed guidelines for reporting pastoral sexual abuse, see the Center for Women and Religion, *A Clergy Abuse Survivor's Resource Packet*, 3d rev. ed., November 1993 (2400 Ridge Road, Berkeley, CA 94709).

39. See Arthur Gross-Schaefer and Jan Singer, "Clergy Sexual Misconduct: A Call for a Faithful, Not a Fearful, Response," *Congregations: The Alban Journal* (May/June 1993), 13–14. Helpful articles on legal issues include T. E. Denham and M. L. Denham, "Avoiding Malpractice Suits in Pastoral Counseling," *Pastoral Psychology* 35/2 (1986), 83–93; Deborah M. House, "Clergy Sexual Misconduct: The Church's Legal Liabilities," *Circuit Rider* (September 1992), 8–9; Donald C. Clark, Jr., "Sexual Abuse in the Church: The Law Steps In," *Christian Century*, April 4, 1993, 396–98.

40. Draft work by the Sexual Ethics Task Force of the Episcopal Diocese of California, Spring 1992.

41. Nathaniel S. Lehrman, "The Normality of Sexual Feelings in Pastoral Counseling," *Pastoral Psychology*, 49–52.

42. Charles Rassieur was already advocating this approach in 1976 in *The Problem Clergymen Don't Talk About*. Note that, in the light of more recent learnings about abuse, Rassieur's consideration of reporting sexual feelings to a counselee is almost always ill advised.

43. William E. Hulme, "Sexual Boundary Violations of Clergy," in *Sexual Exploitation in Professional Relationships*, ed. Glen O. Gabbard (Washington, D.C.: American Psychiatric Press, 1989), 189–90.

44. David J. Rolfe, "The Destructive Potential of Psychological Counseling for Pastor and Parish," *Pastoral Psychology* 34/1 (1985), 61–68.

45. E.g., Patrick Carnes, *Out of the Shadows: Understanding Sexual Addiction* (Minneapolis: CompCare, 1983).

46. Rutter, *Sex in the Forbidden Zone*; Sissela Bok, "Lies Protecting Peers and Colleagues," in *Lying: Moral Choice in Public and Private Life* (New York: Vintage/Random House, 1979), 161–66.

47. For example, see the appendix in Fortune, *Is Nothing Sacred?* For churches struggling to harmonize sexual ethics policies with canonical and constitutional disciplinary requirements, pioneering work has also been done, for example, in the Episcopal Church dioceses of Minnesota, Chicago, Boston, Los Angeles, and California, and in a number of synods of the Evangelical Lutheran Church in America. A model in the Roman Catholic Church is being developed in the Archdiocese of Chicago.

48. For a more detailed guideline for elements to be included in a denominational policy, see Center for Women and Religion (2400 Ridge Road, Berkeley, CA 94709), "Clergy Abuse Survivors' Packet," 3d rev. ed., November 1993.

49. Details of appropriate diagnosis and treatment of professional sexual misconduct are exhaustively presented in Gary Schoener, Jeanette Milgrom, John Gonsiorek, Ellen Luepker, and Ray Conroe, *Psychotherapists' Sexual Involvement with Clients: Intervention and Prevention* (Minneapolis: Walk-In Counseling Center, 2451 Chicago Ave. South, Minneapolis MN 55404), 1989.

50. Excellent resources are now being developed for congregational healing in the aftermath of clergy sexual abuse. See, e.g., materials developed by the Rev. Chilton Knudsen, Pastoral Care Officer, Episcopal Diocese of Chicago, 65 E. Huron St., Chicago, IL 60611. In particular, Knudsen has developed a wheel representing "Dimensions of Congregational Healing," including shock, denial, bargaining, anger (scapegoating), depression/sadness, anger (righteous rage), and acceptance/integration. See also Chilton Knudsen, "Trauma Debriefing: A Congregational Model," in *MCS Conciliation Quarterly* (Spring 1991), 12–13; Nancy Myer Hopkins, "Symbolic Church Fights: The Hidden Agenda When Clerical Trust Has Been Betrayed," *Congregations: The Alban Journal* (May/June 1993), 15–18.

51. For excellent training resources for denominations and congregations, contact the Center for the Prevention of Sexual and Domestic Violence, 1914 N. 34th St. #105, Seattle, WA 98103. In particular, I have found two training videos to be invaluable: "Not in My Church" for general education, and "When You Cross the Line," especially for clergy.

CHAPTER 7: CHILD SEXUAL ABUSE

1. Not her real name. Certain details have been altered to protect her confidentiality, but the essentials of the story are true. By permission.

2. Marian Wright Edelman, Children's Defense Fund, Washington, D.C. See Edelman, *Families in Peril: An Agenda for Social Change* (Cambridge: Harvard University Press, 1986), and *The Measure of Our Success: A Letter to My Children and Yours* (Boston: Beacon Press, 1992).

3. Roland Summit, "Beyond Belief: The Reluctant Discovery of Incest," *Sexual Assault and Abuse: A Handbook for Clergy and Religious Professionals*, ed. M. Pellauer, B. Chester, and J. Boyajian (San Francisco: HarperSanFrancisco, 1987), 173.

4. Roland Summit, "The Child Sexual Abuse Accommodation Syndrome," *Child Abuse and Neglect* 7 (1983), 177–93.

5. David Finkelhor, *Sexually Victimized Children* (New York: The Free Press, 1979).

6. Summit, "Beyond Belief," 177.

7. Lenore Terr, *Too Scared to Cry: Psychic Trauma in Childhood* (New York: Basic Books, 1990), 538–89.

8. Ibid., 248.

9. Elaine Westerlund, *Respond to Incest: In Memory of Nancy* (Boston: Women in Crisis Committee, The Episcopal Diocese of Massachusetts, 1987), 9–10.

10. Cf. Leonard Shengold, "Child Abuse and Deprivation: Soul Murder," *Journal of the American Psychoanalytic Association* 27 (1979), 538, citing Brandt Steele, "Violence within the Family," in *Child Abuse and Neglect*, ed. R. Helfer and C. Kempe (Cambridge, Mass.: Ballinger, 1976), 3–23. K. McIntyre, "Role of Mothers in Father-Daughter Incest. A Feminist Analysis," *Social Work* 26 (1981), 462–66.

11. See Westerlund, *Respond to Incest*, 9–10; Summit, "Beyond Belief," 173, 183.

12. Diana Russell, "The Incidence and Prevalence of Intrafamilial and Extrafamilial Sexual Abuse of Female Children," *Handbook on Sexual Abuse of Children*, ed. L. E. A. Walker (New York: Springer, 1988).

13. Ibid. See also David Finkelhor, "Risk Factors in the Sexual Victimization of Children," *Child Abuse and Neglect* 4 (1980), 265–73.

14. Suzanne Sgroi, "Sexual Molestation of Children: The Last Frontier in Child Abuse," *Children Today* 4 (May–June 1975), 20.

15. Sandor Ferenczi, "Confusion of Tongues Between Adults and the Child: The Language of Tenderness and of Passion," *Final Contributions to the Problems and Methods of Psychoanalysis* (New York: Basic Books, 1955), 155–67; cited in Judith Herman, *Trauma and Recovery* (New York: Basic Books, 1992), 107.

16. Shengold, "Child Abuse," 539.

17. Ibid., 552.

18. Ibid., 541, also citing Ferenczi, "Confusion of Tongues," 165.

19. Shengold, "Child Abuse," and elaborated more recently in his book *Soul Murder: The Effects of Childhood Abuse and Deprivation* (New York: Fawcett Columbine, 1989).

20. Shengold, "Child Abuse," 537.

21. Ibid., 551.

22. Ibid., 537.

23. Ibid., 535, citing Anselm von Feuerbach, *Kaspar Hauser* (1832), 55–56.

24. Heidi Vanderbilt, "The Children," in "Incest: A Chilling Report," *Lear's*, February 1992, reprint edition, 4.

25. Diana Russell, *The Secret Trauma: Incest in the Lives of Girls and Women* (New York: Basic Books, 1986), 70, also citing Gail Wyatt's study of 248 African American and white women in Los Angeles County, 1985; Diana Russell, Rachel A. Sherman, and Karen Trocki, "The Long-Term Effects of Incestuous Abuse: A Comparison of Afro-American and White American Victims," in *Lasting Effects of Child Sexual Abuse*, ed. Gail Wyatt (Beverly Hills: Sage, 1988); Anthony Urquiza and Lisa Marie Keating, "The Prevalence of Sexual Victimization of Males," in *The Sexually Abused Male*, ed. Mic Hunter (New York: Lexington Books, 1990); David Finkelhor, "Risk Factors in the Sexual Victimization of Children," *Child Abuse and Neglect* 4 (1980), 265–73.

26. Russell, *The Secret Trauma*, 70.

27. Ibid., 60.

28. Studies by Finkelhor and J. Landis, summarized in Judith Herman, *Father-Daughter Incest* (Cambridge, Mass.: Harvard University Press, 1981), 13; also extrapolated from statistics for female perpetrators in Russell, *The Secret Trauma*, 218, also citing Finkelhor, *Sexually Victimized Children*.

29. V. DeFrancis, *Protecting the Child Victim of Sex Crimes Committed by Adults* (Denver: The American Humane Association, Children's Division, 1969; David Finkelhor, *Sexually Victimized Children*, cited in David Finkelhor, *Child Sexual Abuse: New Theory and Research* (New York: Free Press, 1984).

30. I have been asked why I include child sexual abuse in my course on violence against women, and in this book, since boys are also victims of sexual abuse and incest. I include it because it is so pervasive in women's lives, and because these proportions place it clearly on the spectrum of male violence against females in our culture. There is no doubt, however, that boys are molested as children and teenagers, and there is no question that the harm, devastation, and lasting consequences are as serious as for girls. There is also the suggestion that sexual abuse of boys has been underreported and underestimated by experts. For a fine book on men dealing with sexual abuse as children, see Mike Lew, *Victims No Longer: Men Recovering from Incest and Other Sexual Child Abuse* (New York: Harper & Row, 1990).

31. Florence Rush, "The Freudian Coverup," *Chrysalis* 1 (1977), 31–45; Judith Herman, *Father-Daughter Incest* (Cambridge, Mass.: Harvard University Press, 1981); Jeffrey Masson, *The Assault on Truth: Freud's Suppression of the Seduction Theory* (New York: Farrar, Straus and

Giroux, 1984). For an account of the impact of this research on the psychoanalytic community, see Janet Malcolm, *In the Freud Archives* (New York: Knopf, 1984).

32. Sigmund Freud, "The Aetiology of Hysteria," *Collected Papers* 1 (1896), ed. P. Rieff (New York: Collier, 1963).

33. "Almost all my women patients told me that they had been seduced by their father. I was driven to recognize in the end that those reports were untrue and so came to understand that the hysterical symptoms were derived from fantasy and not from real occurrences" (*The Complete Introductory Lectures on Psychoanalysis* [1933] [New York: Norton, 1966], 584, cited in Summit, "Beyond Belief," 188). Contrast this with Freud's earlier assertion in a letter to colleague Wilhelm Fliess, "I have come to the opinion that anxiety is to be connected not with a mental, but with a physical consequence of sexual abuse." M. Bonaparte, A. Freud, and E. Kris, eds., *The Origins of Psychoanalysis: Letters to Wilhelm Fliess, Drafts, and Notes: 1877–1902* (New York: Basic Books, 1954), 79–80, quoted in Rush, "Freudian Coverup," 34–35, and Summit, "Beyond Belief," 187.

34. Herman, *Trauma and Recovery*, 18.

35. Russell, *The Secret Trauma*, 82, making reference to such groups as the Rene Guyon Society and the North American Man/Boy Love Association (NAMBLA).

36. If from one in five to one in three women in the United States are sexually abused before reaching adulthood, then as many as 19 to 32 million women are abused (Margot Silk Forrest, editor of *The Healing Woman*, personal communication). How many are seen for therapy?

37. Finkelhor, *Child Sexual Abuse*, 16–17.

38. For a more thorough discussion of these distinctions, see Russell, "Can Incest Be Nonabusive?" in *The Secret Trauma*, 38–55.

39. Vanderbilt, "The Children," 3.

40. Renee Fredrickson, *Repressed Memories: a Journey to Recovery from Sexual Abuse* (New York: Fireside/Parkside-Simon and Schuster, 1992), 22.

41. Patrick Gannon, "Treating Multiple Personality Disorder," paper presented at CPC Fremont Hospital, Fremont, Calif., March 1993.

42. Frank W. Putnam, Jr., "Dissociation as a Response to Extreme Trauma," in Richard Kluft, ed., *Childhood Antecedents of Multiple Personality* (Washington, D.C.: American Psychiatric Association Press, 1985), 65–98; Patrick Gannon, "Treatment of Multiple Personality Disorder"; Bennett G. Braun, "The BASK Model of Dissociation: Clinical Applications," *Dissociation* 1/2 (1988), 116–23.

43. Gannon, "Treating Multiple Personality Disorder."

44. Fredrickson, *Repressed Memories*, 24.

45. Herman, *Trauma and Recovery*, 1.

46. Stephanie Salter and Carol Ness, "Buried Memories, Broken Families," *San Francisco Examiner* series April 4–9, 1993; "Rush to Judgment," *Newsweek*, April 15, 54–60.

47. John Briere, *Therapy for Adults Molested as Children: Beyond Survival* (New York: Springer, 1989), 53.

48. Judith Herman, in the *Harvard Mental Health Letter*, cited in Karen Olio, "Facts, Fiction and Fantasy," *The Healing Woman* 2/4 (August 1993), 5.

49. Herman, *Harvard Mental Health Letter*, 5.

50. Roland Summit, "The Child Sexual Abuse Accommodation Syndrome," 188.

51. Ellen Bass and Laura Davis, *The Courage to Heal: A Guide for Women Survivors of Child Sexual Abuse* (New York: Harper & Row, 1988), 81.

52. Most recently this viewpoint has been promoted by an organization called the False Memory Syndrome Foundation. "False Memory Syndrome" is a term, which, unlike "battered women's syndrome" or "child sexual abuse accommodation syndrome," has no scientific studies or clinical trials behind it, although some studies on memory and suggestibility by legitimate researchers such as Ulric Neisser (studies of the Challenger crash and the 1989 San Franscisco earthquake), Alison Clarke-Stewart (University of California at Irvine), Stephen J. Ceci (Cornell Dept. of Developmental Psychology), and Elizabeth Loftus (University of Washington) have been cited by the group to support its claims. There is real value in these studies for the understanding of

how traumatic and especially nontraumatic memory are (differently) formed, and of the importance of nonleading questioning in assessing legal allegations. The purpose of such studies is *not* to quash genuine reporting and to perpetuate society's long-standing climate of disbelief and blame of victims. A letter published in *The APA Observer* and signed by seventeen psychologists from highly regarded research institutions reads in part: "In particular we object to the term 'false memory syndrome,' a non-psychological term originated by a private foundation whose stated purpose is to support accused parents. . . . Individuals who claim that memories of abuse are always true or always false are taking a political or legal stand. At the very least, their claims are scientifically unwarranted." Cited in Olio, "Facts, Fiction and Fantasy," 4. A critical view of the history of victimization reveals that sexual abuse has been "discovered" and then discredited on a cycle of approximately every thirty-five years. See Roland Summit, "Beyond Belief"; and also Herman, "A Forgotten History," in *Trauma and Recovery*, 7–32. For a careful critique of each of the claims of the False Memory Syndrome Foundation, see Olio, "Facts, Fiction and Fantasy."

53. Lenore Terr, "Early Memories of Trauma: What Happens to Early Memories of Trauma? A Study of Twenty Children under Age Five at the Time of Documented Traumatic Events," *Journal of the American Academy of Adolescent Psychiatry* 27/1 (1988), 96–104.

54. Briere, *Therapy for Adults*, 54; see also Leonard Shengold, "Did It Really Happen? An Assault on Truth, Historical and Narrative," in *Soul Murder: The Effects of Childhood Abuse and Deprivation* (New York: Fawcett Columbine, 1989), 32–40. On the issue of "what really happened," see also chapter 9.

55. See Fredrickson, "Made Up or Real?" in *Repressed Memories*, 158ff.

56. D.W. Winnicott, *The Maturational Processes and the Facilitating Environment* (London: Hogarth Press, 1965); Herman, *Trauma and Recovery*, 110.

57. Compiled from E. Sue Blume, "The Incest Survivors' Aftereffects Checklist," in *Secret Survivors: Uncovering Incest and Its Aftereffects in Women* (New York: John Wiley & Sons, 1990), xviii–xxi; John Briere, "Core Effects of Severe Abuse," in *Therapy for Adults Molested as Children*, 39–50; Renee Fredrickson, "Symptom Checklist," in *Repressed Memories*, 48–51; Bass and Davis, *The Courage to Heal*, 34–54; and survivor's stories told to me.

58. As maladaptive as it may appear, self-abuse, which is often seen in cases of more severe sexual abuse histories, is a way in which survivors can penetrate the numbness of dissociation and feel—something, anything. Self-mutilation usually follows a predictable sequence: dissociative state (often in reaction to an event that triggers a repressed memory), followed by agitation and compulsion to self-injure, numbness during the act itself, and then a feeling of discharge, relief, or calm. The subsequent pain produced serves as both a distraction from the memory of the trauma and a physical replacement for emotional pain. The injury is a dissociative act, steering the conscious mind away from actually remembering or feeling the earlier abuse. See Herman, *Trauma and Recovery*, 109; Briere, *Therapy for Adults*, 24–28. While it may look like a suicidal gesture (and should be assessed for dangerousness the same way), it is actually a gesture toward being more alive: "I needed to see if I was still real, if I could still hurt" (Sandra Butler, *Conspiracy of Silence* [San Francisco: New Glide, 1978], 45, cited in Briere, *Therapy for Adults*, 27).

59. Briere, *Therapy for Adults*, 44–45.

60. While controversial among the battered women's movement, there is in this category some clinical suggestion that victims of severe child abuse may also be at higher risk for subsequent abuse by adult partners because of damage to boundaries and lack of healthy socialization to recognize signs of danger. Care must be taken not to use this as a rationale for blaming the victim: "She asked for it" or "She provoked it." Nor does this theory describe all battered women or explain why battering occurs. Also, this clinical theory must be qualified by the recognition that *all* women, by virtue of their universal indoctrination into a sexist culture, are at least to some extent socialized to have weak boundaries and muted capacities to sense danger and protect themselves.

61. Alice Miller links the empathy required for a career as a psychoanalyst—arguably applicable to other helping professionals as well—with childhood exploitation by narcissistically

disturbed parents in *The Drama of the Gifted Child*, trans. Ruth Ward (New York: Basic Books, 1981), 22–23; see also Thomas Maeder, "Wounded Healers," *The Atlantic*, January 1989, 37–47.

62. Term from Henri Nouwen, *The Wounded Healer* (New York: Doubleday Image, 1972).

63. David Finkelhor, *Child Sexual Abuse*, 47, citing studies including Nicholas Groth and A. Burgess, "Sexual Trauma in the Life Histories of Rapists and Child Molesters," *Victimology* 4 (1979), 10–16. Finkelhor points out that although studies show up to 32 percent of offenders with a background of childhood sexual trauma, this does not mean that molestation causes people to become offenders: "Most children who are molested do not go on to become molesters themselves. This is particularly true among women, who whether victimized or not rarely become offenders" (47).

64. Finkelhor, "Risk Factors"; Russell, *The Secret Trauma*; Russell, "Incidence and Prevalence of Intrafamilial and Extrafamilial Sexual Abuse of Female Children," *Child Abuse and Neglect* 7 (1983), 133–46. Finkelhor and Russell have revisited this debate more recently and affirm that the small abuse rates for women offenders are reliable: "There is every reason to believe that child sexual abuse is primarily perpetrated by males and that male perpetrators may be responsible for more serious and traumatic levels of sexual abuse than female perpetrators" (Russell, *The Secret Trauma*). The question then is, Why are so many experts in the field arguing that the number of female perpetrators has been seriously underestimated? They posit two reasons: First, that clinicians are seeing more cases of sexual abuse by females—however, the number of cases of all types of sexual abuse is increasing in the same proportions. Secondly, researchers and clinicians remain ideologically uncomfortable with the idea of male preponderance and seek for reassurances that seem to have less political implications. Finkelhor and Russell, "Women as Perpetrators," in Finkelhor, *Child Sexual Abuse*, 171–85. Approximately 70 percent of male victims were abused by men. Urquiza et al.

65. E.g., Vanderbilt, "The Children."

66. Finkelhor, *Child Sexual Abuse*, 173, describing the National Incidence Study figures.

67. Ibid.

68. Nicholas Groth, with H. Jean Birnbaum, *Men Who Rape: The Psychology of the Offender* (New York: Plenum Press, 1979), 146. See also Suzanne Sgroi, "An Approach to Case Management," in *Handbook of Clinical Intervention in Child Sexual Abuse* (Lexington, Mass.: Lexington Books, 1982), 1ff. The issue of whether sexualization, power, or both are the motivations for sexual abuse is discussed in Finkelhor, *Child Sexual Abuse*, 33–35.

69. Recent research by David Finkelhor and Linda Meyer Williams on characteristics of incest offenders is summarized in Vanderbilt, *The Children*, 12–13. For more detailed clinical considerations, see Finkelhor, *Child Sexual Abuse*, 33–52.

70. See Finkelhor, *Child Sexual Abuse*, 38–39, on "emotional congruence."

71. Ruth Mathews, St. Paul, Minn., cited in Vanderbilt, "The Children," 14.

72. Groth with Birnbaum, *Men who Rape*, 192.

73. bell hooks, "Feminist Movement to End Violence," *Feminist Theory: From Margin to Center*, 118–19.

74. Eleventh-century "Collect for Purity," Book of Common Prayer, 323.

CHAPTER 8: RITUALISTIC ABUSE

1. Caryn Stardancer, excerpt from "Dear Doctor," in *Returning to Herself: Poems of Restoration* (Kelseyville, Calif.: H.P.L. Publishing, 1989), 4. Reprinted by permission of Caryn Stardancer.

2. Her name has been changed.

3. James Ward, also cited below.

4. California Consortium of Child Abuse Councils (CCCAC), conference entitled "Ritual Abuse of Children: Treating the Survivors," with Catherine Gould, Ph.D.; Gloria Speicher, Ph.D.; Sandra Baker, Ph.D.; May Peterson; Sharon Bergeron, MFCC; Pamela Clare-Maurer, MFCC; Linda Walker, LCSW; Paul M. Crissey; and survivors, Sacramento, Calif., June 2, 1989.

5. Some of this art is reproduced in Stardancer, *Returning to Herself*.

6. Lenore Terr, *Too Scared to Cry: How Trauma Affects Children . . . and Ultimately Us All* (New York: Basic Books, 1990), 32.

7. For published testimonies of persons with multiple personalities, see Barry M. Cohen, Esther Giller, and Lynn W., eds., *Multiple Personality Disorder from the Inside Out* (Baltimore, Md.: The Sidran Press, 1991). For a detailed secondhand account of one ritual abuse survivor's experience and recovery process, see Judith Spencer, *Suffer the Child* (New York: Pocket Books/Simon and Schuster, 1989).

8. Jaimee Karroll, Executive Director of Westword Institute, a professional training organization (1563 Solano Ave. #344, Berkeley, CA 94707), explains: "Within the field there is widespread discussion about the need to differentiate between personality fragments and fully established personalities (they are different). Some professionals, as well as individuals with multiple personalities, have not yet learned how to differentiate between a fragment and an actual personality. Fragments tend to be function-specific and lack depth. They are not responsible for managing a strain of history and rarely have much information beyond responsibility for a very specific function. In a situation where there is such a high degree of shattering the majority of parts are probably fragments. If the personality system were to be mapped (a picture/family tree drawn to reflect the structure of the system), the map would probably assist in the differentiation of fragments and actual personalities. Usually, the fragments can be understood as a shattering of a personality split" (personal communication, July 1993). A fragment usually has only a single affect or function. Frank W. Putnam, *Diagnosis and Treatment of Multiple Personality Disorder* (New York: Guilford Press, 1989), 104, citing Richard P. Kluft, "An Introduction to Multiple Personality Disorder," *Psychiatric Annals* 14 (1984), 19–24.

9. Karroll: "Some satanically-seeming personalities are actually helping personalities. By assuming pseudo-satanic allegiance, the personality can then be successful in masking/hiding internal disobedience. . . . Not all satanic personalities are satanic-identified. Many individuals who have progressed in their therapy report that they assumed compliance as a life-preserving measure. . . . The reader should be encouraged to recognize the importance of emotional healing, as opposed to exorcism, which is rarely warranted but often recommended and used by professionals who are not fully informed."

10. Karroll: "I know of no statistic that informs as to the correlation between a sex abuse history, dissociation, and ritual abuse. I believe the incidence of ritual abuse to be somewhat rare. Because of a lack of clarity about the incidence there is a tendency for experts to over- and underestimate. Professionals must be assisted in understanding and accepting that when an individual has a history of sexual abuse there is a possibility there may also be a history of ritual abuse. However, the majority of people with sexual abuse histories probably have not been ritually abused. Additionally, I think providers must be encouraged to address what is accessible."

11. *Ritual Abuse: Definitions, Glossary, the Use of Mind Control*, Report of the Ritual Abuse Task Force of the Los Angeles County Commission for Women, 1.

12. For an overview of the psychology of brainwashing, see Paul A. Verdier, *Brainwashing and the Cults: An Exposé on Capturing the Human Mind* (North Hollywood, Calif.: Melvin Powers/Wilshire Book Company, 1977).

13. Karroll. She cautions: "The victim is forced to perpetrate. That is quite different than being a coperpetrator. The severity of this kind of assault stems from the perpetrators' ability to systematically manipulate the victim into a psychology of responsibility for the violence and/or murders. Usually the perpetrator is successful in his/her effort to force the victim into assuming responsibility for the violence. One of the primary ways a victim suffers is through his/her knowledge of his/her actions during the assault. The crux of the psychological and pastoral work is to help the individual understand the depth of victimization . . . to help them embrace the reality that the perpetrator (a person) successfully dangled them on the edge of sanity and/or life by placing them in a situation where they were forced to harm another or be harmed. This is not the same as coperpetration."

14. *Ritual Abuse: Definitions*, 1.

15. See Jean Goodwin, "Credibility Problems in Multiple Personality Disorder Patients and Abused Children," in Richard Kluft, ed., *Childhood Antecedents of Multiple Personality* (Washington, D.C.: American Psychiatric Association Press, 1985), 1–20.

16. The reported examples are taken from *Ritual Abuse: Definitions*, 2–5, 6, 9, 10; from Judith Spencer, *Suffer the Child*; and from stories reported to me.

17. It is likely that some ritual abuse cults may be classified by police simply as pornography rings because the groups' activities are so often tied with the production of pornography. Sex rings are defined as "a situation in which one or more adults conspire and organize for the purpose of promoting illicit sexual acts with and among minors" and often involve sado-masochistic torture of children. See Daniel S. Campagna and Donald L. Poffenberger, *The Sexual Trafficking in Children: An Investigation of the Child Sex Trade* (Dover, Mass.: Auburn House, 1988). Common characteristics of sex rings are also true especially of intergenerational ritual abuse cults: high level of planning and cooperation among offenders, numbers of victims, longevity of the groups, forced victimization of minors by other children, an extensive range and sophistication of sexual activities, and a potential for spilling over into the domain of public exploitation, e.g., sale of child pornography. See *Sexual Trafficking*, 39–41.

18. American Psychiatric Association, Diagnostic and Statistical Manual, 4th rev. ed. (DSM-IV) (Washington, D.C.: APA Press, 1994), 484–87.

19. DSM-III-R.

20. Frank W. Putnam, Jr., "Dissociation as a Response to Extreme Trauma," in Kluft, *Childhood Antecedents*, 65–98.

21. Bennett G. Braun, and Roberta G. Sachs, "The Development of Multiple Personality Disorder: Predisposing, Precipitating, and Perpetuating Factors," in Kluft, *Childhood Antecedents*, 37–64.

22. Putnam, "Dissociation," 49.

23. Patrick Gannon, "Treatment of Multiple Personality Disorder," presented at CPC Fremont Hospital, Fremont, Calif., May 1993.

24. American Psychiatric Association, *Diagnostic and Statistical Manual of Mental Disorders*, 4th ed. (DSM-IV) (Washington, D.C.: APA, 1994), 484–85. See also American Psychiatric Association, Diagnostic and Statistical Manual, 3d ed. rev. (DSM-III-R) (Washington, D.C.: APA, 1987), 269–72.

25. DSM-IV, 485.

26. Richard P. Kluft, and Catherine G. Fine, Conference "Treating Multiple Personality Disorder," sponsored by Westword Institute, cosponsored by Bay Area Women against Rape, the California Consortium for the Prevention of Child Abuse, and Woodside Women's Hospital, Oakland, Calif., December 5–6, 1991. A tape of this conference is available from Westword Institute, 1563 Solano Ave., Suite 344, Berkeley, CA 94707. Colin Ross, author of *Multiple Personality Disorder: Diagnosis, Clinical Features, and Treatment* (New York: John Wiley & Sons, 1989), adds the following caution about physiological differences between alters: "These are widely observed clinically but not well documented scientifically" (personal communication, September 1993).

27. For a simple overview of alter personalities, see Eliana Gil, *United We Stand: A Book for People with Multiple Personalities* (Walnut Creek, Calif.: Launch Press, 1990). For a much more detailed clinical description, see Frank W. Putnam, chap. 5, "The Alter Personalities," in *Diagnosis and Treatment of Multiple Personality Disorder*, 103–30.

28. Putnam, *Diagnosis and Treatment*, 202–4. The "Inner Self Helper" was first identified by Ralph B. Allison, "Psychotherapy of Multiple Personalities," paper presented at the annual meeting of the American Psychiatric Association, Atlanta, Ga., May 1978, as cited in Putnam, *Diagnosis and Treatment*, 202. See also Kluft, "An Introduction to Multiple Personality Disorder."

29. David Caul, paper presented to the American Psychiatric Association, Atlanta, Ga., May 1978, cited in Putnam, *Diagnosis and Treatment*, 203.

30. Thanks to Jaimee Karroll for this distinction.

31. Kluft, "Introduction to Multiple Personality Disorder."

32. Putnam, *Diagnosis and Treatment*, 114.

33. For a beautiful poem about this experience, see "To My Therapist upon Finding Our Kore," in Stardancer, *Returning to Herself*, 23.

34. Kluft, Conference "Treating Multiple Personality Disorder."

35. Karroll: "Often when there is distress and verbalization about integration as death, not enough time has been spent addressing internal concerns about the prospect of living as "One." Fusion must be carefully prepared therapeutically. See Putnam, *Diagnosis and Treatment*, 306ff.

36. For example, see The Troops for Truddi Chase, *When Rabbit Howls* (New York: Jove, 1990). For an example of testimony about the struggle of integration, from personalities not yet fully integrated, see "Reflections of Selena and Jenny," in Spencer, *Suffer the Child*, 373–75. On integration issues from survivors' perspectives, see chap. 7, "Unification," in Cohen et al., *Multiple Personality Disorder*, 169–80; and from a clinical perspective, see Putnam, *Diagnosis and Treatment*, 298–322.

37. David Caul, "Group and Videotape Techniques for Multiple Personality Disorder," *Psychiatric Annals* 14 (1984), 43–50, cited in Putnam, *Diagnosis and Treatment*, 261–62.

38. Kluft, Conference "Treating Multiple Personality Disorder."

39. For a review of the history of multiple personality disorder as a diagnosis, see Richard Kluft, "Childhood Antecedents of Multiple Personality Disorder: Predictors, Clinical Findings, and Therapy Results, in Kluft, ed., *Childhood Antecedents*, 170–76; and Putnam, *Diagnosis and Treatment*, chap. 2, "History and Definitional Criteria of MPD," 27–36. Also reviewed by Kluft at Conference "Treating Multiple Personality Disorder."

40. DSM-III-R, 271.

41. DSM-IV, 486.

42. Ibid.

43. For example, see L. P., "We Weave the Cloth of Healing," in Cohen et al., *Multiple Personality Disorder*, 166.

44. For an example, see Judith D., "Simply Whole," in Cohen et al., *Multiple Personality Disorder*, 28.

45. Kluft, "The Natural History of Multiple Personality Disorder," in Kluft, ed., *Childhood Antecedents*, 223.

46. Kluft and Fine, Conference "Treating Multiple Personality Disorder."

47. For a detailed clinical description of indicators of multiple personality, see Richard J. Loewenstein, "An Office Mental Status Examination for Complex Chronic Dissociative Symptoms and Multiple Personality Disorder," *Psychiatric Clinics of North America* 14/3 (September 1991), 567–604.

48. Putnam, *Diagnosis and Treatment*, 176–77.

49. This BASK model of dissociation was developed by Bennett G. Braun, "The BASK Model of Dissociation: Clinical Applications," *Dissociation* 1/2 (1988), 116–23, cited by Fine, Conference, and Fine, "Thoughts on the Cognitive Perceptual Substrates of Multiple Personality Disorder," reprint, 2400 Chestnut Street, Suite 610, Philadelphia, PA 19103. In order for abreaction work to be complete, all four levels of the abuse memory must be worked through.

50. For a review of clinical issues surrounding permeability, see Putnam, *Diagnosis and Treatment*, 114–15.

51. Ibid., 124–26.

52. Richard Kluft, "Therapy of Multiple Personality Disorder: A Study of 33 Cases," *Psychiatric Clinics of North America* 7 (1984), 9–29, cited in Putnam, *Diagnosis and Treatment*, 124–25.

53. Gil, *United We Stand*, 13.

54. Kluft and Fine, Conference; Putnam, *Diagnosis and Treatment*, chap. 9, "The Therapeutic Role of Hypnosis and Abreaction," 235–51.

55. A NIMH study demonstrated this phenomenon in approximately 30 percent of cases. Putnam, *Diagnosis and Treatment*, 219.

56. Colin Ross, personal communication, August 1991. Dale Griffis, Tiffin, Ohio, states that in his experience and research in criminology and psychology of ritual abuse, 98 percent of cult leadership is male. Few females rise to that rank, and most who do, do so as part of a husband-

wife team (personal communication, August 1993). Jerry Simandl adds that there are some cults with high priestesses, but the cults are still generally male dominant, and more research is needed (personal communication, August 1993).

57. *Ritual Abuse: Definitions*, 13–14.

58. Karroll, personal communication.

59. Dale Griffis, personal communication, August 1993.

60. See, e.g., Jenny's story in Spencer, *Suffer the Child*, xix.

61. Kluft, at Kluft and Fine, Conference.

62. Marita Bausman, and David O. McCoy, "The Satanic and the Spiritual: Specialized Treatment of MPD Clients," unpublished paper presented April 15, 1988. For a survivor's brief testimony, see also Grace, "The Place of Religion in Therapy," in Cohen et al., *Multiple Personality Disorder*, 110.

63. Bausman and McCoy have presented an excellent discussion of this partnership between clergy and therapist in "The Satanic and the Spiritual."

64. Survivor testimony, CCCAC Conference, Sacramento, June 2, 1989.

65. The modern witchcraft movement, also known as wicca or "the old religion," is generally understood as a peaceful, nature-based goddess religion, which disavows Satanism as part of a completely different, Christian-dependent religious system. For further discussion of the distinction, see Margo Adler, *Drawing Down the Moon* (Boston: Beacon Press, 1979), esp. 51–54, 330ff., also citing Edward J. Moody, "Magical Therapy: An Anthropological Investigation of Contemporary Satanism," in *Religious Movements in Contemporary America*, ed. I. Zaretsky and M. Leone (Princeton: Princeton University Press, 1974), 380–82.

66. Examples are given by Bausman and McCoy, "The Satanic and the Spiritual," 9ff.

67. For a more detailed clinical description of therapeutic issues, see Putnam, *Diagnosis and Treatment*, chap. 7, "Issues in Psychotherapy," 167–96.

68. "A Memorial Service for Those Who Died as Victims of Ritual Abuse and Other Violent Assault," Berkeley, Calif., June 1990, sponsored by Bay Area Women against Rape, Oakland; Center for Women and Religion of the Graduate Theological Union, Berkeley; and St. Cuthbert's Episcopal Church, Oakland.

69. For a discussion of the importance of "the context of a life lived out in committed relationship to God in Jesus Christ in the Christian Church," see James S. Ward, "Ritual and Healing: The Liberating and Rehumanizing Resources of the Church for Ritual Abuse Survivors," unpublished paper presented at University of California, Berkeley, Healing Institute on Ritual Abuse, January 20, 1989, 2.

70. James S. Ward, "The Problem of Ritual Abuse," unpublished paper presented to the California State Social Service Advisory Board, Committee on Child Abuse Prevention, December 8, 1988, 3; and for an in-depth theological rationale, see Ward, "Ritual and Healing," 5ff.

71. For an example of a satanic initiation rite, see Spencer, *Suffer the Child*, 14–21.

72. The question of rebaptism has also been raised. James Ward writes, "Many survivors will have already been baptized, and those whose involvement has been generational will likely have been baptized in a kind of reversal where the same or similar words will have been used, but the intention will be to mock or blaspheme Christian ritual. In this case the intention of the rite determines its validity and rebaptism is entirely appropriate. If there is some doubt . . . then 'conditional' baptism is available. Rebaptism for the sake of simply marking a renewal of faith as an adult . . . is uncomfortably close to a manipulation of Christian ritual, and therefore not a healing act. The sacrament should not be treated like magic or a mere social convenience. Its power is not *ours* to use that way." "Ritual and Healing," 6–7.

73. Ward, "The Problem of Ritual Abuse," 3.

74. For a different view on exorcism, see James G. Friesen, *Uncovering the Mystery of MPD* (San Bernardino, Calif.: Here's Life Publishers, 1991).

75. This is a consensus view of many survivors, therapists, clergy, and experts. See Putnam, *Diagnosis and Treatment*, 113–14. Jaimee Karroll, personal communication, July 1993. Caryn Stardancer, personal communication, August 1993. Putnam also describes clinical methods for

working with persecutory personalities (205–10). See also Elaine Ramshaw, *Ritual and Pastoral Care* (Philadelphia: Fortress Press, 1987), 86.

76. Karroll, personal communication, July 1993.

77. Bausman and McCoy, "The Satanic and the Spiritual," 7.

78. Ibid., 7.

79. This statement has engendered lively debate among friends and clergy colleagues. "If this is not within the scope of expertise of a priest, then whose?" And yet, for many of us trained in a liberal theological tradition, such discussions of evil as an objective force seem foreign and shaky. My acquaintance with ritual abuse survivors more than anything has unseated my previous rational certainty that all evil is of human agency. As one colleague put it: I now see that there may be a door there—but I do not feel qualified to describe what is beyond it.

80. For a clinician's description of his own reasoning behind using an exorcism technique with a patient under hypnosis, see Ralph Ellison, *Minds in Many Pieces* (New York: Rawson, Wade, Inc. 1980), 82ff.

81. This story by permission of the survivor. This resembles the therapeutic technique of "talking through," addressing the entire personality system at once through the host personality, as described in Putnam, *Diagnosis and Treatment*, 197–98, 226–27, also citing Kluft "An Introduction to Multiple Personality Disorder"; Braun, "Use of Hypnosis with Multiple Personality," *Psychiatric Annals* 94 (1984) 39–40; and Caul paper presented to the American Psychiatric Association, Atlanta, Ga., 1978.

82. Bausman and McCoy, "The Satanic and the Spiritual," 10. By permission.

83. James Ward notes that this may have been the only way the one who witnessed the victim's death could outsmart the cult—by keeping them in some sense alive (in their own personality system) (personal communication, September 1993).

84. Ibid.

85. Ward, "Ritual and Healing," 2–4.

86. Ibid., 3.

87. For an example, see survivor Will R.'s poem, "The Beginning," in Cohen et al., *Multiple Personality Disorder*, 5.

88. Ward, "Ritual and Healing, 4.

89. Ibid.

90. Caryn Stardancer, "Communion," in *Returning to Herself*, 46. Reprinted by permission of the author.

CHAPTER 9: THE PASTOR AS "WOUNDED HEALER"

1. Ram Dass and Paul Gorman, *How Can I Help? Stories and Reflections on Service* (New York: Alfred A. Knopf, 1991), 227.

2. Henri Nouwen, *The Wounded Healer* (Garden City, N.Y.: Doubleday/Image, 1972), 81–82.

3. See Thomas Maeder, "Wounded Healers," *The Atlantic Monthly*, January 1989, 37–47.

4. Cited ibid., 39.

5. Alice Miller, *The Drama of the Gifted Child*, trans. Ruth Ward (New York: Basic Books, 1981).

6. I. L. McCann and L. A. Pearlman, "Vicarious Traumatization: A Framework for Understanding the Psychological Effects of Working with Victims, *Journal of Traumatic Stress* 3 (1990), 131–50, cited in Herman, *Trauma and Recovery*, 140. See also Nancy J. Cole, "Stages in Trauma Therapy," *Newsletter of The Center for Trauma and Dissociation*, 4400 E. Iliff Ave., Denver, CO 80222, 1/5 (October 1993), 1. Cole outlines stages of secondary traumatization experienced by therapists working with severely traumatized patients, and suggests coping styles and outcomes.

7. Frank W. Putnam, *Diagnosis and Treatment of Multiple Personality Disorder* (New York: Guilford, 1989), as cited in Herman, *Trauma and Recovery*, 141.

8. Christina Maslach, *Burnout: The Cost of Caring* (Englewood Cliffs, N.J.: Prentice-Hall, 1982), 3–5.

9. Cary Cherniss, *Staff Burnout: Job Stress in the Human Services*, Sage Studies in Community Mental Health, vol. 2 (Beverly Hills and London: Sage Publications, 1980), 17.

10. Maslach, *Burnout*, 35–70.

11. Cherniss, *Staff Burnout*, 18.

12. Maslach, *Burnout*, 35ff.

13. Cherniss, *Staff Burnout*, 75.

14. Maslach, *Burnout*, 56ff.

15. Ibid.; see also James Lowery, Jr., "Well, Effective and Thriving Clergy: Research Report for the Cornerstone Project, Episcopal Church Foundation" (Boston, Mass.: Enablement, Inc., August 1, 1992).

16. Lowery, "Well, Effective and Thriving Clergy."

17. Dorothy McRae-McMahon, *Being Clergy, Staying Human: Taking Our Stand in the River* (Washington, D.C.: Alban Institute Publications, 1992), 72.

18. Oakland Coalition of Congregations, 5843 Foothill Blvd., Oakland, Calif.

19. See Maslach, *Burnout*, 147–48.

20. Ibid., 147–48.

21. Donald R. Hands and Wayne L. Fehr, *Spiritual Wholeness for Clergy: A New Psychology of Intimacy with God, Self and Others* (Washington, D.C.: Alban Institute, 1993), 75–76.

22. Diane Fassel, *Working Ourselves to Death: The High Cost of Workaholism and the Rewards of Recovery* (San Francisco: HarperSanFrancisco, 1990), 117.

23. See Herman, *Trauma and Recovery*, 151–54, on the value of a professional support group.

24. Nouwen, *The Wounded Healer*, 93–94.

25. Dass and Gorman, *How Can I Help?* 195–96.

26. Ibid., 195.

CHAPTER 10: MINISTRY WITH VIOLENT MEN

1. Paul Kivel, *Men's Work* (New York: Ballantine Books, 1992), xx–xxi.

2. I was first introduced to the "Act Like a Man" box during a workshop by Oakland Men's Project at the California Governor's Victim Services Fall Training Conference, Orange, Calif., November 1988; I subsequently assisted presenting this model at a workshop I helped organize for the Episcopal Diocese of California with Harrison Simms and Paul Kivel of Oakland Men's Project (January 1989). This material is now summarized in Kivel, *Men's Work*, 22–40.

3. See Hamish Sinclair, *Prospectus: Training Programs for "Accountable/Advocacy" Batterer Intervention Programs*, Manalive! Training Programs for Men, 345 Johnstone Drive, San Rafael, CA 94903.

4. Donna Garske, citing research at Marin Abused Women's Services, 1717 5th Ave., San Rafael, CA 94901 (personal communication, October 1993).

5. E. Bern and L. Bern, "A Group Program for Men Who Commit Violence towards Their Wives," *Social Work with Groups* 7/1 (1984), 63–76; R. J. Brown and F. L. Chato, "Characteristics of Wife Batterers and Practice Principles for Effective Treatment" (Calgary, Alberta: Forensic Service, Calgary General Hospital, 1984); A. Ganley, "Court-Mandated Counseling for Men Who Batter: A Three-Day Workshop for Mental Health Professionals" (Washington, D.C.: Center for Women Policy Studies, 1981); and D. Saunders, "Helping Husbands Who Batter," *Social Casework: The Journal of Contemporary Social Work* (1984), 347–53; cited in Anne Ganley, "Perpetrators of Domestic Violence: An Overview of Counseling the Court-Mandated Client," in Marie Fortune, ed., *Violence in the Family: A Workshop Curriculum for Clergy and Other Helpers* (Cleveland, Ohio: Pilgrim Press, 1991), 213.

6. See, e.g., Roland Summit, "Beyond Belief: The Reluctant Discovery of Incest," in Pellauer, Chester, and Boyajian, *Sexual Assault and Abuse: A Handbook for Clergy and Religious Professionals* (San Francisco: HarperSanFrancisco, 1987), 194; Gary Schoener and John Gonsiorek, "Assessment and Development of Rehabilitation Plans for the Therapist," in Schoener et al., *Psychotherapists' Sexual Involvement with Clients: Prevention and Intervention* (Minneapolis: Walk-In

Counseling Center, 1989), 401–4; Jonathan H. Segal, "Erotomania Revisited: From Kraepelin to DSM-III-R," *American Journal of Psychiatry* 146/10 (October 1989), 1261–66. Pedophilia is particularly intractible and, as a general rule, "cannot be cured, only treated." Daniel S. Campagna and Donald L. Poffenberger, *The Sexual Trafficking in Children: An Investigation of the Child Sex Trade* (Dover, Mass.: Auburn House, 1988), 45, citing Chris Corbett, senior counselor, "Together We Can" program, Pittsburgh, Pa.

7. Rich Garcia, MFCC, personal communication, October 1993.

8. The original study was conducted in Minneapolis by Lawrence Sherman and Richard Burk, "Specific Deterrent Effects of Arrest for Domestic Assault," *American Sociological Review* 49 (1984), 261. More recently, an entire issue of *Journal of Criminal Law and Criminology* 83/1 (Spring 1992) has been devoted to arrest as a deterrent, including six replications of the Minneapolis study. Details of the replication studies' results vary according to length of time the effect of deterrence lasts, the amount of police surveillance and follow-up, and contextual issues of race and economics.

9. Summit, "Beyond Belief," 193–94; also citing H. Giaretto, "Humanistic Treatment of Father-Daughter Incest," in *Child Abuse and Neglect: The Family and the Community*, ed. R. Helfer and C. Kempe (Cambridge, Mass.: Ballinger, 1976), 143–57, 155.

10. Judith Herman, "Considering Sex Offenders: A Model of Addiction," *Signs* 13/4 (1988), 695–725.

11. With batterers, it has been observed that even when physical violence is stopped after participation in a rehabilitation program, other behaviors that continue patterns of domination, control, and manipulation continue, and the essential dynamic of the relationship remains unchanged. Donna Garske, Marin Abused Women's Services.

12. Adapted from Barbara Hart, *Safety for Women: Monitoring Batterers' Programs*, Pennsylvania Coalition against Domestic Violence (2505 North Front Street, Harrisburg, PA 17110-1111, 1988), 84–85.

13. Adapted from legislative work of a committee for building standards for court-ordered batterers' programs into California law, under the auspices of the California Alliance Against Domestic Violence. The committee's work drew on Barbara Hart, *Safety for Women: Monitoring Batterers' Programs*, Pennsylvania Coalition against Domestic Violence (2505 North Front Street, Harrisburg, PA 17110–1111), 1988; and County of Los Angeles Domestic Violence Council, *Batterer's Treatment Program Guidelines* (Dept. of Community and Senior Citizen Services, 3175 W. 6th St., Los Angeles, CA 90020), June 1988. For standards, see especially pp. 8ff.

14. For example, Campagna and Poffenberger, *Sexual Trafficking*, make the following statement regarding treatment of child molesters: "Molestation is not a sexual dysfunction; rather it is a power dysfunction" (45).

15. A recent public opinion survey indicates that the general population of men now recognizes that domestic violence is a serious problem but nevertheless has major misconceptions about what constitutes abuse and where it is occurring ("not in my backyard"); most men also know that there are few negative social consequences for abusive behavior, and they are reluctant to intervene even though they have ideas of how to do so, primarily because they do not recognize their own role or responsibility for stopping male violence against women. "Man to Man: A Public Opinion Survey of Men's Knowledge, Attitudes, Beliefs and Behaviors Concerning Domestic Violence," October 1993, Marin Abused Women's Services.

16. For example, see Susan Schechter, *Guidelines for Mental Health Practitioners in Domestic Violence Cases* (National Coalition Against Domestic Violence, P.O. Box 15127, Washington, DC 20003–0127, 1987).

17. Edward Gondolf and David Russell, "The Case against Anger Control Treatment Programs for Batterers," *Response* 9/3 (1986), 2–5; and Richard Tolman and Daniel G. Saunders, "The Case for Cautious Use of Anger Control with Men Who Batter," *Response* 11/2 (1988).

18. Gondolf and Russell, "The Case against Anger Control."

19. Richard Tolman and Daniel G. Saunders, "The Case for Cautious Use of Anger Control with Men Who Batter," *Response* 11/2 (1988), 19.

20. Hart, *Safety for Women*, 101.

21. Ibid., 101–3.

22. Ibid. See also Ganley, "Perpetrators of Domestic Violence," 213. Ganley also includes references to a number of clinical studies of batterers' programs.

23. Based on Hamish Sinclair, "Manalive! Training Programs for Men," and *Prospectus*.

24. Dobash and Dobash, *Women, Violence and Social Change*, (New York: Routledge, 1992), 246.

25. Cf. Sinclair, "Manalive!" and Oakland Men's Project. Rich Garcia cautions: If this is only done in a spirit of doing time or enforced symbolic restitution, it is not likely to effect real change. Many men, however, find it an important reinforcement to all they have already gained in their program.

26. Contra Sonkin and Durphy. For more details on both sides of this debate, see Dobash and Dobash, *Women, Violence and Social Change*, 247.

27. Hart, *Safety for Women*.

28. Harrison Simms (personal communication, June 9, 1988).

29. Based on Anne Ganley, "Cool Downs/Time Outs: A Procedure for Stopping Your Battering" (handout prepared for American Lake VAMC, Tacoma, WA 98493); "MOVE: Men Overcoming Violence" and "Gay Male Domestic Violence" (pamphlets from MOVE/Men Overcoming Violence, 3004 16th St. #12, San Francisco, CA 94103); and Sinclair, "Manalive!" See also Daniel Jay Sonkin and Michael Durphy, *Learning to Live without Violence: A Handbook for Men* (San Francisco: Volcano Press, 1982).

30. Cf. Hart, *Safety for Women*, 91.

31. Ibid.

32. See, e.g., John C. Gonsiorek, who projects a ten- to thirty-month timeline in "Working Therapeutically with Therapists Who Have Become Sexually Involved with Clients," in Schoener et al, *Psychotherapists' Sexual Involvement*, 142. Judith Herman ("Counseling Offenders," 719) recommends at least three years, paralleling alcohol recovery.

33. Kivel, *Men's Work*, and "Men's Work: To Stop Male Violence," pamphlet of Oakland Men's Project, Oakland, Calif.

34. Oakland Men's Project pamphlet, "Men's Work: To Stop Men's Violence," 2.

35. State Justice Institute, "Evaluation of Court-Ordered Treatment for Domestic Violence Offenders," by Adele Harrell, The Urban Institute, October 1991, 92.

36. Ibid., 12.

37. Ganley, "Court-Mandated Counseling," 222.

38. For example, see Schoener and Gonsiorek, "Assessment and Rehabilitation," in Schoener et al., *Psychotherapists' Sexual Involvement with Clients*, 402–4; Donald R. Hands, "Types of Clergy who Sexually Abuse" in "Sexual Addiction, Sexual Abuse and the Clergy," *Clergy in Crisis* (St. Barnabas Center, Rogers Memorial Hospital, Oconomowoc, WI 53066), 17–18.

39. John C. Bush and William Harold Tiemann, *The Right to Silence: Privileged Clergy Communication and the Law*, 3d ed. (Nashville: Abingdon Press, 1989), 178.

40. Ibid., 180.

41. In one state, Rhode Island, the reporting is without names for statistical purposes only. In most cases, reports are made to police. In Arkansas, reports are made to domestic violence advocates.

42. 551 P.2d 334, 131 Calif. Rep. 14 (1976). For discussion of implications of Tarasoff for clergy, see Lindell Gumper, *Legal Issues in the Practice of Ministry* (Birmingham, Mich.: Psychological Studies and Consultation Program, Inc., 1981), 18; Bush and Tiemann, *The Right to Silence*, 172–73. For more details on duty to warn, including Tarasoff (duty to warn), and related cases Jablonski (712 F.2d391, 9th Cir. 1983) (duty to warn based on a prior history) and Hedlund (34 Cal.3d 695, 1983) (duty to inform foreseeable victim of risk to bystanders), see Daniel Jay

Sonkin, Del Martin, and Lenore E. A. Walker, *The Male Batterer: A Treatment Approach* (New York: Springer, 1985), 133–36.

43. Cited in Bush and Tiemann, *The Right to Silence*, 173.

44. Malpractice is professional negligence, and the proof of malpractice depends on established standards of care for the profession. One often cited case, Nally v. Grace Community Church, did for a time establish professional standards of care and grounds for clergy malpractice regarding a case of suicide: a duty to investigate suicidal manifestations; inform the individual's family or others who might be able to help; refer to competent professionals; train and employ competent counselors to secular standards; and make counselors available to the parishioner in question. However, this was overturned by the California Supreme Court (253 Calif. Rep. 97 [1988]) and rejected for review by the U.S. Supreme Court. The California Supreme Court ruling: no duty to refer; no clergy "malpractice" or negligence established; and access to clergy for counseling should be free from state restrictions. See Bush and Tiemann, *The Right to Silence*, 93. For a discussion of the ethical questions involved in Nally, and clergy confidentiality in general, see Margaret Battin, *Ethics in the Sanctuary: Examining the Practices of Organized Religion* (New Haven: Yale University Press, 1990), 20–73.

45. Connecticut, Mississippi, Nevada, and New Hampshire, cited in Richard R. Hammar, *Pastor, Church and Law*, 2d ed. (Matthews, N.C.: Christian Ministry Resources), 180.

46. Kentucky, Maryland, Oregon, and South Carolina, cited in Hammar, *Pastor, Church and Law*, 180.

47. Arkansas, Idaho, Louisiana, and Washington, cited in Hammar, *Pastor, Church and Law*, 180.

48. Ibid.; Bush and Tiemann, *The Right to Silence*, 178–79.

49. Hammar, *Pastor, Church and Law*, 182, which also reports that in State v. Motherwell, 788 P.2d 1066 (Washington 1990), clergy in one state successfully argued that because the state legislature's 1975 amendment of the child abuse reporting law intentionally deleted a reference to clergy, the intent of the law was to exclude them from the mandate.

50. Hammar, *Pastor, Church and Law*, 183–84, which also reports that in at least one case, Fischer v. Metcalf, a state appeals court rejected abused daughters' attempt to sue a psychiatrist who treated their abusing father and failed to report him, because the legislature did not include civil liability under possible penalties for failure to report.

51. Ibid., 181.

52. Gumper, *Legal Issues*, 43; for philosophical discussion of this issue, see Bush and Tiemann, *The Right to Silence*.

53. An important case is *In Re Swenson*, in which the Supreme Court of Minnesota determined that a clergyperson was not required to divulge information told to him privately in the context of voluntary confession and private advice, even though no sacrament of confession was involved. See Bush and Tiemann, *The Right to Silence*, 122–24.

54. Bush and Tiemann, *The Right to Silence*, chap. 13.

55. Larry Spielman, "Confidentiality: Lessons Learned from Real Life," unpublished paper.

56. Bush and Tiemann, *The Right to Silence*, 180.

57. Ibid.

58. William Rankin, *Confidentiality and Clergy: Churches, Ethics and the Law* (Wilton, Conn.: Morehouse Pub., 1990), 50–52.

59. Sissela Bok, "The Limits of Confidentiality," in *Secrets* (New York: Vintage Books, 1984), 120–22.

60. Ibid., 121–22. See also a slightly different version of this argument in Sissela Bok, "The Limits of Confidentiality," *Hastings Center Report* (February 1983), 24–25, cited in Fortune, "Confidentiality and Mandatory Reporting: A Clergy Dilemma?" in *Sexual Assault and Abuse: A Handbook for Clergy and Religious Professionals*, ed. Mary Pellauer, Barbara Chester, and Jane Boyajian (San Francisco: HarperSanFrancisco, 1987), 199.

61. Bok, *Secrets*, 121. Note that Bok makes no special ethical exception for the religious professional in sacramental confession (123).

62. Ibid., 122.

63. Marie Fortune, "Reporting Child Abuse: An Ethical Mandate for Ministry," in Anne Horton and Judith Williamson, *Abuse and Religion: When Praying Isn't Enough* (Lexington, Mass.: Lexington Books/D.C. Heath, 1988), 189–97, and Marie Fortune, "Confidentiality and Mandatory Reporting," 198–205.

64. Fortune, "Reporting Child Abuse," 195. See also Sissela Bok, "Lies Protecting Peers and Clients," in *Lying: Moral Choice in Public and Private Life* (New York: Vintage/Random House, 1978), 161–66.

65. Fortune, "Reporting Child Abuse," 195.

66. Fortune, "Confidentiality and Mandatory Reporting," 203; Fortune, "Reporting Child Abuse," 192–93.

67. Rankin, *Confidentiality and Clergy*, 50.

68. Fortune, "Reporting Child Abuse." Note that anonymous reporting also fails to establish any documentation of having taken responsibility in case of legal liability (per Hammar, *Pastor, Church and Law*, 185).

69. For example, for the complete canons of the Roman Catholic Church concerning the sacrament of confession, see Title IV, cc. 959–997 in Canon Law Society of America, *Code of Canon Law: Latin-English Edition* (trans. of Codex Iuris Canonici), 1983; and *Pedalion/The Rudder of the Metaphorical Ship of the One Holy Catholic and Apostolic Church of the Orthodox Christians, Or: All the Sacred and Divine Canons as Embodied in the Original Greek Text*, 5th ed., trans. D. Cummings (Chicago: Orthodox Christian Educational Society, 1957). The canons of the Episcopal Church do not treat the issue of sacramental confession. However, the *Book of Common Prayer*, which is to be adhered to at all times, states: "The content of a confession is not normally a matter of subsequent discussion. The secrecy of a confession is morally absolute for the confessor, and must under no circumstances be broken" (*BCP*, 446). This is possibly the strongest directive in the *Book of Common Prayer*.

70. Allen Duston, O.P., Dominican School of Theology and Philosophy (personal communication, August 1993). The Orthodox Church carries a similarly severe sentence, either excommunication or defrocking (Leonidas Contos, Patriarch Athenagoras Orthodox Institute, personal communication, November 1993).

71. Anne L. Horton and Doran Williams, "What Incest Perpetrators Need (but Are Not Getting) from the Clergy and Treatment Community," in Horton and Williamson, eds., *Abuse and Religion*, 256–66.

72. "Male Counselors and Female Rape Survivors," *YWCA Rape Crisis Manual*, Mid-Peninsula YWCA Rape Crisis Center, Palo Alto, Calif., September 1989.

73. For example, specific guidelines were developed by one congregation in the case of a lay leader who had abused two children, as described in Carol Adams, "When the Abuser Is Among Us: One Church's Response to a Perpetrator," *Working Together* 14/3 (Winter 1993/Spring 1994), Center for the Prevention of Sexual and Domestic Violence, Seattle, Wash., 1–4.

74. As described in chapter 6 above, note also that in the case of clergy offenders, restoration to Christian fellowship is *not* synonymous with restoration to professional ministry or to participation in the parish(es) in which the abuse occurred.

CHAPTER 11: EMPOWERING WOMEN

1. These are adapted from crisis counselor training at Sojourn: Services for Battered Women in Santa Monica, California, and a crisis counselor training card, "Steps in the Crisis Counseling Session/Call" developed by the author for Mid-Peninsula Support Network for Battered Women in Mountain View, California. There are many similar models used at battered women's agencies across the country. The reader may call his or her local shelter agency for additional information, written materials, and training, with particular emphasis on strategies for crisis response in the local area.

2. A number of similar models for suicide assessment can be carried out very effectively by pastors who do not have extensive clinical training. Resources I have found valuable include Vincent D'Andrea and Peter Salovey, *Peer Counseling: Skills and Perspectives* (Palo Alto, Calif.: Science and Behavior Books, 1983), 87–100; and especially Burl E. Gilliland and Richard K. James, "Suicide: Strategies for Assessment and Intervention," in *Crisis Intervention Strategies* (Pacific Grove, Calif.: Brooks/Cole Publishing Co., 1988), 75–102. For more in-depth reading, the following are classics by the pioneers of the field of suicide prevention and psychology in the 1960s and 1970s: Norman L. Farberow, "Crisis, Disaster, and Suicide: Theory and Therapy," in Edwin Shneidman, ed., *Essays in Self-Destruction* (New York: Science House, 1967), 373–98; Edwin Shneidman, Norman Farberow, and Robert Litman, eds., *The Psychology of Suicide* (New York: Jason Aronson, 1976); Edwin Shneidman, *Definition of Suicide* (New York: John Wiley and Sons, 1985). See also Leo Rangell, "The Decision to Terminate One's Life: Psychoanalytic Thoughts on Suicide," in Ronald Maris, ed., *Understanding and Preventing Suicide* (New York: Guilford Press, 1988), 28–46; and L. E. Fujimura, D. M. Weis, and J. R. Cochran, "Suicide: Dynamics and Implications for Counseling," *Journal of Counseling and Development* 63 (1985), 612–15. For a discussion of the deeper meaning of suicide from a Jungian perspective, see James Hillman, *Suicide and the Soul* (Zurich: Spring Publications, 1976).

3. Shneidman, *Definition of Suicide*, 143–44.

4. Edwin Shneidman, "Preventing Suicide," in Shneidman et al., *The Psychology of Suicide*, 431–32.

5. Ibid., 435–38.

6. D'Andrea and Salovey, *Peer Counseling*, 91.

7. Gilliland and James, "Suicide," 79.

8. Ibid., 80.

9. Shneidman and Farberow, "Facts and Fables on Suicide," Public Health Service Publication No. 852 (Washington, D.C.: U.S. Government Printing Office, 1961), reprinted in Shneidman et al., *The Psychology of Suicide*, 130. Also see chart on relative risk of moderate and extreme depression in D'Andrea and Salovey, *Peer Counseling*, 90.

10. Shneidman, Farberow and Litman, *The Psychology of Suicide*, Gilliland and James, 81.

11. Gilliland and James, 81.

12. Shneidman (*Definition of Suicide*, 143) makes the point that not all suicides are cries for help, nor are they communications of hostility, rage, destruction, or withdrawal. The common interpersonal act of suicide is communication of pure *intention*.

13. John Hipple "Suicide: the Preventable Tragedy," mimeographed monograph (Denton, Tex.: North Texas State University, 1985), cited in Gilliland and James, "Suicide," 97.

14. See Rangell, "The Decision to Terminate One's Life," 35; on the significance of hope in suicidality, see also Hillman, *Suicide and the Soul*, 154–55.

15. Shneidman, "Preventing Suicide," 435.

16. Hillman, *Suicide and the Soul*, 154–55.

17. Gilliland and James, "Suicide," 3.

18. The field of crisis intervention is relatively young. The origins of crisis theory lie in Erich Lindemann's historic study of grief reactions in the aftermath of the Coconut Grove nightclub fire which claimed five hundred lives in 1942. Lindemann first identified that there was a predictable course to grief reactions after a crisis that involved transitory adjustment struggles. Timely crisis intervention could prevent longer-term psychopathological consequences. See Lindemann, "Symptomatology and Management of Acute Grief," *American Journal of Psychiatry* 101 (September 1944), 101ff., and his later book *Beyond Grief: Studies in Crisis Intervention* (New York: Jason Aronson, 1979). Other important references establishing principles and methods of crisis intervention include Gerald Caplan, *Principles of Prevention Psychiatry* (New York: Basic Books, 1964) and W. E. Morley, J. M. Messick, and D. C. Aguilera, "Crisis: Paradigms of Intervention," *Journal of Psychiatric Nursing* 5 (1967), 537ff. The history and development of crisis theory is summarized in Gilliland and James, *Crisis Intervention Strategies*, chap. 1.

19. Taught as part of hotline counselor training, Sojourn Services for Battered Women, Santa Monica, Calif., 1983. Very similar models are presented in the crisis literature described. See especially Gilliland and James, "Steps in Crisis Counseling," in *Crisis Intervention Strategies*, Fig. 2–1; Morley, et al. provide a somewhat more elaborated but similar version in "Crisis."

20. For a more detailed model for just this step of problem-solving, see the "D.E.C.I.D.E.S. model" of D'Andrea and Salovey in *Peer Counseling*. The "D.E.C.I.D.E.S. model" follows the steps (1) define the problem; (2) establish an action plan; (3) clarify values; (4) identify alternatives; (5) discover probable outcomes; (6) eliminate alternatives systematically; (7) select and start action.

21. Ruth Schmidt, "After the Fact: To Speak of Rape," *The Christian Century*, January 6–13, 1993, 16–17.

22. This is a tenet of existential psychotherapy. See, e.g., James Bugental, *Psychotherapy and Process: The Fundamentals of an Existential-Humanistic Approach* (New York: Random House, 1978); and Irvin Yalom, *Existential Psychotherapy* (New York: Basic Books, 1980) and *Love's Executioner* (New York: Basic Books, 1989), esp. 3–14.

23. Vern Haddick, "Facilitative Responding: Based on the Writings of George Gazda," unpublished paper distributed to class at California Institute of Integral Studies, 765 Ashbury Street, San Francisco, CA 94117.

24. Judith Herman, *Trauma and Recovery* (New York: Basic Books, 1992), 52–53.

25. See ibid., 134.

26. Developed by psychiatrists at St. John's Mercy Medical Center, St. Louis, cited in Jerold Kreisman, and Hal Straus, *I Hate You, Don't Leave Me: Understanding the Borderline Personality* (New York: Avon, 1989), 99ff.

27. Professional pastoral counselors are certified in the United States by the American Association of Pastoral Counselors, 9504a Lee Highway, Fairfax, VA 22031-2303.

28. For more information see Michael Dwinell, "How to Choose a Therapist/Counselor" (Cincinnati: Forward Movement, 1991).

29. Evangelical Lutheran Church in America; (Episcopal) Church Insurance Company: "Standards of pastoral practice will require professional [i.e. licensed clinical] consultation or referral for counseling beyond six sessions, along with the proscribing of fees or donations for pastoral care. Anyone charging fees for counseling outside the scope of Church employment must possess appropriate professional credentials and proof of separate professional liability insurance."

30. D'Andrea and Salovey, *Peer Counseling*.

31. Ibid.

32. For an excellent resource for such pastoral training, see Charles Taylor, *The Skilled Pastor: Counseling as the Practice of Theology* (Minneapolis: Fortress Press, 1991).

33. Herman, *Trauma and Recovery*, 34; see also Lenore Terr, *Too Scared to Cry* (New York: Basic Books, 1990).

34. Herman, *Trauma and Recovery*, 74–75.

35. John Maltsberger and Dan Buie, "Countertransference Hate in the Treatment of Suicidal Patients." *Archives of General Psychiatry* 30 (1974), 627, cited in Herman, *Trauma and Recovery*, 143.

36. Cf. Alice Miller, *The Drama of the Gifted Child*, trans. Ruth Ward (New York: Basic Books, 1981), on the importance of grieving the injuries, deprivations, and losses of childhood as a prerequisite for not repeating them.

37. Herman, *Trauma and Recovery*, 155ff.

38. A cooperative model between peer advocates (i.e. shelter and rape crisis workers), licensed psychotherapists, and pastoral counselors recognizes that all three have important, *complementary* contributions to make in a survivor's healing process. For a more detailed discussion of this model of cooperation, see Pamela Cooper-White, "Peer vs. Clinical Counseling: Is There Room for Both in the Battered Women's Movement?" *Response* 13/3 (1990), 2–6; and "The Respective Roles of Shelter Advocate, Pastoral Counselor and Psychotherapist in Working with Battered Women: A Cooperative Model," presented to the national meeting of the Division for Social Ministry Organizations, Evangelical Lutheran Church in America, Chicago, April 1990.

39. Challenge yourself concerning any instances of your own disbelief and process them through the knowledge that historically, even the most experienced experts—such as Freud—disbelieved women's experience. Remind yourself: Incredible, devastatingly brutal things really do happen to women. If disbelief lingers, try to suspend it in favor of the survivor's experience of reality. Suspend your need to pin down the details, or to have clarity about what exactly did happen. Less important than determining literal, forensic fact is the recognition that she is communicating her anguish as clearly as she knows how. Something terrible happened to her. In most cases, that is enough to be sure of.

40. See Elaine Ramshaw, *Ritual and Pastoral Care* (Philadelphia: Fortress Press, 1987).

41. Valerie M. DeMarinis, *Critical Caring: A Feminist Model for Pastoral Psychology* (Louisville, Ky.: Westminster/John Knox, 1993).

42. See e.g., Mary D. Pellauer, Barbara Chester, and Jane A. Boyajian, "Resources for Ritual and Recuperation," in Pellauer, Chester, and Boyajian, eds., *Sexual Assault and Abuse: A Handbook for Clergy and Religious Professionals* (San Francisco: HarperSanFrancisco, 1987), 223–47. Note: Some of these liturgies should be approached with caution, or at least with ample preparation and education—for example, a liturgy focusing on forgiveness (e.g., pp. 237–38), a startling rendering of Psalm 137 which includes, "May we remain victims, if we relax in our captivity and acquiesce to our oppressors" (p. 231), and a liturgy using Native American ritual which raises questions of cultural appropriation (pp. 240ff.). See also Nancy L. Woodworth-Hill, *A Healing Liturgy Especially for Survivors of Abuse*, The Episcopal Church of the Ascension, 16 Linwood Avenue, Buffalo, NY 14209; and "Prayer Service—Toward Justice for Women," in Marie Fortune, *Violence in the Family: A Workshop Curriculum for Clergy and Other Helpers* (Cleveland, Oh.: Pilgrim Press, 1991), 95–103, esp. Kelly Jarrett, "Litany of Acknowledgment" based on Tamar's story in 2 Samuel 13, pp. 101–3, and Caroline Sproul Fairless, "A Litany of Healing," pp. 97–98. For a variety of liturgies focused on justice for women, contact WATER: Women's Alliance for Theology, Ethics and Ritual, 8035 13th St., Ste. 1 & 3, Silver Spring, MD 20910.

43. Caroline Sproul Fairless, "What Does Love Require?: A Family Violence Manual for the Church Community," M.Div. honors thesis, Church Divinity School of the Pacific, Berkeley, Calif., May 1989, 31.

CONCLUSION: THE CALL TO RECONCILIATION

1. Dietrich Bonhoeffer, *The Cost of Discipleship*, trans. R. H. Fuller and I. Booth (New York: Macmillan, 1976), 47–48.

2. Ellen Bass and Laura Davis, *The Courage to Heal: A Guide for Women Survivors of Child Sexual Abuse* (New York: Harper & Row, 1988), 150–51.

3. Laura Davis, *Allies in Healing* (New York: HarperCollins, 1991), 124, citing Alice Miller, *Banished Knowledge* (New York: Bantam, 1991), for an analysis of this phenomenon.

4. See Judith Herman, *Trauma and Recovery* (New York: Basic Books, 1992), 189–90.

5. H. B. Lewis, *Shame and Guilt in Neurosis* (New York: International Universities Press, 1971) and "Shame: The 'Sleeper' in Psychopathology," in H. B. Lewis, *The Role of Shame in Symptom Formation* (Hillsdale, N.J.: Lawrence Erlbaum, 1987), 1–28; cited in Herman, *Trauma and Recovery*, 189.

6. Alice Miller, *For Your Own Good: Hidden Cruelty in Child-Rearing and the Roots of Violence*, trans. H. and H. Hannum (New York: Farrar Straus Giroux, 1984).

7. George Rundle Prynne, "Jesus, Meek and Gentle," *The Hymnal of the Protestant Episcopal Church in the United States of America: 1940* (New York: The Church Pension Fund, 1940), no. 358.

8. Themes of remembering, knowing vs. not-knowing, and breaking silence are pervasive in the work of Holocaust survivor and writer Elie Wiesel. See, e.g., "We Must Remember," in *Against Silence: The Voice and Vision of Elie Wiesel*, ed. I. Abrahamson (New York: Holocaust Library, 1985), 3:192–93; and "The Call to Remember," in *Against Silence*, 1:112–14.

9. Marie Fortune, *Sexual Violence* (New York: Pilgrim Press, 1983), 208–15.

10. Jeffrie G. Murphy lays specific moral grounds for forgiveness in "Forgiveness and Resentment," *Midwest Studies in Philosophy* 7 (1982), 50B.

11. Marie Fortune, *Keeping the Faith: Questions and Answers for the Abused Woman* (San Francisco: Harper & Row, 1987).

12. Ibid., 47–49.

13. Ibid., 49.

14. Fortune, *Sexual Violence*, 211, 213.

15. Bass and Davis, *The Courage to Heal*, 154.

16. Herman, *Trauma and Recovery*, 192.

17. Ibid., 192–93.

18. Philosopher Jeffrie G. Murphy comes to a similar conclusion in "Forgiveness and Resentment," 503–16. He states that forgiveness means letting go of resentment; it is not excuse, justification, or even mercy. It is not obligatory, and even though he outlines five moral grounds and two additional religious grounds for forgiveness, it must always be compatible with self-respect, respect for others as moral agents, and respect for the moral order. Citing Fay Weldon's novel *Female Friends* (London, 1975), he writes, "Women have been taught to forgive and accept where they should have been taught to resent and resist" (515).

19. All the word studies in this chapter were made using Robert Young, *Young's Analytical Concordance to the Bible*, 22d ed. (Grand Rapids: Wm. B. Eerdmans, 1972), 367, 799; *Interpreter's Dictionary of the Bible* (Nashville: Abingdon Press, 1962), 1:314–19, 4:16–17; and Gerhard Kittel, ed., *Theological Dictionary of the New Testament* (Grand Rapids: Wm. B. Eerdmans, 1964), vol. 1. For a different biblical study, see James Emerson, *The Dynamics of Forgiveness* (Philadelphia: Westminster Press, 1964), 101.

20. This same word, *aphiemi*, is used in reference to Jesus' own granting of forgiveness. Much of Jesus' own healing ministry was performed by releasing people from their sins, restoring them to wholeness. To the paralytic (Matt. 9:2ff.), or the leper (Luke 5:20ff.), or the woman whose sins were many (Luke 7:47ff.), he said, "Your sins are forgiven," thereby releasing them into newness of life and fuller participation in the community once again. He was accused of blasphemy by the scribes and the Pharisees for claiming the authority to grant forgiveness, which they ascribed only to God.

21. Rudolf Bultmann, "aphiemi," in Kittel, *Theological Dictionary*, 1:509–12.

22. In Hebrew, *nasa*, "to lift up or away," and *selichah*, "sending away, letting go," and in Greek the verb *apuluo*, "to loose away" (Luke 6:37-38).

23. James Emerson points out that this is not the same as pretending the sin is not there or that it never happened. There is realism in this understanding of forgiveness. God deals with the sin; God does not merely ignore or erase it (personal communication, September 1993).

24. Survivor letter, written as an exercise in therapy and not actually sent to her father. In Lynn Heitritter and Jeanette Vought, *Helping Victims of Sexual Abuse: A Sensitive Biblical Guide for Counselors, Victims and Families* (Minneapolis: Bethany House, 1989), 213–14. Excerpt by permission.

25. Krister Stendahl, *Paul among Jews and Gentiles* (Philadelphia: Fortress Press, 1976), 85, 95, cited in John Patton, *Is Human Forgiveness Possible? A Pastoral Care Perspective* (Nashville: Abingdon Press, 1985), 89, 127–30; and lectures at Harvard Divinity School, Cambridge, Mass., Spring 1982. According to Stendahl, forgiveness is not a major theme in Paul. Paul's "weakness," according to Stendahl, indicated a physical condition and not a moral weakness or sin. Paul's was actually "a rather robust conscience." According to Stendahl, it was the medieval preoccupation with penitence, exemplified in the *Confessions* of Augustine and later taken to personal depths by Martin Luther (himself an Augustinian monk), which pointed the modern church so heavily in the direction of sin, penitence, and forgiveness.

26. Frederick William Faber (1814–1863), "There's a Wideness In God's Mercy," Hymn nos. 469, 470, *The Hymnal 1982* (New York: [Episcopal] Church Hymnal Corporation, 1985).

27. See Patton, "The Discovery of Human Forgiveness," in *Is Human Forgiveness Possible?* 117–45. This may also be compared to the other side of the experience, that of discovering that one is forgiven, which James Emerson (*Dynamics of Forgiveness*) called "realized forgiveness" (cited in Patton, 131–32).

28. The distinction between forgiveness and reconciliation is also developed, from a different perspective, in Vincent Taylor's now classic *Forgiveness and Reconciliation: A Study in New Testament Theology* (London: Macmillan, 1960). While I differ with some of Taylor's interpretations, his exposition of reconciliation as a restoration of fellowship and communion with God—after Ritschl, *Justification and Reconciliation* (1970–74)—coincides with my shift from the individual emphasis in forgiveness to a corporate emphasis in reconciliation. Again, the emphasis in this text is more on the experience of being forgiven than on the act of forgiving, although this is also developed, particularly in reference to New Testament theology.

29. Robert McAfee Brown, "The Possibilities (and Problems) of Reconciliation," *Open Hands* 8/3 (Winter 1993), 4–5.

30. *Young's Analytical Concordance*, 799; see also Friedrich Buchsel, "atallasso," in Kittel, *Theological Dictionary*, 1:251–59.

31. I find resonances of this idea in Emerson, *Dynamics of Forgiveness*: " 'Realized forgiveness,' as a perspective of the ministry of the parish, demands the total community. It requires the total community of believers to mediate the context of forgiveness and it requires the total community of believers to give the instrumentation of that context" (180). Emerson's focus is more on the experience of being forgiven than the activity of forgiving; however, the emphasis on community is similar to the point I am making here.

32. Martin Buber, *I and Thou*, trans. Walter Kaufman (New York: Charles Scribner's Sons, 1970), 67.

APPENDIX

A LITANY FOR HEALING

God of grace, you nurture us with a love deeper than any we know, and your will for us is always healing and salvation.
We praise you and thank you, O God.

God of love, you enter into our lives, our pain, and our brokenness, and you stretch out your healing hands to us wherever we are.
We praise you and thank you, O God.

God of strength, you fill us with your presence and send us forth with love and healing to all whom we meet.
We praise you and thank you, O God.

God of love, we ask you to hear the prayers of your people.
Hear us, O God of life.

We pray for the world, that your creation may be understood and valued.
Hear us, O God of life.

Touch with your healing power the minds and hearts of all who suffer from sickness, injury, or disability, and make them whole again.
Hear us, O God of life.

Touch with your healing powers the minds and hearts of all who live in confusion or doubt, and fill them with your light.
Hear us, O God of life.

Touch with your healing power the minds and hearts of all who are burdened by anguish, despair, or isolation, and set them free in love.
Hear us, O God of life.

Break the bonds of those who are imprisoned by fear, compulsion, secrecy, and silence.
Come with your healing power, O God.

Fill with peace those who grieve over separation and loss.
Come with your healing power, O God.

Restore to wholeness all those who have been broken in life or in spirit by violence within their families; restore to wholeness all those who have been broken in life or in spirit by violence within our Family of Nations; restore to them the power of your love; and give to them the strength of your presence.
Come, O God, and restore us to wholeness and love.

Let us now name before God and this community gathered those, including ourselves, for whom we seek healing.
(The congregation may call out names).

We lift up before you this day all those who have died of violence.
(The congregation may call out names of those who have died.)

That they may have rest
In that place where there is no pain or grief, but life eternal.

O God, in you all is turned to light, and brokenness is healed. Look with compassion on us and on those for whom we pray, that we may be re-created in wholeness, in love, and in compassion for one another.
AMEN.

Developed by the Rev. Caroline Sproul Fairless, as part of "What Does Love Require?: A Family Violence Manual for the Church Community," M. Div. honors project, Church Divinity School of the Pacific, May, 1989. Fairless is an ordained Episcopal priest, and is currently Vicar at Holy Family Episcopal Church, Half Moon Bay, California. Used by permission.

INDEX OF NAMES

318 | INDEX OF NAMES

INDEX OF SUBJECTS

ACKNOWLEDGMENTS

Excerpts from *Trauma and Recovery* by Judith Lewis Herman, M.D., copyright © 1992 BasicBooks, A Division of HarperCollins Publishers, Inc. Reprinted by permission of BasicBooks and HarperCollins.

Excerpts from *Therapy for Adults Molested as Children: Beyond Survival* by John Briere, copyright © 1989 Springer Publishers, Inc., New York. Reprinted by permission.

Poem "Communion" copyright © Caryn Stardancer. Reprinted by permission.

Excerpt from "Beyond Submission and Toward Surrender: The Evolving Female Self," an unpublished paper by Mary Tennes, Ph.D., presented at the 1993 Redefining the Givens Seminar Series.

Excerpt from "After the Fact: To Speak of Rape" from the January 6–13, 1993 issue of The Christian Century, copyright © 1993 The Christian Century. Reprinted by permission.

Excerpt from "Feminist Movement to End Violence" from *Feminist Theory: From Margin to Center* by bell hooks, copyright © 1984 South End Press. Reprinted by permission.

Excerpts from *Men's Work* by Paul Kivel, copyright © 1992 Hazelden/Ballantine. Reprinted by permission.

Excerpts from "Child Abuse and Deprivation: Soul Murder" by Leonard Shengold from *Journal of the American Psychoanalytic Association* Vol. 27 no. 3 (1979). Reprinted by permission of International Universities Press, Inc.

Excerpt from "Men's Work: To Stop Men's Violence," copyright © Oakland Men's Project. Adapted from *Men's Work* by Paul Kivel. Reprinted by permission of Oakland Men's Project.

Excerpt from *Safety for Women: Monitoring Batterers' Programs* by Barbara Hart, copyright © 1988 Pennsylvania Coalition against Domestic Violence. Reprinted by permission.

"Power and Control Wheel" and "Non-Violence Wheel" from Domestic Abuse Intervention Project, Duluth MN. Reprinted by permission.

"Is Your Relationship Healthy and Non-Abusive?" from Marin Abused Women's Services, San Rafael CA. Reprinted by permission.

"Johari Window: A Graphic Model of Awareness in Interpersonal Relations" adapted from *Group Processes: An Introduction to Group Dynamics* by Joseph Luft (Palo Alto: National Press Books, 1963). Reprinted by permission of Mayfield Publishing Company.

Excerpt from "Reflections of the Thomas Hearings" from *Center for Women and Religion Newsletter* (Nov. 1991), copyright © 1991 Center for Women and Religion. Reprinted by permission.

"Litany for Healing" from "What Does Love Require: A Family Violence Manual for the Church Community," M. Div. Honors Thesis by Carolyn Fairless, Church Divinity School of the Pacific, May 1989. Reprinted by permission.

Excerpt from *Helping Victims of Sexual Abuse: A Sensitive Biblical Guide for Counselors, Victims, and Families* by Lynn Heitritter and Jeanette Vought, copyright © 1989 Bethany House. Reprinted by permission.

From "The Satanic and the Spiritual: Special Treatment of MPD Clients" by David McCoy and Marita Bausman (unpublished paper). Used by permission.

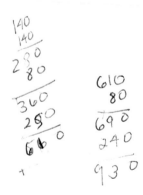

140
140
———
280
80
———
360
280
———
660

+

610
80
———
690
240
———
930